Business Week

Guide to
THE BEST
BUSINESS SCHOOLS

FIFTH EDITION

Business Week

OTHER BUSINESS WEEK GUIDES BY McGRAW-HILL

Business Week

Guide to
THE BEST
BUSINESS SCHOOLS

FIFTH EDITION

John A. Byrne
Senior Writer, BUSINESS WEEK

with a team of
BUSINESS WEEK Editors

McGraw-Hill

New York   San Francisco   Washington, D.C.   Auckland   Bogotá
Caracas   Lisbon   London   Madrid   Mexico City   Milan
Montreal   New Delhi   San Juan   Singapore
Sydney   Tokyo   Toronto

Library of Congress Cataloging-in-Publication Data

Byrne, John A.
    Business Week guide to the best business schools / John A. Byrne
with a team of Business week editors.—5th ed.
       p.   cm.
    Includes index.
    ISBN 0-07-009472-1
    1. Business schools—United States—Evaluation. 2. College
choice—United States—Handbooks, manuals, etc. 3. Master of
business administration degree—United States—Handbooks, manuals,
etc. I. Business week. II. Title.
HF1131.B95 1997
650'.071'173—dc21
                                            97-11436
                                               CIP

1 2 3 4 5 6 7 8 9 0 DOC/DOC 9 0 2 1 0 9 8 7

ISBN 0-07-009472-1 (PBK)

The sponsoring editor for this book was Susan Barry, the editing supervisor
was Jane Palmieri, and the production supervisor was Suzanne W. B. Rapcavage.
The book was designed by Michael Mendelsohn of MM Design 2000, Inc., and
was set in Minion by North Market Street Graphics.

Printed and bound by R. R. Donnelley & Sons Company.

McGraw-Hill books are available at special quantity discounts to use as
premiums and sales promotions, or for use in corporate training programs. For
more information, please write to the Director of Special Sales, McGraw-Hill,
11 West 19th Street, New York, NY 10011. Or contact your local bookstore.

 This book is printed on recycled, acid-free paper containing a
minimum of 50% recycled, de-inked fiber.

CONTENTS

Preface ix

1. WHY GO FOR THE MBA? 1
What Are MBA Students Like? 4
All MBAs Are Not Created Equal 6
A Top MBA Degree Rarely Comes Cheap 8
Seek a School That Matches Your Interests 10
Tour the Campus Without Leaving Home 10

2. HOW TO GET INTO ONE OF THE BEST B-SCHOOLS 13
Zipping Through the Application Forms 15
Preparing for the GMAT 16
Should You Take a GMAT Prep Course? 19
Creating Your Personal Marketing Strategy 21
Crafting the Perfect B-School Essay 22
To Interview or Not 25
Managing Your Recommenders 26
How to Get a School to Foot Part of the Tuition Bill 27

3. RANKING THE B-SCHOOLS 30
Business Week's Top 25 Business Schools 31

4. B-SCHOOLS BY THE NUMBERS 45
GMAT Scores 46
B-School Selectivity 47
Full-Time Enrollments 48
International Enrollments 49
Women MBA Enrollments 50
Minority Enrollments 51
Pre-MBA Annual Pay 52
Starting Pay Packages 53
Outstanding MBA Loans 54

5. THE TOP TWENTY-FIVE   55

1. University of Pennsylvania (Wharton)   56
2. University of Michigan   61
3. Northwestern University (Kellogg)   67
4. Harvard University   73
5. University of Virginia (Darden)   80
6. Columbia University   86
7. Stanford University   92
8. University of Chicago   98
9. Massachusetts Institute of Technology (Sloan)   103
10. Dartmouth College (Tuck)   109
11. Duke University (Fuqua)   115
12. University of California at Los Angeles (Anderson)   121
13. University of California at Berkeley (Haas)   127
14. New York University (Stern)   133
15. Indiana University   139
16. Washington University (John M. Olin)   145
17. Carnegie Mellon University   150
18. Cornell University (Johnson)   156
19. University of North Carolina (Kenan-Flagler)   163
20. University of Texas   170
21. University of Rochester (Simon)   175
22. Yale University   180
23. Southern Methodist University (Cox)   186
24. Vanderbilt University (Owen)   191
25. American Graduate School of International Management (Thunderbird)   197

6. THE RUNNERS-UP   203

Babson College (F. W. Olin)   204
Brigham Young University (Marriott)   208
Case Western Reserve University (Weatherhead)   211
Emory University (Goizueta)   215
Georgetown University   218
Georgia Institute of Technology (DuPree)   222
Michigan State University (Broad)   225
Ohio State University (Fisher)   229
Pennsylvania State University (Smeal)   232
Purdue University (Krannert)   236
Rice University (Jones)   240
Texas A&M University (Mays)   243
Tulane University (Freeman)   247
University of Georgia (Terry)   251
University of Illinois at Urbana-Champaign   254
University of Iowa   258
University of Maryland at College Park   262

University of Minnesota (Carlson)   266
University of Notre Dame   270
University of Pittsburgh (Katz)   274
University of Southern California   278
University of Tennessee at Knoxville   282
University of Washington   286
University of Wisconsin—Madison   290
Wake Forest University (Babcock)   294

7. THE BEST BUSINESS SCHOOLS OUTSIDE THE UNITED STATES   **299**

U.S. B-Schools versus European B-Schools   301
Things to Consider Before Applying Abroad   302
Yet Another Option for an International Experience   303
The European Institute of Business Administration (INSEAD)   306
London Business School   308
Western Business School   310

Index   313

PREFACE

You have in your hands the fifth edition of what has now become the bible for all students and observers of the best graduate schools of business. Hundreds of thousands of applicants have relied on earlier versions of this guide for its storehouse of straight facts and analysis on the top programs. Indeed, many B-school deans and corporate recruiters view this up-to-date guide as a strategic study of their business. This latest edition is the most comprehensive of them all.

For this guide, the magazine used its most recent surveys of graduates and corporate recruiters as a starting point. Then the staff interviewed hundreds of students, alumni, recruiters, faculty members, and deans to draw out the strengths and weaknesses of the top schools. The result is a product that reveals far more information and intelligence on the best programs than exists anywhere else.

The guidebook is an outgrowth of BUSINESS WEEK's biennial ranking of the best business schools that began in 1988. Since then, the magazine has carved out management education as an important and critical area of coverage. That mission extends beyond the pages of the magazine. On America Online, for example, BUSINESS WEEK has an extensive area dedicated to the coverage of the best business schools and sponsors frequent conferences with current MBA students, deans, admission and placement directors, and applicant advisers. You can download the transcripts of more than 50 online conferences, which are full of information and advice. And there's even a series of 50 message boards on which applicants, students, and BUSINESS WEEK staff interact on a daily basis, including a section in which BUSINESS WEEK Senior Writer John A. Byrne answers any and all questions posted regarding management education. A good deal of this additional information is also available via Internet on BUSINESS WEEK's web site at www.business-week.com.

Byrne, who created the BUSINESS WEEK ranking of the top schools, has directed the magazine's coverage of this area for well over a decade. A veteran business reporter and writer, he is also the author of *The Headhunters, The Whiz Kids,* and *Informed Consent.* Byrne conceived and wrote much of what you'll read in this book.

Staff Editor David Leonhardt regularly covers the business school beat for the magazine. He has made a major contribution in reporting, writing, and editing many of the B-school profiles in the book, and he also played a key role in the research for the cover story. Jennifer Merritt, a BUSINESS WEEK intern, also contributed to the reporting and writing of school profiles. Judi Crowe greatly assisted in analyzing the results of thousands of completed questionnaires from the magazine's polls. Lourdes Hernandez proved invaluable at the difficult task of sending out most of the surveys and inputting much of the data into computers. Managing Editor Mark Morrison supervised the project.

Guide to
THE BEST
BUSINESS SCHOOLS

FIFTH EDITION

WHY GO FOR THE MBA?

Feeling a little like Dilbert lately? Trapped in a maze of corporate politics and cubicles where everyone seems to get ahead except you? Are you overwhelmed by bureaucratic rules and bosses promoted beyond their level of competence? Weary over all the dislocations in the workplace? Or simply more ambitious for yourself and your career? If you can answer yes to any of these questions, you've no doubt thought about returning to school for an MBA. The degree isn't a surefire guarantee for success in the world of business, but when granted from a top university it can provide a measure of personal security that can help greatly in what has become an uncertain world. No wonder so many people want an MBA.

In recent years, in fact, business schools have been in the midst of quite a bull market. At virtually all the best schools, applications, GMAT scores, and starting-pay packages for MBAs are setting an all-time record. An avalanche of MBA wannabes, more eager than ever to have their résumés stamped, have overwhelmed the admissions offices of the leading schools since the early 1990s. BUSINESS WEEK's Top 25 schools processed 80,766 applications in 1996 alone, up 33 percent in just two years and far higher than the previous peak of 64,647 in 1990. The average GMAT score of the latest incoming class at the Top 25 hit a record 644, up 35 points in the past decade.

Every school posted an increase in applications. The largest swell occurred at the Massachusetts Institute of Technology's Sloan School of Management, where an applicant pool of 3012—up 80 percent between 1992 and 1996—vied for just 325 seats. Applications to No. 1 Wharton have soared 46 percent, to a record 7389 in 1996, stunning admissions officials, who scrambled to keep up. At one point, it took the school an entire month to fulfill a telephone request for an application. Stanford University sent invites for its Class of 1998 to only 1 in 14 applicants.

The applications avalanche at top programs reflects both a race to quality schools and a rising demand among employers for MBAs. "The gap between the top schools and the second tier is widening," says Meyer Feldberg, dean of Columbia University's business school. "It's simply harder to justify going to a good second-tier school for the same costs."

> An avalanche of MBA wannabes have overwhelmed the leading schools.

Also critical, however, is that employers believe the wave of innovation that has swept through business schools in recent years has made MBA graduates more valuable than ever. "Ten years ago, these schools made little if any effort teaching leadership or teamwork," says James Gottshalk, who recruits MBAs for US West Inc. "Today, they are doing a much better job in these areas."

Sure enough, recruiters responding to BUSINESS WEEK's survey in 1996 hired 8100 MBAs, up 7.6 percent from 1994. Not only are companies hiring more B-school graduates, but they're also willing to pay them a lot more for their expertise. Median pay for a graduate of a Top 25 school jumped 16 percent, to $81,569; the median package for grads at five schools is now $100,000 or more; and the average number of job offers per student has risen to 3, from 2.6 in 1994.

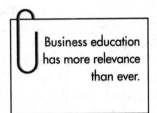

Business education has more relevance than ever.

Whatever the job prospects, the promise of a business school education has more relevance today than ever. In response to complaints from Corporate America, schools have added more courses on "soft" skills, such as leadership and teamwork. They are placing greater emphasis on globalization and information technology. They're also trying to teach business as a whole instead of a set of disparate functions, and they're breaking down the walls that have long separated academia from the real world of business. "I think we're bringing more value to students today than we did in the past because of these changes," says B. Joseph White, dean of the University of Michigan's business school.

Today is certainly an advantageous time to attend a top business school because you'll have the opportunity to be both a participant in and a beneficiary of these changes. Even more important, the MBA still remains the one advanced degree to prepare you for life in the corporate or entrepreneurial world, to give you a head start against the competition, and to help you stand out in the managerial crowd. The payback from your investment may take a little longer today, but the right MBA can often lead to a more exciting career and a fatter paycheck. It can provide a foundation from which to launch a successful business. It can even be a ticket to a high-powered job running your own company.

These are all good reasons for why so many people continue to rush off to get an MBA. Yet, the most basic question you need to ask is this: Is it worthwhile to invest as much as $150,000 (a sum that includes your loss of income and cost of tuition) and two years of your life to get this degree? With very few exceptions, all the graduates of the top schools answer this question in the affirmative. They describe their two years of graduate study as one of the high points of their lives: meeting bright new friends, sharing new experiences, discovering horizons and careers they never knew existed. A good B-school education also imparts a level of confidence and maturity that years of actual work experience could never deliver. "It's like drinking from a fire hydrant," explains one Stanford University graduate. "There is so much intense learning and growing going on, both inside and outside the classroom."

The skills and knowledge you accumulate in a good MBA program teach you to think and analyze complicated business problems. The experience fosters enduring friendships and business contacts with exciting, dynamic people from around the world. It opens doors to some of the world's great organizations, including the highest-paying public and private corporations, consulting firms, and investment banks. Some graduates gleefully report doubling their salaries after spending two years in a top B-school program.

Yet because many prospective students fail to do the preparatory homework, they end up wasting a lot of time and a lot of money. At the outset, they don't find out what an MBA can and can't do for them. They fail to properly evaluate a particular school or program to discover what it can deliver. They don't adequately analyze the costs of going to school against the likely benefits. The upshot: Many MBAs find the rewards of their degree elusive. Much to their chagrin, it fails to deliver on a better job, a bigger salary, and great opportunities to ascend the corporate ladder.

> MBAs today are as common as Dilbert cartoons.

How come? Truth is, MBAs today are as common as the Dilbert cartoons in your local newspaper. American schools alone graduate some 85,000 new MBAs every year, up from just 49,000 in 1980, and only 4814 in 1960. With visions of big promotions and heady salaries dancing in their heads, hordes of people have gravitated to the B-school world. Many of them felt disadvantaged at work without the degree. Many others, particularly those with liberal arts backgrounds, felt they needed some business instruction to be successful in Corporate America. Still others, trapped in unfulfilling careers they were aching to escape, saw the MBA as the ticket out.

It wasn't. The so-called "Passport to the Good Life" became little more than a frustrating dead end. Perhaps they put too much hope and too many expectations on a piece of paper. "An MBA degree is not a magic wand that transforms inexperienced and immature undergraduates into licensed managers," says Arnoud De Meyer, an associate dean at INSEAD, the European Institute of Business Administration in Fontainebleau, France. "I have never met a company recruiter who hires MBAs; they hire people with high potential. An advanced degree is only part of a total package of education and experience, as well as the motivation to work in a particular industry."

If you boast high potential and want an advanced degree in business to seize the advantage, you're holding the best possible guide to take the guesswork out of one of the most important career decisions you'll ever make. Not merely a ranking of schools or a series of flimsy profiles written from slick brochures, this guide is a tell-it-like-it-is scouting report on the best of the bunch. For years, as many as 50 schools claimed they were among the Top 25, and well over 100 institutions told prospective applicants they were in the Top 50. To be sure, too many schools jumped on the MBA bandwagon because it became something of a fad to offer the degree. That's why more than 700 institutions grant MBAs in the United States alone, up from 370 in 1974. Not only was it the degree to have, it was the degree to have to succeed. And it's true that in some professions, notably consulting, banking, and consumer packaging, an MBA can be nearly a necessity.

WHAT ARE MBA STUDENTS LIKE?

Remember the stereotypical image of MBAs in the 1980s? They were supposed to be highly ambitious, narrow-minded climbers who were overly competitive and out for a quick buck. Forget that image. If it was ever true, it certainly hasn't been true for a very long time. At the best schools, MBAs are a broad and diverse mix of people. A recent graduating class from Northwestern University's Kellogg School of Management boasted someone who was hijacked in the Philippines by rebels, a *Sports Illustrated* reporter, a story editor from Metro-Goldwyn-Mayer, a professional soccer player, a dean of students for a girls' prep school, and a former Seattle Seahawks cheerleader. Stanford University's Class of 1998 boasts several Olympians—including a gold medal water polo player, a finalist in the Sundance Film Festival, a record company founder, a U.S. Marines platoon commander, a project manager for a national labor union, and a financial analyst for the National Football League.

Like many MBA candidates, some of these people never really planned a career in business and grew unhappy with what they were doing for a living. Maybe you're a musician, artist, engineer, lawyer, doctor, or teacher. Is the MBA a good investment for the career switcher? A degree from a top school can make the transition to the business world a lot easier. It will not only give you a taste of what business is all about, it may also provide the contacts you need to land a viable job when the educational experience is complete. Indeed, some MBA-recruiting companies like the different perspectives that people from law or medicine can bring to business. If you're really tired of what you're doing, a quality MBA can be a pass to this new and different world.

There are other kinds of career switchers, too. These are people who already have good jobs in business, but don't want to stay in the same industry or career for the rest of their lives. An MBA degree may be a tougher choice in this case. Don't expect any guarantees that the MBA will allow you a fresh start. If you have had valuable experience in an industry or a company, you'll find an MBA more worthwhile if you build upon that previous experience—not just toss it away in the hopes of doing something completely different. A chemist for a drug company may well want to return to the pharmaceutical industry in a business management position in finance or marketing. Those who want to divorce themselves from their previous experience face a tougher road.

Increasingly, too, there is a new kind of MBA student—the would-be entrepreneur. Many now view B-school as a useful "boot camp" in which you learn the nuts and bolts of business, make a slew of networking contacts, and get a corporate job where you'll spend your first three to five years before launching your own company. Responding to a growing interest in entrepreneurship, B-schools have launched a bevy of courses that make it possible to do your own thing sooner in life than you ever expected. Widely available courses instruct how to assemble a business plan; raise money from venture capitalists and other investors; incorporate your business and produce, market, and sell a product. Some schools, such as UCLA, Babson, Carnegie Mellon, and the University of Southern California, have developed complete programs in entrepreneurship. And some schools even help link graduating students with potential financial backers. The upshot? Dozens of businesses have been started by recent MBA graduates, from restaurants and coffeehouses to computer

> An MBA may not allow you a fresh start.

5

and electronics firms. Obviously, none of these courses confer immediate success. That's up to you.

ALL MBAs ARE NOT CREATED EQUAL

Despite the inevitable ups and downs of the economy, the MBA degree has retained its value. Anyway you look at it, it's the graduate degree of choice among the corporate elite. Every year, an increasing number of chief executives of the largest corporations hold the degree. Most brand-name companies consider the MBA to be something of a screen for the best and brightest young people around the world. That's why they recruit so many MBAs and why they so willingly pay them handsome salaries and bonuses. The combination of a top degree and an employment history with a Hewlett-Packard or Citicorp can make a big difference on a résumé. Executive headhunters today say that their clients often specify that the MBA is a prerequisite for top management positions.

When should you go to business school, then? The succinct and difficult answer is when you can get into one that's good enough to make a meaningful difference to you and your career. Years ago, most applicants applied to an array of schools, from those where they considered admission to be something of a slam dunk to those that were clearly "stretch" schools. Today, many applicants focus in on a handful of the very best. If they fail to get through the admissions screen, they simply wait and reapply. The reason: With growing recognition that quantity-over-quality thinking has gotten American management in a lot of trouble, a better idea has taken hold. The MBA is more crucial, or less, depending on which school confers it. "When people talk about the MBA, they tend to talk about the generic degree," says Thomas F. Keller, former dean of Duke University's Fuqua School of Business. "But the MBA is not a standardized product, and a lot of programs don't offer much value."

Little-known institutions with small MBA programs that lack accreditation probably aren't going to give you either a quality business education or a hefty starting salary. Neither will most part-time evening MBA programs where the dropout rates are high and you fail to move through the program with a cohort group of bright students. "The initials don't mean anything," insists John W. Rosenblum, dean of the Jepson School of Leadership Studies at the University of Richmond. "The sooner we stop writing MBA and start acknowledging it's as meaningless as a BA, the better off we'll be. What counts is where did you get it. We have too many people studying for MBA degrees without careful thought as to why, and we have too many schools offering MBAs without careful thought as to why."

If you want a worthwhile MBA, you have to get it from a school with a reputation for quality and prestige—whether it's known worldwide, throughout the United States, or only regionally. BUSINESS WEEK customer satisfaction surveys of alumni have found that the greater the reputation of the school, the more likely you are to be more than satisfied with your results. You might even want to ignore the big national schools if your goal is to take over the family business or simply to gain basic business knowhow. In some cases, an MBA from a state university could turn out to be far more valuable than one from Harvard. Why? Because you'd make more relevant business and government contacts to further your career in the area. And you would graduate without all that heavy debt.

Exactly who goes to business school these days? When you count both full- and part-time programs together, you find that students range in age from 21 to the early 50s, though the biggest single age group is 28 years old. About one-quarter are at least 31 years of age, while only 7 percent are at least 40. Men easily outnumber women: At the University of Michigan or Harvard Business School, roughly one in every four students is a woman; at Carnegie Mellon, it's less than one in five. Students are predominantly white. One recent study by the Graduate Management Admission Council found that only 8 percent of MBAs are black and 4 percent are Hispanic. At Chicago, only 5 percent of the students are minorities today. It's less than 10 percent at such top schools as Northwestern, Dartmouth, Indiana, and Carnegie Mellon. Instead, you're more likely to find ethnic and foreign diversity in the large percentages of students who hail from non-U.S. countries. At Wharton, 30 percent of the MBA students are from outside the United States. At the University of Rochester's business school, some 46 percent of the students are from foreign countries.

Most of the better schools prefer that MBA candidates have three or more years of full-time work experience under their belts before applying. Your chances of gaining admission to a good program fall significantly without work experience. Many MBAs who lack time in the real world say they regret not having waited before going to B-school. Having already lived through many of the

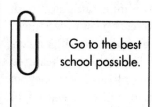

Go to the best school possible.

issues you'll investigate in a graduate business education gives you a valuable reference point to use as you study business. It also makes your comments and insights in the classroom more meaningful to a discussion. And the quality of your work experience is often used by the better schools as a key admissions criterion. The better the company and the experience, the more likely it will open the door to a top-flight MBA program.

A TOP MBA
DEGREE
RARELY
COMES CHEAP

Other than buying a house, going to grad school is probably the single largest investment a twenty- or thirty-something will make. Think about it. In addition to nearly 50 grand for two years of tuition at many top schools, most MBA students give up twice that in lost earnings. The total cost usually runs to six figures; at Harvard Business School, the most expensive of them all, the median is $183,300. That number helps to put into perspective the starting pay and bonus packages for a Harvard MBA, which averaged $113,545 in 1996. Expect to pay about $24,000 a year in annual tuition at the best private schools that exude MBA prestige. Add a few thousand more for books and other expenses, and the total cost, including lost earnings, can easily exceed $150,000. Quite a bit of money for a business education and a piece of parchment. That's why, in fact, so many top MBAs flock to the world of management consulting and investment banking. They pay graduates the highest starting salaries and bonuses and that money is often sorely needed to pay off a pile of loans.

If you work the averages, however, a degree from a Top 50 school should have enabled you to land a job that paid a starting salary and bonus of nearly $70,000 in 1996. Simple calculator math will tell you that it might take a few years to recoup your investment in lost earnings and tuition. Truth is, however, that an MBA is certainly worth the cost—especially at the top 50 or so schools featured in this book. Despite those two valuable years and all that money, an MBA from a leading school pays for itself within five to eight years—including the two years you spend in school. The economic advantage you initially gain from the MBA, moreover, is usually maintained throughout your career. A study by University of Rochester professor, Ronald N. Yeaple, found that the average post-MBA annual salary growth during the first five years after graduation ranges from 10 percent for lesser-known schools to nearly 30 percent for the best schools. Chicago's MBA grads see their salaries rise by an average of 25 percent annually for the first five years after graduation; at Rochester, it's 17 percent. Those are rates of increase that should be compared against average raises in the meager 5 percent range for most white-collar professionals in recent years.

And it's more likely to give you a better shot at attaining what most people seek in their first job after B-school: interesting work, good chances for promotions, solid pay, clear responsibilities, friendly coworkers, job security, and challenging problems to work on. Besides, you can't feed into a calculator the increased confidence and psychological comfort an MBA may give you as a business executive or manager. One Harvard grad likens it to a vacation in Europe: "Can you justify its payback? No. But does it broaden your horizons, give you a new perspective on the world? Is it valuable? Of course."

There also are ways to limit the degree's cost. Students at state schools pay substantially less tuition than those at private schools. If you're a resident of Texas, for example, you could get a degree from the University of Texas at Austin for under $10,000 in tuition—over two years! That's a mere fraction of what the degree would cost you at Northwestern or Wharton. The same is true at such top schools as Indiana University or the University of North Carolina, arguably the best value in MBA education. At North Carolina, even a nonresident of the state pays only $14,332 a year in tuition—nearly half what you'd pay at any top private school. Compare that to neighboring Duke University, where the annual bill is $23,690. And in many cases, nonresidents are eligible to pay resident tuition in their second year of graduate study.

That's a pretty compelling argument in favor of the public university. Few students want to graduate with $50,000 or more debt on their backs. But also remember that the graduates of public universities seldom bring home the highest starting salaries. A Wharton graduate brings home a starting median pay of $100,000, while a grad of North Carolina gets a median pay of $77,250. Besides the basic salary and bonus, moreover, elite MBA grads often get a spate of other perks that range from moving expenses and guaranteed year-end bonuses to new cars and as much as two years' reimbursement of tuition. A degree from Wharton or Northwestern is far more likely to bring these bennies than one from Indiana or Texas.

Cost, then, is certainly one criterion in deciding whether you can go for an MBA and where you should go. But there are lots of other critical considerations, too. While a school's overall standing

The cost of an MBA is a deciding factor.

is important to the value of its degree, you also should think about what you want to gain from an education. Do you want a job in finance? marketing? manufacturing? human resources? Some schools have reputations for being the absolute best in a particular field. If you're interested in entrepreneurship, for example, it would be hard to beat the programs at Babson, Wharton, or UCLA.

Within the top tier of business schools, the issue for prospective students is not which school is No. 1 or No. 7, but how well the school's strengths and culture fit your needs. Keenly interested in international business and want to attend a U.S. school? The top 10, judged by graduate satisfaction: Thunderbird, Berkeley, Georgetown, Wharton, New York University, Tulane, MIT, Michigan, and Columbia. What about the best schools for information technology? The top 10 are Carnegie Mellon, MIT, UCLA, Berkeley, Texas at Austin, Duke, Dartmouth, Maryland, Rochester, and Wake Forest. You should also know that Harvard is in the process of remaking its MBA program around the use of technology. The best for leadership skills? Harvard, Kellogg, Virginia, Wharton, UCLA, Michigan, Southern Methodist, Washington University, Vanderbilt, and Stanford.

Before applying to any school, do your homework. Go beyond the slick brochures and promises made by the marketing staff of these schools. Treat it the way an MBA would in a typical case study. "You should gather all the information about placement, the quality of the school, and do a business analysis of it," suggests Robert L. Virgil, former dean of Washington University's Olin School of Business. "If you're investing two years of your life and a lot of money, I think you should visit the school when it's in session. Attend a class or two, talk to the students, grab a recruiter during a coffee break to find out what he or she thinks the place is like. Then, look at yourself in the mirror and see if you really match up with the school."

There's also a new, interesting alternative to the on-campus visit: the virtual tour. Like thousands of enterprises trying to sell their goods, business schools have gone online, making it easier than ever for prospective students to glean the information they need from a computer screen. Say you live in Seattle and want to take a look at Duke University's B-school in North Carolina. Just log on to the World Wide Web and call up the Fuqua School of Business web site. There you'll find everything from the nitty-gritty on the MBA curriculum to detailed biographies of faculty members. The

SEEK A SCHOOL THAT MATCHES YOUR INTERESTS

TOUR THE CAMPUS WITHOUT LEAVING HOME

web addresses for the top schools are on the front page of each school profiled in this guidebook. For America Online subscribers, an easy way to tap into B-school Web sites is to enter AOL's BUSINESS WEEK area, which features direct links to nearly 75 of the best schools, including more than a dozen international management schools.

Some of these sites, such as the Haas School of Business at the University of California at Berkeley, are full of colorful art that give you a glimpse of the campus, its classrooms, and lecture halls. They will tell you everything you need to know about the academic community, the social and recreational amenities in the area, and the school. The Haas site even allows you to check the performance of the student investment club's portfolio. New York University's site boasts interesting page links, including one to a game, Guess the Dow.

But don't get too content sitting in front of your computer screen. After all, cruising the Web can't take the place of a campus visit, and with a slow modem, it can take several frustrating hours just to get through a single site. Many B-school sites, moreover, are little more than slick electronic marketing brochures. You'll discover no comparative information on how a school stacks up against its competitors, nor will you find even the smallest hint of negative news. But that's why you bought this guidebook.

Other advice: Before selecting which schools you might want to attend, chat candidly with recent graduates. If you already have your heart set on becoming a consultant at McKinsey & Co., it would be wise to find a McKinsey staffer who is an alumnus of the school you want to attend. Most alumni and/or admissions departments will help you locate recent graduates. Wharton goes so far as to send all applicants a directory of alumni who have volunteered to share their firsthand knowledge of Wharton by telephone. Applicants can call Wharton MBAs by location, company, and undergraduate school from Argentina to Venezuela. Remember, however, when speaking to alumni, that graduate schools of business have changed so dramatically in recent years that alums who have been out of the school for five or more years may not have a good feel for the current MBA program. "We're changing so rapidly, they don't know what the school is all about today," says Donald Jacobs, dean of Northwestern's Kellogg School.

Consider, too, how a particular school's method of instruction suits your personality. At Harvard, you could find yourself strain-

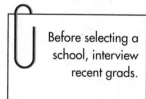

Before selecting a school, interview recent grads.

ing to make your voice heard in classroom discussions that account for most of your grade. If you're not good at scrambling for attention in a class of 90 very competitive students, you'll likely be better off at a school such as Dartmouth's Amos Tuck. There's more emphasis there on how well you work in small teams and on cooperation instead of competition. On the other hand, if you're very aggressive and enjoy the thrill of a contest, you should go to one of the more competitive schools, such as Columbia or Chicago. (See Chapter 3 for BUSINESS WEEK's survey of top graduates and what they say about their schools.)

You won't find large numbers of terribly disappointed people. MBAs from the top schools generally offer positive endorsements of the experience—whether they are freshly minted or have been out for a number of years. Most have little doubt that the time and expense of getting the degree were well worth it. They say they forged friendships and contacts that will endure through a lifetime; they linked up with new jobs that paid better money and offered greater opportunities for advancement than the positions they left. Some consider it the most important and formative decision they've made in their lifetimes.

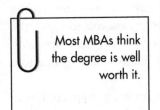

Most MBAs think the degree is well worth it.

HOW TO GET INTO ONE OF THE BEST B-SCHOOLS

So you want to go to business school. Once you have narrowed down your choices, you face a daunting pile of work. You'll have to arrange on-campus visits to check the schools out. You'll have to schedule, in most cases, a personal interview with a school's admissions office. You'll have to study and prepare to take the grueling Graduate Management Admission Test (GMAT). And you'll have to carefully fill out an application form for every school to which you apply.

This isn't something you do at the last minute. Some admissions directors suggest that you start this process a full year or two before you actually apply. Of course, few people allow themselves that much time. But it would be wise to begin seeking information on schools in the spring—a little more than a year before you would enroll in an MBA program. Read the school profiles in this book. Check out the Web sites of the schools in which you're interested. Send away for literature. Attend an MBA Forum, an event for prospective students that begins in late September and ends in late November. More than 100 schools attend the forums, sending admissions personnel and program literature. They are held in Cleveland, Boston, Houston, Washington, D.C., Chicago, New York, Los Angeles, and San Francisco. Another set of international forums are held in January in Paris and Frankfurt, and in May in Tokyo and Hong Kong.

What will the schools use to evaluate you? B-schools generally look at academic factors such as your undergraduate grades and scores on the GMAT. They also consider leadership ability, special talents, background characteristics, motivation, work experience, and career interests. These factors are less tangible, and it's harder to predict how they'll be weighed by admissions committees. But work experience can often tilt a decision in your favor, especially if you can use it to detail vividly how you've worked well with other people or successfully handled a crisis of one kind or another. So could well-written essay answers or a good showing in a personal interview.

Above all, hedge your bets by applying to half a dozen or so schools—and try to apply early if you can. Most schools list their final deadline for admissions between March 1 and June 1. But you

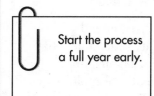

Start the process a full year early.

can be at a disadvantage if you mail in your application so late in the game. Ideally, you should try to get it in by early January to gain admission for the fall semester or quarter. Duke University's B-school admissions staff begins reading applications on December 1 and continues to admit students until the class is full. Under that system, the earlier you apply the better off you are. "If people waited until our final deadline, they would have virtually no chance of being admitted," says Anne Sandoe-Thorp, director of admissions for Duke. "If you're an average candidate, your chances go down significantly the later you wait." That's not always the case. But it is always better to apply early—before the admissions staff is deluged with applicants.

It's helpful to create a calendar-based plan of what needs to be done and when. That will put you on a schedule that will allow you to manage the process. It also will help you meet critical deadlines. Here's an example:

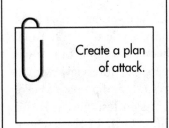

Create a plan of attack.

Spring or Early Summer: Narrow down schools, check out Web sites, request program literature and applications, and set up on-campus visits for the early fall.

August: Enroll in a six-week GMAT prep course or set aside two months to practice the test at home.

September: Begin to visit campuses, attend classes, chat with current students and faculty. Attend an MBA Forum, if there is one in a nearby city. Do an admissions interview, if allowed before you file an official application.

October: Take the GMAT. Begin the application process, filling out the forms, requesting undergraduate transcripts, creating a personal marketing plan for yourself, crafting answers to essay questions, choosing recommenders.

November: Visit more campuses. Schedule the bulk of your personal interviews. Begin to file your applications with the schools.

December: At first, complete the applications for schools that are not at the very top of your list. Save the best for last, when you can approach them having had more practice and experience. In almost all cases, it's better to file early—but not too early when you'll compete with the overanxious overachievers—and never in the last round. Ask for personal interviews at schools which refused to do an interview before an application is filed.

ZIPPING THROUGH THE APPLICATION FORMS

One of your first challenging assignments? Set aside about 10 hours to complete each mind-numbing, head-scratching 20-page application. That's maybe 50 hours of hard slogging for the typical MBA candidate, who applies to three to five schools. Make sure every application is neatly typed, and that your name, birthplace, and social security number fit just right.

Or at least that is how it used to be. Modern technology has found an answer for the application blues. Multiple application software now allows you to do something no typewriter has ever done: enter those pesky vitals each school demands in one fell swoop. "Using software probably saved me 30 to 40 hours of work," says Christopher Gosk, who applied to half a dozen schools and went to the University of North Carolina. "It would have been a nightmare otherwise."

The single best product for all this is something called MCS Multi-App. For just $50, the software allows you to apply to as many as 54 of the best schools—virtually all of them listed in this guidebook. It is sold on disk in Windows 3.1 or Windows 95 versions or can be downloaded from the Web. You can contact the firm at 800-516-2227.

How does it work? After you mark the schools you are applying to, a screen prompts you to begin typing. You'll start by entering simple information, like your name and address, and move on to work experience and academic records. Once you've filled it all in, the program distributes the information to each application that needs it. Say you are applying to Stanford, Wharton, and Michigan. When you open the Stanford University file to complete the application, all the information you entered in the first phase transfers over. Half your application is completed before you start.

It will take about 45 minutes to complete the common questions before you can move to questions specific to a single school. Here, Multi-App offers you a dangerous little option: With a keystroke, you can copy an essay written for one school to any application. You'll then have to customize the essay manually for each school. At a time when most B-schools hear from far more qualified applicants than they can accept, it's a better idea to write essays that are truly school-specific. "The danger of these software packages is they make the application process look generic, when there are different rules for every school," says Samuel Lundquist, former director of Wharton School's admissions office.

With a laser printer, the completed forms look strikingly similar to the paper versions put out by the schools. Some B-schools, such as Duke and Harvard, estimate that 25 percent of their 1995–1996 applicants used the commercial software programs. "It saves us the time and money of creating our own software, and it makes applying to business school easier for students," says James Miller, assistant director of admissions at Harvard. "What's not to like about it?"

PREPARING FOR THE GMAT

No matter how you slice it, your chances of getting into a good school are very dependent on how well you score on the Graduate Management Admission Test (GMAT). Four times a year, in January, March, June, and October, more than 200,000 people have routinely sat for four hours with number two pencils in hand, filling in answers that will largely decide what kind of school they can apply to. Beginning in October of 1997, however, this ritual will change in a dramatic way when the test goes electronic in the United States. You will then be able to take the test when it's convenient—by appointment at a nearby testing center. Everyone in the world should be able to take the GMAT by computer by the year 1999.

Candidates will sit at computers, log in demographic information, and the test will pop up on the screen. Questions will be selected randomly so no two tests will be alike. In fact, if a test-taker gets an answer wrong, the next question will likely be at the same level of difficulty. Consistent right answers move you to levels of more difficulty. You'll type in answers and the scores for the verbal and quantitative sections will be generated minutes after you finish. The analytical writing piece of the test is expected to come a week later. Year-round access to the GMAT should allow schools to make quicker decisions on applications.

Every accredited B-school requires the GMAT as part of the admissions package and admissions officers typically give anywhere from a 20 percent to 40 percent weight to the score alone. If you manage to eke out only the average score of 494, from a range of 200 to 800, your chances of making it into a top school are pretty slim. You really need to score above 600 to seriously entertain the idea of making it into a Top 25 school. And you need to score no less that 580 to walk through the door of one of BUSINESS WEEK's Runners-Up schools—excellent graduate business institutions that tend to be overshadowed and therefore hidden from view by the frenzy to land a spot in the Top 25. True, Northwestern accepted one applicant in 1996 with a GMAT as low as 410, and the University of Michigan as low as 500. But the average at the schools was 660 and 645, respectively. Remember, too, that a high GMAT alone isn't going to get you into a top school: Northwestern rejected half of its applicants with perfect 800 GMAT scores in 1996. Still, you want to score as high as you can.

If your test score doesn't quite measure up, don't surrender just yet. It's possible that you could be rejected from one school based on your GMAT score and be accepted by a Top 25 school with the same score. Why? Some schools, feverishly working to boost their reputations by appearing selective, will simply toss you out of their admit pool. They are using GMAT averages as a marketing tool to attract better candidates. Other schools, already assured of their quality reputation, might pay more attention to other parts of your application—work experience, essays, personal interviews, and undergraduate grades.

Many admission directors, too, look beyond the overall GMAT score to see how well or poorly you did on the quantitative and verbal sections of the test. Yale University's B-school, for instance, accepts students who on average fall within the 94th percentile on the verbal part of the GMAT. Yale's non-U.S. students, however, typically score only in the 70th percentile. But their "quant" scores are so high it doesn't make much of a difference overall. The reverse is often true of U.S. applicants, who don't do nearly so well on the math.

Fewer than 10 out of the more than 269,000 tested ace the GMAT in any given year. Fewer than 2000 people score 700 or above on this test. A score in the low 500s would put you into the 60th percentile, while a score of 600 would propel you into the 89th percentile. So a difference of 100 points can move you up into elite-school status. That's why it's important to spend some time gaining familiarity with the test before you take it. Most test-takers simply buy a workbook and use the sample tests in it for practice. One in four goes to the trouble of taking a formal preparation class.

If you fail to score high, don't give up.

Although you can take the test as often as you like, the schools to which you apply will see all your grades. So it's generally not a good policy to take the GMAT itself for practice. You don't send schools the rough drafts of your essay answers, and you don't walk into an interview with jeans and uncombed hair. If you're going to practice for the GMAT, you should do it either in a preparation course or by buying some of the old tests from the Graduate Management Admission Council. This organization also sells *The Official Guide for GMAT Review,* which contains actual tests, for $13.95, and personal computer software to help study for the exam for $59.95. (The address is Graduate Management Admission Test; Educational Testing Service; P.O. Box 6103; Princeton, New Jersey 08541). At the least, you need to get the GMAT Bulletin of Information to register for the test and gain essential information about it. (You can telephone GMAT at 609-771-7330 for the free bulletin.)

The GMAT looks like most other entrance exams. The math is tougher than you found on your old SATs, but the basic format of the test is the same. Still, if you haven't seen much algebra and geometry since high school days, you'll need to do lots of prep work. The verbal sections test your ability to understand and evaluate what is read. The quant sections measure basic math skills as well as your ability to solve quantitative problems and interpret the data in graphs, charts, and tables. In 1994, GMAC officials added a pair of essay questions to the test. The grading on this portion of the exam is based on how well you present logical arguments and express ideas that are "correct, concise, and persuasive."

What to expect? In the first essay question, you'll be asked to analyze a given issue. The GMAT will contain a statement followed by a series of questions. Here's an example:

> People often complain that products are not made to last. They feel that making products that wear out fairly quickly wastes both natural and human resources. What they fail to see, however, is that such manufacturing practices keep costs down for the consumer and stimulate demand.

After reading the statement, you'll be asked the following:

Which do you find more compelling, the complaint about products that do not last, or the response to it? Explain your

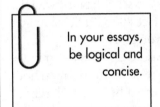

In your essays, be logical and concise.

position, using relevant reasons and/or examples drawn from your own experience, observations, or reading.

The second essay question requires you to analyze an argument. The GMAT again will provide a statement followed by several queries you have to answer. Example:

The computerized, on-board warning system that will be installed in commercial airliners will virtually solve the problem of midair plane collisions. One plane's warning system can receive signals from another's transponder—a radio set that signals a plane's course—in order to determine the likelihood of a collision and recommend evasion action.

After reading and digesting this bit of esotericism culled from a magazine, you'll be asked to discuss how logically convincing you find this argument. You'll need to analyze the "line of reasoning and the use of evidence in the argument" and suggest ways to strengthen the argument.

This essay section is graded separately from the multiple-choice questions, with scores ranging from zero (unscorable because the writing is illegible, or the test-taker failed to write on the assigned topic) to six (outstanding). Each essay is scored by two people, and you'll get an average of the scores from the two graders. You're given a full hour to respond to these two essays, while roughly three hours of the test are devoted to the verbal and quant sections of the exam.

SHOULD YOU TAKE A GMAT PREP COURSE?

Need some advice to up your score? Don't bother with coaching books that contain simulated GMAT exams. Get copies of the real things and practice with them. You need to become "fluent" in test-taking, knowing exactly what to expect when you step into the testing center to take the exam. That's the goal in most prep courses. A key to this is attaining a level of comfort with the test itself. Buy a stopwatch and practice as much as you can, taking timed tests. Review the answers and analyze the parts of the test you had wrong. Look for patterns and correct them. After a few practice tests, you'll be ready to approach the exam more systematically. "The best advice on how to prepare is to familiarize yourself with the GMAT and what it tests," says Robert Levy, national director of graduate programs for Kaplan Educational Services. "Whether you decide to prepare with a course, software, or a book, the key is walking into the test and not being faced with any surprises."

If you can rule out one or more of the five answers on the multiple-choice questions, you generally should guess. But be aware that your odds of guessing the right answer are not necessarily one in four or five. Each section of the GMAT typically flows from the easiest questions to the most difficult. Therefore guessing could be less productive toward the end of a GMAT section.

Is it worth the money to take a prep course? Probably so—especially if you lack the self-discipline to practice and study on your own. Going to a classroom on a regular basis with other MBA hopefuls helps to keep you motivated and directed toward the goal of doing the best you can on this important test. One firm claims that its average students increase their GMAT scores by 70 points after taking its six-week review course. (That's the difference between what a student scores on the first diagnostic test and the final one given to them.) But if you do take a course, it makes sense to do it no more than two months before you sit down with the real GMAT. This is the equivalent of training for a race. You don't stop two months before the race.

A class will lighten your wallet to the tune of between $750 to $900, depending on where you live—but both the Stanley H. Kaplan Educational Center, the nation's largest coaching service that offers a course with 11 sessions, and the Princeton Review, Inc. actually offer financial aid to offset the cost. You'll have to go to the trouble of filling out a financial aid form, but it can be worth it. Kaplan offers unlimited financial help, while the Review discounts its classes an average of $100 for those who prove financial hardship.

Which firm offers the better course? That's hard to say. So much depends on the individual instructor and how well he or she can motivate you in the classroom. Courses often meet in small groups once a week in the early evenings or on the weekends. Instructors analyze typical mistakes made on actual GMAT tests, then work those areas to death. If you're weak in geometry questions, you'll get drilled on the subject. There are also workshops of six to eight people held on weekends, sometimes on Sunday mornings. Expect to spend about 24 hours in class and another 18 hours in workshops. A one-on-one tutoring service is also available for

If you lack self-discipline, take a prep course.

over $1000. To get more information on the Review courses, call 800-333-0369, or check their web site at www.review.com. To obtain more information on the Kaplan courses, call 800-KAP-TEST, or check their web site at www.kaplan.com.

If you do enroll in one of these prep courses, it helps to start before classes begin. Get Kaplan or Princeton Review to give you the study materials a few weeks before you start so you have the time to familiarize yourself with them. There are usually so many books and tests that it's virtually impossible to do all of them during the course. Another bit of advice: If you have the option, take the longer of the two prep courses. Some applicants complain that the shorter course is simply too compressed and hurried.

CREATING YOUR PERSONAL MARKETING STRATEGY

Getting through the admissions screens at the top business schools requires not only a good GMAT score, time, and effort. It also requires a strategy. As applications rise higher and higher, it's getting tougher than ever for applicants to differentiate themselves from the masses. To enhance the odds of success, it's necessary to create a strong personal marketing campaign for yourself. You do this within the confines of your admissions interview, your application—especially your answers to essay questions, and through your recommenders.

Consider the strategy of Phil Carpenter, a Stanford MBA: "When I was applying to business school, I developed a positioning strategy based on what I thought made myself unique. I was a liberal arts major, yet had plunged into the fray of Silicon Valley and over the course of three years had become fairly technical. I therefore positioned myself as the liberal arts guy with a technical twist, and provided evidence to show just how my combination of strong written and verbal skills, plus a solid technology background, made me not only a unique candidate but one who had been very successful in my chosen field of high-tech marketing."

Carpenter, who has since co-authored the superb *Marketing Yourself to the Top Business Schools,* reinforced this image of himself through his selection of recommenders. One of them was the chief executive of the start-up company he worked for before business school. Another recommender was an art history professor whom he got to know during his undergraduate studies. Yet another was a Stanford Law School professor who had known him since he was a child. Together, they helped to position him as the "liberal arts guy" with a technical bent.

"The key to differentiating yourself is to try to put yourself in the role of the admissions officer evaluating your application file," advises Steve Christakos, former director of admissions at Northwestern's Kellogg School. "Too often, unsuccessful candidates have trouble presenting themselves with a sense that they're going to be evaluated against other applicants. For example, rather than discuss what you've accomplished as an investment banking analyst, you may wish to address your more unique characteristics in terms of your potential contributions in an entire business school class. Trying to differentiate yourself on the basis of what you did as an analyst is hard to do when so many other people have the same work background. But you may be able to talk and write about the confidence and conviction demonstrated as editor of a newspaper you started in college, or the unusual maturity you were forced to display as a teenager when you were left at home as the oldest of four siblings."

CRAFTING THE PERFECT B-SCHOOL ESSAY

It's your answers to a school's essay questions that provide the single best opportunity to position yourself to an admissions staff. Many of the best schools want to get to know the real you. That's why one of the most critical parts of the application process is the section of essay questions. They don't want bland and boring answers. They don't want vague and unspecific examples. They want insight into what makes you tick, why you're motivated to get the MBA, and what you're likely to accomplish with it. Base your essay on specific experiences, people, and influences from your life. When you draw on those unique experiences, your essays will be as unusual as your personal experiences. The more detail, the better.

What can you expect? The University of Michigan's Business School hits you with four mandatory essay questions and gives you the option of responding to a fifth one as well. Here's a sample: "The year is 2010, and the annual edition of *Who's Who* includes your biography. What does it say, beginning from the time when you completed your MBA degree?" Or how about this one: "You are the manager of a product line which has, since its introduction 10 years ago, been extremely popular with consumers and very profitable for your firm. However, your research team has advised you of a long-term study which shows that the product may lead to health problems in consumers 5 to 10 years after they purchase it. Due to increased competition in the rest of your company's industries, the company will be forced to close down a part of its operations, leading to widespread layoffs, unless it continues to manufacture and market this product. What are the issues facing the company, and how would you approach the situation?"

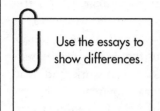

Use the essays to show differences.

Those queries are pretty much straightforward. But the admissions directors at some schools almost seem to delight in thinking up unusual questions to ask applicants. One recently asked potential students to write a succinct description of how they handled real-life ethical challenges. Another asked applicants to describe the details of failures in their careers.

Applicants to the University of Pennsylvania's Wharton School found themselves puzzling over some of the more novel essay questions:

- "What one non-professional activity do you find most inspirational, and why?"
- "Write about a time when you experienced change within an organization. Identify and evaluate your role in the process."
- "Describe a personal achievement that has had a significant impact on your life."

How should you answer such questions? Your essays should show how different you are, not how great you are. To stand out among countless applicants who all work capably in their jobs, tell how you have tutored underprivileged children. Discuss the influence your father has had on you, or your role as a guitarist in a rock band or a cellist in a classical quartet, or write about your biggest failure and what you learned from it. "Don't view your essay as an academic article or a business memo, but as a human interest story about yourself," advises Linda Abraham, a consultant who guides applicants through the essay process. "Use anecdotes and analysis."

Accomplishments count, but schools also use essays to assess your personal goals and values. So discuss an accomplishment in terms of the obstacles you overcame to achieve it. It's not enough to write about leading a project team or the challenge in directing people of diverse backgrounds. You need to discuss specifically what challenges you faced dealing with someone who didn't accept or respect you. Use personal experiences that reveal strength of character, leadership qualities, and personal integrity. Too frequent use of the word "I" and too rare use of the word "we" in recording your accomplishments can put off some B-school admissions officers. Sensitive to criticisms that MBAs are too self-centered, many schools today emphasize teamwork and read essays with an eye toward ferreting out the egomaniacs.

Don't plan to knock off the essays in a single evening. Completing a set should take 20 to 40 hours of thinking, organizing, drafting, and polishing. On each essay, stick to the point you want to make. To get some idea of what to emphasize, look over the school's brochures—they often contain clues about what kinds of students are wanted. (Those with managerial potential? diversified skills?) Play up how well you fit their bill.

"Most candidates tend to use a grab-bag approach, hoping they'll hit on something that clicks with us," adds Christakos. "We don't want people to ramble on." Be succinct and to the point. A good rule of thumb is to stay within 10 percent of the suggested upper word limit. Figure out the themes you will need to fully answer a question or essay topic, and don't wander or overwrite. Admissions staff, weary from reading through thousands of pages of this stuff, favor quality over quantity. Duke University's Fuqua School of Business was shocked when it received a four-inch-thick package via Federal Express from an overzealous applicant. The application materials were in a three-ring binder that included a table of contents, with charts detailing what the applicant had done so far with his life and where he planned to go. The package drew plenty of chuckles, but no special consideration.

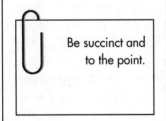

Be succinct and to the point.

Honesty is vital. "Don't play games," advises Karen Page, who runs a Learning Annex seminar for MBA applicants in New York. "Play up everything you've done for what it's worth, but don't cross the line to lie or cheat." Admissions staff aren't likely to check on your facts, but they've read through so many applications that they can sense when something doesn't quite add up.

If you know a graduate of the school, ask him or her to read your essays before you turn them in. What about attention-getting ploys like writing in crayon or sending a videotape? Some applicants are bold enough to try them. Rather than complete an essay, one UCLA applicant, an avid runner, sent a picture of himself with the headline: "How badly do you want to go to UCLA?" The picture showed him with a victorious smile, completing the New York Marathon in record time. That, too, drew a few laughs around the office. But as a rule, most admissions directors dislike gimmicks.

TO INTERVIEW OR NOT

In recent years, a new wrinkle has appeared in the applications process: a personal interview. Northwestern University's Kellogg School was the first B-school to interview every applicant to its full-time program—more than 6000 of them in 1996—in one-hour sessions in places as far-flung as Tokyo and Kuala Lumpur. The reason? Kellogg officials don't believe it's possible to assess a person's composure, articulateness, or leadership ability from test scores or past grades. To put the interview into perspective, it's interesting to note that 644 Kellogg applicants for the Class of 1994 scored over 700 on their GMATs. But only 32 percent of them were offered admission. Many observers believe that the reason Northwestern is a favorite among corporate recruiters is because it screens its candidates well, thus bagging the best of them.

Now, other top schools are giving more candidates the once-over. Michigan, Florida, and Chicago claim to interview virtually all MBA applicants. In 1996, for example, Harvard conducted personal interviews with 65 percent of its admitted class, up from 38 percent only a year earlier. In putting together Harvard's Class of 1999, the school expects to interview 75 percent of the admitted class. Some schools allow alumni to interview and file reports on candidates, others prefer that only a select group of admissions staff conduct the questioning.

What should you expect? In general, interviewers want to try to evaluate leadership and communication skills. In non-U.S. applicants, the schools are also looking to evaluate English-speaking proficiency. "I'm most interested in motives," says Steven DeKrey, director of the MBA program at the University of Florida. "I'm after the whys and the decisions that brought the candidate here. Why this school? Why management? I'm looking for the individual who has made his or her own decisions. Someone who isn't aimed at me because of a boss or someone else." In early 1997, Harvard asked applicants to describe a conflict at work and how they dealt with it, their leadership styles, and their goals and objectives in 10 years.

Seek an interview if you think it would be helpful to plead your case in person—especially if you're articulate and think you can demonstrate some leadership qualities. "All we know about you is what you put on paper," reasons Michael Hostetler, a former dean at Duke. "So it's the applicant's best way to make sure we have as accurate a picture of him or her as possible." Conversely, however, it could be the kiss of death. If you're not likely to do well in an interview situation, by all means avoid it. "Anyone who interviews poorly is a fool to do a nonrequired interview," admits DeKrey. A poor performance during an interview can cancel all your hopes for admission to a good school.

MANAGING YOUR RECOM- MENDERS

Most applicants don't give enough attention to the people they ask to recommend them for MBA admission. If you can get a successful alum to write a letter on your behalf, do it. Generally, though, you should ask people who know you well. Advises Harvard admissions director, Jill Hubbell Fadule: "Ask people who you have worked with closely who can comment on your ability to work with others and manage others and who have some insight into your long-term potential. We have a problem with applicants who feel that they need the most senior person they know or who they have ever run into write their letters of recommendation or that they should only get letters from our alumni. But the quality of the relationship is more important. The person needs to know the applicant very well in order to do a good job answering our questions. We get letters from Ted Kennedy and others who may have run across a candidate in a blue moon. That only wastes a data point that an applicant could have used to provide more valuable information."

It goes without saying, of course, that you should make sure that whoever you ask for a reference will give you a good one and will send it in on time. That's not as easy as you might think. Some B-schools ask particularly specific questions of recommenders, and ask that they mail their questionnaires to the schools separately and in private. Harvard, for example, even requires them to rate you on a scale of "Unusually Outstanding/Top 2 percent" to "Poor/Bottom Third" on such characteristics as integrity, intellectual ability, self-confidence, maturity, and your ability to work with others. Make sure that your references have a positive view of your abilities and talents.

You also need to prepare recommenders for the assignment. You should provide them with background material on you, including your résumé. "If you have finished all or parts of your application, share that material with your recommenders," says Carpenter, co-author of *Marketing Yourself to the Top Business Schools.* "If not, I do recommend that you put together a quick memo that outlines why you feel you need to pursue the MBA, and what it will do to help further your goals. Some background on what you have been doing in your professional life will be particularly useful for a professor who may not have heard from you in a while. By all means, give your recommenders preparatory information—it helps you to manage the message."

HOW TO GET A SCHOOL TO FOOT PART OF THE TUITION BILL

Getting into a good B-school is hard enough. It requires smarts, motivation, and maturity. It also requires money, and lots of it. MIT's Sloan School of Management charges $22,700 for annual tuition. In 1986, the school's yearly tuition was $11,200. How do most full-time MBAs meet the staggering costs? One study showed that they borrowed half of the cost and squeezed a quarter of it from their parents. Scholarships account for only 11 percent of the total bill for male students, but cover 25 percent of the female MBAs' bill. Minorities are also more likely to get a greater proportion of their tuition from scholarship funds.

The best way to get financial help is to ask for it, and ask early. That means your application should arrive as soon as the admissions office begins to accept them. Ask the admissions staff and student aid office about the scholarships offered. Inquire whether work-study or graduate assistantships are available. Most scholarships are based on either merit or need, so you have to prove one or the other—and it's best to provide evidence of both. It's also sometimes possible for a top applicant to gain greater financial aid from a second-tier school than a brand-name one. Why? B-schools that lack Top 25 status may dangle big bucks in front of strong candidates they otherwise might not be able to attract. Consider Nick Grasberger, who had three years of work experience with USX Corporation and a spinoff company, Aristech Chemical Corporation. Besides the solid work background, he was a dean's list scholar at Notre Dame and scored a 680 on the GMAT.

He was set to go to Wharton after gaining acceptance there, but then the University of Pittsburgh offered him a full-tuition scholarship and a $250-a-month stipend even though he hadn't asked for any financial aid at all. Pitt hands out six of these "Associate Fellow" scholarships a year. "I had always had my heart and mind set on Wharton," says Grasberger, "but I may have had to borrow $50,000 to go there." He opted for Pittsburgh, graduating from the 11-month program and joining H.J. Heinz.

New York University's Stern School and many other schools have their version of the Pitt program. Stern, for example, made 30 offers to applicants in 1994 under its Dean's Scholars program, which provides full or partial funding ranging from $5000 to $15,000 a year. "You need to compete in a lot of ways, and we've learned that people are sensitive to price and to the personal attention they get," says George Daly, dean of Stern. Starting in the fall of this year, for example, Cornell's Johnson School will award full-tuition, two-year Park Fellowships to 30 entering MBA students. The fellowships, funded by the Park Foundation, are named for the late media entrepreneur Roy H. Park. This is an incredible deal for highly qualified applicants: Not only is your full tuition paid for, but you also get a stipend to cover basic living expenses, books, and supplies. The idea behind the fellowship is to allow Cornell to compete more aggressively for the best students. Those selected for the fellowships must "demonstrate exceptional promise for academic and professional success. Strong consideration will be given to candidates whose academic and work experience demonstrate exceptional leadership capabilities, a devotion to public service, and a keen concern for environmental issues."

Of the 140 students in Carnegie Mellon's Class of 1996 who applied for financial aid, 120 got scholarships and grants that averaged $5800 each for their first year. At Northwestern's Kellogg School, 20 to 25 percent of the class gets some scholarship money. But there are very few full scholarships, and most of those are for minorities. About 68 percent of the MBAs at Duke get financial assistance, 40 percent of them scholarships that average about $7000 a year. If you can't get a scholarship, try for a low-interest loan from the school. Some schools use a central application service such as the Graduate and Professional School Aid Service. If a loan is required, you can write for a form from GAPSFAS, CN 6660, Princeton, New Jersey 08541. You'll need to complete the form and send it back to Princeton. The service will analyze your resources and send its analysis to the schools of your choice. Check with the admissions or financial aid offices to find out what each requires.

Another option gaining greater attention is the "MBA Loans" program run by the Graduate Management Admission Council.

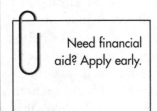

Need financial aid? Apply early.

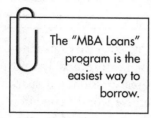

The "MBA Loans" program is the easiest way to borrow.

The program ties together federal, need-based loans and private loans in a one-stop-shopping approach. Students who apply for help under this program are simultaneously considered for all federal loan programs as well as private loans, eliminating the need to fill out numerous applications. GMAC asserts that its single lending source provides low guaranteed fees and low interest rates. For more information, contact GMAC at 800-366-6227.

You might not like the idea of going into hock to pay for your MBA, but if it's the only way to pay the bills, it might be worth it. In most cases, you won't have to worry about repaying the debt until after you graduate and get that lucrative job.

RANKING THE B-SCHOOLS

Rankings of any kind are controversial, whether they rate automobiles or pizzas. Because rankings measure quality and, therefore, prestige, they tend to arouse great passion and spark much interest. In an increasingly competitive world, reputation counts for a lot. That's why so many people are intrigued by rankings and why rankings cause such a stir.

In the business school world, there are only two closely watched and followed rankings, both done by magazines: the biennial BUSINESS WEEK ranking and the annual *U.S. News and World Report* ranking. These polls measure very different things, which is why the results can vary significantly. BUSINESS WEEK, for example, bases its ranking of the best schools on extensive surveys of graduates and corporate recruiters. *U.S. News* bases much of its ranking on admissions and placement data, including average GMAT scores and starting salaries of MBAs provided to the magazine by the schools.

Until BUSINESS WEEK began to rate the schools on customer satisfaction in 1988, most rankings had been based largely on the reputation of the schools' professors and their published work in academic journals. Typically, B-school deans or faculty were asked to list the top schools in order of personal preference. A school's academic prestige usually loomed large in such ratings, and the deans and faculty members tended to give lots of weight to a school's reputation for academic research. There's no disputing that research is vital both to a school and to American business. But traditional surveys gave short shrift to a school's teaching excellence, the quality of its curriculum, or the value of its graduates to Corporate America.

BUSINESS WEEK adopted a strikingly different approach: It surveys both the graduates of top schools and the mainstream MBA recruiters who hire them. In effect, the survey measures how well the schools are serving their two markets—students and their ultimate employers. The 1996 graduate poll was randomly mailed to 7235 MBAs from 51 of the most prominent schools in the country. We received 4830 replies to the 36-question survey, a response rate of 67 percent. The views of the Class of 1996 were then supplemented with those collected by the magazine in 1994 and 1992 to

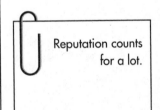

Reputation counts for a lot.

form a graduate ranking. All told, the responses of 14,150 graduates were factored into the ranking. The poll of corporate recruiters was mailed to 326 companies that actively recruit these graduates from the campuses of the best schools. In 1996 alone, these companies hired 8100 MBAs. BW received 227 replies, a 70 percent response rate. The result:

BUSINESS WEEK'S **TOP 25 BUSINESS SCHOOLS**

OVERALL RANK	1994 RANK	CORPORATE RANKING	GRADUATE RANKING	GRADS EARNING OVER $100,000	AVERAGE JOB OFFERS
1. Wharton	1	1	4	49%	3.1
2. Michigan	6	3	3	24	3.5
3. Northwestern	2	2	8	45	3.8
4. Harvard	5	4	9	62	4.2
5. Virginia	12	11	1	41	2.7
6. Columbia	8	6	16	39	2.7
7. Stanford	4	7	11	59	3.3
8. Chicago	3	5	23	32	2.9
9. MIT	10	8	13	52	3.6
10. Dartmouth	13	12	7	52	2.7
11. Duke	11	10	10	23	3.1
12. UCLA	9	17	2	33	3.1
13. Berkeley	19	16	5	33	2.9
14. NYU	16	9	21	14	2.4
15. Indiana	7	13	17	3	2.8
16. Washington U.	NA	20	12	0	3.3
17. Carnegie Mellon	14	26	5	23	3.3
18. Cornell	15	18	20	17	2.9
19. North Carolina	18	27	14	12	3.1
20. Texas at Austin	17	15	28	5	2.9
21. Rochester	NA	38	18	9	2.6
22. Yale	NA	30	22	34	2.8
23. Southern Methodist	NA	43	15	5	2.8
24. Vanderbilt	NA	40	19	9	2.3
25. Thunderbird	NA	23	26	4	2.3

How does this ranking differ from others? The 1996 list by *U.S. News & World Report* found that the best schools were, in order: (1) Stanford, (2) MIT, (3) Wharton, (4) Kellogg, (5) Harvard, (6) Chicago, (7) Dartmouth, (8) Columbia, (9) Duke, and (10) Berkeley. The rest: (11) Virginia, (12) Michigan, (13) New York University, (14) Carnegie Mellon, (15) Cornell, (16) UCLA, (17) North Carolina, (18) Texas at Austin, (19) Yale, (20) Indiana, (21) Purdue, (22) Emory, (23) Rochester, (24) Maryland, and (25) Georgetown.

What accounts for the differences? The *U.S. News* ranking is largely based on numerical data. Student selectivity, determined by such things as average GMAT score, undergraduate grade-point average, and acceptance rates, accounted for 25 percent of the ranking. Placement success alone accounted for 35 percent. It was determined by the percentage of MBAs employed at graduation, those employed three months after graduation, median starting base salaries, and the ratio of recruiters to graduates. The remainder of *U.S. News*'s ranking is based on two reputational surveys sent to B-school deans and MBA program directors as well as corporate recruiters.

What both rankings have in common is that they identify the best schools in the country, regardless of where each school ranks. That is helpful information to assist applicants in narrowing down their choices. Even more helpful, however, is more detailed information on how each of these very good schools is differentiated from the others. Applicants can make the best choices by carefully looking over BUSINESS WEEK's graduates' survey findings to see how these schools truly differ from one another. Would you thrive in a culture that emphasizes competition? If so, the charts on the following pages will tell you that the most obvious Top 25 choices are Columbia and Chicago. If you'd prefer a school with a strong cooperative culture, at the top of your list should be Dartmouth and Washington University. Would you rather have leading-edge professors at the top of their fields in research? If so, you should zero in on Carnegie Mellon and MIT. If, on the other hand, you'd prefer the absolute best teachers, then you should look carefully at Virginia, Dartmouth, and Carnegie Mellon. The charts give you a clue to these and many other critical factors. Each chart shows the 1996 survey results from 25 of the 51 schools at which graduates were surveyed—the 12 that got the best scores on each question and the 12 that received the worst. If you're interested in a school that failed to make the charts, you can safely assume that the school scored in the "average" range—neither excellent nor poor.

Look closely at the detailed information, not just the rankings.

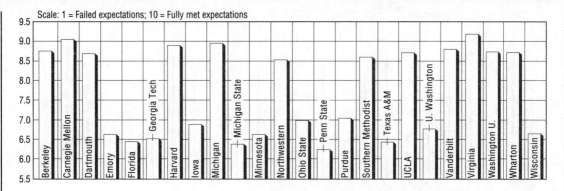

Scale: 1 = Failed expectations; 10 = Fully met expectations

1. To what extent did your MBA experience fulfill or fail to meet your expectations of what a good program should be?

MBA candidates at the top business schools are tough and discriminating customers. They often quit good-paying jobs to go to graduate school, and they pay top-dollar tuition rates. Understandably, they arrive at the schools with high expectations. Which MBA programs do the best job of satisfying those expectations? The top five are Virginia, Carnegie Mellon, Michigan, Harvard, and Vanderbilt. The laggards? Penn State, Michigan State, Texas A&M, Florida, and Georgia Tech.

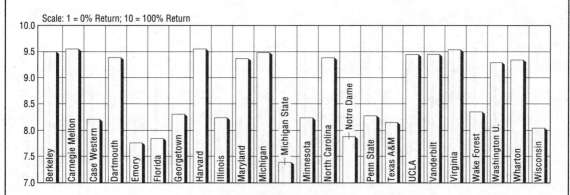

Scale: 1 = 0% Return; 10 = 100% Return

2. Do you believe your MBA was worth its total cost in time, tuition, and lost earnings?

A graduate business education might very well be the most expensive purchase of your life after a house. The average student at the top 50 schools quits a job paying about $38,000 a year and can pay well over $50,000 in tuition and fees. With the average score on this question hitting a record 8.8, the Class of 1996 was quite happy with what it got for this hefty investment. Harvard, Carnegie Mellon, Virginia, Berkeley, and Michigan grads led the pack in this category. Michigan State, Emory, Florida, Notre Dame, and Wisconsin were at the other end.

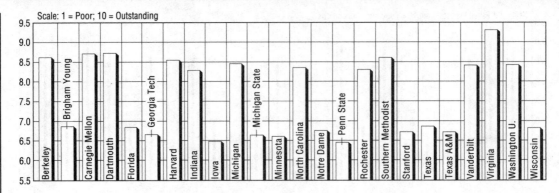

Scale: 1 = Poor; 10 = Outstanding

3. How would you rate the quality of teaching in core courses?

What's taught in every MBA core curriculum are the fundamentals: finance, accounting, marketing, statistics, and organizational behavior. Even though these basic skills are critical, many schools put junior profs in these core classes, partly because the veterans prefer to teach higher-level electives. Which schools boast superb core teachers? Virginia, Dartmouth, Carnegie Mellon, Berkeley, Southern Methodist, and Harvard. On the other hand, Penn State, Iowa, Minnesota, Michigan State, and Georgia Tech have a lot to learn. Top 25 schools near the bottom: Stanford and Texas.

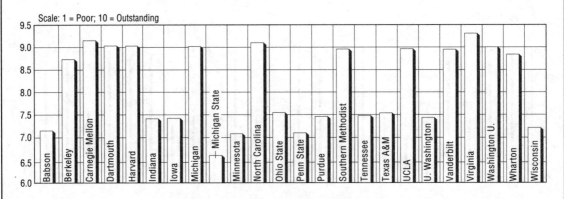

Scale: 1 = Poor; 10 = Outstanding

4. How would you rate the quality of the teaching in elective courses?

After you learn the basics, a school's ability to deliver in-depth knowledge in key areas makes or breaks an MBA education. It's the elective offerings at any school that allow students to custom-design the degree to their personal career goals. The professors at Virginia, Carnegie Mellon, North Carolina, Harvard, and Dartmouth earn the best reviews. The teachers at Michigan State, Minnesota, Penn State, Babson, and Wisconsin have to try harder. The only Top 25 school to score near the bottom: Indiana.

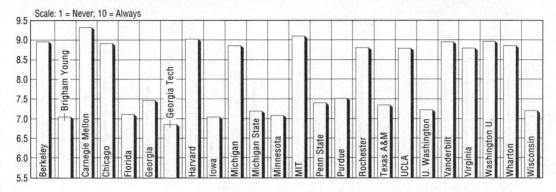

Scale: 1 = Never; 10 = Always

5. Were your teachers at the leading edge of knowledge in their fields?

Schools that rely too heavily on executives for adjunct faculty run the risk of putting a prof in front of a class to tell little more than old war stories. It's not only important to maintain a balance of the theoretical and practical, it's also critical for a school to boast teachers who are at the leading edge of thinking in management, finance, and marketing. Grads felt this to be particularly true at Carnegie Mellon, MIT, Harvard, Berkeley, Chicago, and Wharton. They were less certain of it at Georgia Tech, Iowa, Brigham Young, Minnesota, and Florida.

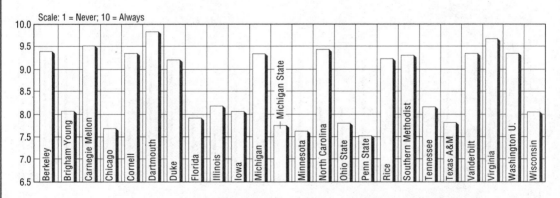

Scale: 1 = Never; 10 = Always

6. Were the faculty available for informal discussion when classes were not in session?

Professors at the best B-schools have a great gig: Corporations want them as consultants and publishers want them to write business books. But profs need to balance those lucrative outside interests with the demands of their students who not only want them in the classroom, but also want time outside the class. Which schools' faculty seems most available to help students after class? Dartmouth leads this key teaching quality, followed by Virginia, Carnegie Mellon, North Carolina, and Berkeley. On the other end are Penn State, Minnesota, Chicago, Michigan State, and Ohio State.

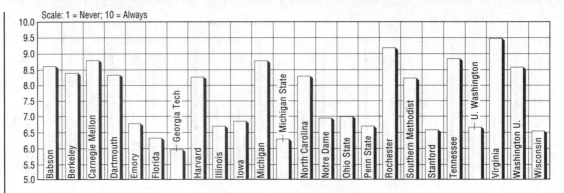

Scale: 1 = Never; 10 = Always

7. To what extent was the coursework integrated as opposed to being taught as a cluster of loosely related topics?

Most business problems have marketing, financial, and operations implications. Yet, most MBA programs view problems from narrow functional perspectives. That's why so many curriculum makeovers have focused on the need to integrate the basic business disciplines. Who's doing the best job? Virginia, Rochester, Tennessee, Carnegie Mellon, and Michigan. Graduates at Georgia Tech, Michigan State, Florida, Wisconsin, and Stanford believe their schools don't do nearly as well.

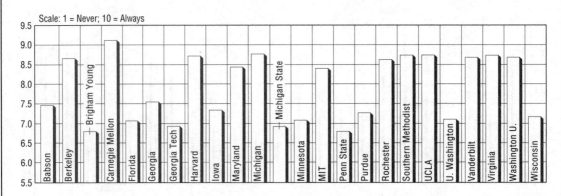

Scale: 1 = Never; 10 = Always

8. How current was the material/research presented in class for discussion and review?

While a lot of the research in academia is rather esoteric, a good deal of it is vital to a school and to American business. Professors who conduct leading-edge research, however, should be able to transmit some of it to their students in the class. If that research work fails to filter down into the classroom, students can hardly benefit from it. Grads think Carnegie Mellon, Michigan, UCLA, Southern Methodist, Virginia, and Harvard do the best job of getting current research and topics into courses. Brigham Young, Penn State, Michigan State, Georgia Tech, and Florida need to work at it.

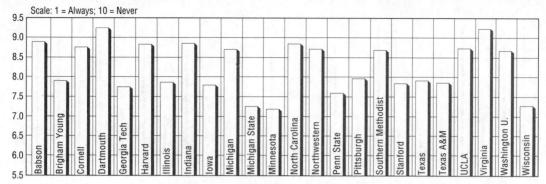

Scale: 1 = Always; 10 = Never

Schools (left to right): Babson, Brigham Young, Cornell, Dartmouth, Georgia Tech, Harvard, Illinois, Indiana, Iowa, Michigan, Michigan State, Minnesota, North Carolina, Northwestern, Penn State, Pittsburgh, Southern Methodist, Stanford, Texas, Texas A&M, UCLA, Virginia, Washington U., Wisconsin

9. Do you believe the faculty compromised teaching in order to pursue their own research?

What drives academia is research. Teachers are largely rewarded with promotions and tenure on the basis of their own study and publication of it in scholarly journals. Much of it, unfortunately, is either meaningless or inaccessible to the average manager. Few excellent teachers gain tenure if their research doesn't please colleagues; virtually all excellent researchers get tenure even if they can't teach. Grads say the schools that get this right are Dartmouth, Virginia, Babson, Indiana, North Carolina, and Harvard. At the bottom are Minnesota, Wisconsin, Michigan State, Penn State, and Georgia Tech.

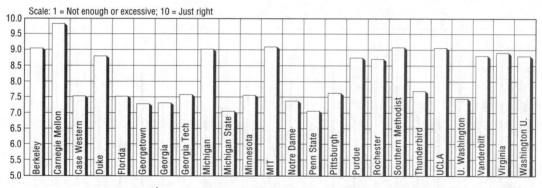

Scale: 1 = Not enough or excessive; 10 = Just right

Schools (left to right): Berkeley, Carnegie Mellon, Case Western, Duke, Florida, Georgetown, Georgia, Georgia Tech, Michigan, Michigan State, Minnesota, MIT, Notre Dame, Penn State, Pittsburgh, Purdue, Rochester, Southern Methodist, Thunderbird, UCLA, U. Washington, Vanderbilt, Virginia, Washington U.

10. As a result of the program, how would you assess your ability to work with computers and other analytical tools that affect your ability to manage?

Managing information has become an important part of business and life. B-schools have responded to this challenge in different ways, but it's vital to learn how to use computers, networks, and analytical tools to help you become a better manager. Carnegie Mellon grads say they're most comfortable here, followed closely by MIT, Southern Methodist, UCLA, and Berkeley. Bringing up the rear? Michigan State, Penn State, Georgetown, Georgia, and Notre Dame. The only Top 25 school near the bottom: Thunderbird.

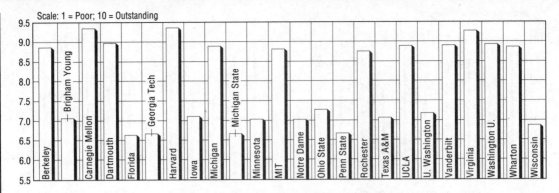

Scale: 1 = Poor; 10 = Outstanding

11. **How would you assess the school's performance in providing you with numerous ways of thinking or approaching problems that will serve you well over the long haul?**

If you take away anything from an MBA program, it should be a systematic way of solving business problems. When a manager or executive confronts a difficult decision, he or she should have a framework or way of thinking available for weighing the pros and cons. Graduates think that Carnegie Mellon, Harvard, Virginia, and Dartmouth do the best job in this department. MBAs were less satisfied at Florida, Michigan State, Georgia Tech, and Penn State.

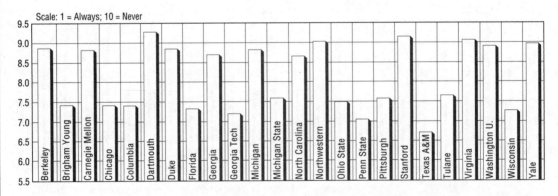

Scale: 1 = Always; 10 = Never

12. **Do you feel your classmates emphasized individual achievement at the expense of teamwork?**

There was a time when nearly everyone assumed that MBA students were almost all cut-throat competitive. That's hardly the case these days, even at Harvard where students are graded on a curve. But some schools go out of their way to encourage highly cooperative, rather than competitive, cultures. The schools that do the best at fostering friendly cooperation? Dartmouth, Stanford, Virginia, Northwestern, and Yale. The most competitive schools? Texas A&M, Penn State, Georgia State, and Wisconsin. Columbia and Chicago are the only Top 25 schools near the bottom.

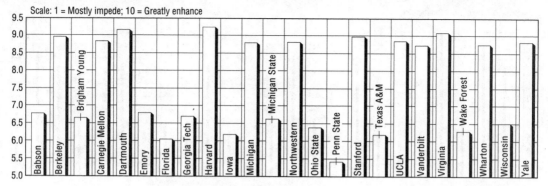

Scale: 1 = Mostly impede; 10 = Greatly enhance

13. Did the caliber of your classmates impede or enhance the learning process?

A funny thing happens when you ask MBA graduates to assess their experience on campus. They almost always say that they learned as much, if not more, from their fellow classmates as from their professors. The quality and mix of people a school invites into a program are critical to the learning process. Which schools' graduates thought the most of their classmates? Not surprisingly, Harvard leads the pack, followed by Dartmouth, Virginia, Stanford, and Berkeley.

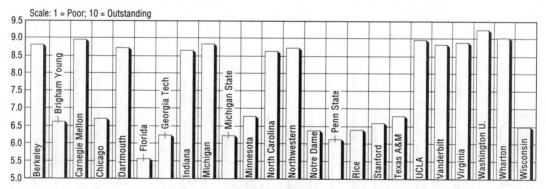

Scale: 1 = Poor; 10 = Outstanding

14. How would you judge the responsiveness of the faculty and administration to students' concerns and opinions?

"Customer service" and "total quality" get a good deal of attention in MBA classrooms around the country. But many students have found that these can be nearly nonexistent concepts when applied to the schools they attend. Some deans and faculty go so far as to say that students aren't customers at all—even though some of them are investing well over $100,000 to get their degrees. Which schools have it right? Washington University, Wharton, UCLA, Carnegie Mellon, Virginia, and Michigan. The deans of Florida, Penn State, Michigan State, and Georgia Tech need to hear a few lectures on customer service. Stanford and Chicago were the only two Top 25 schools near the bottom.

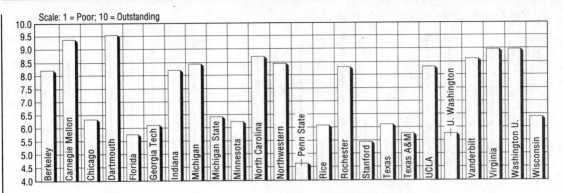

Scale: 1 = Poor; 10 = Outstanding

15. How would you assess the responsiveness of the school in meeting the demand for popular electives?

Since you'll only spend two years on campus getting your degree and the first year will largely be consumed by required courses, time to enroll in key electives is limited. Many students complain that courses they looked forward to were oversubscribed. The upshot: They lost out on coursework they badly wanted. Which schools do the best job of assuring such things don't happen? Dartmouth, Carnegie Mellon, Washington University, Virginia, and North Carolina. The worst? Penn State, Stanford, University of Washington, and Texas A&M.

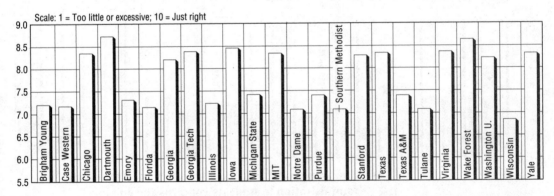

Scale: 1 = Too little or excessive; 10 = Just right

16. How would you appraise your school's efforts to bring you into contact with practicing professionals in the business community?

Because of their locations in urban centers, some schools can lure extraordinary business talent into classrooms and lecture halls. Others try so hard they overcome the disadvantage of being tucked in an out-of-the-way place. Encouraging such contact is a good idea to enhance learning and job networking. Which schools do too little of this? Wisconsin, Tulane, Southern Methodist, and Notre Dame. The best? Out-of-the-way Dartmouth largely because of an aggressive executive-in-residence program.

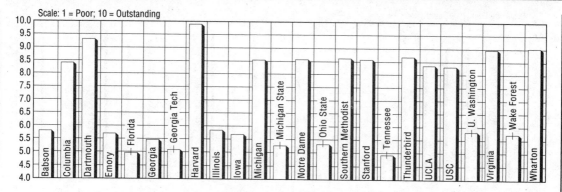

Scale: 1 = Poor; 10 = Outstanding

17. How would you judge the school's alumni network and connections that can help you throughout your career?

MBAs should graduate not only with a degree and a job, but with the contacts that will help them succeed throughout their lifetimes. Indeed, what most distinguishes the very best programs from the others is often the value of a school's alumni network and its willingness to help fellow alums. The best? Harvard, Dartmouth, Wharton, Virginia, and, surprisingly, Thunderbird. The worst? Tennessee, Florida, Georgia Tech, and Michigan State.

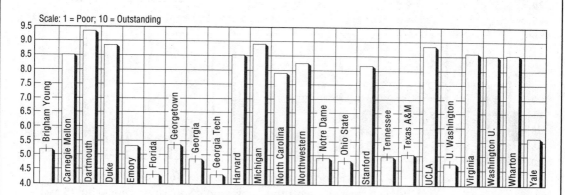

Scale: 1 = Poor; 10 = Outstanding

18. How would you judge the aggressiveness of the school in helping you with summer job placement or a summer internship?

The summer between the two years of an MBA program is an important time. Most MBAs land internships that allow them to sample an industry or a function and gain valuable experience for the ultimate job hunt. This is an opportunity to pad your résumé, too. Which schools work hardest to get their students the most opportunities for summer employment? Michigan, Duke, UCLA, Virginia, Wharton, and Harvard top this list. At the bottom? Florida, Georgia Tech, and the University of Washington.

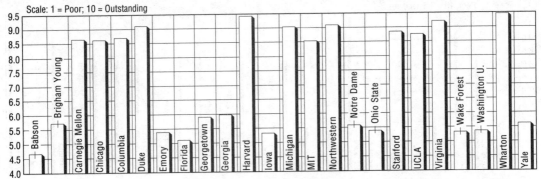

Scale: 1 = Poor; 10 = Outstanding

19. How would you characterize the number and quality of firms recruiting on your campus?

The job market for MBAs has been exploding in recent years largely due to heavy hiring by consulting firms and finance companies and the return of many industrial recruiters. Who's doing the best job in attracting a large number of diversified, brand-name companies to campus? Not surprisingly, Wharton and Harvard sit at the top of this list, followed by Virginia, Duke, Northwestern, and Michigan. At the bottom? Babson, Florida, Wake Forest, and Iowa. The only Top 25 school in the rear: Yale.

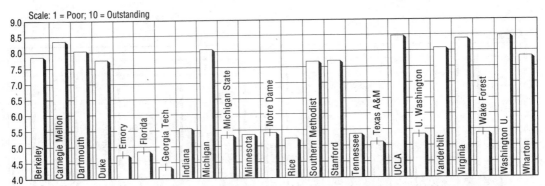

Scale: 1 = Poor; 10 = Outstanding

20. If the organizations you targeted for employment did not recruit on campus, how would you assess your school's assistance in supporting your independent search for a job?

Most of the companies that recruit on campus are looking for MBAs to fill entry-level positions. That's especially frustrating to older, more experienced graduates, who sometimes find themselves overqualified for mainstream MBA jobs. So which schools provide the most help to these older grads or those who seek less-traditional positions can be an important indicator of the quality of a career services office. Which schools rate best? UCLA, Washington University, Virginia, Carnegie Mellon, and Vanderbilt. The worst? Georgia Tech, Emory, Florida, Texas A&M, and Rice University.

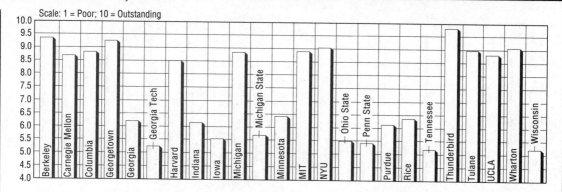

Scale: 1 = Poor; 10 = Outstanding

21. Based on your own personal level of satisfaction, please appraise your school's efforts to include international business topics in the MBA program.

Of all the business buzzwords circulating these days, globalization is way up near the top of the list. Many schools are exposing students to far more material on how the global business environment impacts local companies. Grads at Thunderbird, Berkeley, Georgetown, Wharton, and New York University give their schools the best grades for satisfying their interests in international business. MBAs at Tennessee, Wisconsin, Georgia Tech, and Penn State were the least satisfied on this dimension.

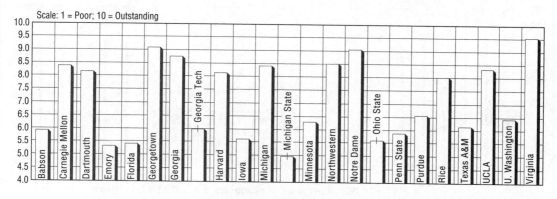

Scale: 1 = Poor; 10 = Outstanding

22. Based on your own personal level of satisfaction, please appraise your school's efforts to include ethics in the MBA program.

Many people argue that it's impossible to teach ethics. If so, it hasn't held back many of the nation's top schools from trying to instill a sense of right and wrong in MBA students. Not surprisingly, the two school winners in this category are among the very few B-schools that offer mandatory, graded ethics courses: Virginia and Georgetown. The weakest in satisfying grads' appetites for ethics in the program: Michigan State and Emory.

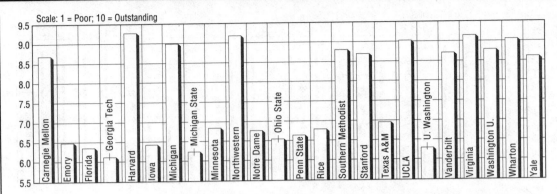

Scale: 1 = Poor; 10 = Outstanding

23. Based on your personal level of satisfaction, please appraise your school's efforts to include leadership topics in the MBA program.

Leadership: How it's obtained, cultivated, and used has been one of the most popular topics in business management for years. One school after another has launched leadership exercises, seminars, and courses in response to corporate demands. Who leads this fast-changing area? Harvard, Northwestern, Virginia, and Wharton top the charts. Graduates were less satisfied at Georgia Tech, Michigan State, and the University of Washington.

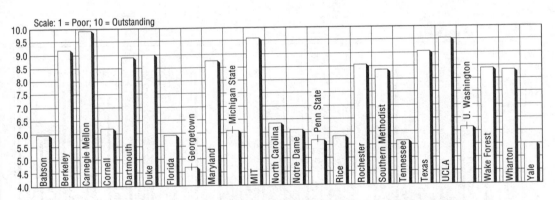

Scale: 1 = Poor; 10 = Outstanding

24. Based on your personal level of satisfaction, please appraise your school's efforts to include information technology concepts in the MBA program.

Advances in technology have revolutionized the practice of management in the past decade. So schools have been working overtime to better integrate computers and their use in the MBA curriculum. Which schools do the best job of exposing their students to the power of information technology as a tool in decision making and management? Carnegie Mellon, MIT, UCLA, and Berkeley top the list. Less successful, if not dismal, are Georgetown, Yale, Tennessee, and Penn State.

B-SCHOOLS BY THE NUMBERS

There are many ways to select a business school and just as many ways to look at one. Here we use numbers and statistics to provide a quick glimpse of the best 50 schools. Some of this data is available from the business schools that routinely publish plenty of their own stats. But a lot of the information made available here was gathered specifically by BUSINESS WEEK from the latest crop of MBA graduates. What also makes these numbers valuable is that they provide direct comparisons among the best schools. Instead of looking at a GMAT average or another number in isolation, you'll see exactly how a school you're interested in compares with its peers.

You'll find a wealth of data in these pages. You'll discover which of the top schools are the most selective and, therefore, the hardest to get into. You'll find out which schools boast the largest enrollments, the highest and lowest percentages of international students, women, or minorities. You'll find out how much money an MBA graduate from each of these schools is likely to command in the job market. And you'll discover which schools' graduates leave campus with the largest loans hanging over their heads.

None of this information constitutes a ranking, nor is any of this data used when BUSINESS WEEK compiles its own rankings of the top schools. But it may help applicants to see how the schools in which they're interested fit into the overall scheme of things. Note that a single asterisk indicates a BUSINESS WEEK estimate.

Stats provide a quick glimpse of the best schools.

GMAT SCORES

No part of the admissions process causes more angst and paranoia than the Graduate Management Admission Test (GMAT). Nearly 300,000 people register to take it every year because every business school requires the test's results from applicants. As imperfect as they are, GMAT scores may be the single best indicator of student quality. How much weight do admissions officers put on a GMAT score? Between 20 and 40 percent. Generally, average scores for the top schools continue to climb. Here are the numbers for the Class of 1998:

TOP 25 SCHOOL	AVERAGE GMAT	RUNNERS-UP SCHOOL	AVERAGE GMAT
Stanford	690*	Maryland	640
Chicago	685	Georgetown	634
Harvard	680*	U. Washington	634
Yale	676	Georgia Tech	633
Dartmouth	669	Georgia	630
Wharton	662	USC	630
Columbia	660*	Emory	626
Northwestern	660	Brigham Young	621
Virginia	660	Tulane	621
Berkeley	652	Penn State	616
UCLA	651	Rice	613
MIT	650	Ohio State	612
Duke	646	Notre Dame	611
NYU	646	Michigan State	610
Michigan	645	Wake Forest	609
Carnegie Mellon	638	Texas A&M	608
Cornell	634	Illinois	605
Texas	631	Case Western	603
Indiana	630	Minnesota	602
Rochester	630	Purdue	602
North Carolina	630	Tennessee	600
Vanderbilt	615	Babson	599
Washington U.	606	Wisconsin	597
Southern Methodist	600	Iowa	589
Thunderbird	572	Pittsburgh	585*

B-SCHOOL SELECTIVITY

Another critical indicator of a business school's quality is the number of applicants it accepts and rejects. Stanford, partly because of its small size but mostly because of its high standards, leads the pack in rejecting the most applicants. It turned down 93 percent of its applicants for the Class of 1998. Generally, it has gotten harder than ever to get into a top school. Two years ago, for example, Wharton accepted 23 percent of its applicants. In 1996, it accepted only 15 percent. Columbia's acceptance rate fell to 14 percent from 25 percent. Texas's acceptance rate fell to 18 percent from 35 percent in 1994.

TOP 25 SCHOOL	APPLICANTS ACCEPTED	RUNNERS-UP SCHOOL	APPLICANTS ACCEPTED
Stanford	7%	Maryland	19%
Berkeley	13	Purdue	23
Harvard	13	Georgia	23
Dartmouth	14	Georgetown	30
Columbia	14	Penn State	30
MIT	14	Ohio State	31
Northwestern	14	Tennessee	31
Wharton	15	Emory	33
Duke	17	Wisconsin	34
UCLA	17	Minnesota	36
Texas	18	Tulane	37
North Carolina	19	USC	38
Virginia	19	U. Washington	38
NYU	20	Case Western	39
Chicago	23	Georgia Tech	40
Yale	23	Illinois	41
Cornell	25	Michigan State	41
Michigan	28	Wake Forest	41
Carnegie Mellon	31	Notre Dame	45
Rochester	36	Rice	45
Vanderbilt	42	Texas A&M	46
Washington U.	44	Iowa	47
Indiana	45	Babson	48
Southern Methodist	62	Brigham Young	51
Thunderbird	75	Pittsburgh	67

FULL-TIME ENROLLMENTS

The size of an MBA program is an important attribute of a school's culture. In the large MBA populations at Harvard, Wharton, Thunderbird, and Columbia, it's easy to be an anonymous student. That's less true at Dartmouth College or Wake Forest, where everyone knows each other by their first names. Generally, most schools have been quietly increasing their enrollments—even while they accept fewer applicants. The Top 25 school with the biggest increase in full-time enrollment? MIT, which has squeezed an additional 217 students into its school since 1994.

TOP 25 SCHOOL	FULL-TIME ENROLLMENT	RUNNERS-UP SCHOOL	FULL-TIME ENROLLMENT
Harvard	1779	Illinois	566
Wharton	1533	Wisconsin	556
Thunderbird	1420	Georgetown	465
Columbia	1255	USC	460
Chicago	1189	Maryland	380
Northwestern	1146	Babson	359
Michigan	828	U. Washington	358
Texas	824	Case Western	310
NYU	800	Purdue	298
Stanford	725	Pittsburgh	296
MIT	717	Penn State	277
Duke	700	Emory	270
UCLA	625	Minnesota	270
Indiana	598	Ohio State	270
Carnegie Mellon	538	Michigan State	264
Cornell	513	Rice	262
Virginia	499	Notre Dame	261
Berkeley	478	Brigham Young	260
Yale	461	Texas A&M	229
North Carolina	427	Georgia Tech	220
Vanderbilt	427	Tulane	212
Rochester	412	Wake Forest	203
Dartmouth	377	Iowa	201
Washington U.	290	Tennessee	181
Southern Methodist	272	Georgia	172

INTER-NATIONAL ENROLLMENTS

With so many schools claiming a global emphasis, this list quickly shows you which institutions have been most receptive to large numbers of non-U.S. students. Rochester leads the Top 25 schools with 46 percent, while Iowa surprisingly tops the list of Runners-Up schools with nearly half of its MBA candidates from outside the United States. Overall, the percentage of non-U.S. students in elite MBA programs continues to rise. Washington University posted the largest increase of any Top 25 school in the past two years, jumping a full 23 points to 39 percent. Iowa climbed 26 percentage points since 1994 to 49 percent.

TOP 25 SCHOOL	INTERNATIONAL STUDENTS	RUNNERS-UP SCHOOL	INTERNATIONAL STUDENTS
Rochester	46%	Iowa	49%
Washington U.	39	Pittsburgh	37
Carnegie Mellon	38	Illinois	35
MIT	37	Maryland	35
Berkeley	35	Ohio State	32
NYU	35	Babson	31
Thunderbird	33	Case Western	31
Yale	31	Georgia Tech	31
Wharton	30	Tulane	31
Cornell	28	Tennessee	29
Harvard	27	Wisconsin	28
Michigan	26	Michigan State	27
Stanford	25	Purdue	27
Columbia	24	Georgetown	26
Northwestern	24	Penn State	26
Chicago	23	Texas A&M	26
Vanderbilt	23	Notre Dame	25
Southern Methodist	22	USC	23
UCLA	20	Emory	21
Duke	19	Georgia	21
UNC	19	U. Washington	20
Texas	17	Brigham Young	17
Indiana	16	Minnesota	17
Dartmouth	16	Wake Forest	15
Virginia	12	Rice	14

WOMEN MBA ENROLLMENTS

A few years ago, some business school deans expressed concern that fewer women were going to get their MBAs. These stats show that the downturn in enrollment was largely a temporary phenomena caused by the influx of more international students. Still, the percentage of women enrolled in the top MBA programs varies widely in Top 25 schools, from a high of 36 percent at North Carolina to a low of just 19 percent at Carnegie Mellon. The same is true among the Runners-Up schools. Tennessee tops the list with more than half of its MBA candidates female, while Brigham Young is at the bottom with 19 percent.

TOP 25 SCHOOL	WOMEN STUDENTS	RUNNERS-UP SCHOOL	WOMEN STUDENTS
North Carolina	36%	Tennessee	51%
Columbia	35	Iowa	50
Thunderbird	35	Wisconsin	36
Berkeley	34	Babson	35
Cornell	32	Georgetown	35
Northwestern	31	Maryland	35
Duke	30	U. Washington	35
Dartmouth	30	Case Western	33
Washington U.	30	Michigan State	33
Stanford	30	Ohio State	33
Virginia	29	Illinois	32
Southern Methodist	29	Pittsburgh	31
Yale	29	USC	30
MIT	28	Tulane	29
Wharton	28	Wake Forest	29
UCLA	27	Emory	28
Harvard	26	Notre Dame	28
NYU	26	Georgia	28
Rochester	26	Texas A&M	28
Michigan	25	Minnesota	27
Texas	25	Georgia Tech	26
Vanderbilt	24	Penn State	26
Chicago	23	Rice	24
Indiana	23	Purdue	21
Carnegie Mellon	19	Brigham Young	19

MINORITY ENROLLMENTS

With all the talk about cultural diversity in the workforce these days, it's interesting to see how the schools stack up when it comes to enrolling minority students in their programs. These percentages are for black, Hispanic, and American Indian students from the United States. Among Top 25 schools, Stanford has posted the biggest gain, jumping to No. 1 with 25 percent, from only 10 percent in 1994. The biggest surprises: the dismal record on minority recruitment at Carnegie Mellon and Chicago. Carnegie fell 3 percentage points in two years to just 2 percent, while Chicago plummeted 13 percentage points to 5 percent.

TOP 25 SCHOOL	MINORITY STUDENTS	RUNNERS-UP SCHOOL	MINORITY STUDENTS
Stanford	25%	USC	33%
Virginia	20	Georgia Tech	23
Harvard	19	Penn State	17
North Carolina	16	Rice	16
Wharton	16	U. Washington	15
MIT	15	Babson	14
Michigan	15	Wisconsin	12
Yale	15	Case Western	12
Texas	14	Maryland	12
Columbia	12	Texas A&M	12
Duke	12	Emory	11
Berkeley	11	Ohio State	11
Cornell	11	Tulane	11
Thunderbird	10	Purdue	10
UCLA	10	Michigan State	10
Northwestern	9	Georgia	9
Rochester	9	Notre Dame	9
Dartmouth	9	Minnesota	8
Indiana	8	Tennessee	8
NYU	8	Georgetown	7
Vanderbilt	7	Illinois	7
Washington U.	6	Iowa	7
Chicago	5	Wake Forest	7
Southern Methodist	5	Pittsburgh	6
Carnegie Mellon	2	Brigham Young	0

PRE-MBA ANNUAL PAY

Schools routinely focus on GMAT scores as an indicator of the quality of applicants. But another important measure that is seldom known is how much money applicants make before getting into business schools. The larger the bucks, the more likely the candidate left a meaningful job in a demanding environment. It's also more likely that candidates earning more money have more valuable work experience to contribute to classroom discussion and debate. Another way to look at these numbers: applicants to the best programs have to give up a lot when they decide to go to an elite graduate business school. So here are the median figures on what MBAs at the top schools made before getting their degrees.

TOP 25 SCHOOL	PRE-MBA PAY	RUNNERS-UP SCHOOL	PRE-MBA PAY
Harvard	$55,000	Southern California	$40,000
Stanford	54,000	Georgetown	36,000
Dartmouth	45,000	Purdue	36,000
Northwestern	45,000	Rice	35,500
MIT	45,000	Georgia	35,000
Wharton	45,000	Minnesota	35,000
UCLA	45,000	Tennessee	34,500
Berkeley	44,000	Babson	34,000
Chicago	44,000	Georgia Tech	33,500
Columbia	44,000	Pittsburgh	33,500
North Carolina	43,000	Case Western	32,000
Virginia	40,000	U. Washington	32,000
Yale	40,000	Maryland	31,000
New York	39,000	Emory	30,000
Michigan	38,500	Notre Dame	30,000
Carnegie Mellon	37,000	Ohio State	30,000
Duke	37,000	Wisconsin	30,000
Cornell	36,750	Michigan State	29,500
Texas	36,000	Iowa	29,000
Indiana	35,000	Illinois	28,000
Rochester	35,000	Wake Forest	28,000
Washington U.	34,000	Penn State	27,000
Southern Methodist	30,000	Texas A&M	25,500
Thunderbird	30,000	Brigham Young	25,000
Vanderbilt	30,000	Tulane	25,000

STARTING PAY PACKAGES

A quick glimpse at these numbers explains why so many people still want to get an MBA. The Class of 1996 from these top 50 schools landed jobs with median starting pay packages approaching $69,000. Indeed, the median pay hit six figures at six schools, up from only Harvard and Stanford in 1994. Thanks largely to continued heavy recruiting by consulting firms, MBAs captured more than hefty salaries and sign-on bonuses. Many of them received such bennies and perks as stock options, free cars, interest-free loans, round-trip airline tickets, relocation and housing allowances, tuition reimbursements up to two full years, and guaranteed year-end bonuses—all of which BW includes in the total pay package. That's why these figures tend to be higher than those reported by the schools.

TOP 25 SCHOOL	TOTAL PAY	RUNNERS-UP SCHOOL	TOTAL PAY
Harvard	$110,640	Georgetown	$70,000
Stanford	108,000	Southern California	70,000
Dartmouth	105,000	Emory	65,000
MIT	102,750	Purdue	65,000
Wharton	100,000	Rice	63,000
Northwestern	95,000	U. Washington	62,150
Columbia	88,850	Case Western	60,500
Chicago	86,000	Minnesota	60,000
Berkeley	85,000	Pittsburgh	57,650
UCLA	85,000	Babson	57,500
Virginia	85,000	Brigham Young	56,500
Yale	83,050	Notre Dame	56,100
Michigan	81,400	Tennessee	56,080
Carnegie Mellon	81,180	Georgia Tech	56,050
Duke	78,000	Ohio State	56,000
North Carolina	77,250	Wake Forest	56,000
New York	75,000	Maryland	55,000
Cornell	70,000	Michigan State	53,500
Texas	69,000	Iowa	52,950
Indiana	67,000	Penn State	52,000
Rochester	65,000	Illinois	50,000
Washington U.	62,750	Georgia	48,750
Southern Methodist	62,350	Tulane	48,450
Vanderbilt	59,000	Texas A&M	47,000
Thunderbird	57,000	Wisconsin	46,800

OUTSTANDING MBA LOANS

When you're making the decision to quit a good-paying job and go back to school for two years, you'll probably scratch your head wondering how you'll pay for that high-priced education. The simple answer: borrow money. These numbers reflect the average outstanding loans for graduates in the Class of 1996. It's not a pretty picture. Harvard grads, for example, leave school with average loans of about $47,600. The lightest debt loads are generally carried by MBAs who graduate from public universities. Among the Top 25 schools, Texas's MBAs owe the least, at an average of $23,000—less than half the debt at Harvard.

TOP 25 SCHOOL	OUTSTANDING LOAN	RUNNERS-UP SCHOOL	OUTSTANDING LOAN
Harvard	$47,595	Babson	$42,107
Chicago	47,335	Georgetown	39,763
Northwestern	46,037	Wake Forest	34,973
Wharton	45,550	Tulane	34,909
Vanderbilt	44,553	Southern California	34,242
Stanford	43,724	Emory	30,350
MIT	42,664	Case Western	29,021
Dartmouth	42,652	Notre Dame	28,365
New York	41,694	Rice	27,707
Yale	39,177	U. Washington	24,447
Duke	38,769	Wisconsin	22,711
Cornell	37,014	Pittsburgh	21,909
Thunderbird	36,174	Minnesota	20,621
Carnegie Mellon	34,506	Illinois	19,839
Columbia	34,392	Michigan State	19,626
Virginia	32,415	Penn State	19,408
Washington U.	30,184	Iowa	18,008
Michigan	29,927	Maryland	17,763
Indiana	28,688	Purdue	16,870
Southern Methodist	28,273	Ohio State	16,786
Rochester	26,669	Brigham Young	16,711
Berkeley	25,102	Tennessee	16,635
UCLA	26,909	Texas A&M	16,591
North Carolina	23,336	Georgia Tech	14,635
Texas	22,931	Georgia	11,933

THE TOP 25

The schools on BUSINESS WEEK's Top 25 list offer the best MBA education you'll find in the United States, if not the world. But that may be the only common thread that holds these schools together. Like the differing personalities you'd find in any group of people, each institution boasts its own culture and style. Each has strengths and weaknesses. Each promises students vastly different educations and experiences.

Which one is best for you? Read through the profiles to find out. They start with a snapshot view of the school that provides important information about the school's size, diversity, cost, selectivity, standing in the polls, and how much its graduates command in the marketplace. We also identify the most outstanding faculty, singled out by the latest graduating class; tips for applicants; and candid comments on the school and its pros and cons from the Class of 1996.

There are other interesting statistics here: not only how many applicants are rejected by the school, but how many of those who are accepted reject the school that sent them an invitation. Wharton, for instance, accepts 15 percent of those who apply, but enrolls 71 percent of the applicants it agrees to admit. The University of Michigan's business school, meantime, accepts 28 percent of its applicants, but enrolls only 44 percent of them.

Virtually all of these figures apply to the class that entered in the fall of 1996 and will graduate in 1998. An asterisk next to any number indicates that the figure is a BUSINESS WEEK estimate. The lists of each school's outstanding professors are also based on the results of the magazine's graduate survey. A professor who received four stars was singled out as a best teacher by 20 percent or more of the respondents; three stars, 15 to 19 percent; two stars, 10 to 14 percent, and one star, under 10 percent.

> Each school has its own culture, style, strengths, and weaknesses.

1.
UNIVERSITY OF PENNSYLVANIA

UNIVERSITY OF PENNSYLVANIA

The Wharton School
104 Vance Hall
Philadelphia, Pennsylvania 19104
E-mail address: mba.admissions@wharton.upenn.edu
Website address: http://www.wharton.upenn.edu/

Corporate ranking: 1	Graduate ranking: 4
Enrollment: 1533	Annual tuition & fees: $23,608
Women: 28%	Room and board: $8515
Non-U.S.: 30%	Average GMAT score: 662
Minority: 16%	Average GPA: 3.42
Part-time: none	GPA range: 2.4 to 4.0
Average age: 27.7	Average years of work exp.: 3–4
Applicants accepted: 15%	Accepted applicants enrolled: 71%
Median starting pay: $100,000	Average starting pay: $101,760

Teaching methods: Lecture, 55%   Case study, 30%   Projects, 15%

Contact:
Robert Alig
Director of Admissions
and Financial Aid
102 Vance Hall
3733 Spruce St.
215-898-3430
*Final application
deadline:* April 10

There may have been a few moments when Thomas P. Gerrity had second thoughts. During the summer of 1996, he was climbing toward the majestic peaks of the Grand Tetons in Wyoming. Some 5000 feet in the air, he had to do a belly crawl across the face of the mountain, his fingers scrabbling for a grip on the granite. "It was a moment of truth," he says.

Gerrity, dean of the University of Pennsylvania's Wharton School, easily made the maneuver and later reached the summit to witness a strikingly beautiful sunrise. Gerrity scaled the heights yet again in 1996 by leading Wharton to the pinnacle of BUSINESS WEEK's B-school ranking for the second time in a row. And he didn't just hang on by his fingernails. The dean significantly strengthened the school's lead among corporate recruiters and gained the fourth-best marks in BUSINESS WEEK's graduate poll to stay ahead.

Wharton's overtaking Northwestern for the No. 1 slot in 1994 was largely the result of major changes, begun in 1991, to its once-rigid MBA curriculum. Gerrity, a former Rhodes scholar, MIT professor, and consultant who had come to Wharton a year earlier, made the education more relevant and pragmatic. He placed greater emphasis on "people skills," added global perspective, and urged profs to teach business in a more integrated fashion. Those changes allowed Wharton to capture the title as the most innovative business school in America in BUSINESS WEEK's survey of corporate recruiters. These efforts are continuing, and a major initiative in globalization is expected to be launched in late 1997. Among other things, the project will employ technology to team

Wharton students with others at business schools around the world in assignments and field projects.

Increasingly, though, the hallmark of Gerrity's administration is his effort to make Wharton, the oldest school of business, a living, experimental management laboratory for its students. "This is a real organization, a model for organizing change out in the real world," he says. "So we're making it a terrific part of the program for students. 'Empowerment' is an overused word, but it relates here."

For years, much of academe has viewed students as a necessary distraction from the mission of advancing knowledge through scholarly research. But soon after arriving at Wharton, Gerrity began using market researcher Opinion Research Corp. to survey the views of first- and second-year students every year. The results led to numerous changes and persuaded him to invest far more time in communicating with students. "We were patting ourselves on our backs a couple of years ago, but the surveys showed us that students still didn't feel connected or didn't particularly understand the vision for the school," Gerrity recalls.

Now, Wharton students sit on and regularly participate in virtually every committee, having a voice in everything from curriculum reform to facilities planning. "We have 6000 to 7000 hours of work experience sitting around here," says Vice-Dean Bruce Allen, who, together with Gerrity, has met with students in lunches, open forums, and meetings—135 in 1996 alone. "We would be fools not to capture that talent and put it to work."

Over an 18-month period from 1995–1996, for example, student committees have worked closely with Gerrity to analyze future space requirements for the business school. One result: Gerrity has won approval for a new $100 million B-school complex of classrooms and meetings halls. Now, MBA students are involved in the actual design of the new building as well.

The dean has also used MBAs to get better performance out of his professors. Each entering class at Wharton appoints a dozen student academic representatives who regularly report "problem" teachers and curriculum miscues to the administration. Many professors now find themselves routinely huddled in "quality feedback circles" with students ready to criticize their classroom performance on a weekly basis.

Although the school's teaching scores in BUSINESS WEEK's survey still lag behind such leaders as Dartmouth, Virginia, and Harvard, overall teaching quality has dramatically improved. Wharton's profs now rate among the very best in elective classes and near the top in being at the leading edge of knowledge in their disciplines. The attention to teaching is hardly lip service. In 1995, for example, one prof was quickly yanked out of a core finance course after student complaints of poor performance. "I couldn't imagine that happening five years ago," says G. Richard Shell, a Wharton professor. "I have this image of a big hook coming onstage if you fail to perform. We expect to be held accountable."

So at Wharton you can expect a highly responsive administration to student concerns and priorities. You can also expect a truly innovative and modern MBA education. Incoming students arrive in early August, four weeks before the official start of the fall term to ensure that students from diverse backgrounds all begin on an equal footing. You are given courses in basic accounting, microeconomics, and statistics. If you have a liberal arts background, these sessions will help ease the jitters of entering a rigorous MBA program. If you have a business background, they can help you prepare for exams to waive out of several core courses and take more electives. About 75 percent of first-year students gain waivers out of classes. The four-week program also includes mini-courses in nine different languages, mini-electives in such topics as the History of Business and Classics of East Asia, a two-day leadership retreat, brown bag luncheons to help you use a financial calculator or surf the net for business basics, and plenty of opportunities to bond with classmates at barbecues, parties, and other social gatherings.

Your first year at Wharton is organized into four six-week quarters. Each first-year class is divided into cohorts, sections of 60 students each who take all the core courses together. Groups of three cohorts are gathered in clusters, which become a class within a class. Each cluster shares the same team of core professors who work together to integrate the coursework and coordinate student workload. In the first-semester Leadership course, you will work alone and in five-person teams on such soft skills as managing differences, power and authority, ethics, and communication. In the second semester, your team will be assigned a 12-week-long field application project in which your analysis of a real-world problem will be presented to executives actively involved in the case. You'll also get to select from a set of six half-semester courses that Wharton calls a "core bracket course" in such topics as information, innovation and entrepreneurship, geopolitics, risk and crisis management, technology, and the environment and the firm.

Finally, Wharton provides first-year students an optional Global Immersion Program, a four-week overseas experience preceded by six weeks worth of introductory lectures in a country or region critical to the world economy. In recent years, groups of students have gone to China, Japan, Russia, South America, and Europe. These trips, however, are hardly cheap, adding as much as $5000 to your education bill. In your second year, you'll be able to pursue one of the most extensive offerings of elective courses by any business school in the world in pursuit of one of over two dozen majors. In any single academic year, Wharton offers 189 different electives, more than three times the number offered by Harvard or Dartmouth and more than twice the number offered by Stanford and Cornell. The breadth of the offerings can over-

whelm people. You can major in everything from actuarial science and arts management to international finance and public and nonprofit management. You also can create your own major with faculty approval.

Yes, Wharton is the No. 1 school for finance. But Wharton is and always has been much more than a finance school, having established itself among the leaders in general management, entrepreneurship, global management, real estate, health care management, and marketing. The school's famous Lauder Institute, which offers an MBA/MA in international studies, is arguably the single best global management experience anywhere—besting a degree from any of the top European business schools or from any U.S. business school claiming to offer a truly international MBA. A joint venture between the B-school and the university's School of Arts and Sciences, this 24-month program allows students to focus on one of five areas of the world, including East Asia, the former Soviet Republics, Latin America, the United States, or Western Europe. Students spend about 25 percent of their time abroad, including a cultural immersion program before the start of their Wharton classes and a summer internship with a multinational company that requires extensive use of a foreign language. Wharton also offers international exchange programs with 10 non-U.S. business schools during which you could spend a full semester abroad as part of the school's regular MBA program. Each year, moreover, about 40 Wharton students pursue other dual-degree programs in such areas as communication, engineering, law, medical sciences, nursing, and social work.

For a school of this size and scope, Wharton does a surprisingly good job of holding down nasty competition among its highly ambitious students. Make no mistake about it: Wharton isn't as cozy and cooperative as Dartmouth, Stanford, Northwestern, or Yale, but it isn't nearly as competitive as Columbia or Chicago. At least that's according to BUSINESS WEEK's latest survey results.

Outside of class, students often tend to scatter, because they live in apartments and homes all around the campus and Philadelphia. Many MBAs live in either Center City, a 10-minute ride by bicycle, or West Philadelphia, an area that has seen better days. Indeed, in 1996, several students found themselves victims of crime in the area. Wharton has set aside a dozen floors of Grad Tower B for MBAs alone and dubbed it the "Living Learning Center." About 350 students reside in the on-campus dormitory, making it easy for them to organize in study groups, get advice on courses, or simply find a companion for a late-night snack.

Friendships forged in cohorts often carry through the remainder of the program and into the plethora of Wharton's social activities. Every Thursday at 4:30, it's happy hour at the MBA pub in Steinberg Conference Center (named for Reliance Group chairman and undergrad alum Saul Steinberg). First-year MBAs tend to prefer Murphy's, a joint with a great jukebox seven blocks west of the campus. A ritualistic fixture of Wharton life is a big celebration once a semester called "Walnut Walk." After mid-terms, MBAs don a combination of formal attire and shorts and begin the bar crawl on Second Street, winding their way through as many as 20 pubs, ending up at a sobering 3 a.m. breakfast.

PLACEMENT DETAILS

Well before the dean hands you your degree, you'll already know exactly where you'll work because Wharton boasts one of the best career services offices of any business school. In 1996, 317 corporations and organizations came on-campus and conducted 10,000 interviews with members of the Class of 1996. Wharton also posted 1190 jobs by correspondence alone. All told, it was a very good year: Wharton grads averaged 3.1 job offers each—not exactly Harvard's 4.2 average, but pretty darn good—and the median starting pay package hit $100,000. Only graduates at four schools did better in 1996: Harvard, Stanford, Dartmouth, and MIT.

Five top management consulting firms led the companies hauling away the most Wharton MBAs in 1996: McKinsey (44); Bain & Co. (32); Booz Allen & Hamilton (28); Andersen Consulting (22); The Boston Consulting Group (21); Lehman Brothers (17); Goldman, Sachs (16); Merrill Lynch (14); Deloitte & Touche (14); Bankers Trust (12); and Coopers & Lybrand (22).

OUTSTANDING FACULTY

Jeremy J. Siegel (****—economics); *Franklin Allen* (***—finance); *Dave Reibstein* (**—marketing); *Howard Kaufold* (**—finance); *Michael Gibbons* (*—finance); *Fhmuel Kandel* (*—finance); *William Tyson* (*—legal studies); *Lawrence Hrebeniak* (*—strategy); *Joseph Gyourko* (*—real estate & finance); *Robert Holthausen* (*—accounting & finance).

APPLICANT TIPS

You can improve your odds of getting in by applying early. Applicants who wait until the final deadline are likely to find that Wharton has already accepted the vast majority of its students. In early 1997, for example, Wharton was accepting 19.2 percent of its applicants for the Class of 1999—well above the previous year's 15 percent acceptance rate, even though applications at that point were nearly 18 percent higher. This is important info to consider, especially since applications to Wharton have risen by 46 percent between 1994 and 1996. Wharton evaluates applications starting in mid-November until its final deadline in early April. The school promises a decision within about eight weeks after receiving an application.

Visit the campus and request an interview with admissions, especially if you believe you can make a good personal impression. Wharton schedules personal admissions interviews from June to mid-December and from January to the end of April. You can schedule an appointment by calling 215-898-6183.

If you have a computer and access to a laser printer, Wharton provides free admissions software for applicants who use MS DOS 3.3 or better. Requests for the software on either a 3 1/2" or 5 1/4" diskette should be made in writing and faxed (215-898-0120) or mailed to the admissions office.

Contact:
Robert Alig
Director of Admissions and Financial Aid
102 Vance Hall
3733 Spruce St.
215-898-3430
Final application deadline: April 10

WHARTON MBAs SOUND OFF

The PC laboratory was always crowded during the semester, preventing us from doing assignments. The school is proud of establishing a new PC room. However, adding fewer than 30 computers for 1500 MBA students, excluding undergrads, did not work. Despite large needs the course which teaches us how to use the Internet was not held this spring term. Some professors did not accept E-mail questions.

Wharton provides a great mix of lecture and case teaching, which means that we are not as facile at case studies as Harvard, but we also avoid the Harvard problem of students getting good at cases rather than business. The school's reputation would definitely improve if it were not located in Philadelphia and had a better physical plant.

The alumni network is enormous, impressive, diverse, and responsive. Throughout my two years, I have been in touch with at least 25 alumni who have been helpful on project work, career guidance, and other matters. The level of involvement with the business world and the emphasis on reality is incredible.

The true strength of my education came from outside the classroom—participating in programs such as the Global Immersion Program and the exchange program. These programs not only allowed me to experience and see what issues are important to the international business community and explore the global marketplace, but they allowed me to challenge myself in a way I never expected.

Wharton has a low-key atmosphere that fosters teamwork and learning and de-emphasizes grades. There were multiple extracurricular activities such as: Christmas in April, improving homes, the Investment Management Club, managing a $100,000 portfolio with 11 students, and Whalasa, the Wharton Latin American Students Association providing exposure to Latin American culture.

2.
UNIVERSITY OF MICHIGAN

UNIVERSITY OF MICHIGAN

The University of Michigan Business School
Ann Arbor, Michigan 48109
E-mail address: umbusmba@umich.edu
Website address: http://www.bus.umich.edu

Corporate ranking: 3
Enrollment: 1886

Women: 25%
Non-U.S.: 26%
Minority: 15%
Part-time: 1059
Average age: 27
Average years of work exp.: 4
Applicants accepted: 28%
Median starting pay: $81,400

Graduate ranking: 3
Annual tuition & fees:
   resident—$17,030
   nonresident—$23,180
Room and board: $6800
Average GMAT score: 645
GMAT range: 500 to 800
Average GPA: 3.3
GPA range: 2.3 to 4.0
Accepted applicants enrolled: 44%
Average starting pay: $86,155

Teaching methods: Lecture, 45%   Case study, 35%   Projects, 20%

Contact:
Judith Goodman
Director of Admissions
313-763-5796
Application deadlines:
December 1 (priority)
January 1
March 1

Before you consider the Michigan School of Business Administration, it's important to get a few things out of the way. Despite its No. 2 ranking, the school is not nearly as prestigious as Wharton or Harvard. Its MBAs earn less on average than graduates at other top schools—though the gap is shrinking. The student body, while obviously talented, lacks the fire power of those at rivals like Northwestern and Wharton, where MBAs boast higher GMATs and more impressive work experience.

If any of that turns you off—and it well may—Ann Arbor is not the place for you. But if it doesn't scare you, you are in for a treat. Michigan offers one of the finest MBA educations in the world. Over the last five years, it has improved more than any other top-10 school. It now offers an education that's superior to the one you'd get at other schools with fancier names, according to surveys of both corporate recruiters and students. You can emerge from here with world-class skills in marketing or finance, operations or general management. The administration bends over backward to respond to student concerns, even causing one professor to leave in a huff and accuse Dean B. Joseph White of being too responsive.

The school does "a really good job of admitting students who have their feet planted on the ground," says Saundra Banks-Loggins, vice president for recruitment services at Wells Fargo Bank in San Francisco. "Michigan knows how to woo employers and also give their students the confidence, but not the arrogance, that they're a hot commodity."

Indeed, Michigan's four-place jump to No. 2 was the biggest surprise in the BUSINESS WEEK survey. But it didn't come from nowhere.

For years, Michigan had a slight image problem, making it hard for the school to stand out in the established world of B-schools. Northwestern originally built its reputation by being the best school in marketing. Harvard did the same in general management, and Wharton boasted its strength in finance. So when White took over in 1991 as Michigan's dean, he needed to push the school into the forefront of B-school innovation. The vehicle for that journey? Curriculum reform. A former Cummins Engine Co. human resources exec, he quickly made curriculum innovation a signature of his deanship, launching, among other things, a business version of medical-school residency in which student teams work at sponsoring companies on special projects. In this seven-week program, known as Multidisciplinary Action Project (MAP), students work hand-in-hand with corporate managers. Executives from companies such as Boston Consulting Group, Federal Express, Motorola, and Xerox helped design the one-of-a-kind program. White considers the project to be a period of real-world training under close supervision.

Central to those concepts is the notion that students are true partners in the educational process. White takes this concept to the hilt, sometimes drawing criticism for the level of power students have at the school—like from the professor who left the school. Regardless, students are number one at Michigan, and changing with the business world is the goal.

MAP is a key part of the first-year curriculum. "It goes right to the heart of the weaknesses of MBA programs," White says. "Typically, schools don't do a good job on cross-functional stuff which is so vital in business. We also have neglected the area of operational effectiveness. How do you achieve an increase in productivity, time cycles, etc. And, third, we haven't helped

students transfer knowledge into action. MAP addresses all three areas."

How does it work? At North American Phillips Corp., for example, a student team recently mapped out and examined the company's relationship with its suppliers. The team's recommendations lowered costs, speeded up orders, and improved relations with vendors. The bad news: Don't expect to see any money for your work. Unlike the usual summer internships MBAs use to help pay their tuition bills, these apprenticeships are geared to specific projects and supervised by faculty and a committed team of corporate managers. "We wouldn't dream of medical school without making rounds, internships, and residencies," White argues. "By the end of the decade, I believe there won't be a business school that doesn't add this."

White also revamped the entire structure of Michigan's program. He broke the 14-week term in half, forcing professors to pare their courses down to the essentials. The shorter terms give Michigan an edge because the school can quickly change with the flow of the business world. The shorter formula, for example, has allowed the school to launch new seven-week electives in topics that weren't worth a full 14 weeks, such as customer satisfaction and environmental policy. He also added as optional 30 hours of Executive Education–style leadership modules in such topics as creativity, managing influence, negotiations, and team building.

Two years ago, many skeptics asked whether White could sustain Michigan as the B-school world's innovator. The school's jump in the rankings—from sixth to second—proves that White did more than just keep the school up to par. He pushed the school into the same category as its more famous rivals thanks to satisfied students and raves from Corporate America. Only Harvard, for example, joined Michigan in landing on the top 10 favorite hunting ground list in all four major subjects: finance, general management, marketing, and operations. Michigan

MBAs also won raves for their ability to work as team players and think globally. Among Top 25 schools, only Wharton offers a more innovative curriculum, according to corporate recruiters.

That indicates that although many schools are moving to adopt new ideas and concepts, few have moved as swiftly or as effectively as Michigan. White encourages creative changes in what is already one of the best B-schools in the country. The school's infrastructure is one example. It's housed in a handsome seven building complex that features modern classrooms and lecture halls as well as a state-of-the-art computing center and business library. There is still at least one area that needs work, though: the information technology program.

Michigan is also attempting to stay on the leading edge for training managers to deal with Workforce 2000, the still-floating buzz word for managing cultural and racial diversity in the workforce. The reason: Nearly one of every six students is a minority, and *The Journal of Blacks in Higher Education* deemed Michigan the best B-school for blacks. Plus, one-fourth of Michigan MBAs are international students. Not bad for a state school in the Midwest. What's more, the B-school is by no means isolated from the university's vibrant academic community. Some decide to get their MBAs here simply because they want to be in Ann Arbor, one of the nation's leading college towns. As long as you don't mind cold weather, it's hard to beat its combination of university-town culture and small-town charm. The atmosphere has made the city a popular place for entrepreneurs and retirees—so much so that housing can be hard to find and somewhat expensive. The pace of housing construction has trouble keeping up with the demand, and some students spend nearly as much as New Yorkers for a place to live. Parking is no picnic, either.

Students at Michigan find a generalist's approach to management, where nobody is forced to major in any given discipline. If they want, though, students can specialize in areas such as accounting, finance, marketing, and organizational behavior. Many of the B-school's professors have joint appointments with the university's departments of psychology, sociology, economics, or law. Michigan also offers several joint master's programs in areas as varied as music and engineering. MBAs are free otherwise to take up to 10 hours of credit in another school in the university. White also abandoned Michigan's letter grading system, but the switch is largely cosmetic. The current system uses words (Excellent, Good, Pass, Low Pass, Fail) in an effort to encourage teamwork and discourage competition. You have to figure, though, that MBAs are smart enough to translate "Excellent" to an "A" and "Pass" to a "C."

You'll start your first year with an introductory lab that assesses your strengths and weaknesses. Then you'll be shipped off to Detroit or a place like the high unemployment city of Benton Harbor. It's part of a new weeklong Leadership Development Program that has swallowed the old global citizenship program. Whether these efforts are just field trips into the inner city or are actually the incubator for a generation of socially conscious executives is hard to predict. But to most at Michigan, it doesn't make much of a difference. Regardless, they argue, moving students off sheltered campuses and exposing them to real social problems is critical.

Michigan has gotten plenty of corporate support for its emphasis on community service. As part of their orientation, students hear speeches from top career execs who challenge them to retain a commitment to society after they graduate. Executives also join the students on their trips into the community. After the day spent with paintbrushes and brooms, teams of students launch optional yearlong consulting projects for nonprofit groups. They create business plans, install accounting systems, and target potential donors for fund-raising.

The first term of the core curriculum focuses on the basics: business economics, financial accounting, marketing, statistics, and corporate strategy. The second term takes the first three of these subjects and requires students to apply them to business problems, while adding courses in international business and finance.

Once the new calendar year begins, MAP falls into place, accounting for 25 percent of the core curriculum. For it, faculty from four areas—accounting, operations, human resources, and information systems—team-teach four courses in their fields for seven weeks. Then there's one week's worth of preparation before the internships begin with the companies. The week is treated like an executive education seminar. Students get a three-inch notebook of readings, exercises, and cases on operational improvement and process analysis. Some executives actually come into the classroom and teach it. And throughout all of this activity, you'll still be working on your community action project and attending executive skills workshops.

In the second year, you'll get to choose from among 60 14-week electives and 65 7-week classes. A 7-week course in either ethics or law is the only required elective. A final requirement of the core is Corporate Strategy II. Besides the more typical array of B-school offerings, there are also field project courses and business language courses in French, Spanish, and Japanese. There are, of course, opportunities to study abroad. The William Davidson Institute allows students to study emerging economies from Eastern Asia to Eastern Europe. The Africa Corps sends MBAs to South Africa, Uganda, and Ghana. There are also exchange programs with eight European business schools, from the University of St. Gallen in Switzerland to Britain's London Business School.

When you're in Ann Arbor, you are sure to have an active social life. Semesters often kick off with a party at Charlie's, a favorite bar, where students consume as much beer and pizza as possible. Michigan doesn't hold classes on Fridays, which students consider to be an advantage over Northwestern, which gives students Wednesdays off. At U of M, the weekend starts Thursday night with beer at Rick's, where a pitcher costs little more than two bucks. Also popular are O'Sullivans and ScoreKeepers. And the Brown Jug is the place to be in the wee hours of the morning. The town also goes a little bit nuts over the Wolverines sports teams, making them somewhat of an obsession. The B-school association purchases blocks of tickets so students can sit together at football and basketball games, and the B-school always has tailgate parties.

PLACEMENT DETAILS

Unlike other Top 25 schools such as Wharton, Columbia, and NYU, you won't find a well-worn path between Ann Arbor and Wall Street. Many of the school's grads with an interest in finance are more keen to work in the field at Kraft, General Foods, or Ford than at Morgan Stanley or Goldman Sachs. Only 14.7 percent of MBAs found jobs in banking and financial services in 1996. White is constantly trying to increase the visibility of his grads, and he does that with several trips to New York, both with students and on his own to peddle his grads to the big guys.

Top hirers from among the 163 companies that came to campus in 1996: Deloitte & Touche (15 grads); Ford Motor (15); Ernst & Young (14); Intel (14); Coopers & Lybrand (13); Hewlett-Packard (9); Procter & Gamble (9); Booz Allen & Hamilton (7); United Technologies (7); Citibank (6); Chase Manhattan (6); and Kraft (6). The average student took home $81,400 in the first year out of Michigan. That trails Wharton and Harvard by about $20,000, but it's on par with other top public schools, like Berkeley and UNC. There's a difference, though. In terms of tuition, Michigan is public in name only. It charges more than $23,000 a year for out-of-state students and more than $17,000 for Michigan residents. On average, students leave Ann Arbor with $30,000 worth of debt. In other words, this may be a wonderful business school, but compared to its rivals it's not the best bargain.

So White faces a huge challenge. True, he's already built the program substantially, boosted its national reputation, and won the respect of both students and faculty. Now he needs to keep up with private-school rivals that have deeper pockets and—barring an unlikely cut in tuition—convince Corporate America to pay his grads a bit more.

OUTSTANDING FACULTY

William Lovejoy (***—operations management); *Rajeev Batra* (**—marketing); *David Butz* (**—economics); *M.P. Narayanan* (**—finance); *C.K. Prahalad* (**—strategy); *Victor Bernard* (*—finance); *Andrew Lawlor* (*—entrepreneurship); *Pierre Dussauge* (*—strategy); *Sugato Bhattacharyy* (*—finance); *Jeffrey Abarbanell* (*—accounting).

APPLICANT TIPS

Michigan heavily weighs GMAT scores, work experience, and undergraduate academic records. The school maintains, however, that it is less concerned with the precise content of a student's earlier education than with the overall record of achievement. That's a call to emphasize whatever your achievements have been on the job or outside work.

It's wise to apply early if you can. If you get your application in by December 1 you can get a decision by February 15. For more info, you can fax the admissions office at 313-763-7804. Eight of every 10 applicants are interviewed by the school, so if you're personable and articulate it would be in your favor to show up for an interview. To schedule one, call admissions at 313-763-7805.

Contact:
Judith Goodman
Director of Admissions
313-763-5796
Application deadlines: December 1 (priority); January 1; March 1

MICHIGAN MBAs SOUND OFF

It's no irony that Michigan developed the National Consumer Satisfaction Index. The administration is genuinely interested in satisfying its main customers, the students. I'm amazed at how many times the school asked the students how things were going, including mid-term and end-of-term, teacher evaluations, and informal get-togethers with the dean.

The school put too much emphasis on teamwork, general management, and organizational behavior. Such a policy would be welcomed by executive program students. But the school is reluctant to support finance, accounting, and manufacturing-related courses. The school is not so enthusiastic to improve our number-crunching skills. The school is so aggressive in modernizing its program that it forgets to improve students' basic quantitative abilities.

The school's generalist format is well-suited for people wishing to become operations managers, company presidents, and CEOs. However, individuals looking to become investment bankers and CFOs will not find the required depth in UMB's finance course offering.

Our deans are the dynamic duo. Joe White is a great champion of the school, and he sells it to anybody who listens. Ted Snyder is more low-key, but he is hard at work behind the scenes on student satisfaction and faculty recruiting issues. The faculty are incredibly broad and deep. Michigan students are down-to-earth, very hard working team players who don't have a me-first attitude. People have a sense of humor here. They also have a lot of character.

A weakness I found in the program is that many 14-week classes did not have enough depth. It seemed that some classes in a 14-week course were filler. On the other hand, 7-week courses were very intense and every class provided value.

The school is very student-driven. If a course is in demand, the school will open new sections; if there is interest in a new subject, the school will create courses in it; if there are complaints about how something is functioning, the school—from the dean to the staff in the admissions office—will work diligently and sincerely to resolve the problem and will seek out student participation in crafting a solution.

**3.
NORTH-
WESTERN
UNIVERSITY**

NORTHWESTERN UNIVERSITY

J.L. Kellogg Graduate School of Management
Leverone Hall
Evanston, Illinois 60208
E-mail address: kellogg-admissions@nwu.edu
Website address: http://www.kellogg.nwu.edu

Corporate ranking: 2	Graduate ranking: 8
Enrollment: 2546	Annual tuition & fees: $23,025
Women: 31%	Room and board: $9630
Non-U.S.: 24%	Average GMAT score: 660
Minority: 9%	Average GPA: 3.3
Part-time: 1400	GPA range: 2.03 to 4.0
Average age: 28	Average years of work exp.: 5
Applicants accepted: 14%	Accepted applicants enrolled: 9%
Median starting pay: $95,000	Average starting pay: $98,830

Teaching methods: Lecture, 33%   Case study, 33%   Projects, 34%

Contact:
Michele Rogers
Director of Admissions
and Financial Aid
847-491-3308
*Final application
deadline:* March 23

After more than two decades in the job, Dean Donald P. Jacobs shows no signs of tiring of his role as the legendary leader of Northwestern University's J.L. Kellogg School of Management. Indeed, he has a few tricks up his sleeve to win back the No. 1 ranking Kellogg earned in three consecutive biennial BUSINESS WEEK polls from 1988 to 1992.

Jacobs, who took over the B-school in 1975 and has since outlasted the deans of every Top 25 school, has outlined a new strategic plan for Kellogg that places greater emphasis on global management, advanced technology, entrepreneurship, and an ever-improving basic curriculum.

Not that anything is terribly wrong at the powerhouse school that slipped to third place in 1996, behind Wharton and Michigan. Corporate recruiters are still overwhelmingly satisfied with the school's graduates. They believe Kellogg graduates have the best interpersonal skills and work best in teams. They also say that Kellogg grads have the best marketing skills and third-best general management skills (behind Harvard and Stanford). In addition, Kellogg was ranked third (behind Wharton and Michigan) for having the most innovative curriculum. Students, too, believe they are getting a top-notch education. Although there are some gripes, they are minor. The fall simply reflects that other very good schools have caught up.

Arguably the most successful B-school dean of this era, Jacobs established the model of the modern business school in the early 1980s. At the time, elite schools such as Harvard, Stanford, Chicago, and Wharton were content to ignore the demands for MBAs who could better lead and motivate others. Jacobs ignored tradition, building and nurturing a culture driven by co-operative learning and student empowerment. It worked like a charm. And Kellogg's rivals have since hopped on the bandwagon, overhauling their curricula to be more responsive to their own MBAs and to Corporate America. It's no stretch to call Jacobs a revolutionary behind the last decade of widespread B-school reform.

So why the slow descent from No. 1? Simply put, when you start a trend, you can often fall victim to the copiers, as Jacobs has quickly found out. If the competition sees a good thing and ignores its significance, they doom themselves. But this is not so in the ever-changing B-school world, and schools like Wharton, Michigan, and Harvard have hopped on the boat Jacobs pushed out to sea in the 1980s. And now that he knows it, Jacobs is trying to predict and cultivate the next best trend, including keeping the school diverse and culturally rich—something he started to do years ago.

Incoming students get a quick taste of how Kellogg is different when they arrive early for the preorientation outdoor adventures right after Labor Day. In 1996, more than 400 students were involved in these one-week bonding trips. Incoming students and second-years went backpacking in Colorado, California, Wyoming, Arizona, Utah, and Nevada; biking in California; canoeing in northern Canada, Missouri, and the Boundary Waters; sailing on Chesa-peake Bay; and even scuba diving in the Cayman Islands and Bonaire. The trips are a great way to meet your classmates and get the inside scoop on Kellogg, but they also lighten your wallet by up to $1000.

These voluntary adventures precede CIM (Conceptual Issues in Management), a week-long program organized and run entirely by as many as 200 second-years. This event, which starts in the third week of September, is now much more common at business schools, but was an early hallmark of the Kellogg program. Students begin arriving on Sunday to walking tours of the campus and downtown Evanston, as well as a reception that evening for those who are married. There's an outdoor field activity; a business simulation game; sessions on cultural diversity, negotiations, and team building. There are also a series of intensive math reviews that meet every day for students suffering from math anxiety.

Classes begin immediately after the last week of September. Kellogg classes, which meet twice a week for an hour and 40 minutes, are scheduled on a quarterly basis with three quarters a year. The quarter system is rigorous and unforgiving. No classes are scheduled on Wednesday, a good day to sleep in, take a swim in the sports and recreation center, laze at the lakefront park, or work on group projects. You need 23 courses to graduate and you can waive out of core courses if you qualify, but must replace them from more than 100 electives and advanced classes. Most Kellogg MMs (instead of the MBA, grads receive a Master's of Management) major in 2 or 3 of 17 areas, from marketing to international business to public nonprofit management. Four courses are required in any given major. If you already own an undergraduate business degree, Kellogg has a program that would allow you to get a master's in one year.

To keep Kellogg on the leading edge, Jacobs is pushing a new international focus. He has launched three international executive MBA programs in France, Germany, and Israel to better expose his faculty to global topics, launched a new international speaker series, and expanded alumni clubs abroad. Now, every one of Kellogg's seven academic departments has at least one course that deals with international issues and each department has infused global examples throughout all course offerings. Students can also take not-for-credit language classes taught by university faculty. The courses—in Japanese, French, German, and Spanish—cost an extra $150 each and are held from 5 to 7 p.m. in Leverone Hall after regularly scheduled business classes.

Jacobs has also allowed students to create specially designed, two-quarter international independent study courses, focusing on a country of their choice. With a faculty sponsor, students arrange a syllabus, assume responsibility for guest speakers, determine research topics, and identify key issues facing industries in their chosen nation. Students complete the coursework in the winter quarter, then travel to the selected country over spring break for a two-week group consulting project and international study tour. In the spring quarter, students put the finishing touches on their studies and present them to faculty and visiting executives. Last year, students in the Peru class ended up spending an entire day with President Alberto Fujimori, traveling the countryside in his private jet and visiting villages and towns across Peru.

Moreover, Kellogg has caught up with the traditional elites in attracting international applicants. In 1996, the school received 1106 foreign applications from 82 countries. A respectable 24 percent of students boast foreign passports from 39 countries. In 1992, only 16 percent of the B-school's students were from abroad. Adding to the international mix is the fact that nearly 60 percent of the school's American students have lived, studied, or worked overseas.

Though Kellogg was something of a laggard in the use of advanced technology, Jacobs is now expanding the use of technology media in classrooms, developing new courses on the impact of technology on business, and recruiting a top scholar for a new chair in info tech. The 1994 addition of Andersen Hall, the former home of the school of education and social policy, also has made a big difference. Andersen, linked to Leverone Hall next door, brought with it four new computer-wired classrooms, 15 group study rooms, and a computer lab. Still, Kellogg requires all incoming students to have their own laptops.

Of all of these new areas of emphasis, however, perhaps none is getting as much attention right now as entrepreneurship. The dean is expanding faculty and course offerings in this area, seeking more funding for entrepreneurial/venture capital summer internships, and exploring links with other areas of the curriculum, such as a look at entrepreneurship internationally. Broadening interest in startups led Jacobs to add a sequence of courses and a major in entrepreneurship. Nine profs now teach the subject, up from three in 1994. About 42 percent of the current students express an interest in the field. Besides classes in the basics of new venture formulation, would-be entrepreneurs can dive into such courses as Introduction to New Products and the Entrepreneur and His/Her Social Environment. These days, more than 25 percent of all students are members of the school's Entrepreneur and New Venture Club.

Through all these changes, one very important thing remains the same: the Kellogg team concept. It brings the campus to life through an extraordinary display of student entrepreneurship and involvement. Student involvement in the governance of the school has been, and should continue to be, one of the key drivers of Kellogg's success. There are a whole set of mechanisms—some formal, some informal—to solicit and act on student input. For one, the dean has an open-door policy, brown-bag lunches abound, and faculty and staff actively participate in student activities and conferences. There are also Dean's forums, and numerous committees, all run by students. The students even conduct their own exit surveys on graduates.

Since 1994, students have conceived and implemented five different programs, including LEAP—Learning Through Experience in Action Program—a 10-week consulting assignment/course with area corporations; Kellogg Corps, a Peace Corps type volunteer program for grads, through which recent grads spend their summers doing pro bono consulting projects in developing countries around the world; and Chicago Tours, a series of student-organized trips to Chicago businesses for observation and networking.

Kellogg, named after the son of the breakfast cereal founder, built its reputation on marketing. But the school does have an outstanding reputation in general management, manufacturing, and finance. Many grads think the finance instructors are the best of all teachers at the school. And there are still other areas of specialty: Kellogg offers a three-course sequence in total quality management, including a practicum in which students work with a company's managers or public school administrators to implement quality efforts. For those interested in a career in not-for profit, the school boasts a powerful Nonprofit Management Program that even challenges Yale or Stanford's offerings with 14 electives. Students gain summer stipends if they take lower-paying public or nonprofit positions between the first and second year. And there's a loan forgiveness program for graduating students taking jobs in public or nonprofit sectors. That loan forgiveness fund was amply boosted when 82 percent of the 1996 graduating class pledged a whopping $350,000 as a class gift.

For aspiring gearheads, the school offers a two-year Master of Manufacturing Management degree, which successfully graduated its first class in 1992. This joint program with the university's McCormick School of Engineering is an attempt to help restore America's competitive edge. The program's main classroom and lab is the university's Technological Institute. In 1996, some 60 students graduated from the program, which includes a guaranteed manufacturing internship over the summer.

The Kellogg campus isn't as self-contained as some others, but it's pretty impressive nonetheless. Leverone Hall, the primary six-story center of the building, overlooks lush Deering Meadow, an expanse of grass and oak trees. The new Andersen Hall building is state-of-the-art, with a four-story, 3000-square-foot atrium that is the center of student life. Kafe Kellogg, a restaurant in the atrium, is a convenient place to grab lunch or coffee. It also serves as party central on some nights. The nearby Deering Library, a Gothic structure that looks as if it has been transplated from turn-of-the-century England, boasts intricate stained-glass windows and its own librarian and is attached to the university's main library. Two blocks away is the Allen Center, the executive education wing. The McManus Living and Learning Center, renovated in the early 1980s, is on the southern edge of the campus and houses a third of the students, who vie for a spot there via lottery. Jokingly dubbed the loving and lusting center by students, it has played an integral part in nurturing Kellogg's group culture and cooperative spirit.

Every Friday afternoon, the keg is tapped and seems to flow forever at 4:45 p.m. in the atrium for the weekly TGIF session. In the spring, the weekly ritual adjourns to the meadow directly in front, where frisbee throwing and soccer remain the sports of choice. At times, the Kellogg experience can resemble a big undergraduate party, though Northwestern itself is far from a party school. Many grads say Kellogg is the place to be if you are married: Chicago is full of great job opportunities, and the school's myriad of student-run organizations go out of their way to include significant others and children (including several parties, like the fall beach luau on the shores of Lake Michigan behind the recreation center).

There are plenty of places to go for a beer or a good dinner nearby in Evanston or an el-ride away in downtown Chicago or Roger's Park. Tommy Nevins and the Keg are popular Evanston hangouts, but beware—you must purchase food to buy beer. It's another strange Evanston law, just like the one that says you must bag your own food at Burger King. Evanston was a dry city until 15 years ago. In fact, Prohibition was founded in this staunchly stuffy town by Frances Willard. Every year, undergrads hold a party in her honor—with lots of heavy drinking.

Back on campus, most students overbook themselves with extracurricular activities. Business with a Heart, Kellogg's do-good MBA group, raised more than $70,000 in 1996 for charitable causes. Some built homes for low-income families, staffed homeless shelters, and collected and distributed clothing for the less fortunate. All these programs get plenty of coverage in the *Merger,* Kellogg's lively student newspaper.

Kellogg is big on networking and helping alums, too. The school boasts a computer service for alums who can dial in for job opportunities. Kellogg has had a paid consultant since 1991 who focuses exclusively on alumni placement. There are workshops on career planning, résumé writing, interviewing, and successful networking. In the future these services will become even more important to Kellogg's 38,000 alums in 85 countries. There are 58 alumni clubs around the world, half outside the United States, and the doings of alums occupy 20 or more pages of *Kellogg World,* the alumni magazine published three times each year.

PLACEMENT DETAILS

In 1996, 300 companies came on campus to recruit Kellogg grads and conducted about 15,000 interviews. The school says only 5 percent of the class had no job offers at graduation. The trend toward consulting continues with 34 percent of the class of 1996 heading into that field. Corporate finance and product management were next in line, accounting for roughly 13 percent of the graduating class each. Top employers: McKinsey (33); Ernst & Young (18); Boston Consulting Group (17); A.T. Kearney (17); Booz Allen & Hamilton (14); Hewlett Packard (13); Citibank (12); Diamond Technology Partners (10); Deloitte & Touche (9); and Andersen Consulting (8).

What's interesting about these stats is that McKinsey, the premier management consulting firm that pays the highest starting pay packages for MBA grads, is increasingly relying on the school for talent. Two years ago, only 16 Kellogg grads joined the firm. In 1992, just 14; in 1990, 12; in 1988, 10. The big leap to 33 hires in a single year by the most prestigious recruiter of MBAs is a powerful endorsement of the school and its graduates. If Jacobs's new strategic plan works, Northwestern might well find itself at the top of the heap yet again.

OUTSTANDING FACULTY

David Besanko (****—management and strategy); *Tim Thompson* (****—finance); *Mohambir Sawhney* (****—marketing); *Louis Stern* (***—marketing); *Steven Rogers* (***—entrepreneurial finance); *Sunil Chopra* (**—managerial economics); *Ann McGill* (**—marketing); *Tamu Thiagarajan* (**—accounting); *Larry Revsine* (**—accounting); *Martin Stoller* (**—organizational behavior).

APPLICANT TIPS

Kellogg was the first school, and still remains one of the very few, that attempts to interview all of its applicants. If you aren't likely to come across well in a personal interview, your chances of getting in will be pretty slim. In other words, your GPA and GMAT—no matter how strong—won't, on their own, let you in the door. That's especially true because Kellogg puts a lot of weight on your ability to communicate and get along with others. Like most top-tier schools, Kellogg places a high value on full-time work experience. The admissions committee evaluates your potential for a management career by carefully reviewing not only your experience but also your accomplishments at work, in the military, and in extracurricular activities. "We look for active, bright, caring people," says Dean Jacobs. "We don't have loners with sharp elbows for students."

You can improve your odds of securing an invitation by applying early. Because applications are reviewed on a continuous basis, your chances of gaining acceptance and lining up financial aid and housing may fall if you wait until the last minute to apply. Indeed, Kellogg's first application deadline is December 1, even though its final deadline is nearly four months later.

Kellogg also is one of the few schools that provides free software to help you more easily fill out the application and to apply for a scholarship. The school hands out disks for both Macintosh and MS-DOS users. There is, however, no advantage or disadvantage to completing your application via disk. Requests for the DiskApp software should be made in writing to the admissions office by fax at 708-491-4960. Or you can get it via modem by calling 312-644-5007. The diskettes come in four versions: 5 1/4-inch or 3 1/2-inch high-density DOS, Macintosh high density, and 3 1/2-inch high-density Windows.

Contact:
Michele Rogers
Director of Admissions and Financial Aid
847-491-3308
Final application deadline: March 23

KELLOGG GRADS SOUND OFF

To me, it seems Kellogg did the ultimate—it got me to overcome my psychological fears of finance and helped me land a great job in the field. To this end, the faculty in the Finance Department had the most significant impact.

They have all been extremely accessible and more than willing to help, no matter how basic my questions. Placement was helpful. I found it frustrating at times that some students seemed to think placement was supposed to get them a job instead of providing access and tools.

The true value of Kellogg is its focus on teamwork-oriented assignments. Leveraging the knowledge and experiences of fellow classmates has been the single most valuable method of advancing my managerial skills and general business knowledge. Kellogg truly treats the student as the ultimate customer and provides an ideal environment for personal and professional development.

Kellogg offers outstanding opportunities to be part of the school. You can work in the admissions office, collaborate with admissions on strategic issues, do research with professors, organize conferences, and initiate tangible change in all activities aimed at improving student facilities.

The spirit of this place is amazing. People genuinely want to help each other to learn and to get jobs. Being cutthroat competitive with your classmates in not something you find here. Even during the midst of recruiting, people help each other with interview skills, résumés, and contacts, even when they're going after the same job.

4.
HARVARD UNIVERSITY

HARVARD UNIVERSITY

Graduate School of Business Administration
Soldiers Field
Boston, Massachusetts 02163
E-mail address: admissions@hbs.edu
Website address: http://hbs.harvard.edu

Corporate ranking: 4	Graduate ranking: 9
Enrollment: 1779	Annual tuition & fees: $23,840
Women: 26%	Room and board: $6175 + meals
Non-U.S.: 27%	Average GMAT score: *680
Minority: 19%	Average GPA: 3.5
Part-time: None	GPA range: 2.6 to 4.0
Average age: 27.5	Average years of work exp.: 4.9
Applicants accepted: 13%	Accepted applicants enrolled: 88%
Median starting pay: $110,637	Average starting pay: $113,544

Teaching methods: Case study, 75% Lecture, 15%
Projects & simulations, 10%

Contact:
Jill H. Fadule
Director of Admissions
617-495-6127
Application deadlines:
November 13
January 8
March 5

Within a week of moving into his spacious new office in Morgan Hall in the fall of 1995, new Harvard business school Dean Kim B. Clark dispatched his first message to the faculty—via electronic mail. The note raised eyebrows not necessarily because of what it said—that Clark was launching a new technology initiative—but because his predecessor had never used E-mail. Indeed, even after Harvard encouraged MBAs to communicate via computer, former Dean John H. McArthur had refused to get an E-mail address because he didn't want students to inundate him with messages.

Clark is not only creating a new open culture, but he's also using technology to remake the world's most influential business school. So far, he's surprising both insiders and outsiders with how rapidly he's bringing change to an institution that reveres tradition and ritual. And the early payback on his strategy is clear: Harvard climbed one notch in the 1996 ranking as grads gave their new dean a resounding thumbs-up for his dramatic changes in the MBA program. In addition, there was a big rise in satisfaction due to the new technology initiative. Corporate recruiters ranked Harvard graduates as having the best general management skills, in the top five for marketing and operations skills, and in the top ten for finance skills.

It's about time. In recent years, many critics have argued that Harvard B-school, like so many U.S. corporate giants, was increasingly out of step with fast-moving changes in the business world—changes that nimbler B-schools were leaping to address. With information technology playing a more central role in the economy, the only computer lab for students was closed in 1993. With corporations operation on a global stage, Harvard remained startlingly insular: Just 10 percent of all case studies involved international business. And in an era when forward-thinking managers were flattening hierarchies and fostering teamwork, America's high church of management education remained a sclerotic bureaucracy that seemed to do everything in its power to promote rivalry rather than cooperation among its students.

Through it all, it's true, Harvard's prestige remained high: This year, a record 8056 applicants are vying for just 880 seats in the class, and 88 percent of those accepted will attend, the highest "yield rate" in business education. But the B-school was clearly a fading icon, losing ground to the likes of Stanford, Wharton, and Kellogg. Two years ago, it fell to No. 5 in BUSINESS WEEK's biennial survey—its lowest ranking ever.

When University President Neil L. Rudenstine named Clark dean in September of 1995, some observers thought the reserved and methodical professor would move slowly. Others saw Clark, who had spent 25 years at Harvard as a student and professor, as too much of an insider to shake things up.

By all accounts, though, the tall, youthful Clark has moved forcefully to bring the business school up to speed. He has announced plans to invest $185 million in a major overhaul of the business campus. The proposed plans call for a redesign and expansion of the world's largest business library, the construction of a new classroom building with four amphitheaters, a new 67,000-square-foot campus center for MBAs, and two new dormitories for executive education students. This is an incredible expansion plan for a B-school campus that already boasts 27 buildings, including its own fitness center and chapel.

He has invested more than $12 million in a high-tech initiative that promises to transform the school and establish it as a leader in infor-

mation technology. Already, 92 percent of exams are conducted on computers, and the school is using multimedia technology to recreate its trademark, the case-study method. The goal: to pump out 500 online cases over the next five years. If Harvard succeeds, it will transform the way business is studied in B-school and corporate classrooms around the world, because it sells 4.8 million case studies a year to outsiders.

To help spur such innovations and speed decision making, Clark has decentralized authority, ditching committees and task forces where proposals often languished for months or years. And he has mounted an all-out attack on rigid rules—one of which prohibited faculty from ordering Post-it notes in any color other than yellow.

Clark is even changing the way the school screens applicants. Reversing a decision made by McArthur over a decade ago, he is again requiring the Graduate Management Admission Test (GMAT). Under fire for churning out investment bankers and consultants, Harvard had dropped the test, which measures analytical skills, in the belief that it favored students who would choose those careers. But graduates continued to shun Corporate America, while the school lost a key tool for gauging applicants.

Although many of these moves will merely bring Harvard abreast of competitors, Clark is winning plaudits for style and content. "Neil Rudenstine hit a home run in picking this guy," says Thomas S. Murphy, retired chairman of Capital Cities/ABC Inc. and head of Harvard's visiting committee. "Kim knows exactly where he wants to go and how he is going to get there." Rivals, too, have good things to say. "He's a scholar, a dedicated teacher, and a people person," says Michael Spence, dean of Stanford University's School of Business. "And he's moving decisively."

Even the B-school faculty—perhaps the largest single conglomeration of outsized egos and intellects anywhere in business—is applauding. "Kim understands technology and its power like few people do, and he is catapulting us into the future with it," says Michael Jensen, a professor who heads the organization and markets group.

Acknowledging that "some things needed to be changed," Rudenstine says Clark, an insider who never held a leadership position, was the ideal person for the job. "He was not invested in making lots of the earlier administrative decisions," adds Rudenstine. "Yet he was in a good position to understand what had to be done."

Incoming students are in a good position to benefit from these changes—especially those in the MBA curriculum, the result of a three-year review begun under McArthur in 1992. While the faculty nixed some of the more radical recommendations, it approved several dramatic alterations. So far, these have had their greatest impact on the so-called January cohort, the class of 253 students who enrolled in January of 1996 for a new, shorter, 16-month program that eliminates time for a summer internship.

The new option began with Foundations, two and a half weeks of lectures, projects, and case studies in quantitative methods, leadership, ethics, and business history. To foster a sense of belonging, the new students were divided into groups of 16, which were reshuffled throughout the exercises. By the end of Foundations, each student said he or she already knew on average 50 percent of classmates. The B-school is providing Foundations on a pass/fail basis to ease new students into its competitive culture, long reinforced by a forced grading curve in which 10 percent of the students in every class get the lowest grades. The school says it is still evaluating whether to change or abolish the grading system—which was among the earlier recommendations that failed to gain acceptance. The Foundations innovations were rolled out to all entering students in the fall of 1996.

To encourage greater integration of the basic business disciplines, the required curriculum in the first year is being delivered by just 19 professors who meet together regularly. In the past, it took 85 faculty members to deliver the first-year program. "You can't do cross-area curriculum innovation with a group of 85 people," says Leonard Schlesinger, the Harvard prof who is architect of Foundations and who was a contender for the deanship. "It just doesn't happen. But now there are 19 of us sitting around a table together planning our day-by-day interaction with students as opposed to focusing all our energies on our individual courses. More classes are now team-taught by faculty from different disciplines and include more group exercises and projects to help students develop teamwork and leadership skills. As recently as three years ago, some MBAs complained that they participated in just three group assignments over two years. Students now say they have as many as two dozen team projects in the first year. Early reviews are positive. "It made the school smaller and more flexible because the courses were taught by fewer faculty," says Patrick Criteser, an MBA student in the new January cohort. Adds another, former McKinsey & Co. analyst Sumir Chadha: "You get a sense that all the professors are talking to each other now. They know what the other professors are teaching every day, and there's more integration of the courses."

Virtually all of the second year at Harvard is devoted to acquiring more in-depth knowledge in a field of your choice. The school offers students a rich array of 60 classroom electives and 11 field studies. About 56 percent of the elective courses are new in the past three years, from Managing in the New Health Care Industry to The Business of Sports. Harvard's professors—who as a result of case-study teaching are a pretty dynamic and engaging bunch—are among the very best teachers in all of business academe. Add these incredible strengths to the most student-responsive administration Harvard has had in years and you get a superb learning environment that is undergoing a profound transformation as a result of technology.

Clark's decision to invest some $12 million on his technology initiative—far more than the annual budgets of most graduate B-schools—has astounded observers. "It's just incredible for a school to spend $11 million on anything in six months," says David Blake, former president of the American Assembly of Collegiate Schools of Business. "But it's one thing to get computers around the place," Blake adds. "It's another to use them in an innovative way."

In fact, Clark hasn't simply opened the school's hefty checkbook. He is using technology to create a greater sense of community among the 1704 MBA students, 174 faculty, and 500 staffers and to reaffirm Harvard's commitment to the case-study approach. The B-school now has a new info infrastructure with a single campuswide E-mail system that is fully compatible with the Internet. And Clark has put new computers on the desks of most faculty and staff and built a state-of-the-art computer lab with six desktop publishing stations and 100 Macintosh and IBM computers that can deliver digital video on the desktop.

Many other schools have more computers or are using technology differently. Carnegie Mellon University's business school, with a quarter as many students, boasts 12 computer labs with 150 machines. MIT's Sloan School has a $3 million computerized trading room—the equal of anything on Wall Street—that enables students to analyze market data and test trading strategies. But no other B-school dean has articulated a vision of using technology as a tool of reinvention as Clark has. A harbinger of how Harvard plans to capitalize on its investment can be glimpsed in Developing, Managing, and Improving Operations, the first paperless class in the school's history. Students can use the Web to access all of the course's teaching materials, including class schedules, case studies, supplemental readings, assignments, and teaching notes. After each class, David M. Upton, a gung-ho, young prof who is among the leaders of the technology initiative, puts up his slides for students to download.

Harvard claims that within a year, every MBA course will be online.

Upton also has developed Harvard's first electronic case study for MBAs. Based on a Beijing Pacific Dunlop Textiles Ltd. sock-making factory in China, it illuminates how Harvard plans to use multimedia to develop and teach case studies. With the click of a mouse, students can view videos of executives discussing the troubled Beijing company or examine key processes inside the noisy plant. Students can also use an online simulation to see how changing production schedules will affect the plant's revenues, inventory, and costs. Says Upton: "This will help us make the case method more relevant than ever."

F. Warren McFarlan, a senior associate dean who is overseeing the technology transformation, envisions Harvard profs routinely lugging video equipment along on research trips. He expects to develop 100 paperless cases in each of the next five years. McFarlan believes he can create these electronic cases for an average of $35,000, only 15 percent more than the typical cost of a paper case.

Clark's high-tech focus will extend well beyond the classroom, promising to change every aspect of the business school, from the way it runs Baker Library to how it links up with its rich and powerful alumni. Next year, all entering students will receive lifelong E-mail addresses intended to link them with one another during their school years and let them stay in touch after graduation. Corporate recruiters will be able to search a database of upcoming grads.

As part of the B-school's new openness, Clark's administration is seeking students' views on every aspect of the program. Clark has named Steven C. Wheelwright chair of the MBA program and charged him with seeing to it that the administration no longer turns a deaf ear to students' concerns. In addition to making himself available via the Net, Clark has held many dinners and meetings with students. "It's not just Dean

Clark who is more accessible," says MBA student Rilla Delorier. "His other administrators have become more visible and more approachable."

There have been some bumps, of course. When the school announced the resumption of the GMAT requirement, some MBAs groused that they had not been consulted. "We have a lot of skin in the game," says Paul D. Conforti, a first-year student. "We're major stakeholders and want to give our opinions."

PLACEMENT DETAILS

Throughout all of this, however, the most elite corporate recruiters never lost their enthusiasm for Harvard grads. Some 310 companies recruited on-campus or at local hotels in 1996, and another 1000 job opportunities were posted by correspondence (excluding alumni jobs and executive recruiter postings). Harvard is the only business school that declines to name its top employers, but you can essentially count on every mainstream MBA recruiter in the world to come to the school. McKinsey & Co. almost always hires the single largest group of grads. In 1996, that came to roughly 80 MBAs, or nearly 10 percent of the class.

What of the future? Because one-third of the school's tenured professors will be retiring over the next five years, Clark has an extraordinary opportunity to remake the faculty. He expects to reach out to Harvard's medical and government schools to create new programs in health and nonprofit management. And he plans further innovations in the curriculum, putting more field projects and interdisciplinary teaching into courses. "We've just barely scratched the surface," says Clark.

True transformation, of course, doesn't come easily. But Clark is off to a fast start at an organization that has long resisted change. The faculty can be sure that it will receive lots of E-mail from this dean in the future.

OUTSTANDING FACULTY

Andre Perold (****—finance); *Tom Piper* (***—financial reporting and control); *Bill Sahlman* (***—entrepreneurship); *Richard Tedlaw* (**—business history), *Michael Jensen* (**—economics), *Scott Mason* (**—finance); *Jeff Rayport* (**—service management); *Regina Herzlinger* (*—accounting); *Elon Kohlberg* (*—managerial economics); *Thomas McCraw* (*—business history).

APPLICANT TIPS

Applications hit a new record in 1996 when the school got more than 8000 for fewer than 800 openings. The school reinstituted the GMAT requirement, after doing away with it for several years. It's also interviewing more applicants than ever: Admissions Director Jill Hubbell Fadule expects the school to interview 75 percent of its entering class in 1997, up from 65 percent a year earlier and only 38 percent in 1995. If you receive an invite for an evaluative interview, consider it a positive sign: they are given only after admissions reads your application, and roughly 60 percent of those interviewed in 1996 were admitted. Also, in 1996 only 25 percent of the entering class got in without the 45-minute interview.

What to expect? At Harvard, the interview is not informational. It's used to further evaluate you as a candidate. You'll be asked questions to elicit actual experiences, risks taken, difficult decisions you've made in your life, and tough feedback you've been given. You may be asked if you failed at something and what you learned from the experience. You may also be asked questions that will allow Harvard to evaluate how you deal with ambiguity and how imaginative you are. Harvard promises decisions on applicants within two weeks from your interview date.

Other pointers: Invest at least a week simply to fill out what is one of the more involved application forms of any school. Especially critical are your answers to Harvard's eight essay questions, each requiring a succinct half-page or full-page answer. Examples: "Describe an ethical dilemma you have experienced firsthand. How did you manage and resolve the situation?" Or: "Describe a setback, disappointment, or occasion of failure that you have experienced in your professional life. How did you manage the situation?" How to answer them? Says Admissions Director Fadule: "They should answer them as if the questions were asked of them by a good friend. They shouldn't get so focused on this being a business school application and that they should narrow their scope of how to answer the question. Be candid. We need to understand the whole person. People who overthink or who craft their responses do themselves a disservice because we don't get to know the true person behind the application."

Harvard prefers that your recommenders be people who you have worked with closely and who can comment on your ability to work with others. It's not important to have a "name" recommender. It's also not critical to have a senior executive of a company be a recommender. The quality of your relationship to your recommender, however, is important.

Admissions allows applicants to observe a first-year class from October through April, providing you call 617-495-6127 at least 24 hours in advance to ensure that a student host can be arranged. Harvard also holds information sessions daily at 3 p.m. on Mondays, Wednesdays, and Fridays during the school year at the admissions office in Dillon House. Harvard does not offer an IBM-style disk-based application but will accept a Macintosh version from Apply Software Systems Inc. at 800-93-APPLY. It will set you back about $40. For written applications, the school suggests that you insert a piece of cardboard in a 9-inch by 12-inch envelope to ensure that your application isn't bent or damaged in the mail.

The school has four decision periods, starting in early November and ending on March 5. Harvard discourages telephone calls regarding your application, but provides helpful feedback to rejected candidates who were either interviewed by admissions or who came close to getting in.

Contact: Jill H. Fadule
Director of Admissions
617-495-6127
Application deadlines: November 13, January 8, and March 5

HARVARD MBAs SOUND OFF

Harvard was my first choice due to its reputation and network worldwide that is unmatched. A lot of students from other countries were here for the same reason. If you want to start your own business later on, it gives you a real edge internationally if you want to raise capital from people in the network. Dean Clark has been very responsive to improve a lot of complaints regarding administration.

The teaching at HBS is phenomenal. Faculty show a relentless zeal for challenging students to make the most of themselves. Students are constantly driven to "think out of the box," and always ask "why," without accepting the most common "good answers." I describe my experience at HBS as having learned the "good questions" and then knowing "how to ask them" and "when to listen." HBS pursues lifelong learning through its dynamic classroom environment.

The network is excellent at Harvard. During my job search, I had over 95 percent of all alumni return my phone calls when I was conducting an independent job search. They provided specific information and contacts, the +/– of companies/jobs, and useful "next steps." In addition, the professors are extremely focused on teaching. Unlike my old undergrad school which focused on research, HBS ensures that professors emphasize teaching.

An alumnus of HBS told me the value of your MBA is that it "provides you with a wealth of information to amplify and enhance your interests and the opportunity to pursue them." I wouldn't have had half of the opportunities nor interests without HBS.

The administration has vaulted itself off the charts in redressing some historic problems with responsiveness. Dean Clark holds forums constantly and answers E-mail within 24 hours. Problems voiced by students are dealt with by student/administration teams very quickly. Investment and commitment to technology is massive. The highest caliber of classmates makes the program. Case discussions assume the aura of a "mini United Nations," as students from around the world weigh in with local perspectives. The program does not live up to its negative stereotypes. Team focus: many group projects include a timed mid-term exam, group papers, computer simulations, and study groups. The grading system is an asset that prevents "inflation," and actually de-emphasizes grades (since 80 percent get the middle grade) and promotes real learning.

5.
UNIVERSITY OF VIRGINIA

UNIVERSITY OF VIRGINIA

Darden Graduate School of Business Administration

P.O. Box 6550

Charlottesville, Virginia 22906-6550

E-mail address: darden@virginia.edu

Website address: http://www.darden.virginia.edu

Corporate ranking: 11	Graduate ranking: 1
Enrollment: 499	Annual tuition & fees:
	resident—$11,819
Women: 34%	nonresident—$19,627
Non-U.S.: 12%	Room and board: $11,600
Minority: 20%	Average GMAT score: 660
Part-time: none	GMAT range: 460 to 790
Average age: 27	Average GPA: 3.1
Average years of work exp.: 4	GPA range: 2.01 to 4.0
Applicants accepted: 19%	Accepted applicants enrolled: 49%
Median starting pay: $85,000	Average starting pay: $92,895

Teaching methods: Lecture, 10%   Case study, 75%   Projects, 15%

Contact:

Jon Megibow

Director of Admissions

800-UVA-MBA1

or 804-924-7281

Final application

deadline: March 15

for fall

Some fans of the University of Virginia's Darden School of Business liken the MBA program to the more famous one up north at the Harvard business school. Like Harvard, it's a school that boasts superb teaching from professors who generate sometimes heated discussions in their classrooms through the case-study method. The similarities end there, however. Virginia is cheaper, harder, smaller, and more cooperative.

As it turns out, those are powerful differences that Dean Leo I. Higdon, Jr., successfully leveraged since arriving here in October of 1993. His leadership vaulted the school an incredible seven spots, to fifth, by gaining ground with the corporate recruiting community and winning BUSINESS WEEK's top prize in graduate satisfaction. The only problem: Soon after moving the school up to its highest rank ever, Higdon announced he was leaving the school to become president of rival Babson College.

Too bad. During his short tenure at Darden, Higdon, a Chicago MBA, and his staff went off on a major benchmarking expedition, comparing and analyzing virtually everything Darden does against the best of its B-school rivals to see how it can become better. Among other things, he met with nearly 150 corporate recruiters to win them over. "They have a voice and need to be heard," explains the former investment banker. The visits worked like a charm and put completely to rest a bit of turmoil in recent years. In early 1992, for example, an outside committee concluded that the business school was a "hostile climate" for women faculty, and an anonymous group of African-American students also alleged that Darden was none too friendly an environment for minorities.

Dean Higdon and his predecessor, John Rosenbloom, moved swiftly and effectively to deal with these complaints, though some MBAs think the school has gone overboard to be what they call "politically correct." Seven of Darden's last 10 faculty hires have been women, and 2 of the 10 are minorities. In 1993, the school hired its first woman to hold an endowed chair: Professor Patricia H. Werhane, an ethics scholar. The Graduate Women in Business Network, a support group for women graduate B-school grads, recently voted to establish its permanent headquarters at Darden. And the school is 1 of 10 business schools in a consortium created to increase the enrollment of minority students. Some 17 percent of the Class of 1996 is composed of minorities, up a full 10 points from only 7 percent two years earlier.

Despite the earlier controversy, however, the school has always remained a first-rate institution with a dynamic, caring faculty and bright, hard-working students. The quality of teaching here is among the best in the world, as good as or even better than Dartmouth and Harvard, North Carolina, and Cornell. Indeed, BUSINESS WEEK's surveys—from 1990 to 1996—show Virginia to be among the very top schools with the highest satisfaction ratings on teaching measured by BW. That has been true in both the elective and core offerings, as well as on such things as faculty accessibility outside the classroom.

How can Virginia be so good? It's because excellence in teaching has long been the sine qua non for tenure and promotion at Darden. Most other schools are happy just to promote and reward scholars—not teachers. As Sherwood C. Frey, one of Darden's best professors, puts it: "You could be the best researcher in the world, but you can't get tenure here if you aren't a good teacher." Hopefully, this is an area no dean will ever change.

Like Harvard, Darden is a "case-study" school that offers graduates a general management education. Many of the professors here are Harvard Business School expatriates who prefer the casual informality and intimacy of Darden over their alma mater in Boston. The differences are evident at the start of every weekday morning, when at 9:30 faculty and students gather in the lobby of the B-school for coffee and talk. When you attend one of the core courses, you'll find yourself in a class with 60 students—a full one-third smaller than Harvard's classes. So students get more "air time" to voice their opinions in class. They're also more likely to know each other, and the faculty is far more inclined to know them. With class discussion accounting for 50 percent of your grade, that's a critical consideration.

When you're in a class of 240, instead of roughly 800 as at Harvard, you're also less likely to feel so fiercely competitive. At Darden, students are not as prone to be victims of "chip shots"—the cutting remarks made by classmates at Harvard and other schools to score points with a professor. "When it happens, you'll see someone swinging an imaginary golf club to make it clear to everyone that it was a chip shot," says Richard M. Paschal, a Darden alumnus. Without Harvard's forced grading curve, there's no disadvantage in contributing to the learning of a classmate. People actually speak of a "Darden community"—a highly supportive environment where students pull each other along.

This cultural advantage occurs in an academic village in an environment as quaint and rich as the Charlottesville area. Looming in the background are the foothills of the Blue Ridge Mountains and the Shenandoah Valley—land idyllic enough to attract a slew of Beautiful People, from Jessica Lange to Sissy Spacek. Darden's MBAs take advantage of the area's beauty by going to The Barracks (a popular stable about five miles from the grounds) for horseback riding in the mountains and to Wintergreen for skiing.

Within view of the campus is Thomas Jefferson's Monticello, an architectural masterpiece that greatly influenced the look of most of the university buildings. Within this classic environment is the Darden School—a rectangular three-story building that some say looks like a modern textile mill. Across a tree-lined courtyard sits the university's law school. A new Jeffersonian-inspired home for the business school was completed in 1995.

More differences between Harvard and Darden exist in the innovative, integrated curriculum. Each teacher in the first year belongs to one of four groups of profs who all teach the same section of 60 students. There's a programmed feel to the curriculum. As former dean Rosenblum puts it, "Our courses go for three weeks, stop, come back for another three weeks. It's more of an integrated, shuffled-deck kind of experience. There's a flow of learning that goes through the core curriculum."

In the dreaded quant course, for example, you'll cover decision analysis, discounted cash flows, and probability in September. The next month, there are no classes in quantitative analysis. Instead, you'll pick up the start of your courses in operations and finance. Come November, quant classes begin again just as classes in accounting, marketing, business, and the political economy take a breather.

With such an intricately linked schedule, no one can waive out of any of the core courses. CPAs must sit through accounting; former plant supervisors must attend the first level operations course. All told, the first year contains nine required courses, including what is the only graded, 20-session class in ethics at a major school. There's also a course in Analysis and Communication in which students must make five speeches to small groups, write five business memos and reports, and learn group presentation skills.

While most B-schools, including Harvard, are still grappling with how to incorporate ethics into their programs, Darden is clearly a pioneer in the field. In addition to the required course in ethics for MBAs, the school blends the subject into courses in accounting, marketing, and operations. A 20-year-old Olsson Center for the Study of Applied Ethics also creates teaching materials, tracks scholarships in business ethics, and sponsors seminars on the subject for executives. R. Edward Freeman, who heads up these efforts, is widely regarded as one of the preeminent scholars in business ethics.

Your second year begins with one of two new required 1.5-credit courses, Concepts of Strategy, intending to integrate the concepts and perspectives of the first-year courses. Then there's Leading Strategic Change, a course designed to help students develop leadership skills and attitudes.

Another less controversial requirement in the second year is a "directed study" that allows students to take one of six different options from international field projects in consulting with corporate sponsors such as PepsiCo, British Petroleum, and General Motors to researching and writing a case study for inclusion in Darden's curriculum. About 40 percent of MBAs here ace the program to study abroad. You'll round out the year with a series of required and voluntary electives that can be chosen from a catalog of about 60 courses. They range from Leslie E. Grayson's Management of International Business to Thomas C. MacAvoy's Innovation and Technology Management.

Expect to work hard in these and all the courses at Darden, which throws far more work at students than Northwestern, Chicago, Harvard, or Stanford. "The first year was hell," says Richard A. Longstaff, who graduated in 1992. "It's the only time in my life I worked 16 hours a day." Through the years, graduates have rated the school's program among the toughest of them all in the BW survey. So intense is the experience in the first year that 65 to 80 hours of study per week is the norm. You'll have to study and dissect 14 cases a week. Students who routinely got A's as undergraduates find it difficult to ace their courses at Darden. "The workload reaches a point at which students are unable to give any more due to exhaustion and burnout," says a Darden alum. "At the overload point, the relationship between effort and learning breaks down and students are merely going through the motions." The school maintains that the hellish work pace forces students to learn to better manage their time.

In the late 1980s, one Darden student compared the grueling first year to a fraternity hazing. He had a point: Up to 8 percent of those who enrolled in the program failed to complete it. Sensitive to complaints that he was running an academic "boot camp," then-Dean Rosenblum made several alterations. First-year students now prepare 25 fewer cases than earlier due to a deliberate reduction in the number of classes. And they don't have to endure Saturday exams or Saturday deadlines for papers for the required communications course. Not too many years ago, Darden actually held classes on Saturdays, as well. Although Darden schedules more classroom hours than any other leading business school, an effort has been made to make the workload more manageable. Often the school now has only two classes on Wednesdays for first-years, more travel days for second-year students, and daylong program events on a specific issue for first-years. Now, 98 percent of those who enroll at Darden complete the program.

It's still hardly a cakewalk. But students get help—and lots of it. When candidates are admitted to the school, the admissions staff often suggests an accounting or statistics course over the summer. On day one, second-years guide group discussions of case studies to show the newcomers how it is done. On the first weekend, all students and faculty gather for a schoolwide picnic to get to know one another. The dean hosts students at a series of eight receptions during the first month of school. And every Darden student is assigned a faculty adviser and a big brother or sister.

Among several joint-degree programs, Darden boasts a unique MBA/MA in Asian Studies that can be earned in three years. The program features customized foreign language courses and six months of independent study in either Japan or a Chinese-speaking country. One major caveat: The third year adds another $30,000 to the cost of the regular MBA program. Darden hopes to launch similar programs in Europe and Latin America over the next couple of years.

When these joint-program MBAs return to campus, they're likely to bemoan the quality of the food in the cafeteria in the B-school, jokingly dubbed "Cafe Death." All the more reason, MBAs say, to order out from Pizza Hut in Charlottesville. When MBAs here work up a thirst, they're apt to stroll down to Sloan's, a popular bar only a three-minute walk from school, or the Biltmore Grill.

Most MBAs live in private housing within walking distance of the university because Darden lacks sufficient dormitory facilities. In Charlottesville, you can still rent a spacious two-bedroom apartment for little more than $500 a month. As many as half of Darden's students end up in Ivy Gardens, a seven-minute stroll from the B-school and the site of the first-years' "100 case party" celebrating the 100th case of the first semester. These apartments, however, became the subject of a highly critical story in the campus newspaper in 1991. The article reported student complaints about everything from rental rates to the treatment of security deposits. Some MBAs even live out in the country in cottages during their second year. Students' working spouses, however, may find it rough to get a job in town. You just don't have anywhere near the professional opportunities that would exist in New York, Boston, Chicago, or L.A.

Even so, there has long been a greater sense of camaraderie among students, spouses, and faculty than is possible at a large urban school. Professors and students team up to play pick-up basketball games. Every Friday at 5 p.m., MBAs trek to the Graduate Happy Hour that brings together 300 to 500 graduate students from all over the university. There's an annual Chili Cook-Off, an occasion that may cause some indigestion but remains one of the school's most popular events. The Birdwood Picnics, the Foxfield Races, the International Food Festival, and the Darden Follies offer a bit of distraction and relief from the heavy workload. The social event of the second semester is clearly the Spring Ball. The small size of the class, the intimate nature of the educational experience, and all these events help to foster a cozy, close-knit culture. One measure of the esprit de corps is the record $230,000 gift given to the school by 94 percent of the Class of 1996.

PLACEMENT DETAILS

In 1996, 187 companies recruited second-year students on campus, conducting 4287 interviews—or roughly 17 job interviews per graduate. Another 345 job opportunities were posted by correspondence. Darden MBAs had in hand an average 2.7 offers at graduation. The top employers of the Class of 1996: Renaissance Solutions, Inc. (9); Coopers & Lybrand (8); Deloitte & Touche (6); Ernst & Young (6); American Management Systems (5); Booz Allen & Hamilton (5); AT&T (5); Boston Consulting Group (4); Capital One Financial (4); and Procter & Gamble Co. (4). With strong companies like that behind this school and with the progress Higdon has already made, the opportunities should continue to expand for this mini-Harvard of the South.

OUTSTANDING FACULTY

Susan Chaplinsky (****—finance); *Robert F. Bruner* (****—finance); *Robert J. Sack* (****—accounting); *Sherwood Frey* (***—statistics); *E. Richard Brownlee* (**—accounting); *Edward Davis* (**—operations); *Mark R. Eaker* (**—international finance); *Robert Spekman* (**—marketing); *Bob S. Harris* (**—finance); *John L. Colley, Jr.* (**—management).

APPLICANT TIPS

Getting into Darden is tougher than ever. In 1996, the school received a record 2622 applica-

tions and admitted MBAs with an average GMAT of 658, up 30 points in three years. With its leap in the rankings, applications are likely to go up even higher. So don't count Virginia as an easy school. On-campus interviews are critical to the application process at the University of Virginia. As the school puts it: "We look for individuals with strong interpersonal and communication skills, as these are essential for success in both a case method teaching environment and in positions of broad managerial responsibility." Virginia, in fact, won't review your application until you have an interview.

So you should consider this as a necessary, first step. The only possible exception is for international students. Schedule an interview as early as possible. Virginia begins interviewing in mid-September and stops in mid-March, and appointments are made on a first-come, first-served basis. To schedule an interview, contact the admissions office at 800-UVA-MBA1 or via fax at 804-924-4859.

Use the interview opportunity and your answers to the four mandatory essay questions to show admissions that you are what the school says it seeks: "a multidimensional individual." Darden wants candidates "whose academic ability, leadership potential and experience, and personal qualities indicate that they can contribute to and benefit from our program."

The school has three application periods. The first one ends on December 2. But applicants who apply by February 3 get a welcome or turndown by March 14. If you wait until the final March 14 deadline, you may not hear from the school until two months later. Applications received after March 14 are considered on a space-available basis.

Contact: Jon Megibow
Director of Admissions
800-UVA-MBA1 or 804-924-7281
Final application deadline: March 15 for fall

DARDEN MBAs SOUND OFF

There is excellent preparation for a career in general management. The level of curriculum integration is outstanding. The case method can be an inefficient way to learn for some (myself included). Too much class time was spent discussing multiple wrong ways to do things, rather that having someone demonstrate the right ways (especially true in highly quantitative courses). To its credit, the school is revising the curriculum to provide "mini-lectures" in certain first-year courses.

There is the long-term impact of the case method to consider. After two years of three cases a day, five days a week, and listening to 65 students' comments, Darden students learn how to listen. On the other side of the coin, the case method forces students to think about what they want to say, and say it with grace, style, and understated confidence. Darden students receive considerable praise from fellow students for well-crafted comments.

A comparison of the old and new Darden buildings is a perfect metaphor for how the school's culture has changed. The former facility was a less-than-hospitable, quasi-Bauhaus 1970s box. Today's Darden, and the new Darden building, is comfortable, friendly, and, at least to me, inspiring.

Darden is a school in which professors never teach. The most popular professors act really well as "good talk show hosts." They write very few text books, seldom publish papers. . . . In fact, students learn from each other. This is good! But, professors get all the credit. In class, there are very few international issues discussed. Dean Higdon is trying to make changes, however.

The case method used at Darden and Harvard allows a student to gain a lifetime of experience in just two short years. I am not sure that some of my younger classmates have yet to realize the powerful knowledge that Darden has provided them to utilize as they pursue their various interests and careers. While a few complain of the heavy workload, I wouldn't have traded a single moment of my time at Darden.

The student body is cohesive and, through the curriculum, has ample opportunity to work with each other to discover the challenges of working with different people who have differing viewpoints and work ethics. The school is completely dedicated to the development of quality business leaders. It does so through providing outstanding courses and visiting professional guests. The students' voice is largely responsible for the changes that are made in the curriculum thereby enhancing the experience of students and faculty members.

Due to the school's policy of not allowing CPAs to opt out of accounting, and investment bankers from finance, the bar is set high enough to challenge every student. The high quantitative emphasis at Darden is not widely known by recruiters. But through discussions with other MBA students from top 10 schools, and my experiences working with other summer associates, the program's tough spreadsheet orientation is one of the most effective of any school. The facilities of the new school are just unbelievable for their functionality and architectural beauty.

Darden does an excellent job of integrating courses to support cross-functional learning. The teachers are truly dedicated to education and excel in the classroom. In addition, they are regularly available outside of the classroom for discussion. The Dean is committed to making Darden an enduring institution and the broad level of alumni support is also indicative of Darden's ambitions. While Darden still has a "boot camp" mentality, I still managed to meet my fiancée in the first year!

6.
COLUMBIA UNIVERSITY

COLUMBIA UNIVERSITY

Graduate School of Business

105 Uris Hall

New York, New York 10027

E-mail address: gohermes@claven.gsb.columbia.edu

Website address: http://www.columbia.edu/cu/business

Corporate ranking: 6	Graduate ranking: 16
Enrollment: 1380	Annual tuition & fees: $23,830
Women: 35%	Room and board: $9390
Non-U.S.: 24%	Average GMAT score: 660
Minority: 12%	Average GPA: 3.3
Part-time: None	GPA range: 3.0 to 3.8
Average age: 27	Average years of work exp.: 4.5
Applicants accepted: 14%	Accepted applicants enrolled: 70%
Median starting pay: $88,850	Average starting pay: $92,550

Teaching methods: Lecture, 40%   Case study, 40%
Group projects, 20%

Contact:
Ethan Hanabury
Director of Admissions
212-854-1961
Application deadlines:
November 1 (spring)
February 2 (summer)
April 20 (fall)

First the good news: Extensive improvements in Columbia B-school's aging building mean elevators actually get you to the second floor faster than the stairs and temperatures are finally tolerable in a once too-cold, too-hot facility that only the cockroaches seemed to like.

Now the even better news: Dean Meyer Feldberg's plans for a new state-of-the-art building have finally come to fruition. The state-of-the-art building, to be shared with the university's law school, will open in the fall of 1998. Of course, nothing goes off without a hitch in New York, and before the school broke ground for the new building on Amsterdam Avenue at 115th Street, it had to build the U.S. government a new post office to replace the one on the land Columbia bought for its new facility. Now that's a complicated mouthful—but in the city that never sleeps, you'd expect a B-school that can keep up with the fast-paced confusion.

Columbia is certainly doing that. In fact, there's not all that much bad news in Morningside Heights these days. What goes on inside the walls of Columbia's B-school building is even more impressive than the plans for the new facility. Feldberg, who left the presidency of the Illinois Institute of Technology to become dean in mid-1989, has led Columbia through a dramatic transformation. His $100 million capital campaign has raised the school's endowment to $80 million and provided funds for the new building. He launched a new MBA program immodestly dubbed "The Curriculum for the 21st Century," while carving out a niche for Columbia as an international business school. And the school that used to accept half its applicants four years ago now accepts only one in seven.

Finance is this school's strong point, and with Wall Street only a subway ride away, Columbia capitalizes on its prime location. But be prepared to keep up with a rigorous two years. Having the ability to do several things at once is essential to this B-school's educational experience. The northern Manhattan campus certainly doesn't provide a pleasant or reflective environment like rolling hills in Durham, North Carolina, or Charlottesville, Virginia. Going to school in New York City is an education in itself, Feldberg tells the entering class each year.

One thing is for sure, though, when you leave this program, you will be able to deal with any problem from a global perspective. Every class is taught with an international slant, taking management from a simple U.S.-centric theme into a worldwide venture. Seventy percent of Columbia MBAs are fluent in more than one language.

Columbia had long been viewed as a cut-throat environment. In the past, students could go through the entire first year without having to work with another student. Feldberg decided to change this and implemented a cluster system. Now, the class is divided into sections of 60 students. This cluster is further broken down into study groups of 10 students and stays together through the first year. Feldberg says this gives a sense of community to the school without taking away the idea of healthy competition.

Besides the new building, the big news is Columbia's revamped MBA program. Entering students are required to own notebook computers so that each becomes computer literate in business applications and databases. More than 300 data jacks can be found in all study areas, conference rooms, classrooms, and even in the deli and library, so that MBAs can connect to the school's network no matter what else they're up to. That said, students complain the network itself is still not top-notch. But it should improve. Finance exams are now done on computers and turned in via network. Students are beginning to register for classes on computer, as they do at many schools. The fall of 1996 marked the opening of the new Dow Jones Telerate Trading Room, a top-notch facility that will provide students with hands-on experience in the use of live market data feeds and the Dow Jones Telerate data and analysis platform.

Corporations are giving the new curriculum a thumbs-up. In BUSINESS WEEK's corporate poll, the school moved up one spot, to No. 6 this year, allowing the school's overall rank to move from eighth to sixth. Not surprisingly, Corporate America particularly likes the finance grads who come out of Columbia. Only Chicago and Wharton get better marks here. But marketing is a strength, too. Recruiters place the school seventh as a hunting ground in this area.

The reforms are a result of intensive study and survey work. In early 1990, a pair of committees composed of senior faculty, administrators, and students began to ask various constituents to help redefine the institution's mission. The group gathered data from 2000 alumni, 100 recruiting companies, nearly 1000 students, and 100 of its own professors. They also ran focus groups of managers, meeting with executives from American Express, Bankers Trust, General Electric, Merck, and others.

The result of the effort—the first comprehensive review of Columbia's program since the early 1960s—was the curriculum that made its debut in 1992. The program puts more emphasis on managing and less on crunching numbers. It requires students to learn communications, plus quantitative and computer skills, before beginning the program. Then, in year one, every MBA has seminars on presentation skills, team building, and writing proficiency.

More importantly, the program tries to integrate into the first-year core curriculum four key themes: globalization, total quality, ethics, and human resources management. Not exactly buzz words you'd expect at a school famous for its finance jocks. The goal is for each theme to absorb at least 12 class sessions, with slightly more for international issues. In a few instances, a single case study is being simultaneously taught over three separate classes, so that MBAs can see how finance, marketing, and management fit together. An integrative group project at the end of the first term allows students to see how the disciplines play a role in any business decision. "This was a very painful undertaking," says Feldberg. "But it wasn't effective the way it was and we wanted these four themes to tie the entire first year together because one or two courses wasn't enough."

The biggest challenge in the curriculum change has been working with the faculty. Columbia is asking narrowly trained professors to view business problems more broadly and to work together across disciplinary areas. Teachers are being challenged to alter their teaching methods to a more engaging, Socratic style as more case studies and group projects are dumped into the core. The transition has been anything but easy, because Feldberg has had to deal with an antiquated culture, one in which academic intellectualism has long assumed greater importance than the business of learning. The curriculum has also forced the faculty to cooperate to redesign their core courses. Professors now work together, trying to redesign coursework from the presentation to final exam.

At the same time, hiring procedures now pay more attention to teaching, professor evaluations have been redesigned, and faculty are more closely monitored. Outstanding teachers are now recognized by newly established teaching awards. Perhaps the single most important move to improve teaching was Feldberg's appointment of Safwam Masri as vice dean for the MBA program. A masterful teacher, Masri is trying to improve the art around the school. Many students say there's no one better for the job.

It's a job that still needs doing. According to the survey of the class of '96, the quality of teaching at Columbia ranks well below that at rivals like Virginia, Dartmouth, Michigan, and Chicago. It is particularly uneven in the core, students say. "Some poor professors have fallen through the cracks," says one '96 grad. Comments another: "The school must do a better job screening visiting professors. Two [whom I had] were excellent, and two I thought were nothing short of abominable." And, despite Feldberg's claims, the curriculum isn't much more integrated than it was two years ago—and is a lot less integrated than at many other top schools.

Teaching is enhanced by Columbia's rather sizable contingent of adjunct professors, who bring real-time experience to the classrooms. A First Boston analyst, one of the top three covering the computer industry, teaches a security analysis class. An elective on leveraged buyouts is taught by Bill Comfort, head of Citibank's venture capital unit. And other professors utilize the proximity of the business community in their classrooms. The value investing class features such heavy hitters as Warren Buffett, Mario Gabelli of the Gabelli Group, and Michael Price, president of Mutual Series Fund, Inc.

Ask a student or faculty member what the best thing is about Columbia, and the answer will likely be "New York." Ask what the worst thing is, and you may then get the same reply. Like the Big Apple itself, Columbia offers glamour and excitement, but it is not for the thin-skinned or faint-hearted. It's true that the famous Harlem neighborhood, just west of the B-school, is in the middle of an attempt at revitalization. And, as students will doubtless hear hundreds of times as Mayor Rudolph Giuliani—Rudy to the natives—begins his campaign for re-election in '97, the crime rate around the city has dropped considerably. It's now lower than many smaller cities less known for urban danger. Don't try to fool yourself, though: if you don't like city life, you won't like Columbia.

That said, there aren't too many places where you could attend a finance class taught by a corporate raider, lunch with a visiting Wall Street banker, and take in a Broadway show on the same day. It's hard to overstate the wealth of opportunities available to MBAs in the nation's cultural and financial capital. Columbia is the kind of place where you can pick up *The New York Times* and read about a deal made by somebody who spoke to your class just the day before.

Another big advantage is the flexibility Columbia offers students. The school allows MBAs to begin its program in any one of three terms each year. It is possible to complete the degree in 16 months, but most students use the summer term for an internship rather than classes. You also can exempt yourself from core classes by exam, and they don't have to be replaced with similar electives. With nine full courses and two half-courses, the integrated core comprises half the workload for the degree. In year two, students choose from among 150 electives, as well as graduate courses offered at other schools at Columbia University. The B-school has 13 joint degree programs with other arms of the university. Two more are in the works.

MBAs can concentrate in any one of 13 areas of study, including accounting, media, and management. They can focus further, say, on "investment management" under a finance concentration or "management consulting" under a management of organizations concentration. These days, up to 60 percent of the class takes on two concentrations. The school also offers mini-courses in more than 50 languages, including French, German, Italian, Spanish, Chinese, English, and Japanese. But the classes aren't cheap. On top of the $24,000 you pay in annual fees, the school asks you to shell out between $330 and $355 for a three-hour Friday session.

The availability of foreign language classes has helped Feldberg reconstruct Columbia into one of the premier schools for international business. His biggest boost, however, came in 1991 when Jerome A. Chazen, a founding partner of Liz Claiborne, Inc. and a 1950 alum, donated $10 million for an Institute of International Business. This center is tying together all of the school's efforts to globalize: it publishes an expanded journal of world business, ensures that the core courses boast a hefty international component, and is expanding exchange programs with non-U.S. business schools. (There are now 18 such programs and 12 international studies trips.)

Closer to home, Columbia itself has all the amenities of an Ivy League school, including a grassy quad surrounded by temples of learning. Many Columbia B-school students live on the Upper West Side, a neighborhood filled with trendy restaurants and bars catering to both yuppies and intellectuals. By all means, avoid the dormitory allocated to the B-school.

A typical week at Columbia ends in the first-floor Uris Deli, where happy hour is held every Thursday night. After a few beers, students will break up into groups and go their separate ways, some heading down the West Side, others to the Village or Little Italy. Some MBAs hang out at the West End Gate at 113th and Broadway, where beat writer Jack Kerouac once carved his name in a table. Since there are no classes on Fridays, students use the three-day weekends to escape from the city or work part-time. The highlight of Columbia's social season is the annual spring ball, an MBA version of the senior prom—complete with designer evening gowns, stretch limos, and ritzy dinners. The locale for the event changes annually and has included such historic landmarks as the New York Public Library, Federal Hall, and Tavern on the Green.

Just a cursory glance at Columbia's hefty alumni directory underscores its strong reputation in finance. For years, the school has been a factory for the big-league commercial banks and giants of the financial service world. Some 356 of the school's alums draw their paycheck from Citicorp alone. Chase Manhattan Bank employs 277, while Merrill Lynch has 178 on its payroll. Other major employers of alums: Goldman Sachs (160), IBM (156), AT&T (152), Morgan Stanley (131), Bankers Trust (125), Prudential

(122), J.P. Morgan (117), American Express (112), and Smith Barney (106).

PLACEMENT DETAILS

The school's career services office gets good reviews for helping students connect with the job market—unless you're looking to get a job with a company that doesn't recruit on campus. That's a weakness. But for any student who hasn't found a job by graduation, Tom Fernandez, director of placement, holds a Monday group meeting to help and offer advice. With 98 percent placement at graduation, attendance is usually low. After all, 291 companies recruited on campus in 1996 (73 more than in 1995), doing 6742 interviews with second-year students. And more than 1600 job opportunities came into the office through the mail—including 218 international opportunities. Still, some students fault the office for not attracting enough non-American companies with international jobs.

Wall Street's upswing had a big impact at Columbia, since so many of its graduates gravitate to the world of finance. No wonder Columbia was one of only eight schools whose graduates won starting pay packages that averaged more than $85,000 in '96.

Lehman Brothers led the pack in recruiting, with 21 hires, more than double the number of Columbia grads it hired in 1994. Not far behind was Booz Allen & Hamilton (19). Then came Citibank (17), Merrill Lynch (16), J.P. Morgan (16), Goldman Sachs (15), Coopers & Lybrand (13), CS First Boston (12), Bankers Trust (10), American Express (10), Ernst & Young (10), and Deloitte & Touche (9).

That impressive lineup of committed recruiters has much to do with Columbia's reputation. But Feldberg, a master networker, must get some of the credit. He's well-connected to the New York business community. Every year he hosts about 10 cocktail parties for students, alums, and executives from the school's Board of Overseers. He also conjured up a "Take a Student to Lunch" program to link working alumni with students. Of course, Feldberg understands those meals can be a two-way street: while the alums talk about their jobs, students can tell them all about the good things happening at the other end of Manhattan.

OUTSTANDING FACULTY

John Whitney (****—management); *Bruce Greenwald* (****—finance); *Larry Selden* (***—finance); *John B. Donaldson* (*—finance and economics); *Suresh Sundaresan* (*—finance and economics); *David O. Beim* (*—finance); *Bob Bontempo* (*—management); *Paul Glasserman* (*—management science); *Ronald Schramm* (*—finance and economics).

APPLICANT TIPS

Columbia is one of the few top business schools to give students the opportunity to begin their studies in May, September, or January. If you want to apply for May admittance, you must file your application before February 1. If you want to begin in January, you must apply before November 1. For the September start, you have until April 20. The deadlines for non-U.S. students are even earlier for all three periods.

The admissions staff says it "values applicants who have demonstrated leadership ability and who also work well as members of a diverse team." It also looks for candidates "who show high levels of initiative, good judgment and integrity," and it expects candidates "to have clear and realistic goals for the future." Applicants would be wise to address these valued characteristics in filling out the application form and in answering the five required essay questions.

Columbia sponsors information sessions for applicants led by an admissions officer and a current MBA student. Prospective students also are welcome to visit classes Monday through Thursday. For further details, contact the admissions office at 212-854-1961 or via fax at 212-662-6754.

Contact: Ethan Hanabury
Director of Admissions
212-854-1961
Application deadlines: November 1 (spring); February 2 (summer); April 20 (fall)

COLUMBIA MBAs SOUND OFF

The best thing about Columbia Business School is recruiting, without a doubt. If you want to work in finance, there is no better school to attend. All the major investment firms recruit at Columbia. Location is a major plus. It makes it easy for firm visits.

Dean Feldberg and Safwan Masri are an incredible combination. They look after student needs and ensure that world class researchers remember that they are teachers as well. I praise Mr. Masri for his efforts to improve teaching quality.

Columbia is not a hand-holding school. There's a lot to do and experience, but it's up to the students to make sure they take advantage of as many opportunities as possible. The dean has made great progress in creating an atmosphere of trust and cooperation, particularly through the use of the cluster system. For me, the only negative is that the school is too focused on the finance curriculum. But that is its forte so it's understandable. This is definitely the school to go to if you want to work on Wall Street.

Columbia has an advantage that no other top B-schools have . . . New York City. My teachers during my last two semesters included managing directors at Bear Stearns, Smith Barney, Morgan Stanley, and Lehman Brothers. They bring incomparable knowledge and practical wisdom to the classroom.

The school has developed a phenomenal entrepreneurial program that is incredibly popular. Outstanding professors actually help students find the seed money to launch new businesses. Global study trips are also first-rate.

Columbia's location is a huge asset for anyone interested in international business or finance. Quality of life sucks here, but the access is incomparable. Because of the focus on finance, we admittedly lose sight of other important areas like marketing and human behavior/management (where consequently the faculty is generally not as strong). Although many finance jocks dismiss it, the final, cumulative core course "strategy" is terrific and really addresses multifaceted management issues.

Columbia's administration goes the extra mile and never lets a problem go unresolved or forces an unsatisfactory solution. If you know where you want to be, Columbia will break down walls to help you get there.

7.
STANFORD UNIVERSITY

Contact:
Marie M. Mookini
Director of Admissions
415-723-2766
*Final application
deadline:* March 15
for fall

STANFORD UNIVERSITY

Graduate School of Business
350 Memorial Way
Stanford, California 94305-5015
E-mail address: MBAinquiries@gsb.stanford.edu
Website address: http://www.gsb.stanford.edu

Corporate ranking: 7	Graduate ranking: 11
Enrollment: 725	Annual tuition & fees: $23,100
Women: 29.5%	Room and board: $11,400
Non-U.S.: 25%	Average GMAT score: *690
Minority: 25%	Average GPA: n/a
Part-time: none	GPA range: n/a
Average age: 26.3	Average years of work exp.: 3.9
Applicants accepted: 7.4%	Accepted applicants enrolled: 81.3%
Median starting pay: $108,000	Average starting pay: $111,250

Teaching methods: Lecture, 30%   Case study, 40%   Projects, 30%

The Stanford Business School is a magisterial institution in a magical setting. The students here are among the most cooperative and least competitive of any top school of business. They are known for their diversity instead of their sameness. Unlike Harvard, there's no grading curve to promote vicious competition. Nor are grades publicly posted or allowed to be disclosed to corporate recruiters. Only at graduation is the top 10 percent of the class announced. The classes are smaller and more intimate, too. And its location in California lends to its different approach. "There's an informality at Stanford," says Jeffrey Pfeffer, one of the most popular professors here. "It's partly the difference between the West and the East. And one of the caps on our enrollment is that our biggest classrooms hold only 70 people."

Students often refer to the campus as the farm—a throwback to when the campus was indeed a farm and racehorse-breeding ranch a century ago. Stanford clearly boasts one of the most handsome campuses in the country. Not far off from the business school looms the university's charming trademark, the Hoover Tower. The B-school is housed in a four-story building in the center of the university's 8200-acre campus. It's a modern anomaly among the campus's arcaded quadrangles of Spanish-style buildings topped by red tile roofs. The three-story Littlefield Center, more in keeping with Stanford's architecture, is home to the school's faculty. These days there's little evidence of the October 1989 earthquake that abruptly disturbed this tranquil setting. Though no one at the school was seriously injured, the B-school suffered millions of dollars in extensive damage. Classes were canceled for two days; the library, heavily damaged, was shut down for the remainder of the school year and a satellite facility was opened in relatively unscathed Littlefield.

Even the earthquake, however, couldn't keep students away. One in five Stanford MBAs turn down Harvard to come here and study amid the redwoods and palm trees. What they find at Stanford is a pure and unadulterated general management program. No single group of faculty overwhelmingly dominates others. With the exception of health care, Stanford has resisted industry-funded centers of research popular at Wharton and other schools partly because they encourage too much specialization.

But while they attend one of the world's most selective business schools, students quickly find that Stanford lacks the flexibility of many competitors—including Chicago, Kellogg, and Wharton—and the school's emphasis on scholarly achievement has prevented Stanford from rivaling such schools as Dartmouth, Harvard, and Virginia in the quality of the teaching. Indeed, graduates of 44 of the 51 schools polled by BUSINESS WEEK were more satisfied than Stanford MBAs with the quality of teaching in the core curriculum. That dubious distinction made Stanford the only Top 25 school near the bottom of BUSINESS WEEK's satisfaction ranking in core teaching.

These are the major reasons why Stanford lost ground in the BUSINESS WEEK poll in 1996, dropping to seventh from fourth. The school came under criticism from graduates that were less satisfied with the teaching quality and unhappy with the administration's efforts to allay the problems. "It's very, very uneven," says Stephen R. Pamon, Jr., a grad who works at McKinsey & Co. Stanford allows many senior professors to teach specialized courses, letting basic instruction suffer. In some classes, Pamon grouses, "Kids are basically teaching themselves. You take the syllabus and textbook and go to work."

The emphasis on research over teaching—also borne out by the BUSINESS WEEK survey—contributed to the recent decision by James Collins, one of the school's best and hottest professors, to quit. "Stanford's aim is to anchor the end of the continuum toward academic rigor," says Collins, who with a colleague has written the best-seller *Built to Last.* "There are schools that have a real blend of research and teaching, but Stanford doesn't put those on an equal footing."

Such complaints have come up again and again, from BUSINESS WEEK's first surveys in 1988 to 1992. The pages of the school newspaper, *The Reporter,* have overflowed with complaints about the issue. At times, students have been known to abandon the classrooms of core teachers who were so bad they couldn't clearly communicate their ideas to students. Before these latest complaints, however, it seemed that the school was dealing with the troubles. In 1994, the teaching ratings went up significantly for the first time after Stanford began to pair greener professors with stars to team-teach some classes. But those efforts failed to go far enough, according to graduates. "We have done an enormous amount to try to make sure the teaching is as good as we can make it," retorts Dean A. Michael Spence. "The fact that we haven't been able to eliminate these incidents is a source of great frustration."

Too bad, because so much of what Stanford does is so good. A new curriculum—launched in 1992—is still getting good reviews from students. Although the changes are far from dramatic, the fine-tuning puts greater emphasis on human resources issues and gives students more flexibility in scheduling their programs. Stanford elminated Macroeconomics and combined Decision Making under Uncertainty and Data Analysis into a single course. It also added a new class in human resources management as the twelfth core course. These alterations trimmed the course requirements for graduation to 25 from 27. Students may take more electives than the minimum, since the new graduation requirement is considered a floor, not a ceiling.

The slightly lighter workload, Stanford believes, gives first-years the option of taking electives during both the winter and spring terms—an important change, because more and more of the students here are studying foreign languages and are interested in dual degrees. In 1996, Stanford graduated a bumper crop of dual-degree grads, including 15 who walked away with JD/MBAs, 10 with MBAs and the MA in education, and 1 who earned an MBA with a master's in Latin American studies. The redesign also resulted in a leadership skills program, which sounds a bit like the one Chicago installed back in 1989, composed of noncurricular activities and related elective courses.

Students can waive out of several of the required core courses by taking and passing a proficiency exam before school starts, but they must substitute an elective for any class they avoid. Without a requirement to major or specialize in any given field, they're free to take electives anywhere they want. A few second-year MBA students spend their spring quarter studying at the Center for Technology and Innovation in Japan as part of the university's relatively new academic program in Kyoto. The program involves academic coursework in language, culture, and economic and political systems, and is followed by a summer internship with a Japanese firm (but students must have Japanese language skills before enrolling). Mostly, however, they select from the B-school's own novel array of electives from Creativity in Business and Japanese Marketing to Managing Strategic Alliances and Topics in Philanthropy.

Maybe it's the sun-drenched sandstone buildings, the lush grounds, or the clear, crisp air. Maybe it's just a bit of that Silicon Valley entrepreneurial spirit. But Stanford seems to excel at continually coming up with new ideas and courses. Some 55 percent of the 83 electives offered in 1996–1997 are new courses developed in the past three years. They range from Marketing on the Internet to Genius and Folly in Organizations. Another novel offering: Learning to

Lead, a two-quarter course with a summer internship taught by four professors, including Jerry Porras, an associate dean. The course brings 40 first-year students into the nitty-gritty of leadership, requiring MBAs to read and study business leaders on paper and in action. One evening a week, students meet to engage in leadership exercises and role-playing. During the summer internship, MBAs go off to "observe leaders at work." A theme of the second quarter coursework is the "leader as change agent"—requiring a major project in which students apply the learning they've gained in the course and internship.

MBAs also have good things to say about Stanford's Public Management Program, which in recent years has eclipsed Yale University's well-known efforts in public service. Designed for MBAs interested in the public and nonprofit sectors, the program consistently attracts a significant chunk of students. MBAs seeking a PMP certificate must complete the regular B-school core, plus three public management courses from among 20 electives in the field. The emphasis on public management has another unusual twist: MBAs who land lucrative corporate internships over the summer months often pledge to donate some of their earnings to help subsidize classmates who work for nonprofit groups. There's also a loan-forgiveness program for students who take jobs in the public sector after graduation.

Few students enrolled in the program are headed for permanent jobs with nonprofits, but they want a sense of public policy issues. "This is a business school, after all," says James Thompson, the program's director. "The proof is not what they'll do immediately after getting the MBA. People will go to McKinsey or Hewlett-Packard and after a few years they may go to the nonprofits." Some 30 of the 361 MBAs graduating in 1996 completed the coursework for the certificate.

Another certificate program is geared toward students interested in global business. Developed by four students in the Class of 1994, the program awards Global Management Program certificates to those who complete 4 of some 20 electives with an international focus, including two courses beyond those needed for the MBA degree. The program also is a focus for student activities that range from overseas study trips to speeches by leaders of international institutions and governments. Some 35 MBAs graduated with the certificate in 1996.

MBAs here engage in a broad range of extracurricular activities, from raising funds for the homeless to competing in every sport from dart throwing to soccer. Compadres is the preferred Mexican restaurant. For a pleasant dinner, especially when a recruiter is picking up the tab, MacArthur Park in downtown Palo Alto is hard to beat. A ritual of MBA life is the Tuesday evening get-together at Old Pro on El Camino Real in Palo Alto. Forsaking many of the yuppie bars of Silicon Valley, Stanford students take over the joint, even calling the place Arjay's after former B-school dean Arjay Miller, who lifted the school to number one in some rankings during his tenure.

You wouldn't ordinarily expect MBAs from the most selective B-school in the country to hang out at The Old Pro. Black-painted plywood covers the windows of the place to protect the glass when the crowd becomes unruly. Neon beer signs light the outside sidewalk, flashing the names Strohs, Michelob, and Miller into the busy street. Silver duct tape seals the gashes in the bar stools. But then, this is Stanford, and that's why its MBAs are so different from the run-of-the-mill products other schools produce. It's a pity this school is still struggling to figure out how to hire both outstanding scholars and teachers.

PLACEMENT DETAILS

Despite the recent ups and downs of the California economy, Stanford MBAs continue to fare extremely well in the job sweepstakes. Some 253 companies recruited second-year MBAs at Stanford in 1996, doing about 3887 interviews. Another 928 job opportunities were posted by correspondence from more than 500 firms. Pretty impressive numbers for a graduating class of 361 students. That's a major reason why Stanford MBAs averaged 3.3 job offers at graduation. The median starting-pay-and-bonus packages of $108,000, including perks, were bested only by Harvard grads, who got just a couple of thousand dollars more.

Not surprisingly, consulting firms, which typically dangle the big bucks in front of MBAs, are hiring the single biggest chunk of Stanford grads. The top employers of the Class of 1996: McKinsey & Co. (25); Mercer Management Consulting (10); Boston Consulting Group (13); Bain & Co. (11); Goldman Sachs (6); Netscape Communications (5); Donaldson, Lufkin & Jenrette (5); Procter & Gamble (4); Sun Microsystems (4); and J.P. Morgan (4).

In some ways, it's surprising that Stanford doesn't do better than seventh in BUSINESS WEEK's corporate poll. School officials theorize that the small size of the graduating class makes it a more competitive hunting ground for recruiters, who sometimes return to headquarters empty-handed because job offers outnumber Stanford MBAs. They may be particularly bothered because a good chunk of the class accepts jobs with Silicon Valley startups and smaller firms that employ fewer than 1000 workers. Many of these companies are not surveyed by the magazine because they do not hire significant numbers of MBAs and can't compare Stanford's candidates with those from other institutions.

Given Stanford's location, however, technology looms large, and a sizable number of MBAs gain jobs in the computer biz. Many of the visiting speakers also hail from the world of high tech, from NeXT CEO and Apple founder Steve Jobs to Sun Microsystems founder Scott McNearly, who graduated from Stanford. Andrew Grove, chairman of successful chipmaker Intel, now teaches as a lecturer in the fall quarter.

OUTSTANDING FACULTY

James C. Van Horne (****—finance and banking); *Irv Grousbeck* (****—entrepreneurship); *Constance Bagley* (****—business law); *David Kreps* (****—economics); *Srikant Dattar* (***—accounting); *Paul Pfleiderer* (**—finance); *Robert Burgelman* (**—strategic management); *Garth Saloner* (**—strategic management); *Jim Patell* (**—accounting); *Ed Lazear* (*—economics and human resources management).

APPLICANT TIPS

There is no other business school in the world that rejects a larger share of its applicants than Stanford. In 1996, the school turned down 93 percent of the candidates who applied for admission. Many of these applicants were rejected not because they weren't fully qualified to attend the school, but because it can enroll fewer than 370 students a year.

So how do you beat those odds? Stanford seeks applicants who boast strong academic aptitude and managerial potential. The school maintains that it has no minimum GMAT or grade point average requirements. Still, more than 75 percent of Stanford's admitted candidates have overall GMAT scores above 650. And more than most of the other Top 25 schools, Stanford seems to give an edge to higher GMAT candidates.

Because admissions wants proof of an applicant's ability to handle quantitative concepts, it will look closely at your undergraduate grades and GMAT scores in analytical areas. Also, make sure that whoever writes your letters of reference addresses both your managerial achievements to date and your potential as a leader. You should be aware that the school works to modify "a community of diverse backgrounds and interests." Applicants should tailor their essay questions to address Stanford's desire to modify student diversity.

Apply early if you can. The first of three decision periods for applicants ends in early November. The second admissions deadline is January 3, even though you have until the final March 12 deadline to apply. Stanford "strongly encourages" applicants to apply in the first or second round. The school does not offer its own applications on diskettes, but it accepts applications on disks modified by two private companies. Macintosh users can buy a disk application for Stanford from Apply Software Systems at 800-93-APPLY. A Windows or DOS version runs $40 from MBA MULTI-App at 800-516-2227. Applying by disk is optional, however, and does not give applicants an advantage.

Contact: Marie M. Mookini
Director of Admissions
415-723-2766
Final application deadline: March 15 for fall

STANFORD MBAs SOUND OFF

Stanford undoubtedly has the best research faculty of any business school. Unfortunately, teaching is neglected at Stanford, and it often comes in a poor second to research. The problems with the teaching in the core have persisted over many years, and the lack of effective steps to remedy the situation is an obvious indication of how low a priority teaching is.

The lack of a strong commitment to diversity in anything other than admissions can make Stanford a difficult place for an African-American student to spend two years. Specifically, the lack of African-American faculty, African-American case subjects, and the lack of cohesiveness among the minority students are issues that the GSB must address.

I have had an incredible experience at the GSB. It is an extremely cooperative, supportive environment which has helped me make the transition from a high school math teacher in Harlem to investment banking. I would recommend Stanford to everyone.

Stanford is a majestic and wonderful place, a virtual heaven on earth. The educational quality is high, but the true value of the experience was the wonderful and immensely talented classmates. Stanford has the lowest acceptance rate of any B-school, and it is evident from your first day here.

Coming to Stanford Business School and getting an MBA here is the best (greatest bang for the buck) thing I have done in my life. For anyone who wants to manage a hi-tech company, there is absolutely no better school than Stanford—access to Silicon Valley is perhaps Stanford's greatest asset. The biggest thing I got was my increase in self-confidence. At the GSB I have been able to talk to, discuss ideas, and in some cases openly disagree and argue with CEOs who are managing high growth major companies. The opportunity to compare my intellect to them and to realize that they are really not that much "smarter" than you is a great chance. I now know that I can do as well as any of the top CEOs I have met. I know that I and most of my classmates will be successful at what they do.

My primary interest in attending Stanford was to be exposed to high-tech and entrepreneurship. Aside from being an outstanding general management program, Stanford truly excels in teaching students about critical business issues in the high-tech industry and exposing and encouraging them to pursue entrepreneurship. Having Andy Grove, CEO of Intel, teach a high-tech strategy class is like learning about the auto industry from Henry Ford—it's truly awesome!

I'm still dismayed at some of the absolutely godawful, atrocious teachers I suffered through. "How bad were they?" you may ask. Well, let's just put it this way: if they were a car, they'd only have three wheels. Even worse, potential opportunities to improve teaching have been squandered by the school administration. For example, the best teacher by far whom I had was Rohit Deshpande, a marketing professor who was visiting from the Tuck School. Over 40 of his 120 students took the effort to beg the administration to hire Deshpande and improve the notoriously bad teaching in the marketing department. I've heard from reliable sources that the school administration began making moves to hire him (he had publicly stated that he would love to come to Stanford) when other faculty vetoed the nomination on the grounds that Deshpande's research was not strong enough. Well, that's an anecdote which illustrates where the GSB places its priorities in the old teaching vs. research dilemma.

The Stanford MBA experience has been worth every penny, including opportunity costs. I have been extremely impressed with the quality and diversity of my classmates, and have learned a tremendous amount just from interacting with them. The MBA has also allowed me to make a successful career transition from investment banking to entertainment. Being a Stanford MBA has opened a tremendous amount of doors for me to professionals in a wide variety of industries.

Stanford is the perfect environment for people of different skill levels to mix because grades and test scores aren't emphasized, making it easier for people to take risks and take courses that aren't in areas of expertise. The strongest academic areas are accounting, entrepreneurship, strategy, finance, and leadership/interpersonal dynamics.

8.
UNIVERSITY OF CHICAGO

UNIVERSITY OF CHICAGO

Graduate School of Business
1101 East 58 Street
Chicago, Illinois 60637
E-mail address: admissions@gsb.uchicago.edu
Website address: http://www.uchicago.edu

Corporate ranking: 5	Graduate ranking: 23
Enrollment: 2697	Annual tuition & fees: $24,655
Women: 23%	Room and board: $9520
Non-U.S.: 23%	Average GMAT score: 685
Minority: 5%	Average GPA: 3.4
Part-time: 1508	GPA range: 2.1 to 4.0
Average age: 27	Average years of work exp.: 4.2
Applicants accepted: 23%	Accepted applicants enrolled: 57%
Median starting pay: $86,000	Average starting pay: $90,096

Teaching methods: Lecture, 50%   Case study, 25%   Projects, 25%

Contact:
Don Martin
Director of Admissions
773-702-7369
Application deadlines:
December 2
January 15
March 14

It took a slap in the face to get one of the nation's most prestigious business schools to listen to its students again.

In 1996, the University of Chicago's Graduate School of Business (GSB) was not exactly one of the nation's happiest campuses. Dean Robert Hamada's administration allowed too many part-time students to transfer into the full-time program, crowding classrooms and shutting MBAs out of popular electives. Corporate recruiters and students alike were forced to deal with an incompetent career services office. Faculty were harder to track down for informal chats than at virtually any Top 25 school.

So the class of '96 got its revenge. It hammered the school on the bi-annual BUSINESS WEEK survey of grads, dropping Chicago's student satisfaction rank from 4th all the way down to the 23rd. The school's overall rank fell from 3 to 8. "A program has to have everything to be the best: strong academic training, high-caliber students, excellent faculty/student relationship, superb leadership from the administration," says one '96 grad. "U of C lacks the last two."

Comments like that caused the dean and his team to perk up their ears. Then they took action. On November 12, 1996, Hamada and Deputy Dean Robin Hogarth sent memos to students, faculty, and staff outlining plans for wide-reaching reform. "First, by way of a 'mission' statement, we are announcing that the GSB will strive to be at the top of all rankings," they wrote, "including those surveying our students, which means that we must deserve it." The memo said Hogarth would now concentrate strictly on the full-time program and that a new deputy dean's post would be created to oversee the school's well-respected part-time MBA. Staff members—like career services officers and other administrators—would be evaluated by students, and the results would be published, just as they are for professors. The career services office, meanwhile, would get additional funds and two new boards—one filled by recruiters, the other by students—would advise it. And in a move patterned directly after Wharton, Hamada said students would play a large role in the design of a new classroom building. "Stay tuned," the memo concluded, "more to come."

So the question facing prospective students at GSB is clear: which Chicago are they applying to? The poorly run bureaucracy where students get little help applying for jobs? Or the newly nimble elite school that also promises one of the best quantitative business educations in the world?

Probably a little bit of both. The fact is, in terms of academic power, the neo-Gothic campus in the south side neighborhood of Hyde Park is hard to match. The B-school faculty boasts two Nobel Prize winners, while the university as a whole has five. The school's Ph.D. programs are among the top in the country. And last year GSB wooed four of the hottest young junior professors in the country to boost an already envied finance department. One of the new profs had to be proclaimed an official genius to be allowed to stay in the United States, rather than returning to his native England. Another, Ming Huang, holds a doctorate in physics from Cornell, in addition to the one he earned in finance at Stanford. But catch Huang walking across the campus on a given day, and he's just as likely to talk to you about pro basketball as he is to launch into a discussion on the theory of pricing.

That's the type of image the school wants to project: a rigorous academic environment that also permits flexibility. In decades past, Chicago was seen as a largely theoretical B-school which sat on the opposite end of the management education spectrum from Harvard and its case studies. But since the late 1980s, GSB has made major strides to change that. It has rounded out a strong quantitative program with more focus on interpersonal skills. The change is the result of soul-searching started in 1988 when students began to challenge the density of the school's curriculum. An internal study came to the sobering conclusion that Chicago underemphasized day-to-day problem solving as well as the skills needed to manage people.

The school then took the unusual step of empowering its own students to create a mandatory, noncredit leadership program that greets first-years when they arrive. It's now known as LEAD (Leadership Exploration and Development), and it's as much a part of life at Chicago as those gargoyles that sit atop the buildings. Students are introduced to problem-solving techniques and then immediately sent off to use them during a 24-hour project called the Dean's Challenge.

Corporate sponsors, including Amoco, Andersen Consulting, Citibank, and Kraft, do more than foot the bill for the program. Managers from these firms are enlisted to participate, run sessions, and critique the numerous workshops and exercises in team building and leadership. The idea: to better balance the academic theory in Chicago's curriculum with "soft" management skills. Some rival deans pooh-pooh the changes because they are outside the school's mainstream curriculum, but Hamada and his predecessor, John P. Gould, wisely chose not to tamper with the basics of the program. If they had, the faculty would have slowed the process of change dramatically.

Precisely because LEAD is not integrated into the curriculum, it is reinvented every year. The latest version includes role-playing business simulations and is the result of brainstorming by 50 Chicago students who were given a budget and complete responsibility for designing and implementing the program. How does it work? The first-year class is divided into 12 cohorts of about 60 students. Each group is assigned four second-year students, who the guide the frosh, and a faculty member to offer advice.

There's a half-day seminar on business presentation and communication by Beach-Savard consultants, a one-day outdoor exercise that resembles Outward Bound, and a small-group project promoting the same teamwork skills, which lasts for an entire quarter. Then comes the Dean's Project, which, in a recent incarnation, required each of the 60-student teams to devise a plan for a new international business located in at least two countries. The ideas are vetted by alumni and profs, who play venture capitalists. When it's all done, the teams sit down and analyze their decisions and interaction.

It's no accident that the project was an international one. Chicago has a major, and growing, presence in this area. In June 1995, the school launched a two-year International MBA program, which combines traditional MBA courses with special courses on international business issues. Students take courses in culture, history, and politics and must master at least one foreign language. They'll also need to spend at least six months studying in a foreign country. In the summer of '96, students had internships for Goldman Sachs in Tokyo, Siemens in Munich, and the Argentinean government in Buenos Aires. Meanwhile, in the spring of '96, the first class of the International Executive MBA program graduated. While this puts another strain on professors' time, it also gives them a broader perspective to bring back to the full-time students in Hyde Park.

What surprises many people is the large degree of flexibility built into Chicago's program. This is one of the few B-schools that will allow you to substitute core courses with higher-level electives if you have mastered the material elsewhere. The only required classes are Managing in Organizations and LEAD. To get the MBA, though, you must complete 21 courses—no matter how many you waive. Most MBAs do it over six 11-week quarters spread out over two years, though it's possible to cram everything in a year-and-a-half. Either way, you can take evening courses with part-timers in the new $44

million Gleacher Center that opened in 1994. It's a great facility in the middle of Chicago that a number of TV networks used as a base for broadcasts during the 1996 Democratic Convention. No wonder: the views of the city's architecture are fantastic. Amazingly, though, the school didn't see fit to give any windows to the classrooms.

From the downtown center to the main campus in Hyde Park, you'll never doubt that you're in a city while at the University of Chicago. There a huge range of cultural options—from the Chicago Symphony Orchestra to Michael Jordan's Chicago Bulls—just a short subway ride away. At the same time, the campus also borders some rough neighborhoods that warrant caution. Chicago's B-school is a cluster of three classic buildings linked together on the 172-acre university campus. Students flip frisbees or toss softballs around on the outside Midway, which reaches to Lake Michigan from the campus. MBAs tend to hang out at Ida Noyes Hall, two blocks from the B-school. Many of them live at International House, the university dorm two blocks away, or in apartments or homes in Hyde Park. The really smart ones also spend some time at Medici's, a neighborhood restaurant where, for a few bucks each morning, you can get a tasty breakfast, read the papers, and drink as much orange juice as you want—as long as you squeeze it yourself.

During their time at GSB, students can choose a concentration, most in bread-and-butter fields like accounting, business economics, financial management, international business, human resources management, marketing, and statistics. The newest track is analytical finance, taught by 20 faculty members, many of whom are the academics who've made the school's finance department famous. Indeed, recruiters say no other school's MBAs can match the finance skills of GSB grads. Overall, in fact, Chicago's ranks fifth in the view of the nation's largest employers of MBAs. It trails only Wharton, Northwestern, Michigan, and Harvard.

PLACEMENT DETAILS

But H.R. executives don't come away from the windy city all smiles. Fully one out of five recruiters surveyed this year said Chicago's office of career services was among the nation's very worst. "They've replaced people at every level over the past year, and the problems are still there," said one. "They are absolutely the most frustrating place to deal with." Students agree: "We tried to figure out on our own what the hell to do. They just didn't care," says one '96 grad. Hamada has vowed—once again—to fix the problems, and the advisory boards are likely to be a good start. The job shouldn't be too hard, though, since the product they're selling is a such a solid one.

Corporate America clearly believes that Chicago's reputation for imparting strong analytical and quantitative skills is deserved: 44 percent of the class of '96 took jobs in finance. About one in three became consultants, while only 9 percent assumed marketing positions (far below the portion that the schools suburban neighbor to the north sends into the discipline). The biggest alumni hangouts over the years? Some 231 Chicago MBAs are on the payroll at Amoco, 220 at AT&T, 191 at First Chicago/NBD, 190 at Arthur Andersen, and 186 with the U.S. government. Other big employers: Motorola (178), the university itself (149), Citicorp (146), Goldman Sachs (140), and IBM (138).

That kind of high-level infiltration certainly helps with networking. Chicago grads walked out of school, on average, with 2.9 job offers in 1996—above the 2.8 average for the Top 50. The average student took home $86,000 in the first year out. Two hundred eighty-five companies (26 more than in 1995, but still about 10 fewer than in 1990) came to campus, conducting 12,000 interviews. Leading the pack of enthusiastic recruiters: Booz Allen & Hamilton (18), McKinsey & Co. (15), Ernst & Young (15), Deloitte & Touche (13), and Merrill Lynch (12).

Quite a group, in spite of all the troubles at Chicago over the last two years. It shows that GSB remains a top-notch school, even if it does have a good bit of housekeeping to do.

OUTSTANDING FACULTY

Steven N. Kaplan (****—entrepreneurial finance); *Mark Mitchell* (****—corporate finance); *James Schrager* (****—entrepreneurship); *Yacine Ait-Sahalia* (***—finance); *Sanjay Dhar* (***—marketing); *Robert Vishny* (**—finance); *Abbie Smith* (**—accounting); *Kent Daniel* (**—corporate finance); *Peter Klenow* (*—economics); *Marvin Zonis* (*—management).

APPLICANT TIPS

If you're a member of a minority group, make a beeline to this top-flight business school. The reason: Chicago's record on minority recruitment in recent years should make this highly selective school more eager to accept qualified minority applicants. In 1996, only 5 percent of its full-time students were minorities, down from 6.5 percent in 1992. The same may also be true for female candidates. Among the Top 25, Chicago is near the bottom, having just 23 percent of its students female. Contrast that with nearby Northwestern, which has enrolled 31 percent of its class with women. Overall, Chicago puts considerable weight on GMAT scores, although in recent years it has begun to interview virtually all of its applicants to assess their interpersonal abilities. You can improve your odds by applying early, and if you need or want a scholarship, the school recommends that you apply by the January 15 deadline. Chicago also lets students apply using a 3 1/2-inch high-density diskette for Macintosh, DOS, or Windows. Simply call the admissions office at 312-702-7369 or fax your request for application materials to 312-702-9085.

Contact: Don Martin
Director of Admissions
773-702-7369
Application deadlines: December 2, January 15, and March 14

CHICAGO MBAs SOUND OFF

Teaching quality was not consistently good. U of C has some excellent professors and some horrible ones. The administration is not responsive to student concerns. The facilities really need a face-lift. But without my U of C degree I could not have achieved my goal of a career in marketing.

Most professors really care about the success of their students. One professor I didn't know helped me out during a tough and technical 24-hour period of my summer internship. I called a stats professor out of the blue to help me understand an unusual occurrence in my data. He spent several hours working on the problem with me right on the spot.

I found it to be an outstanding training ground for general management. The school has made great strides in strengthening its marketing and behavioral sciences faculty. When its quant strength is added to the mix, the result is a school that may be uniquely qualified to train top-notch general managers who can solve rigorous analytical problems.

Despite the strong, diverse, flexible, and rigorous curriculum, I cannot unequivocally recommend Chicago to others. The reason? The administration. . . . Those in charge are unqualified, inexperienced, and in many cases unaware of reality inside and outside the school's community. As a result, the needs/wants of students are ignored.

Our career-services office is virtually useless. If you are desperate enough to take the time to meet with them, they have nothing useful to say, nor do they have the ability to remember any dealings you may have had with them in the past.

Based on conversations with peers at other schools during my interviewing process, I was surprised at how little they knew about finance. For me, terms like "duration and convexity" were second nature. Chicago helped prepare for my sales and trading job more than expected.

The Chicago MBA program is one of the best in the world. But U of C does not appear to make a sincere effort to recruit minority MBA students. The class of 1996 had only 26 full-time and 1997 only about 12. The outlook does not look good for 1998.

The recruiting process is excellent for consulting and I-banking, but fairly limited on the corporate side. Chicago's only weakness is location. Hyde Park is actually quite nice, but incredibly boring.

Chicago provides its students with the finest possible business education, which, contrary to popular opinion, is a well-balanced blend of theory and practice. The school, however, fails to attract students with leadership potential. Students are typically narrow-minded individuals in pursuit of consulting and investment-banking jobs and have absolutely no extracurricular interests, social skills, or leadership potential.

Chicago is no longer simply a quant school. There are still rigorous finance and econ classes, but faculty and course offerings are extremely well-rounded in marketing, organizational behavior, and strategy.

9.
MASSACHUSETTS INSTITUTE OF TECHNOLOGY

MASSACHUSETTS INSTITUTE OF TECHNOLOGY
Sloan School of Management
50 Memorial Drive
Cambridge, Massachusetts 02142-1347
E-mail address: masters@sloan.mit.edu
Website address: http://web.mit.edu/sloan/www

Corporate ranking: 8	Graduate ranking: 13
Enrollment: 717	Annual tuition & fees: $22,700
Women: 28%	Room and board: $14,000
Non-U.S.: 37%	Average GMAT score: 650
Minority: 15%	Average GPA: 3.5
Part-time: none	GPA range: 3.0 to 4.0
Average age: 27.4	Average years of work exp.: 4.4
Applicants accepted: 14%	Accepted applicants enrolled: 12%
Median starting pay: $102,750	Average starting pay: $100,870

Teaching methods: Lecture, 50%   Case study, 50%

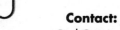

Contact:
Rod Garcia
Director of Admissions
617-253-3730
*Final application
deadline:*
February 3 for fall

Think of MIT's Sloan School of Management and a series of images quickly come to mind. Lester Thurow. Quant jocks. Technology. A rigid curriculum heavily flavored by finance and economics classes. A master's thesis. A small, intimate class.

Forget it. Thurow, a popular economist and prolific writer, is no longer Sloan's dean. Liberal arts majors can move with ease through the new, highly flexible curriculum. You can now get your master's here without having taken a single course in technology. For the first time in the school's history, Sloan allowed students in 1994 to skip a once-required thesis for its MS in management and instead gain an MBA. Eighty-four percent of students took the school up on that offer in 1996. And the school admitted its largest class ever—422 strong—in the fall of 1996, twice the size of its entering classes in the late 1980s.

The changes have come under Glen Urban, who has been at Sloan since 1966 and quietly served behind Thurow as deputy dean from 1987 to 1991. Like the globe-trotting Thurow, Urban is something of a Renaissance man. He has sailed his yacht along the East Coast from Nova Scotia to the Caribbean, helicopter-skied in the Bugaboos, explored out-of-the-way places like Easter Island, and sculpted steel, marble, and stone structures. And, like Thurow, he articulates a compelling vision for the school: to provide "innovation-driven companies with people who are analytic and technical, who are team builders and know how to lead."

Thurow, of course, brought much attention to Sloan. He hired faculty experts in other cultures and countries, lured a greater percentage of non-U.S. students to the school, and focused the school's efforts around the themes of technology and global business. His single greatest accomplishment was MIT's highly regarded Leaders in Manufacturing program, an intense, 24-month experience allowing students to earn master's degrees in both manufacturing and engineering. The centerpiece of the program is a six-month management internship at one of 13 sponsoring U.S. manufacturers, including Alcoa, Boeing, Chrysler, Eastman Kodak, and Motorola. The program's immodest mission: to help the United States recapture world leadership in manufacturing, long a neglected area of study at most business schools. In 1996, only 55 of the 408 who applied for the Leaders program were accepted. Now, other B-schools, like Northwestern University and the University of Michigan, have started similar programs.

Urban, who took over the deanship in mid-1993, was an immediate beneficiary of Thurow's hard work. Just nine months after he succeeded Thurow, Urban saw *U.S. News & World Report* rank the school No. 2, behind only Stanford. It rose to No. 1 in '95 and slipped, barely, back to No. 2 in 1996—but by a mere and insubstantial one-tenth of a point. They were the highest spots the school has ever grabbed in a national survey (largely because its students boast high GMAT scores and because of the school's stellar placement stats). "I inherited a school in good shape," says Urban.

Indeed, he did. To improve it, Urban rolled out a new, innovative curriculum that emphasizes integration and leaves more room for electives. One result: the school made major gains in connecting coursework across the classes between 1994 and 1996, according to surveys of Sloan grads. Fully implemented in 1995, the curriculum forces students to complete all core requirements in the first semester. They then spend the final three drawing from a pool of nearly 100 electives. "Sloan was very tightly controlled and thus allowed hardly any flexibility in the first semester, which enabled us students to

establish common, strong, basic backgrounds," says one '96 MBA. "The curriculum was very flexible in the last three semesters, providing great balance."

The one-term core consists of a half-dozen "interlocked subjects." Translation: faculty meet regularly to plan the integration of subjects and the overall balance of the program. You'll take a trio of "perspectives" courses during the term. Economic Analysis for Business Decisions teaches key microeconomic principles for business and industry analysis; Data, Models, and Decisions keeps to MIT's quantitative reputation and teaches students how to use data to make smart decisions. Organizational Processes focuses on the firm of the future. The three remaining subjects in the core are basic B-school fare: financial and managerial accounting; communications; and strategy. Students move through the fall semester in cohorts, which include faculty mentors who keep in regular contact with the group. Class projects are assigned to teams during a two-week orientation, and they work together on them through the term.

In the spring, students can design their own programs or enroll in one of six career-focused tracks. Two of those—information technology and manufacturing—have been introduced in the last two years. The other four—financial engineering, financial management, entrepreneurship and new product development, and strategic management and consulting—are more established. In any of the six, you must choose four half-semester subjects from a set of six. Then you're free to sample any of Sloan's 110 electives. You also can take up to three courses in other MIT departments—or at Harvard, which is just a few stops away on Boston's version of a subway, the T. Sloan will even give you full credit for language and political science classes.

In the management track, you're required to take a minimum of 90 units of class credit over the three noncore semesters. An average full-semester subject earns 9 units of credit, and a typical term brings between 54 and 60 units to a student. So even the management track leaves time for other electives as early as your first year. Tracksters also take a professional seminar where groups of faculty, students, and outside managers meet together over two semesters to share experience and ideas. Each ProSeminar includes summer internships that reinforce the classroom learning.

These are fairly innovative changes at an already superb business school. So why does Sloan still trail rivals like Wharton and neighboring Harvard in the BUSINESS WEEK survey? For years, Sloan graduates griped about the quality of teaching, a critical component of BW's rankings. Teaching at MIT now receives marks that are well above average among the 51 schools surveyed by BUSINESS WEEK—but they still trail the top echelon by a good margin. Among the relative weaknesses: faculty could do a better job of being available for informal discussions outside of class, and most Top 10 schools receive higher scores for integrating work across courses.

MIT's technical image can still intimidate liberal arts majors, so prospective students should visit the campus, attend a few classes, and seek out MBAs to hear about their experiences. "There seems to be a notion that the curriculum at Sloan emphasizes the quantitative aspect of business," says one '96 alum. "However, some of the most popular courses are those dealing with organizational behavior and ethics." Sloan holds recruiting sessions, bringing together potential applicants and alumni, throughout the United States and in several foreign countries. The school also holds an open house after the admissions season, designed to woo students who have been accepted by other top schools. More than half of eventual students attend an open house. The only academic requirement for attending Sloan, other than a bachelor's degree, is one semester of work in both calculus and economic theory. If you haven't taken those classes, you might want to find the time to do so in the year before you

start. That way you won't be behind from the get-go.

The two-week orientation program is run entirely by students. In one version, organized by second-years to greet the class of 1993, the newcomers were divided into Zoo Groups: blue cheetahs and green zebras, who were managed by second-year Zookeepers. They played Outward Bound–type games, conducted a treasure hunt, feasted on barbeque, and stumbled along a pub crawl to some of Boston's notorious watering holes. When sober, they also attended a Citicorp ethics exercise, case discussions with professors, a workshop on diversity, and a dessert and dancing evening that continued into the wee hours at the Copley Plaza Hotel.

Then real Sloan life begins. The work here can be excessive, and incoming students are told the most important thing they'll learn is the art of selective neglect: figure which assignments are critical and which can be safely shunted aside. MIT's quantative emphasis has traditionally contrasted with the all-case-study method at Harvard, though lately the programs have been moving closer together. MIT's distaste for competition among classmates is demonstrated by its policy of not posting grades.

Sitting next to you in class will be a huge number of engineers and international students. Some 40 percent of Sloanies hold engineering degrees, and no major business school can claim a more diverse student body in terms of home country. Roughly one in four students here is foreign-born, the greatest number coming from the Far East, where an MIT degree is a major status symbol. The school receives about 100 applications from Japanese nationals each year and narrows those down to 40 or so semifinalists. An associate dean then travels to Japan to interview them, looking particularly for outgoing students with leadership potential. To ease the entry of non-U.S. students, Sloan offers a two-week workshop prior to orientation. And to remind everybody of how global the school has become, more than 50 full-size country flags hang in the school's main lobby. "You can't ignore that when you're walking to class," says David A. Weber, former director of the MBA program.

Regardless of where they're from, virtually all students end up with an international learning experience. In the fall of 1996, Sloan began collaborating with two Chinese B-schools: one at Fudan University in Shanghai, and the other at Tsinghua University in Beijing. The school wants to deepen its ties to the world's largest country and help students learn about doing business in the grandest of emerging markets. It also runs—or is planning—collaborations in Chile, India, Mexico, Singapore, Taiwan, and Thailand. In addition, students run their own study tours in which they typically organize pre-trip seminars and enlist two professors to join them on the tour.

There are also numerous signs of MIT's math-and-science culture. A graduate of the program still has the chance to earn the MS instead of the MBA. Buildings here have numbers rather than names. And there's a general idea pervading the curriculum that students should emerge from the school with a solid level of quant know-how. But entrepreneurship has become as much of a buzz word at Sloan as engineering. In 1996, more than 50 interdisciplinary students entered the MIT Business Plan Contest, hoping to win the $50,000 prize. Since 1989, when the competition started, at least 14 companies have emerged from it. Meanwhile, also in '96, the school launched the MIT Entrepreneurship Center, which draws together people from Sloan and other branches of the university to study start-ups. One part of the program: students head into the real world and work in new enterprises, many of which are trying to earn a profit with MIT technology.

The Sloan School of Management is housed in six buildings on MIT's East Campus along the Charles River. Many university buildings have been renovated recently, including Sloan's. Best of all, the Tang Center for Management opened in

September, 1995. The 48,000-square-foot building sits at the corner of Amherst and Wadsworth Streets and houses an auditorium, the career development office, classrooms, and team project meeting rooms. In December 1995, the school also opened a new $3.5 million trading room.

MIT's student body is growing at a similarly fast clip. Long one of the smallest top B-schools, Sloan has more than doubled the size of its entering class to 422 since 1988, with most of the increases coming in the last four years. Back then, Sloan's enrollment was just one quarter of its crosstown rival Harvard. Now, it's about half. It's still smaller than virtually all of its rivals, but the change will certainly affect the character of the school. The worst news is that the faculty will not increase at nearly that clip. That leaves some people worried about the quality of MBA education at the school. "The school has the right size student body," says one member of the class of '96 about his two years at the school, "but it is getting too big." One thing that shouldn't suffer is the quality of the students. Applications shot up 40 percent in 1995 and another 28 percent in 1996. The acceptance rate stands at a paltry 14 percent.

Students typically travel to Sloan via the T's Red Line. The Kendall Square stop has been refurbished as part of a $250 million redevelopment project that includes a new Marriot Hotel and Legal Seafood, the city's signature restaurant. Most of MIT's social whirl is coordinated by the students in the Graduate Management Society, which sponsors cruises on the Charles, ski trips, and a weekly "Consumption Function." Several times a year, international students offer a sampling of the food, drink, and music from their home regions. Such events often include a karaoke night, where students croon golden oldies—usually after several rounds of beer. (In other words, the music may be too painful to listen to if you're fully alert.) Over 25 student clubs and athletic teams offer a range of activities from letting off steam in intramural courses to taking field trips to a Nissan or Saturn plant, the latter being sponsored by the Sloan Auto Industries Club.

Sloanies unwind at the Muddy Charles, a bar that sits a couple of minutes away from campus. Since there aren't many residential areas near MIT, students often go over the bridge to Boston's chic Beacon Hill neighborhoods for drinks and dinner. For housing, students end up scattered all over Cambridge and Boston. From a social perspective, this is not the most closely knit B-school, despite its size. But few can offer the range of easily accessible entertainment and cultural options that MIT does. Cambridge and Boston are filled with fascinating restaurants, bookstores, and open spaces. You'll rarely be disappointed if looking for a concert, art exhibit, or ball game to fill your day.

PLACEMENT DETAILS

Upon leaving Sloan, grads end up at companies across the country—and they're almost always well paid. In 1996, the average grad took home $105,000 (third in the Top 25, after Harvard and Stanford). Some 203 companies recruited Sloan grads in 1996, conducting 2400 on-campus interviews. Some 408 job opportunities were posted via correspondence. The top employers: McKinsey & Co., which hired 24 Sloanies; Booz Allen & Hamilton (9); Boston Consulting Group (8); Intel Corporation (8); A.T. Kearney (7); Bain & Co. (7); American Management Systems (6); Lehman Brothers (6); Merrill Lynch (6); and Deutsch Morgan Grenfell (5).

Dean Urban no longer labors under the shadow of his more famous predecessor. He is clearly putting his own stamp on this prestige school of management.

OUTSTANDING FACULTY

Jeremy C. Stein (****—management); *Robert Pindyck* (****—economics); *Kevin Rock* (****—finance); *Arnold Barnett* (****—statistics); *Paul Healy* (****—finance); *Pete Wilson* (***—finance); *Stewart Myers* (**—finance); *Robert Freund* (**—decision sciences); *Rudy Dornbush* (**—economics); *Rebecca Henderson* (**—management).

APPLICANT TIPS

MIT has one of the earliest application deadlines of any of the top business schools. So if you're interested in attending, apply soon. Given the rigorous nature of this program, GMAT scores and undergraduate grade-point averages in subjects such as math and science are critical. Sloan says it pays "particular attention to the contributions each applicant can make to enhancing the Sloan environment." Translation: In your answers to the five essay questions in the application, you should focus on past achievements that would demonstrate what leadership abilities you could bring to the school.

Sloan likes prestige backgrounds: Among the latest entering class in 1996, 16 had their undergraduate degrees stamped at MIT; 12 at Cornell; 9 each from Brown, Michigan, and Penn; and 8 from Harvard. The largest group had been employed by McKinsey (9).

While the school does not require interviews, MIT strongly encourages them. In 1996, 4 out of every 10 applicants did an admissions interview. "Given our emphasis on both intellectual and interpersonal skills, an interview is a chance for you to demonstrate those important skills that are not easily discerned from your written applications," says the school. Sloan boasts a "master's lunch program" that provides applicants with the chance to have lunch with a current student to learn more about the school. The admissions office also sponsors information sessions most Monday mornings from 9 to 10.

There's also an ambassadors program that arranges information sessions with current students and a chance to attend classes and get a feel for the place. To take advantage of such opportunities, call the master's admissions office at 617-253-3730 or fax 617-253-6405. You can request brochures and applications during the day by calling 617-253-0449.

Contact: Rod Garcia
Director of Admissions
617-253-3730
Final application deadline: February 3 for fall.

SLOAN MBAs SOUND OFF

Sloan's strengths were: the quality and limited size of its student body; its professors and faculty; the team environment; its quantitative and analytical emphasis; its theoretical and case-study balance. Its weaknesses: The career development office focuses on consulting or investment banking, but is very weak in general; the limited number of electives. The strengths definitely outweighed the weaknesses.

The net important plus is the diversity and intelligence of the class. This is not an easy

MBA: Though grades are not particularly important, the workload keeps you busy day after day, week after week. Group work is particularly emphasized. Given the class diversity, it can sometimes be a difficult exercise, but is still quite useful in terms of interpersonal and intercultural skills. The minus of the program: It should improve the quality of teaching in some areas such as marketing.

Economics is often an afterthought for an MBA program, but Sloan's close cooperation with MIT's outstanding economics department gives students the rare opportunity to learn from faculty on the leading edge of the science of markets.

The variety of cultures and nationalities represented really enriched the experience and rounded out the program. Preparing for globalization and the increasing complexity and speed of change through technology were two key elements in Sloan's program. . . . Sloan has made great strides in the last few years to move from a technology-heavy program to a more balanced one.

10. DARTMOUTH COLLEGE

DARTMOUTH COLLEGE

Amos Tuck School of Business Administration
Hanover, New Hampshire 03755-0900
E-mail address: tuck.admissions@dartmouth.edu
Website address:
http://www.dartmouth.edu/pages/tuck/tuckhome.html

Corporate ranking: 12	Graduate ranking: 7
Enrollment: 377	Annual tuition & fees: $23,700
Women: 29.7%	Room and board: $9000
Non-U.S.: 15.9%	Average GMAT score: 669
Minority: 8.7%	Average GPA: 3.39
Part-time: none	GPA range: 2.4 to 4.0
Average age: 26.8	Average years of work exp.: 4.5
Applicants accepted: 13.8%	Accepted applicants enrolled: 49%
Median starting pay: $105,000	Average starting pay: $103,680

Teaching methods: Lecture, 50%   Case study, 40%   Projects, 10%

Contact:
Sally Jaeger
Director of Admissions
603-646-3162
*Final application
deadline:* April 1

Imagine a small, though quaint, New England town. Main street is a collection of brick-facade shops, cozy restaurants, and colonial homes. There's no crime and no congestion. Wherever you go, you're immediately recognized with a welcome smile. People are universally smart, open, and friendly. And everyone is known by his or her first name. If this picture is your version of Nirvana, you can't do any better than Dartmouth's Amos Tuck School.

Yet, the school's greatest advantage has long had the potential to be its most troublesome disadvantage. The school's remote locale in a small New Hampshire town and its small size nurture an ésprit de corps you'll rarely find at major business schools, but it also creates a rather insular place remote from the fast-paced world of business. These days, however, Dean Paul Danos is using satellite-video classrooms to more effectively bring the outside business world onto the isolated campus. He's using technology to import instructors, export classes, and link up with corporate and academic partners.

At the same time, he's working to preserve an unusual culture that combines a caring faculty, bright students, and devoted alumni to make Tuck one of the very best places in the world to get an advanced management education. On the opening day of classes, professors hand over their personal phone numbers and invite students to call if necessary. Second-years host dozens of welcome parties for new students. They even get up early on Saturday mornings to serve their new brethren breakfast in the mess hall before exams. One professor tells of how his students sent his wife flowers and a restaurant gift certificate because he had to work weekends to accommodate an overload of students in a popular class.

Over the years, Tuck has scored consistently high in having one of the most cooperative campuses of any top business school. One reason is that Tuck is small and compact—each class of about 170 students is less than half the size of one at UCLA and a mere fifth of one at Harvard. The full-time faculty numbers only 40, fewer than the tenure-track profs in Wharton's finance department alone. Virtually everyone knows one another by name.

Another reason is that it's *really* isolated. Only prop planes can fly into the tiny airport in West Lebanon, six miles south of Hanover. When the weather turns bad, you face a white-knuckle flight onto the short landing strip that's carved into a mountainside. Boston is a two-hour drive away. Sleepy Hanover rolls up the sidewalks fairly early. The only time people are out late is when they're coming out of the Nugget Theatre on the main street or attending something at the Hop, the college's impressive performing arts center.

The B-school sits on the edge of the Dartmouth campus, bordering the Connecticut River. The cluster of five brick Georgian buildings and two contemporary structures that make up the school is like a private 13-acre encampment at the end of a private road appropriately named Tuck Drive. Byrne Hall, the first new building in 20 years—with more classroom space, breakout rooms, and dining areas—opened in 1993. Underground tunnels and glass-enclosed halls—dubbed Habitrails—connect all the buildings so students needn't venture outside to attend class during the bitterly cold winter months. You could trek from your Woodbury House dorm room to a class at columned Tuck Hall in your slippers. The snow-covered campus makes for a pastoral setting. Students can hear the bronze bells of Baker Tower sound off each hour with such ditties as "Heigh Ho, Heigh Ho" and "Yellow Submarine."

Tradition abounds. Founded in 1900, Tuck is the world's first graduate school of management. Mr. Chips would feel particularly welcome in Stell Hall, the newly renovated student commons, with its cathedral ceiling and carved heavy oak interior. Over the fireplace hangs a fading, formal portrait of old man Tuck, a lawyer and Congressman for whom the school was named.

Tuckies tend to be outdoorsy, exceptionally self-assured, and somewhat preppy. The Dartmouth Skiway, a small ski resort some 20 minutes away in Lyme, is the downhill run of choice. There's ice skating on nearby Occom Pond. There's also hiking on Mount Moosilauke on the edge of the White Mountains National Forest, rowing and canoeing on the Connecticut River, or a slew of intramural sports from ice hockey and rugby to basketball and squash. The college also runs a golf course, boathouse, and riding stable available to Tuck students. In winter, both an MBA Hockey Tournament and a three-day Alpine ski racing event draw rival B-school teams from leading schools in the United States and Canada.

That incredibly wide range of outdoor activity isn't equaled in the MBA course offerings. Tuck offers a general management program, with the emphasis on how different functional areas come together. People who are looking for hard-core functional or theoretical experiences probably want to avoid the school, which discourages over specialization. That also means there are far fewer electives from which to choose. Tuck is the only prestige B-school without a Ph.D. program in business, a fact that leads some academics to pooh-pooh the intellectual rigor of the place. Truth is, it discourages narrow thinking and cultivates a commitment to teaching that is nearly unrivaled.

While many B-schools have been unraveling their programs of late, Tuck is not undertaking any significant changes. The first week features sessions on business ethics, small-group dynamics, an outdoor exercise in teamwork, honor code issues, and discussions on career assessment. Then, the welcome party ends quickly with the first of a trio of 10-week quarters a year in the fall, winter, and spring. During the first year, Tuckies take a set of 13 required courses that cover the business basics. The core classes meet in three sections of about 60 students each, with new student class sections rearranged each term. Classes meet twice a week for an hour and a half each session. Every term has an "integrative learning exercise" in the first year, including a three-day business simulation exercise and an integrated business theme module.

Unlike other schools, Tuck discourages students from waiving out of the core courses that make up the heart of the program. The reason? Like Harvard and Stanford, the school believes that nonaccounting types can benefit from having CPAs in the same classroom. Additionally, more of the work in these courses is applied, rather than theoretical. It's also not easy to take nonbusiness classes at Dartmouth College because it's on a different class schedule than Tuck, which offers more than 50 electives a year.

These days, teamwork has become an overused buzzword on B-school campuses. With the exception of Northwestern, however, few really immerse their students in it like Tuck. A huge amount of the classwork here is done in groups. In the first quarter alone, MBAs do four major team projects in Managerial Economics, Management Communication, Marketing, and Decision Analysis. Virtually all first-year students live together in Woodbury House and Buchanan Hall, so non-U.S. students, who now make up 20 percent of the enrollment, can't gather in subcultures here as they might in other places.

Besides, Tuck makes it almost impossible for that to occur. The capstone event for first-year MBAs is the major consulting project that begins in late November. Teams of students are assigned real clients with real problems, mostly small businesses, town governments, and school districts. They have to meet with the client, study his or her problem or opportunity, and produce a report of recommendations as part of the Managerial Economics course. They then present the final results of their work in an oral presentation to clients, outside consultants, and Tuck faculty as part of the Management Communication course. In the past, Tuckies have tackled marketing and distribution for Catamount Brewery, a local microbrewery; completed a feasibility study to help Plymouth, Massachusetts, lure new business to town; and worked on a report for Vermont Yankee's nuclear facility.

In the first year, a major event is the Tycoon Game. Part folly, part learning experience, the contest is played out by students each spring. Tycoon, a management simulation exercise, is the capstone that allows teams of students to run their own companies and learn from their successes and failures in a risk-free environment. There are six teams to each "industry," and they compete against each other for industry dominance. Students select their own strategies, then choose tactics to battle the competition over 10–14 "quarters."

Even though you play with funny money, this is hardly Monopoly. No one wants to go "belly-up," so everyone works hard to make their company the top performer in the game. Students devise strategies, trying to make savvy investment, production, and marketing decisions that will make their companies the most profitable. A typical decision: whether to sell your clocks abroad. If few companies invest in the foreign market, you could make a killing overseas. But if everyone else jumps into the export business, the competition could cost you your shirt. Advertisements that hail the virtues of the different clock companies in the game—the industry of choice—inundate the campus.

For those longing for an international adventure, in 1988 Tuck launched a management program with the International University of Japan. As a Tuck MBA, you could spend a second-year term enrolled in the school as an exchange student. Or you could get into another formal exchange program with the London Business School or Escuela Superior de Administracion in Barcelona, Spain. There's also the possibility of doing a quarter at INSEAD in Fontainebleau, France, arguably the best non-U.S. business school in the world.

Even if, like most students, you stay at Tuck, you'll get a good amount of international exposure. The school claims that more than a third of all course content is international. It has a stash fund for faculty who want to travel abroad to do research on international business issues. Tuck has put more global executives on its advisory board, and is adding more international offerings as electives. The faculty, meantime, is attempting to use more of its own case studies, weeding out as many Harvard cases as possible.

One thing Tuck doesn't have to worry about is the instruction. The quality of teaching here is exceptional—far better than Northwestern, Stanford, or Chicago. The teaching in both the core and the electives offerings is among the best any business school in the world can offer. The plain reason: For years, the school has awarded professors with pay increases, promotions, and tenure on the basis of their ability to teach in the classroom. Teaching is not compromised for research endeavors. Few major business schools have paid as much attention to teaching quality as Tuck.

No wonder the faculty wins plaudits from students for its accessibility, enthusiasm, and overall quality. The low student-to-faculty ratio encourages frequent interaction with profs. Learning often continues outside the classroom during informal chats at "Tuck Tails"—regular mixers with faculty and students. When courses are oversubscribed at other schools, students are typically told: "Tough luck. Try next time." At Tuck, teachers with popular courses are often expected to add to their workload by offering

extra sessions if the students want them. One recent graduate noted that one professor agreed to teach an extra section of a popular course even though he had to schedule it to start before 8 a.m. "Student interests usually take precedence over the faculty," says one Tuck professor. "The first-year program is set up so that students can take all their classes in the morning and go skiing in the afternoon. If you have a 7:40 a.m. class, you might have to get up at 4 a.m. to prepare for it and get to school. The bottom line is that the students prefer that schedule, so it won't be disturbed."

That rare level of commitment from the faculty extends beyond graduation. Graduates routinely mention that they often call on professors to discuss business problems months and even years after they leave the campus. Second-year students often host dinners in their apartments for professors. When grads return to campus, they frequently stay at the homes of faculty members.

The school also boasts an unusual Visiting Executive program that welcomes more than 30 business leaders each year. They have a two-room office suite in Chase House, attend classes, eat lunch and dinner with students, and participate in discussion groups at night. Recent visitors have included: Procter & Gamble President John Pepper, Champion International Corp. Chairman Andrew C. Sigler, and Disney's Michael Eisner. Some of them will even wander down to swill a beer and catch some grub with students at Cafe Buon Gustaio and Murphy's Tavern—the popular MBA hangouts on the main drag in town.

So what's the downside? The number of elective offerings you can choose from is limited by the school's size. Travel for job interviews is tough. And the diversity and number of companies which recruit at Tuck is limited by its small pool of applicants. Indeed, that's a major reason why Tuck doesn't fare as well as other top schools in BUSINESS WEEK's survey of corporate recruiters.

PLACEMENT DETAILS

In 1996, 131 companies recruited on campus and 610 job opportunities were posted via correspondence. Tuck MBAs averaged 2.7 job offers at commencement, well below the 4.2 high at Harvard. Nonetheless, those offers were among the most lucrative you will find. The Class of 1996 pulled down median starting pay packages of $105,000. Only graduates of Harvard and Stanford did better and not by much: $110,640 and $108,000, respectively.

Not surprisingly, given the huge sums, the largest share of the class was recruited by consulting firms and investment banks. Hiring the most Tuck MBAs were: Bain & Co. (12); Andersen Consulting (10); McKinsey & Co. (6); Coopers & Lybrand (6); AT&T (4); General Mills (4); Intel (4); Booz Allen & Hamilton (3); J.P. Morgan (3); and Merrill Lynch (3). That's an impressive lineup of big-league recruiters who aren't shy about paying big money for talent.

One reason for this success is Tuck's alumni network. Even though the school has fewer than 6900 living alumni, they are amazingly supportive. About 64 percent of Tuck's alums give money to the school every year—the highest participation rate of any graduate B-school. The school publishes an alumni magazine twice a year and asserts that the "Class Notes" section of it boasts more pages of notes per graduate than any other MBA program in the United States.

Tuck alums, when surveyed by BUSINESS WEEK five years after graduation, give the school the highest grades of any for the strength of its alumni network, rating the value of its connections even higher than Harvard and Stanford. But then, that's the kind of loyalty that only a small town atmosphere can bring about.

OUTSTANDING FACULTY

John K. Shank (****—accounting); *Vijay Govindrajan* (***—strategy); *Stephen Powell* (***— information technology); *Clyde P. Stickney* (***—finance); *Phil Anderson* (***—technology); *Rohit Deshpande* (**—marketing); *James Seward* (*—finance); *Kusum Ailawadi* (*—marketing); *Rich Rogalski* (*—finance); *Fred Webster* (*—marketing).

APPLICANT TIPS

The Tuck School seeks applicants with five key attributes: You need to demonstrate that you are creative, cooperative, humane, have leadership ability, and view your career as your central focus. In both your interview and application materials, you should tailor your comments to these characteristics. Indeed, the school publishes a full definition of each of these attributes. Example: "Creative managers not only seek out and promote those quantum leaps that distinguish outstanding organizations from merely good ones, they also demonstrate the courage to stand up for their values and ideas." That's an invitation to describe a situation in which you took an unpopular position and won others over to it.

On-campus interviews are encouraged, but not required. Interviews tend to be focused around your ability to "fit" into the rather unique Tuck culture. Hurry, because you must schedule an on-campus interview a month in advance. The school also offers off-campus interviews in selected cities during the fall and winter as well as alumni interviews around the world. To schedule an interview or get additional information on off-campus sessions, you may contact the admissions office at 603-646-3162.

Tuck uses a rolling decision process with four separate application deadlines. Applications received by December 13 are answered by January 18. Applications that arrive by January 24 are answered by February 21. If you apply by February 21, you'll get a reply no later than March 27. If you wait until the final deadline of

April 1, it may take until May 22 to get an answer from the school.

Contact: Sally Jaeger
Director of Admissions
603-646-3162
Final application deadline: April 1

TUCK MBAs SOUND OFF

It's a bit freaky to walk down the hall and have your marketing professor of only one week and 60 students say hello to you by name. What other B-school allows me to ski, canoe, hike the Appalachian Trail, and study in your backyard, interrupted by humming-birds, blue jays, and deer?

I found the dedication and commitment of the faculty truly remarkable. They were always available, with no prior appointment required, to help in clarifying issues or to advise on classwork or any other matter. Individually, the quant professors were some of the best teachers I have ever had. Tuck students were probably the smartest group of people I have ever met, a source of constant learning and support. The alumni were always there to help, and their loyalty never ceased to amaze me.

Teamwork is the great buzzword at B-schools, but at Tuck it's a way of life. Even in second-year electives, team-based papers and projects often account for greater than two-thirds of one's grade. I felt as if anyone would have helped everyone to learn.

There are very few big egos here. People buy into the teamwork concept. The faculty is unbelievably accessible. Many of them give their home phone numbers on the syllabus.

It is very obvious that the MBA is geared toward the younger, single professional. However, Tuck provided a warm, nurturing environment not only for myself but for my family. At what other school could a student with a flight-attendant spouse and 1-year-old child find the support to not only meet school requirements but also maintain some semblance of family life. Tuck's team-oriented culture easily allowed me the flexibility to succeed.

Many people have asked me how I can spend two years in the snows of New Hampshire. It's an ideal location and setting to spend two years away from the professional world, to fully immerse yourself in your studies, and to have the chance to enjoy the great outdoors.

**11.
DUKE
UNIVERSITY**

DUKE UNIVERSITY

The Fuqua School of Business
Durham, North Carolina 27708
E-mail address: fuqua:admissions@mail.duke.edu
Website address: http://www.fuqua.duke.edu

Corporate ranking: 10	Graduate ranking: 10
Enrollment: 700	Annual tuition & fees: $23,690
Women: 30%	Room and board: $6220
Non-U.S.: 19%	Average GMAT score: 646
Minority: 12%	Average GPA: 3.33
Part-time: none	GPA range: 2.1 to 4.0
Average age: 27	Average years of work exp.: 4
Applicants accepted: 17%	Accepted applicants enrolled: 50%
Median starting pay: $78,000	Average starting pay: $84,020

Teaching methods: Lecture, 33%   Case study, 33%
Projects & simulations, 34%

Contact:
Robert R. Williams
Director of Admissions
919-660-7801
Application deadlines:
December 6
January 10
February 21
March 28

If you stopped by Durham Bulls Athletic Park in the spring of 1996 to take in a baseball game, you would have noticed a baby-faced outfielder named Andruw Jones. For three months that season, the 19-year-old delighted the blue-collar workers, professors, and Fuqua School MBAs who make up the crowd. Then he was gone—off on a remarkably rapid ascent through the hierarchy of baseball. Just four months after leaving Durham, he stepped to the plate in an Atlanta Brave uniform in Yankee Stadium and promptly became the youngest player in World Series history to hit a home run. If Jones lives up to his promise, Durham will soon be able to take a little bit of the credit for training one of baseball's best-known names.

It's a model the Fuqua School is trying to emulate—for the boardroom, of course. In 1992, the school overhauled its curriculum in an effort, said then-Dean Thomas F. Keller, "to graduate the CEOs of the twenty-first century." In terms of their dramatic scope, the changes stack up with those at Wharton and the University of Michigan. Every course in the school's catalog, from the building-block core classes to the electives, underwent major revisions. Each of the four semesters now includes an intensive weeklong leadership course.

Now the next steps fall to Rex D. Adams, a former Mobil Oil vice president who became Fuqua's dean in June 1996. He's not new to Durham, having received his bachelor's degree from Duke in 1962 and served on the B-school's board of trustees since 1979. But he is new to the day-to-day politics of academic life. As he embarks on a plan to expand the faculty by 50 percent in order to offer executive education programs, his chief challenge will be overseeing a transition at a school that grew rather accustomed to one leader.

That leader—Keller, who essentially invented the Fuqua School of Business—described the school as an "innovative, vital, collegial, team oriented" community where people are "pushing and shoving and wanting to go places." A contradiction? Keller didn't think so. The shrewd promoter pushed and shoved Fuqua from relative obscurity to the top tier of the business school world. He took over the job in 1974—only two years after the school graduated its first class of MBAs—and built Fuqua's reputation as a B-school that is one part laid-back Southern charm, another part intense urban ambition.

As a result of the overhaul, first-years are thrown into a "personal development program" that takes a year of coursework in business communications and managerial computing. Students can select 12 or more electives during the two-year program, up from only 8 before. The upshot: The number of hours that students spend in the classroom has increased by a third.

The most visible alteration is the one-week learning experiences that kick off each semester. From the start, the incoming class is divided into four groups and thrown into Team Building and Leadership Development. After a day in class exploring leadership and teamwork, newcomers are shepherded to an outdoor ropes course half an hour south of Durham for team-building exercises. Like the program that first-years at the University of Chicago go through, this is akin to a miniature Outward Bound. The week also features personal assessment exercises, a community service project, and personal career planning. The idea: to get you to think more deeply about what you want to achieve in your career and your life.

The second semester gets to the integrative experience midway through the semester, with a one-week computer simulation on the computer industry itself. Eight teams of 40 students compete against each other. Team members

assume the jobs of managers in finance, marketing, employee relations, operations, and strategy. The exercise is designed to give students the opportunity to apply—in a cross-disciplinary, practical way—what they are learning in the core. Jump-starting the second year is a series of programs that deal with competition and diversity. And the last semester includes a weeklong experience on emerging trends in management, in which MBAs explore strategic issues that have the potential to change business practices in the next decade. Teams research, and then debate, a topic. In 1996, the topic was doing business in Asia, and teams wrote position papers for 40 projects, sponsored by companies such as AT&T, Federal Express, Ford Motor, IBM, Hewlett-Packard, and Microsoft.

Perhaps the most compelling changes in the curriculum, however, concerned the schedule. In the old format, each course met over 14 weeks, twice a week, each time for 1 hour and 20 minutes. Classes still meet twice a week under the new format, but now the marking period has been cut in half to seven weeks, while each course has expanded to 2 hours and 15 minutes each in seven-week terms. The result: contact hours per course fell to 27 hours from 35 hours—but the overall number of classes that each MBA takes has gone up.

One aim of the change was to push faculty members to reexamine the content of their classes, getting them to discard older, less relevant material that may have been in the syllabus for years on end. The longer class format also forced faculty to rethink the way they teach. After all, it's not easy to keep somebody's attention for more than two hours straight. There are now more case studies; assignments are due each day in class; and spot quizzes have replaced mid-term exams. That is a significant change from the Fuqua of yesterday, which featured too many monotonous lectures, few case studies, and few team activities.

At least, that's the idea. The fact is, Fuqua still isn't the B-school to go to if strong core teaching is your most important measure. In 1996, the school received among the lowest scores from grads in the area. Among the Top 25, only the University of Texas and Stanford did worse. "Too many of the core courses are taught by faculty who are either inexperienced or very young," says one '96 grad. "This led to a number of instances in the core curriculum where I felt the quality of instruction was unacceptable." Says another: "The administration exalts research over the quality of teaching in evaluating faculty, and this shows."

Based on his early comments as dean, Adams isn't likely to alter that emphasis. "We can't teach what we don't know," he told the *Financial Times* upon taking the deanship. "Ultimately it is the quality of the research. That is what counts." To be fair, there are mechanisms in place to improve core teaching at the school. Student evaluations of teachers are made public, and a student-led initiative even created midterm evaluations so that professors and students can have a dialogue during a course's lifespan.

So what are the school's academic strengths? For starters, the electives classes get significantly better marks than the core does—but for a Top 25 school, they're still nothing to write home about. But high praise does come to the school's information technology efforts. Students say they leave Fuqua with a greatly enhanced ability to deal with computers and analytical tools. They also note faculty are available for informal discussions away from the lecture hall. Recruiters, meanwhile, say the school is one of their favorite hunting grounds for MBAs in operations and also laud grads' finance skills.

Virtually everyone agrees that Durham is a nice place to spend two years. It's hard for a visiting applicant not to be impressed by the campus and the Research Triangle area. Duke is one of four major universities in the triangle of Durham, Chapel Hill, and Raleigh. (The others are the University of North Carolina, North Carolina State University, and North Carolina Central University.) The mild climate, the relaxed yet intellectual environment, and the modern-looking Fuqua School have powers to charm. The concrete and glass B-school building on the edge on the west campus of the university boasts an airy mall-like environment with trees, horseshoe-shaped classrooms, and a 500-seat auditorium. A new executive education facility—linked to the school by a bridge across a ravine—opened in May of 1989. It's a 10-minute walk to the Duke Chapel, a towering faux-Gothic imitation of many Ivy League buildings, which sits at the heart of the university campus.

Hop in a car, and you can be just about anywhere in the Triangle within half an hour. Like Silicon Valley and Route 128, the area has leveraged its nearby academic resources to woo businesses. You'll never confuse the area for New York or Chicago—but you also won't feel as if you're in the middle of nowhere. Indeed, Durham is a nice compromise between the access a big city provides and the serenity that a tucked-away college town does.

Like most other B-schools, Duke draws heavily upon Corporate America for guest speakers and lecturers. The 1995–1996 lineup of distinguished speakers included: Hugh McColl, chairman and CEO of Nations Bank, in nearby Charlotte; Randall L. Tobias, chairman and CEO of Eli Lilly & Company; and James A. Champy, chairman and CEO of CSC Index.

It's worth noting, though, that as a relatively young program, Fuqua lacks the large alumni network that some rivals boast. The school has graduated about 4500 MBAs since 1972, when it turned out its first class of just a dozen graduates. Still, Keller worked hard to nurture his alumni base into a viable support network. The school has established alumni clubs from Atlanta to San Francisco and New York to Bombay. An attractive alumni magazine, *Exchange,* keeps alums informed of the latest campus happenings three times a year. In 1992, the school also began to pair up first-year MBA students with 125 alumni who volunteered to serve as career mentors.

Perhaps that's the reason why Fuqua students give the school solid marks for helping them establish network connections. Even better, the class of '96 rated the school's career placement office as one of the best in the nation. Only Michigan got higher marks for helping students find a summer internship. Gushes one '96 grad: "Our career services office takes an extremely aggressive approach. It is probably the most daunting example of American organizational might since Operation Desert Storm." The bad news: recruiters are somewhat less satisfied with the way the office serves their needs and give it good, but not great, marks.

Students' satisfaction with their final experience at Fuqua could be one reason they show such loyalty. Each of the last five graduating classes has donated $100,000 or more to the school by commencement. In 1992, the parting gift went to fund permanent recycling stations and to endow continuing language instruction in German and Japanese for MBAs. In 1996, the gift was dedicated to the purchase of new computers and the development of alumni home pages on the Web.

That's a reflection on the "Team Fuqua" culture that sets the school apart from many other B-schools with similar resources. Students play an active role in the school's affairs. They have sat in on the curriculum committee, the MBA programs advisory committee, the admissions committee, the placement committee, and the committee to select the new dean. Fuquons also run and manage The Kiosk, Fuqua's snack bar and store. They arrange numerous trips abroad, including a two-week business tour of 14 leading companies in Japan. And they sponsor a series of wacky games to benefit Special Olympics. In 1996, the Fuqua-MBA Games raised $85,000 for the cause. MBAs from 10 different schools competed in events like the corporate swimsuit relay and the briefcase throw. If that's not strange enough for you, a new tradition began in 1990 with the now-annual Pig Pickin': an open-pit pig roast on an April Satur-

day that the entire university is invited to. All these events are reported in full in *Over the Counter,* the school's monthly newspaper.

On a more regular basis, students scurry to Lakewood Shopping Center, a five-minute drive from campus, where MBAs meet for drinks at T.J. Hoops, a sports bar. There, grads gather to watch the university's Blue Devils basketball team when they play on the road, and an alternate cheerleader usually comes down to lead the crowd. You can also find them at Satisfaction Restaurant & Bar in Brightleaf Square. Every Friday at 5 p.m., MBAs get together in the atrium of the B-school or in the student lounge for beer and snacks. The new R. David Thomas Center for Executive Education offers a delicious—for cafeteria food, that is—all-you-can-eat buffet for $7.85 every day.

Who are you likely to see sitting next to you? It will probably be an American citizen, since only 19 percent of Fuqua students come from other countries—making it only one of six Top 25 schools to fall below 20 percent in this category.

Most MBAs live off-campus in privately owned apartments just a walk or bike ride away. Duke also boasts a complex of Town House Apartments with a swimming pool for graduate students located about three blocks from the main East-West Campus bus line. Fewer than 1 percent of Fuqua students live in university-owned housing. If you have to drive to school, you'll get familiar with the number 751, the nickname for the Fuqua parking lot, about a three-minute walk from school. The lot is so named because it's just off Route 751.

Truth be told, you may spend more time there than you do at Bulls games or Satisfaction because the workload at Fuqua doesn't allow for too much sight-seeing. Under the new curriculum, most students select their first two electives in their second semester. Then they can pick another 10 or 11 in the second year when there is only one required course—in international business. The school doesn't require formal concentrations in any aspect of management, so students are free to choose from any of the 70 electives offered in an academic program. Fuqua does formally list two concentrations: one in accounting, the other in health services management. The latter major was a result of the university's Department of Health Administration's moving to the Fuqua School in 1993. Students can also take up to four courses in other schools or departments at Duke University, including two foreign language courses.

PLACEMENT DETAILS

Where does all this leave Fuqua alums? As befitting a school with a strong info tech program, the most popular landing spot is IBM, where 187 Fuqua alums draw their paychecks—though many of those are grads of the weekend program. After that come Northern Telecom (89), Glaxo Wellcome (53), Merrill Lynch (52), General Electric (51), NationsBank (49), Ernst & Young (46), and Ford Motor (46). More recently, Ernst & Young Consulting led the school's '96 recruiting pack, having signed up 18 MBAs. Also on the list of top recruiters: Deloitte & Touche (18); Procter & Gamble (7); Andersen Consulting (7); Coopers & Lybrand (7); AT&T (7); IBM (6); General Mills (5); First Union National Bank (5); and McKinsey & Co. (4).

Some 244 companies recruited on campus in 1996, conducting 6699 job interviews. About 1300 job opportunities were posted by correspondence. The result: 19 out of every 20 Fuqua grads hold a job offer at graduation. The median pay package ran $78,000—which sounds pretty good until you consider that it's significantly below most schools that Duke considers to be rivals. And that the average MBA at the nearby University of North Carolina at Chapel Hill—who enters B-school earning less than the Fuquons do and pays much less for her education—leaves school making just $750 less than a Duke MBA does.

The bottom line on Fuqua? Like the reputation that the school cultivates, it's mixed. The teaching could use some improvement, and Adams will doubtless face a complicated transition from Keller's two-decade tenure. But this is a top school at a rising university, and it's smack in the middle of one of the most popular regions in the country. In no way would it be a boring place to spend two years. You might even catch the next Andruw Jones as he blows through town.

OUTSTANDING FACULTY

Michael Bradley (****—investment banking); *Simon Johnson* (***—economics); *Peter Brews* (***—international business and strategy); *Panos Kouvelis* (***—operations management); *C.J. Skender* (**—accounting); *James Smith* (**—statistics); *Joseph Mazzola* (*—operations); *Gwen Ortmeyer* (*—management); *S. Viswanthan* (*—finance).

APPLICANT TIPS

The Fuqua School of Business closely examines GMAT scores and undergraduate records, down to course selection, major, and academic trends. The school states that all admitted applicants "must possess outstanding intellectual ability and academic credentials. In addition, they must have demonstrated leadership, interpersonal, and management skills through their professional and extracurricular activities." Obviously, you would increase the odds of getting into Fuqua if you meet these tests and convey the critical characteristics in your application.

Applicants, particularly those in the United States, are "strongly encouraged" to interview on campus with a member of the admissions committee. Interviews are held beginning in mid-September through mid-April. Prospective students are urged to interview as early as possible in the cycle. To arrange an interview, you may contact the admissions office at 919-660-7704 or via fax at 919-681-8026. Applications, by the way, are not read prior to interviews so you'll want to get this over as quickly as possible or clearly state that you will be unable to visit campus for an evaluative interview.

The school says that candidates who apply early have a better chance of gaining admission and of receiving scholarship money. If you complete the application by January 13, Duke will mail you its decision by March 13. If you wait until the final March 31 deadline, you may not get an answer from the school until the end of May.

Applicants without full-time work experience are rarely accepted without an admissions committee interview. The hurdle rate for those without experience is high: about 98 percent of the most recent entering class boasted full-time, post-graduate work experience.

If you want to apply by disk and have a Macintosh computer, you can purchase software from Apply Software Systems by calling MacApply at 800-93-APPLY.

Contact: Robert R. Williams
Director of Admissions
919-660-7801
Application deadlines: December 6, January 10, February 21, and March 28

FUQUA MBAs SOUND OFF

Fuqua's Career Services Office, led by Dan Nagy, has been absolutely stupendous during every phase of the job search. . . . The basic core program is, in my opinion, in need of some adjustments. Too many of the core courses are taught by faculty who are either inexperienced or very young. This led to a number of instances in the core curriculum where I felt the quality of instruction was unacceptable. . . . As a student enters the elective courses, however, he or she is taught by some truly excellent faculty who have both a gift for teaching as well as a strong reputation in their respective fields.

The teaching quality is often inconsistent and the curriculum does a poor job of preparing students for real jobs with real accountability. Too much time was spent on theory as opposed to how to actually implement ideas. Human resources classes are nearly nonexistent. Fuqua does a good job at teaching students how to think, but not how to justify their opinions/findings. The program does not encourage the exchange of ideas. Career services were great if you wanted a large firm, but little was done to help students learn about midsize companies. Fuqua was a valuable experience overall, but not the "think tank" I anticipated.

The quality of life at this school is excellent. The weather is amazing, the golf course is great, and there is plenty to do when you're not working. The environment fosters an excellent work hard/play hard mentality that the students take to heart. I have told a number of incoming students that you will work very hard, but you will have twice as much fun.

The only negatives I can say about Fuqua are these: It has a significantly non-integrated (racially) atmosphere; and some mediocre faculty members in core courses. Everything else about the school is positive.

Probably the greatest strengths in the program lie in its extraordinarily user-friendly administration, its effective general management orientation, and the almost-excessive ethos of collegiality and mutual support.

**12.
UNIVERSITY
OF
CALIFORNIA
AT LOS
ANGELES**

Contact:
Linda Baldwin
Director of Admissions
810-825-6944
Application deadlines:
December 4
January 8
January 31
February 26
April 3

UNIVERSITY OF CALIFORNIA AT LOS ANGELES

John E. Anderson Graduate School of Management
405 Hilgard Avenue
Los Angeles, California 90024-1448
E-mail address: mba.admissions@anderson.ucla.edu
Website address: http://www.anderson.ucla.edu

Corporate ranking: 17
Enrollment: 1160

Women: 27%
Non-U.S.: 20%
Minority: 10%
Part-time: 535
Average age: 27.6
Average years of work exp.: 4.8
Applicants accepted: 17.4%
Median starting pay: $85,000

Graduate ranking: 2
Annual tuition & fees:
  resident—$10,569
  nonresident—$18,963
Room and board: $8150
Average GMAT score: 651
GMAT range: 480 to 790
Average GPA: 3.5
GPA range: 2.7 to 4.0
Accepted applicants enrolled: 55%
Average starting pay: $90,780

Teaching methods: Lecture, 65%   Case study, 35%

The shores of sunny Southern California bring to mind lazy days soaking up the sun, roller blading, bathing-suit clad teens, and an old Beach Boys song. Trends start in Los Angeles, a city full of cultural peculiarities and outrageous taxes. It would seem that the City of Angels would be no place for a business school, but right in the middle of the bronzed beach-goers and belly-button rings lies a top business school not far from beautiful Malibu beach—UCLA's John E. Anderson Graduate School of Management. It's a school that combines the popular mythology of California with the sometimes bewildering quantitative models of the business school world.

There are probably as many students at Anderson who ache to be investment bankers as there are at Harvard or Wharton. But the school's fastest growing area—entrepreneurship—has soared since the 1987 stock market crash and the downward spiral of junk-bond king Michael Milken. The innovative changes won recognition in 1991 when Anderson's entrepreneurship curriculum was named the best in the nation by the Association of Collegiate Entrepreneurs—even though UCLA didn't know it was up for the award. And longtime faculty member William Cockrum is the single best teacher of entrepreneurship in the nation, according to BUSINESS WEEK's poll of recent grads. But it's hard to keep up in a B-school world where everyone is climbing to the top of the new venture ladder.

While Anderson has carved a niche for itself in entrepreneurship, the school fails to impress some recruiters looking for graduates with a strong global view of business. And the school struggles with the California curse—few MBAs want to leave and even fewer out-of-state recruiters want to trek to the West Coast only to find people unwilling to move away. UCLA actually slipped a notch in the corporate recruiters poll even though Anderson's graduates ranked the school second in overall satisfaction for the second time.

The school is trying to catch up, though, reasserting its emphasis on entrepreneurial skills and classes. Smitten by the new venture bug, many students have launched their own businesses, leading the top B-schools. After studying Small Business Management and writing a business plan, a 1992 alum opened a coffeehouse in west Los Angeles with another classmate. The pair saw a need for a coffeehouse catering to university students. The idea caught on.

Now, students sit at the twoPart cafe sipping coffee and find themselves debating not Marxist theory, but rather which small business classes to get under their belts. A pair of 1994 graduates launched Buzz Records, an independent record label. In Entrepreneurship and Venture Initiation, students start out with a case study involving a trio of MBA students who open up a gelato shop in Florida—a case that explores everything from how to hit people up for venture capital money to exactly where to locate your business. The midterm requires an interview with an entrepreneur.

All these courses are just a starting point for the entrepreneurial center, which offers a steady stream of practical programs for students outside the classroom. Through a strong mentor program, students can meet with successful entrepreneurs on a regular basis. There are also internships with venture capitalists. Each spring Anderson holds a contest where student proposals for new enterprises are judged by a panel of venture capitalists. The winners even take

home cash prizes that are not quite large enough to start a business, but certainly enough to enjoy L.A. in style. And the school has been successful in linking some entrepreneurial graduates with local venture capitalists who have bankrolled their businesses.

With 450 members, the school's Entrepreneur Association is Anderson's most popular student group. The club brings guest entrepreneurs and venture capitalists to campus for presentations and sponsors an annual conference on new business start-ups. A small business consulting service sends students out to give management help to entrepreneurs, while a ventures program funds small business ideas developed by students.

Entrepreneurship, of course, isn't for everyone. And even would-be business owners feel the need to get their feet wet in more established companies before setting sail on their own. That's why finance also remains strong at the school, and different events at Anderson allow students to mix with local finance leaders and alumni. But, the key word is local—corporate recruiters complained that the school's graduates have only an average global view of business, and since much of California's business ventures involve the Pacific Rim, UCLA has to be careful not to fall into that specialty crack like its neighbor, the University of Southern California.

If finance and adventures in capitalism are not your cup of tea, don't worry, because the Anderson School also is a great jumping-off point for a career in entertainment management. Where else could you attend class in the morning and drive over to Hollywood to knock on doors after a power lunch?

It's not unusual for students to follow the same path as Elizabeth Wills, a 1989 Anderson graduate who earned an undergraduate degree at Harvard and worked on Wall Street for three years before realizing she was ready for a change. When she came to UCLA, Wills knew she wanted to do something entrepreneurial that involved finance, but she had no idea what. The Anderson school helped her find a summer internship in a small leveraged buyout firm in Los Angeles, where she went to work full-time after getting her MBA.

Many students, like Wills, are surprised that a B-school program surrounded by palm trees offers such a challenging MBA program. And while the Anderson School offers just that, the main attractions are quality of life and price. UCLA is located in the California foothills in Brentwood, the home of the infamous Nicole Brown Simpson and Ron Goldman murders, and borders Bel Air, an exclusive neighborhood whose residents have included Ronald and Nancy Reagan. The atmosphere here is relaxed and friendly. Students catch some rays on the B-school patio while studying or plugging in with a laptop computer.

Another reason the school has been popular in the past was its low tuition rates. But tuition for out-of-state residents has been rising at a fast clip of late, to $18,963 a year. Still, most qualify as in-state residents, who pay only $10,569 in their second year. Dean William P. Pierskalla, a former Wharton deputy dean who joined Anderson in mid-1993, has been trying to privatize the school by hiking tuition fees and pushing for more alumni and corporate contributions to fund operations. The dean hopes to have as much as 80 percent of the school's budget funded privately by 1998, up from less than 50 percent in 1994.

And even though Pierskalla has pushed the tuition rates higher every year, he quickly gained—and kept—the support and admiration of the students. He has expanded the school's board of visitors, making it more than a ceremonial body to tap for fund-raising. Pierskalla has had success in getting outside executives on the board to become more involved in the school and its students. He prides himself on making business partners personal at Anderson. The dean also encourages his faculty to produce research that benefits the ultimate goal—advancement of management practices. And he won't stand for an inadequate teacher, keeping his door open to students' complaints and working quickly to fix any problems.

Like Los Angeles, the Anderson School's population is diverse, with a high percentage of women, international students, and minorities. While other top B-schools have higher numbers for diversity, Pierskalla and his crew have made it one of their top priorities. But, the California curse does show up in enrollment figures. Typically, nearly 40 percent of Anderson's students are from California, and about 60 percent are from the West. But one-quarter of the school's applications come from New York.

And along with sister school Berkeley, UCLA is a popular destination for Japanese students. Anderson receives tremendous support from current and former Japanese students. The bookstore does a healthy business in UCLA sweatshirts, which are status symbols in Japan along with Louis Vuitton handbags and Nike sneakers. The Tokyo alumni club regularly sponsors a reception for students accepted by the Anderson School. Those students also receive a 40-page guide in Japanese explaining the mysteries of Southern California life—how to open a checking account, how to find an apartment, and how to buy a car—penned by a group of second-year students who sent off a group picture of themselves wearing UCLA sweatshirts.

Not every student admitted to UCLA gets this kind of VIP treatment, but the school competes with the best of them by adopting a personalized approach. Everyone accepted here receives a telephone call if they're in the United States and a letter in their native language if they live overseas. Student volunteers handle these little extras, helping to tout the school's image and organize activities. A big reason for this volunteerism: As part of a state university, Anderson doesn't have the resources available to private schools to promote the MBA program to prospective students, alumni, and corporations.

Student participation, both in and out of the classroom, is a hallmark of the school. Pierskalla has turned toward the other B-school customer—the corporate world—working diligently to pull more companies on campus to interview. Anderson, like other top California B-schools, utilizes the piggyback technique to get more interviews for students. By keeping in close contact with other B-schools, Anderson can contact recruiters on those schools' agendas and sometimes convince the company to stay an extra day to interview UCLA MBA candidates.

Students organize most of the Anderson School's interaction with the local business community. The Association of Students and Business (ASB) sponsors lectures by prominent executives; career nights that draw dozens of firms in each industry, such as finance, entertainment, or real estate; and "days on the job," where students turn company employees for a day. ASB's main event is an annual dinner that draws high-level managers from local companies, as well as students and faculty.

At Anderson, teamwork is the king—the result of a redesigned curriculum to foster greater group cooperation among students and faculty. All first-year students now take the same classes at the same time. Under the old system, students were essentially free to take the classes they wanted. This sometimes created a sense that there was a lack of continuity. Anderson operates on the rigorous quarter system, dividing the year into a fall, winter, and spring term. At the beginning of each quarter, the class of some 315 students splits up into sections of between 60 and 65 students. Students take all required core courses for that quarter with their section.

Half of the two dozen courses required for an MBA are core courses. Eight cover areas such as finance, accounting, organizational behavior, marketing, statistics, and economics. To complete the core, students choose from one of two courses concerned with managing people—either Human Resources Management or Managing People in Organizations—and two of three courses covering technical areas such as information systems, macroeconomics and forecasting, and managerial model building.

Students must take at least 8 of the 11 electives within the Anderson School. Three electives can be taken in other UCLA departments. In taking electives, students can choose from traditional disciplines such as finance, marketing, and management sciences—generally regarded as three of the Anderson School's stronger areas—or from interdisciplinary areas such as entrepreneurial studies, international business, arts management, entertainment management, real estate, and not-for-profit/public management.

Teaching hasn't always been a strength at Anderson, and on this go-round, graduate survey data collected by BUSINESS WEEK earned the school a B in teaching—pretty good for a mainstream business school that largely rewards profs for research. That's because the administration has responded quickly to student complaints about poor teaching, removing professors from first-year courses if they fail to measure up. And students rank teaching in the core courses above average. The same is true for the school's wide variety of electives—some 101 choices.

The culmination of the program is a group consulting project that stretches over two quarters. After visiting a business to study a problem, a team of three to five students develops an analysis, writes it up, then makes an oral presentation to company executives. The final task is a written document to the professor of record. Students sometimes gripe that the field study project can distract from their all-important job search, but it is crucial in helping students integrate knowledge acquired in the core courses. Moreover, the consulting arm of the accounting firm of Deloitte & Touche began in 1992 to ante up $3000 in award money for the field study team that "best demonstrates exemplary leadership, teamwork, innovative thinking, and strategic creativity." Deloitte—one-third of whose consultants in downtown L.A. are Anderson grads—also sponsors workshops and a management hotline so that students can tap the expertise of the firm's consultants during their field study projects.

Despite a renewed focus on international management, the school gets only average marks from recruiters when it comes to global education. The school hired Jose de la Torre, who spent 13 years with INSEAD just a few years ago, to develop the international character of its program. Rather than creating a separate international department, de la Torre wants to boost the international content of each functional area.

A key part of UCLA's international strategy is an MBA in international management that includes intensive language and culture study. UCLA launched a 24-month International Management Fellow program that includes 9 months of study and work in a foreign country. During their time abroad, MBAs will attend a foreign university and do an internship with a local company.

PLACEMENT DETAILS

One thing is for sure, recruiters love Anderson's placement department, rating it one of the best of the top B-schools'. Some 160 companies recruited on campus in 1996, doing 5000 interviews with MBA candidates. About 4000 job opportunities were posted via correspondence. The major recruiters: Deloitte & Touche (10); Andersen Consulting (7); Citibank (5); Nestle (5); Price Waterhouse (5); A.T. Kearney (4); Arthur Andersen (4); Hewlett-Packard (4); and McKinsey & Co. (4).

If Hollywood isn't all that apparent in the school's top employers, the influence of the film capital of the world is apparent in Anderson's annual Abaret, a talent show featuring three hours of performance by students and faculty. And the school's location certainly has a huge influence on activities outside of school. With warm weather lingering almost year-round, most social events take place outside, including the Thursday night beer busts held on the school patio. National forests are nearby and just a stone's throw away is the warm California sand and surf. Like other Los Angeles natives, MBA students have big problems finding an affordable place to live and parking spots are even more scarce. Most MBAs live in Brentwood and Santa Monica, beautiful but ultra-pricey neighborhoods. You definitely need a car to survive in L.A., but many UCLA students take the bus to school because of the lack of parking spaces. Other students car pool, and a few have been known to arrive by roller blades or motor scooters. After all, this is L.A.

OUTSTANDING FACULTY

William Cockrum (****—finance); *George Geis* (****—management science); *Bill Yost* (***—operations and technology management); *Tony Bernardo* (***—finance); *Richard Roll* (***—finance); *George Yip* (***—strategy); *Jose de la Torre* (**—international business); *Eric Sussman* (**—accounting); *Victor Tabbush* (**—business economics); *Randolph Bucklin* (**—marketing).

APPLICANT TIPS

Anderson has an edge over some B-schools when it comes to attracting top students because it doesn't place as much emphasis on GMAT scores, rather opting to put more weight on creativity and skill. So mention on your application how you opened your first lemonade stand at six years old and how you started a tutoring program in college. Anderson prides itself on reeling in the dreamers that they perceive as up-and-coming movers and shakers, opting for the quirky successes instead of always turning to the high-scorers for admission.

Personal interviews aren't required, but they are encouraged. UCLA typically interviews fewer than half its applicants, but the school has recently launched a pilot program for alumni interviewing in New York, Boston, Chicago, and Washington, D.C. The expectation is that more and more of UCLA's applicants will get an in-person screening. Interviews through mid-March are usually booked by mid-January. To schedule an appointment, call admissions at 310-825-6944.

The school puts heavy emphasis on your essay-question answers. UCLA encourages applicants to describe themselves candidly and explicitly, with a focus on emphasizing characteristics that are likely to distinguish you from other candidates.

Apply early. UCLA has five admission deadlines and begins to accept applications in October for its first round of acceptances that go out in early January. If you wait until the last minute, you may not hear from UCLA until mid-June.

Contact: Linda Baldwin
Director of Admissions
810-825-6944
Application deadlines: December 4, January 8, January 31, February 26, and April 3

ANDERSON MBAs SOUND OFF

The faculty was consistently impressive. There is something uplifting about seeing your professor quoted in the *Wall Street Journal* or named in the footnotes of major textbooks. There is a terrible shortage of marketing electives. This is because enrollment in part-time and executive programs has grown rapidly, leaving the limited faculty in scarce supply. The elite management consulting firms (McKinsey, Bain, CG, Booz Allen) still do not take Anderson seriously. This is evident in the fact that they either do not recruit here or hire only for international offices.

I am in the unique position of having siblings who received their respective MBAs from Harvard, Stanford, and the University of Chicago. From candid and objective discussions with them, it appears UCLA is close to their respective "product." However, the depth and consistency of this quality is not as deep as at these other institutions.

It's not about money, it's about beer. . . . That is definitely an exaggeration, but Anderson is a very social, fun-loving environment. I enjoyed the tight-knit community, but it could be a difficult adjustment for people who are a bit less outgoing than the norm. The new facility is really quite amazing (I spent one year in the old building and one in the new), with plug-in computer capability at every seat and teacher control which enables instructors to, at the touch of various and sundry buttons, raise and lower screens, project VCR, Mac, or IBM images, or just turn lights on and off for dramatic effect.

I worked with a team of four students on a consulting project for a newly privatized company in the Czech Republic, traveling to Prague numerous times to meet with management and tour the manufacturing facilities. The conclusion of the project was a two-day presentation to the board of directors and senior management. L.A. is an unparalleled location for a business school.

UCLA has a growing exchange program with universities around the world. This is one of the main reasons that I attended Anderson. Its field study project requirement gave me the chance to evaluate India's marketing potential for avionics equipment, work with a completely cross-functional team (marketing, finance, operation management, engineering) and cross-cultural team (Taiwan, China, Indonesia, Singapore, America) to guide an American company's global marketing strategy. This project was accomplished by team members in multiple locations (Hong Kong and Los Angeles) through faxes, E-mail, the Internet, phone calls, and regular mail.

13.
UNIVERSITY OF CALIFORNIA AT BERKELEY

UNIVERSITY OF CALIFORNIA AT BERKELEY

Walter A. Haas School of Business
350 Barrows Hall
Berkeley, California 94720
E-mail address: mbaadms@haas.berkeley.edu
Website: http://www.haas.berkeley.edu

Corporate ranking: 16	Graduate ranking: 6
Enrollment: 740	Annual tuition & fees:
	resident—$10,394
Women: 34%	nonresident—$18,788
Non-U.S.: 35%	Room and board: $10,328
Minority: 11%	Average GMAT score: 652
Part-time: 262	GMAT range: 520 to 770
Average age: 28	Average GPA: 3.42
Average years of work exp.: 4.8	GPA range: 2.17 to 3.98
Applicants accepted: 13%	Accepted applicants enrolled: 51%
Median starting pay: $85,000	Average starting pay: $91,410

Teaching methods: Lecture, 30%   Case study, 40%   Projects, 30%

Contact:
Fran Hill
Director of Admissions
510-642-1405
*Final application
deadlines:*
March 31 for
domestic applicants;
February 14 for
international applicants

It was just another one of those hokey pictures in a local newspaper; hard hats atop their heads, four suits awkwardly posed with blue-and-gold shovels at the groundbreaking for a new building. But this ceremonial event—the September 1992 launching of a new $45 million management complex for the Haas School of Business—had been a critical step in a bold plan to gain greater recognition for Berkeley's B-school.

It was about time. The 56,000 square feet the Haas school had occupied in Barrows Hall was the "most overcrowded, outdated, and inflexible space of any major business school in the country." Who said? Try *CalBusiness*, the school's own alumni magazine. Berkeley's B-school had been operating with about one-eighth the space per student of Stanford and one-third that of UCLA.

By contrast, the new center, which opened in 1995, seems like a palace. Designed by Santa Monica architects Moore Ruble Yudell, the "mini campus" consists of three buildings connected by bridges and surrounding a courtyard located at the eastern edge of the Berkeley campus near California Memorial Stadium. The B-school's new home brings together the school's library, research centers, student computer labs, classrooms, faculty offices, and executive programs.

The new facility isn't the only good news at the B-school by the Bay. In William Hasler's six years as dean, both students and recruiters have grown much more satisfied with the school. The former vice chairman of accounting giant KPMG, Hasler is the first leader in the school's

94-year history to hail from outside the academy. He has prodded the faculty at this research-oriented school to offer MBAs a more real-world perspective. Oddly enough, California's budget crunch has given Hasler a unique opportunity to bring in fresh talent. A system-wide early-retirement program pared business faculty by about a fifth, opening the way in recent years for new teachers from Columbia, Kellogg, and Cornell.

The results have been impressive. Core teaching received significantly better marks than it had in 1994, and Haas now stands fourth in that category, according to BUSINESS WEEK's student satisfaction survey. Indeed, the school now gets marks that are similar to those of Virginia and Dartmouth, the two B-schools best known for strong teaching. "One of Haas's greatest assets was putting some of its best professors in the core classes, instead of hiding them away in only a few elective classes that many students won't take," says one member of the class of '96.

Hasler also appears to have strong support from among Berkeley's alums, who have put up big money to make the new school a reality. The Haas family, which controls jeansmaker Levi Strauss & Co., kicked in $8.75 million for the new management center, bringing its total contribution to $23.75 million, the largest gift in the university's history. The school is named after Walter A. Haas, Sr., a 1910 graduate of the school who was president of Levi from 1928 to 1955.

On the drawing board are efforts to place greater emphasis on globalization and managing technology. Among other things, Hasler created a center for international business management, modeled after those in place at Columbia and Wharton. He'd also like to ensure that MBA students get some overseas experience via semester-abroad programs, consulting projects with international companies, and summer internships.

No matter what he tries to accomplish, Hasler will probably have to move slowly. Berkeley is a huge, cumbersome bureaucracy, and nearly everything here causes a protest, a demonstration, or at least a stir. To his credit, he knows how to manage in a partnership where power is dispersed. That's certainly what he had to deal with at Peat Marwick. And it's what he had to do at Haas. For starters, he had to endure a mind-boggling 200 interviews to win the job. Since then, he's had to deal with the Byzantine politics of public higher education. One example: to build the new center, he fought preservationists who wanted to prevent the school from demolishing a 70-year-old fraternity house.

But Hasler is also working with an institution that has a number of inherent strengths. It boasts a solid faculty and a fairly strong curriculum. The school draws an exceptionally diverse population of bright students. A remarkable 35 percent of the student body comes from outside the United States. More than a third of students are female. One drawback: only one in nine students is an underrepresented minority (African-American, Latino, or Native American). As the premier public university in the melting pot of California, that's particularly surprising.

One of Hasler's priorities has been global business. Berkeley now has the No. 2-ranked program in international business, based on student satisfaction. The Class of 1994 included a dozen graduates from the University of Tokyo alone. One of every four tenure-track faculty members at Haas can be considered international, at least in origin. The school offers 15 exchange programs with schools outside the United States. An international program sees 45 first-year students work on teams in China, Cuba, Spain, Thailand, and Vietnam during the spring term.

Above all, Berkeley remains a free and eclectic place. The commitment to equal opportunity that characterized America during the late sixties and early seventies is very much alive at the university, simply dubbed "Cal" by students and faculty. You can't beat Berkeley for cultural, ethnic, social, and intellectual diversity. About 99 percent of students have work experience, and they seem to know what they want—to make a difference in the world, as corny as that may sound. Failing that, they'll settle for an interesting job with lots of freedom. (Of course, money doesn't hurt either. Haas grads are tied with UCLA's and Virginia's in having the highest post-MBA salary for grads.)

Berkeley's cutting-edge finance faculty draws many of Wall Street's future rocket scientists, but quants can afford to be a little weird, especially when they're making the firm millions of dollars a year. Many Berkeley MBAs gravitate toward high-tech companies like Apple Computer, Hewlett-Packard, and Sun Microsystems, where the corporate culture tolerates and sometimes encourages nonconformism. The thinking seems to be that the person who questions why something is done a certain way may come up with a better, more profitable way of doing it. Berkeley grads who don't land jobs in Silicon Valley often go into business for themselves.

Befitting its diverse student population, Berkeley's B-school emphasizes an interdisciplinary approach to graduate business education. That's the way it has been since 1898 when UC Regent Arthur Rodgers, returning from a trip in Asia, maintained that business education should include faculty and courses from across the university. "I don't believe any other B-school has as many programs that are the products of real joint planning with other units on campus," says former dean, Raymond Miles. "Others may talk about it, but we've been doing it for 90 years."

The B-school offers interdisciplinary programs with the schools of engineering, law, public health, environmental design, and Asian studies. The joint MBA/MA in Asian studies offers special training in languages, political economy, history, and sociology for students interested in both business and Asia. To be accepted into the three-year program, a student must have a bachelor's degree and at least one year of a relevant Asian language. B-school founder Rodgers was convinced that California was the gateway to the Pacific Rim and that Berkeley should prepare its students to become "Pacific statesmen."

Being a liberal never went out of fashion in Berkeley. Much about Haas is a reflection of the overriding environment here, from the school's à la carte MBA program to the liberal grading policies of its professors. Like MIT, the university is known for its strong engineering department, and the B-school has traditionally emphasized quantitative skills. In recent years, there has been some movement toward the qualitative, to the chagrin of some students. Berkeley uses a combination of lecture and case study, with a heavy emphasis on group projects and student cooperation.

There are 11 courses in the core requirements covering areas such as finance, accounting, marketing, organizational behavior, economics, statistics, and information systems. Waivers out of some of these courses are possible. Business and Public Policy, a core requirement taught by David Vogel, Paul Tiffany, and Pablo Spiller, is one of the most popular courses here. Berkeley's strength in this area can be traced back to the sixties, when business and the B-school were under fire from many university students. The protests led to some soul-searching. As a result, the B-school beefed up faculty in the political, legal, and social aspects of business.

No future entrepreneur should go through the Haas School without taking Entrepreneurship, team taught by John Freeman (who has deep research roots in the Bay Area's biotech and computer industries), finance jock Jerry Engel, and marketing guru Adam Berman. The course is centered around a real-life start-up whose principals agree to work with students on a business plan for the company. Several members of Berkeley's finance faculty can speak with extra authority because they are actively involved in the markets. Hayne Leland and Mark Rubenstein are principals in Leland O'Brien Rubenstein Associates, the firm that created portfolio insurance, a trading strategy that uses stock index futures to protect against a decline in equity prices. You'll find no shortage of outstanding teachers at Berkeley (see the listing at the end of the profile).

Along with UCLA, to which it is constantly compared, Berkeley's tuition for nonresidents is among the lowest of Top 25 B-schools. At less than $11,000 for California residents, it's a very good deal. Getting a top-dollar education for a bargain-basement price prompted one recent grad to co-found a fund-raising program where students pledge to the school 1 percent of their first year's salary. More than 50 percent of Haas School students participated in the first year of the program and 75 percent have signed up in the years since. "We decided to give a little something back to the school, and it instantaneously institutionalized," says the recent grad.

The fact that it did gives you a clue about the sharing culture at the Haas School. "Cooperation may well be the hallmark of Haas," believes a recent graduate. "Virtually all major papers were assigned as group projects, and I never personally ran into a classmate who put himself ahead of his teammates. This cooperation also extended to the job search process. If classmates knew of job leads, they usually shared them with others."

That concern for others also translates into a concern for the school and its management. Students take involvement seriously. Through MBA Associates, the student government body, Haas School students make their views known to faculty and administration on such issues as curriculum content, admissions, placement, and publications. MBAA serves as the umbrella organization for all extracurricular activities from the Pacific Rim Club and Women in Management to the Graduate Minority Business Association. These clubs promote a functional area of business by preparing résumé directories, organizing events that bring corporate executives and alumni to campus, and sponsoring "days-on-the-job," where students visit a company to learn about its operations. Students also were responsible for having a core course in communications added to the first year. This replaced an out-of-class oral and written communication requirement. In fact, students are encouraged to create experimental courses and have done so with

Business in the Pacific Rim, as well as Business and the Environment, and others.

Eating ethnic is de rigueur at Berkeley: MBAs frequent Plearn for Thai, Blue Nile for Ethiopian, and the Ajanta for Indian cuisine. MBAs don't crowd Berkeley's famed Chez Panisse restaurant every night, but they make a point of visiting it at least once. More typically, they head to Kip's or Bear's Lair for burgers and pizza. Despite the Bay Area's proximity to the wineries of the Napa and Sonoma valleys, local residents and MBAs are also beer and ale connoisseurs. Triple Rock, which serves beer brewed on the premises, is a favorite. Henry's and Raleigh's are also popular MBA hangouts. San Francisco is only 30 minutes away on the Bay Area Rapid Transit system, or BART, so MBAs often take in the night life there.

Rent control in Berkeley just isn't what it used to be. In recent years, the moderates and the courts have controlled the rent board so now it's hard to find any apartment under $700 a month within a mile of the campus. The university only offers a limited amount of MBA housing and it goes fast.

Berkeley MBAs have a penchant for being entrepreneurial. Indeed, a team of researchers from the B-school and the university's Institute of Personality Assessment and Research began a seven-year personality study of 131 Berkeley MBAs in 1985. The findings: Berkeley MBAs were the third most creative group ever assessed by the institute, falling into what it terms the "entrepreneurial category." "The up side to that is the students are flexible, they take initiative, and are willing to try new things," says Charles O'Reilly, the co-director of the study who has since left for Stanford. "They are probably slightly less desirable for the corporate environment (because) they're likely to do well in situations that value creativity."

To tap into those interests, the B-school's Partnership for Entrepreneurial Leadership matches MBA students with young, high-growth companies for summer internships, followed by project work for credit in their second year. Entrepreneurs' Forums bring participants to the faculty club six or eight times a year for a networking hour with faculty and students. The sessions draw more than 200 venture capitalists, investment bankers, successful and aspiring entrepreneurs, and their lawyers, accountants, and advisers.

PLACEMENT DETAILS

Some 225 companies recruited on campus in 1996, conducting 2500 interviews. Another 5500 job opportunities were posted via correspondence. The major recruiters of the Class of 1996: Deloitte & Touche Consulting (8); Hewlett-Packard (8); Ernst & Young Consulting (7); Andersen Consulting (4); Bain & Co. (3); Booz Allen & Hamilton (3); Boston Consulting Group (3); Citibank (3); McKinsey & Co. (3); and Price Waterhouse Consulting (3).

Berkeley MBAs walked off campus with about 2.9 jobs each—about average for the Top 25. The median starting pay of $85,000 is the same as grads get at such top schools as UCLA and Virginia—and is the highest for any public university business school. It also exceeds what MBAs get at Michigan, Duke, North Carolina, and Cornell. But a good number of the Class of 1996 went up and did their own thing: at least a dozen started Internet-based start-ups. Berkeley gets low marks from recruiters at national corporations, many of whom don't even come to Berkeley, partly because grads just don't want to leave the area. About 60 percent of them take jobs in California, while another 25 percent take posts overseas. They're spoiled by the Bay Area's friendly people, good food, exciting cultural events, and mild—if a bit unpredictable—weather. This means that Berkeley is more of a regional school than many of its neighbors on the list of best B-schools—and the school remains somewhat insecure about this, particularly since that other school to the south is one of the best B-schools in the world. The bottom line

is that if you're looking to land a job with a major company in the Midwest, Northeast, or Southeast, Haas may not be the place for you. But if you're looking to study in a spanking new facility, live in one of the nation's best college towns, and work with one of the more devoted faculties, it just might be.

OUTSTANDING FACULTY

Richard Lyons (****—global finance); *Sara Beckman* (****—management); *Jennifer Chatman* (***—organizational behavior); *David Aaker* (**—marketing); *Andrew Rose* (**—economics); *Hayne Leland* (**—finance); *Brett Trueman* (*—accounting); *Ben Hermalin* (*—economics); *Sankar De* (*—corporate finance); *Rashi Glazer* (*—marketing).

APPLICANT TIPS

Berkeley seeks diverse, intellectually bright applicants. As the school puts it: "Successful applicants exhibit a high level of intellectual performance, a substantial employment history demonstrating potential for a career in management, and personal attributes suggesting leadership, maturity, ethical character, social and civic responsibility, and goal orientation."

Undergraduate grades and GMAT scores are critical. If you have done well in college-level calculus and statistics, you have a significant advantage. Virtually every successful candidate also brings some work experience to Berkeley. More than 90 percent of students have two or more years of professional work experience. Berkeley pays particular attention to the level of responsibility held, as well as to your promotion history and your employer's letter of recommendation.

Because the school conducts few evaluative interviews, you should play up your leadership and interpersonal skills in your answers to the essay questions in the application. Berkeley is looking for examples of initiative, creativity, and resourcefulness in either professional or extracurricular activities. Apply as early as possible. Berkeley begins reviewing applications in November. If you wait until the March 31 deadline, you may not get a response from admissions until the end of May. If you would like to visit the campus and monitor classes, you can schedule your trip by calling the Campus Visitation Program at 510-642-5610. Or you can take a virtual tour via CD, which is available from the school for use on both Windows and Macintosh. Just contact admissions and ask for Berkeley's "Interactive Tour" CD.

Contact: Fran Hill
Director of Admissions
510-642-1405
Final application deadlines: March 31 for domestic applicants, February 14 for international applicants

HAAS MBAs SOUND OFF

Overall, I was very satisfied with Haas. My MBA experience has allowed me to change careers, double my previous salary, and learn finance. . . . Two improvements needed are in recruiting and consistency in teaching quality. One investment bank came to recruit on campus. This shows how weak the recruiting really is. There were some very good and very bad teachers at Haas.

The diversity of the students was amazing: A Pulitzer-prize-winning journalist, an Olympic swimmer, former pro-softball player who also worked at the Fed, former high-tech entrepreneur, former Soviet journalist, Japanese bankers. The list goes on and on. The international students taught me more about doing business abroad than my professors. The entrepreneurial spirit is very strong. Three different Internet-focused companies were founded by students at Haas. They sold them for big bucks. The students have a lot of freedom to start new classes, create organizations to reach out to communities, etc. However, the administration often uses this as a reason to do nothing itself.

With the courses teaching you a way to think and giving you practical tools to use in business, with the incredible people (students, faculty, community) you're constantly surrounded by, and of course the technical training on state-of-the-art equipment, my two years were the most valuable experience I could hope for.

The brand-new building is a terrific asset to the school, as well as an architectural marvel. The facilities are now at the cutting edge of graduate education and the layout has created a true sense of community among students, faculty, and administrators.

Berkeley definitely appeals to a particular "ethos." We are conceited and elite in a way quite distinct from Harvard and Stanford; I think we collectively embrace a unique sense of humanism in the MBA program.

Although I was drawn to the Haas program by the technology and international areas of focus, the diverse student body proved to be even more beneficial to my learning experience. Even in our relatively small class of about 230 students, I had classmates from dozens of countries, every major undergraduate institution, and myriad professional backgrounds. An added bonus of attending Haas is the return on investment: at my new salary I will recoup my total MBA investment, including my forgone salary, in less than two years.

While we send few students to Wall Street and Fortune 500 companies, we instead find ourselves at Silicon Valley start-ups, working abroad, or pursuing "nontraditional" MBA career paths such as environmental management.

14.
NEW YORK UNIVERSITY

NEW YORK UNIVERSITY

Leonard N. Stern School of Business
Management Education Center
44 West 4th Street
New York, New York 10012
E-mail address: sternba@stern.nyu.edu
Website address: http://www.stern.nyu.edu

Corporate ranking: 9	Graduate ranking: 21
Enrollment: 3100	Annual tuition & fees: $22,500
Women: 26%	Room and board: $10,050
Non-U.S.: 35%	Average GMAT score: 646
Minority: 8%	Average GPA: 3.3
Part-time: 2300	GPA range: 2.9 to 3.7
Average age: 27	Average years of work exp.: 4
Applicants accepted: 20%	Accepted applicants enrolled: 10.7%
Median starting pay: $75,000	Average starting pay: $78,895

Teaching methods: Lecture, 60% Case study, 40%

Taking a cue from David Letterman, the Stern School student nudged up to the onstage mike with her own Top 10 list. The topic: Top 10 Reasons to Go to Stern over Harvard Business School.

10. It's $600 a year cheaper.
 9. I'm severely allergic to Ivy.
 8. Would be lost with all that grass on that wide campus.
 7. Harvard is not on the R line.
 6. Wouldn't know what to do with all the money when I graduated.
 5. Always hated the Head of the Charles.
 4. Networking not all it is cracked up to be.
 3. I always wanted to market cat litter for Hartz Mountain Group.
 2. Too many on-campus interviews would interfere with my daily schedule.
 1. Tired of all those drunken Kennedy parties.

Well, okay, so maybe Letterman wouldn't be all that impressed with the self-deprecating wit of Stern's MBAs at their recent annual follies show. But now students can add another reason to forgo Harvard: The school has finally moved out of its dingy quarters near Wall Street onto New York University's main campus in Greenwich Village.

The class of 1994 was the first to arrive at what is called the most expensive building in the history of management education, hearing the wheezing of electric saws and drills as dozens of construction

Contact:
Marry Miller
Director of Admissions
212-998-0613
*Final application
deadlines:* March 15
for fall

workers rushed about to complete work on the $68 million center. Layers of fine dust covered nearly everything. The staircases were still taped closed, and only a few elevators were working. At the time, even a joking student might not have wanted to include the building in the Top 10 list.

But the new management education center, with a cobblestone plaza in front, is helping to transform New York University's Stern School into a formidable competitor for top-tier students. The school's 200-strong faculty, once dispersed over 24 floors in 6 separate buildings, is now housed on 3 floors in a single location. For the first time in the school's history, the faculty actually has its own lounge.

Instead of sitting in hard wooden chairs with arm-top desks in flat classrooms, MBAs now boast of the finest, multitiered, state-of-the-art classrooms available anywhere. The new environment itself imposes different demands on Stern faculty. Professors standing in front of these classrooms genuinely feel that they are on stage and have to perform—something that will put additional pressure on teaching laggards to upgrade their presentation skills.

No less important, the school has launched major changes in the MBA program, to make the Stern curriculum far more relevant and challenging. The design of the new program creates more of an integrated experience where all the courses fit together. And there are new classes that involve more teamwork, globalization, and communication skills.

The person who engineered these dramatic changes is no longer around to see their result. Dean Richard R. West ended his nine-year stint at the head of NYU's business school in mid-1993. West, formerly dean of Dartmouth's Amos Tuck School, brought in the $30 million naming gift from Hartz Group entrepreneur Leonard N. Stern, and bickered with city-planning officials and contractors while getting the new management center up and running. He also led the curriculum revision effort.

George G. Daly, a former White House economist and longtime dean of the University of Iowa's B-school, took over where West left off. Daly is leading the school through a time of transition. While many things have changed, many of the school's attributes will seem the same. The new school in Washington Square remains a big, urban, diverse, and eclectic school with one of the best graduate finance programs in the world. Full- and part-time students may continue to attend the same elective classes—something that many full-time MBAs enjoy, because part-timers often bring real-life perspective to class discussions. As Mitchell Hecht an alum, relates, "I found myself taking classes at night to get certain professors, and in the evening classes you get students who are bond traders during the day who question and challenge some of the classroom theory. The level of dialogue and sophistication is pretty high."

Yet the new center is helping Stern to shake its image as a "night school"—the result of its 1916 roots as a satellite campus on Trinity Place for Wall Streeters who walked to class after work. Such students still account for a large part-time enrollment that the school has deliberately shrunk by one-third, to 2000 students.

For Stern's incoming full-timers, a three-day orientation featuring, among other things, an ethics game and an Outward Bound–like experience in Central Park (if such a thing is possible) kicked off the 1996 school year right before Labor Day. In the new program, cohort groups of 65 students each travel through 12 core courses together—although you can still waive out of a core offering if you've taken the same course as an undergrad. Many of the remaining 8 courses required to graduate will fulfill "major" requirements. Stern students may major in one or more of seven functional areas: accounting, economics, finance, information systems, management, marketing, or statistics and operations research. You can even combine these majors with a further concentration in such areas as international business, operations management,

management consulting, financial engineering, and entertainment, media, and telecommunications. Indeed, two of the newest courses meet the growing interest in the entertainment biz: Strategic Management in the Entertainment Industry and Entertainment Marketing.

After complaints about the quality of teaching in core courses, teaching effectiveness workshops were required for all new teachers and core courses are supposed to be taught by faculty who have proven themselves to be "effective" teachers. Student evaluations of teachers and classes are made public, so that Stern grads can attempt to avoid the worst of the lot by doing a little research. The latest round of BUSINESS WEEK's customer satisfaction polls shows that teaching quality at Stern has improved, though it's rated not much better than average of the 51-plus schools whose graduates are surveyed by the magazine.

It helped that in 1990 West scored a near academic miracle when he got his faculty to pass a promotion and tenure policy that placed as much importance on teaching quality as it did on scholarly research. It was the first time in two decades that the faculty was able to agree on the issue. Eight years earlier, professors here were only one vote shy of approving a policy that would have made research the only criterion for promotion and tenure.

Besides the complaints over teaching, several Stern MBAs maintain that the quality of their classmates isn't always as consistent as it should be, and they say that the large contingent of international students isn't integrated into the school as well as it could be. You'll also hear complaints about the difficulty the placement office has in luring a broader range of corporations to campus to recruit Stern students.

One thing is certain: At Stern, finance is king. A recent study of published research in *Financial Managment* ranked Stern's finance department first in the nation ahead of Wharton, UCLA, Chicago, and Columbia. Stern's finance faculty alone outnumbers the entire fac-

ulty at many B-schools, including Amos Tuck. Almost 20 percent of the school's 135 courses are in the finance area, from Fixed-Income Securities to Venture Capital to Going Public. And Stern grads—despite their complaints about the teaching—almost universally praise the finance faculty.

While nonfinance types might initially cross Stern off their lists, the school boasts a top-notch program in international business. A peek inside the course catalog fails to tell the whole story, since seemingly noninternational courses often include a global aspect. Stern also has a good number of international students. Roughly 35 percent of entering full-time MBAs are not from the United States—that's 300 people from more than 60 different countries from Australia to Peru, including what might be the largest single contingent at a U.S. B-school from Japan—nearly 100 Japanese students. The school even publishes a separate guide for international applicants.

Stern also boasts an internationally oriented faculty. Since 1980, more than 60 percent of the teachers hired by Stern didn't have U.S. passports at one time. Sometimes that's a disadvantage, because some students complain that they have had trouble understanding professors with heavy foreign accents. Even so, the Academy of International Business ranked Stern the nation's top school in 1988 for its international program. The centerpiece of the global slant is an exchange program Stern runs with 26 foreign graduate schools in 21 countries, from the Chinese University of Hong Kong to Sweden's Stockholm School of Economics. Each year, about 60 Stern students trek abroad for at least one semester in the fall of their second year.

For the top students who stay in New York, many enroll in an unusual management consulting course in the second year that stretches over both the fall and spring terms of the second year. In the course, students gain a taste for real-world training as they work as consultants for such companies as American Express Co.,

Digital Equipment Corp., and Sony Corp. At the end of the project, students deliver oral and written reports to high-level executives of each sponsoring company.

Other surprises? Stern boasts a strong program in information systems. From 1980 to 1986, Stern faculty published more articles in the top five management information systems' journals than teachers from any other B-school. Stern's strong showing is largely the result of a highly prolific professor, Henry C. Lucas Jr. At Stern, unlike many other top schools, Information Systems for Management is a required core course, not an elective.

Going to school in New York, of course, can be daunting for some. Stern tries to ease the transition by putting all its first-year students into cohorts of 65 MBAs, each headed by a "Blockhead." Students keep tabs on happenings through the *Stern School Update,* the weekly calendar of lectures, beer blasts, and recruiter visits put out by the office of student affairs. MBAs can also keep abreast of new events through E-mail and Gopher, an on-line info service for Stern-specific news. Student groups range from the Entrepreneurs' Exchange to the Women's Career Forum. MBAs also publish *Opportunity,* the monthly newspaper that attempts to cover the school's ins and outs. It helps that all students are now guaranteed university housing on designated Stern School floors in Alumni Hall on Third Avenue and Tenth Street. About 25 percent of Stern students hole up in university housing.

Stern's new complex is made up of a trio of linked buildings: Virtually all the MBA action occurs in the 11-story Management Education Center (MEC). Then, there's Tisch Hall for the undergraduate program, and the top six newly renovated floors of 100-year-old Shimkin Hall. (The bottom part of the building is occupied by the School of Nursing.) Stern made the absolute most of all the space it could hog. One 200-seat auditorium in the new center boasts a back row higher than the ceiling that gives you the feeling

you're in the upper deck at Yankee Stadium. The "Starship Enterprise Lounge"—the modern-looking student lounge on the third and fourth floors of the MEC—has already become a gathering place for all MBAs. Stern no longer has its own library. Instead, the business collection is on the sixth floor of the university's Bobst Library, the red sandstone building adjacent to the B-school complex. Students can do library searches from within the MEC by logging on to Bobcat, the NYU library database. MBAs can find current periodicals in a fifth-floor reading room.

There's no paucity of restaurants and hangouts in Washington Square. Good vegetarian cooking at cheap prices is available at Apple on Waverly. There's Pluck U on West Third Street for chili, fries, and Buffalo Wings, and Sam's Falafel on Thompson Street for fast food Greek style (with a 15 percent discount to NYU students). Two Boots on Bleeker serves up Cajun-style pizza.

PLACEMENT DETAILS

Professors describe Stern students as down-to-earth: not as intellectually probing as those at Wharton or Stanford, but more aggressive and street-smart. And the vast majority of them are into finance, hardly a surprise given the school's proximity to Wall Street. More than half the MBAs pursue finance majors. Neither is it surprising that as Wall Street turns, so does the business school. Stern's recruiting schedules are typically packed with interviewers from the investment banks, brokerage firms, and commercial banks. The revival of the Street enabled the school to bring in about two job offers each to 86 percent of the Class of 1996 by commencement.

In all, 200 companies recruited on campus in 1996 for permanent jobs, conducting more than 5800 interviews. Some 4600 full-time job opportunities came into the school via correspondence. Citicorp took Stern grads by the truckload, hiring 29 members of the Class of 1996. Other big buyers of Stern talent were Coopers & Lybrand (16); Deloitte & Touche (11); Chase Manhattan Bank (10); Chemical Bank (9); AT&T (8); American Express (8); J.P. Morgan (8); Johnson & Johnson (7); and Morgan Stanley/Smith Barney (5).

Those recruiters are likely to be impressed with the many changes occurring at this New York City school. With a bit of luck, fewer people will need 10 reasons to pick Stern over other top business schools.

OUTSTANDING FACULTY

Aswath Damodaran (****—finance); *William Silber* (****—finance); *John Czepiel* (***—marketing); *Michael Darling* (***—marketing); *Edward Altman* (**—finance); *Roy Smith* (**—finance); *Ingo Walter* (**—finance); *Richard Freedman* (**—organizational behavior); *Michael Capek* (*—management communication); *Gary Simon* (*—statistics).

APPLICANT TIPS

Like its New York City rival, Columbia University, NYU admits full-time MBA students in September for a 21-month program or in January for an accelerated 16-month program. The downside of the shorter version is that you lose the opportunity of gaining a summer internship.

Apply early, and if you want an interview with the admissions staff, make a request within two weeks of submitting your application. Interviews, however, are not required. The school recommends that students complete a semester of calculus and an introductory economics course before enrollment. Obviously, solid grades in such courses—which demonstrate your potential to handle accounting and financial coursework—give you a decided advantage.

Even though the final deadline for admission in September is March 15, full-time applicants seeking financial aid must submit both the financial aid and MBA applications including GMAT scores by January 31. Stern begins its review of applications in January for the fall term and in late August for the spring term. The final deadline for domestic applicants for the spring term is mid-October.

Stern regularly sponsors wine-and-cheese receptions for prospective applicants on selected Mondays from 5:30 to 7 p.m. At these informational sessions, the school makes available a dean or faculty member, an admissions officer, and a Stern student or graduate. To reserve a spot for the reception or arrange a class visit or campus tour, contact the admissions office at 800-272-7373 or 212-998-0600.

Contact: Marry Miller
Director of Admissions
212-998-0613
Final application deadlines: March 15 for fall

STERN MBAs SOUND OFF

I participated in what is called the International Management Program, where I spent one semester (my final one) studying in São Paulo, Brazil. Many of my classmates also participated in this program going to various universities around the world, allowing us to gain a strong understanding of different markets and business environments where we might have an interest. For me, it allowed me to study the Brazilian market and achieve my objectives of finding a job in the finance sector in Brazil.

I only took three electives at Stern because I participated in the International Management Program. Studying in Barcelona was one of the highlights of my Stern experience. I chose Stern because of its obvious commitment to international study and its global perspective.

Stern administration highly values student input on all levels, about all areas of life. For example, a student committee did a benchmarking and reengineering project, on their own, to improve the Office of Career Development. The report was used as a basis for new programs/restructuring and improvements have been tremendous. Student government leaders and Student Group leaders have access to all deans and faculty in leadership. Our views are listened to and often changes result; Deans respond to all E-mail, usually on the same day, sometimes within 24 hours, from all students, faculty, and administration.

In my two years here, I've sat on numerous focus groups held both by the administration as well as by individual departments. I sat in on a marketing department focus group in my first year where we suggested courses in direct mail, arts and media management, and financial services marketing. These courses were available for the next term with top-notch, experienced professors teaching them. I was stunned! They really listened to us and found the resources to make what we suggested a reality. I believe this ability and willingness to reinvest themselves will be Stern's competitive advantage moving forward.

I could see visible improvements in terms of information technology and curriculum while I was there. This school has been continuously improving. Therefore, there might

be some students who are not happy with their Stern experience because they were looking for a well-established and traditional, lecture and case-based business education. However, I personally believe that business education should be flexible, to respond to the changing real business world. I give Stern credit for trying to be responsive.

Not only has the curriculum provided me with a solid grounding in general business principles and, more specifically, in finance (my major), but it has also strengthened my public speaking and interpersonal skills through extensive presentation and group work requirements. The high caliber of my classmates and demanding nature of my professors have caused me to "stretch" my own efforts. Additionally, the receptiveness of both faculty and administration, as well as amazing opportunities to become active in school-related issues have allowed me to truly make a positive, and lasting, impact on Stern. Finally, the Office of Career Development was instrumental in my wildly successful job search. Through on-campus recruiting, I received, and accepted, an offer that was literally for my dream job. If I had it to do over again, knowing what I know now, I would change nothing!

I have been very impressed with the Center for Entrepreneurial Studies at Stern. It currently offers some excellent courses and recently received a large grant enabling it to expand its activities. I believe this is an upcoming department at Stern and is going to start receiving some attention.

**15.
INDIANA
UNIVERSITY**

INDIANA UNIVERSITY

Graduate School of Business
10th and Fee Lane
Bloomington, Indiana 47405
E-mail address: mbaoffice@indiana.edu
Website address: http://www.bus.indiana.edu

Corporate ranking: 13	Graduate ranking: 17
Enrollment: 5998	Annual tuition & fees:
	resident—$8,069
Women: 23%	nonresident—$15,613
Non-U.S.: 16%	Room and board: $5372
Minority: 8%	Average GMAT score: 630
Part-time: none	GMAT range: 440 to 780
Average age: 27	Average GPA: 3.2
Average years of work exp.: 4	GPA range: 2.2 to 4.0
Applicants accepted: 45%	Accepted applicants enrolled: 20%
Median starting pay: $67,000	Average starting pay: $67,770

Teaching methods: Lecture, 33.3% Case study, 33.3%
Projects, 33.3%

Contact:
James Holmen
Director of Admissions
812-855-8006
*Final application
deadline:* March 1
for fall

Have you heard the joke about the student who put up a sign next to the hot-air dryer in one of the school's bathrooms? It read: "Push Button for a Message from the Dean." These days, a lot of B-school deans are blowing excess hot air about the revolutionary changes they've pioneered in management education. In many cases, there's a lot more rhetoric than reality to such boasts. Not at Indiana University's Graduate School of Business. The school has gone to the extremes in reinventing what had once been a basic, no-frills MBA program at one of the better public universities in the United States.

Just how radical? Consider this: In the first year, MBAs receive only two grades—one for each semester. Instead of the usual lineup of functional courses, the first semester's work is more highly integrated in what the school calls a Foundations Core taught by a faculty team of four professors. It's followed in the second semester by a Functional Core taught by a team of five faculty.

The downside of all these changes was that the school may have bitten off more than it could chew. After an eight-place plunge in the '96 rankings, Indiana Dean John Rau announced that he was leaving the school to return to the banking biz. His departure isn't related to the drop, but it may hinder the school's ability to mount a quick turnaround. Most of the drop could be attributed to vastly lower satisfaction scores on BW's graduate survey. Among other things, Indiana earned the dubious distinction of gaining the worst scores for teaching in electives for any Top 25 school. But Indiana also lost major ground in the recruiting survey, dropping five spots to 13th in 1996.

Still, the overhaul was a gallant attempt to remake an MBA program, and what makes it all the more surprising is that it's being accomplished at a school tucked away in southern Indiana—far from the hustle and bustle of Corporate America or the pioneering entrepreneurs of either Silicon Valley or Route 128. The nearest city to rather isolated Bloomington is Indianapolis, about 45 minutes away, and it's hardly a mecca for MBAs. So what propelled Indiana to move so boldly ahead with such dramatic changes in its curriculum?

The school had come in for some heavy criticism from MBAs in BUSINESS WEEK's 1990 poll when IU failed to rank in the Top 20 in the magazine's graduate survey. Overall the school was 15th, thanks to a fairly strong 9th place finish among corporate recruiters. The school took the criticism to heart, speeding a process of change that had begun in 1989 with the appointment of a committee to recommend the future direction of the MBA program. The panel sought the views of students, alumni, industry representatives, leading business execs, and B-school officials.

The effort led to interviews with more than 140 corporate managers and executives. Joseph A. Pica, former director of the MBA program, recalls the comments of one CEO of a top company who said he was struggling with having too many managers who are specialists. "He's got marketing people, finance people, information systems people, and his production people," says Pica. "They're all extremely good at what they do, yet what makes the business really work is when you bring the sum together."

That's exactly what Indiana attempts in this new program, which was launched in the fall of 1992. To meet the needs of incoming students who require extra start-up help in ac-

counting, statistics, and computing, the school now offers short "jump start" courses during the summer. The "preparatory summer" is supposed to provide a more level playing field for all students. A 10-day orientation program kicks off the first year with the typical array of activities, from a teach-building exercise that teaches group problem solving in a wilderness setting at Bradford Woods in Southern Indiana to sessions that promote better awareness of cultural differences and sensitivities as well as their impact on managing the workforce. All students are required to have their own PCs. They get hands-on experience with both mainframes and PCs during orientation week when they take a crash course in spreadsheet analysis and word processing. Through Indiana's computer network, students send messages to classmates and professors by electronic mail. They also can access several databases to help them complete classwork.

To promote more teamwork and cooperation, the school has downsized the entering classes to about 250 from 320. First-year students are grouped into four cohorts of 60 to 65 students. For each two cohorts, a faculty team of four professors will then run the groups through the semester-long Foundations Core—covering accounting, managerial economics, quant methods, and human resources management. Just more of the same under a new label? Not. Faculty teams work with students to aggressively integrate topics, cases, and assignments that span these traditional disciplines. During the first semester, you'll also get "modules" on Power and Negotiation and Applied Business Ethics.

Before the second semester begins, IU deliberately shakes up the cohort groups so you'll meet more of your student colleagues. Then, your group will be assigned a different faculty team of five members to bring you through the Functional Core—designed to explore the relationships among accounting, finance, marketing, operations management, and management information systems. There are no waivers and no breaks for anyone, regardless of their previous experience.

MBAs are enthusiastic about the first-year curriculum changes; however, many are disappointed with the second-year experience. Students say the transition isn't smooth enough—many felt the two halves of the MBA program were separate experiences. There were also complaints about redundancy in the second year. One graduate said he thought a one-year program would have been a better value, since there was so much duplication of basic material. Bringing the second year up to par was a major challenge facing Rau, who became dean in July 1993. Now, that task along with a turnaround will fall to his successor. The school is still looking for a replacement and has since named Dan Dalton interim dean.

IU students can choose from 107 electives. Among the offerings are Bruce Resnick's popular yearlong course, Applied Investment Analysis and Portfolio Management. Students manage a portfolio of $200,000. They screen stocks, study companies, and monitor current events in the fall semester. By January, they put their money where their mouths, rather minds, are, making buy recommendations that they present to the class and an advisory board of IU alums working in the investment business. Finance is the overwhelming major of choice, with 52 percent of students pursuing a concentration in that field. Throughout the program, the three major themes of the curriculum are global, technological, and ethical.

Over the summer months, IU is encouraging students to get involved in "professional development activities," from the more traditional summer internships with corporations to a Washington Campus Program that will give students an opportunity to see the Clinton Administration at work. The university also has well-known foreign language and culture institutes on campus for those bound for careers in international business. Among other things, there are summer internships in Germany, Finland, and Slovenia.

In year two, IU now lets students tailor the MBA to their own interests. You can select a major—requiring four courses in a single discipline—or a double major. You can do a major and a minor, or even design your own concentration of advanced study with a faculty advisor, taking courses outside the B-school. There are only three required courses in the second year: The Legal Environment, Macroeconomics, and Strategic Management. An interdisciplinary major in international business includes language and culture requirements.

All of this experimentation is occurring in an attractive, if isolated, environment. With its rolling green hills and broad-branched trees, the campus could easily be the backdrop for a movie about collegiate life. The university, in fact, was the setting for the hit film *Breaking Away* about the Little 500 bicycle race, an annual fixture of Bloomington life. It's what you'd expect of a quaint town in Indiana with a courthouse square, whose population swells by 36,000 students when the university is in session. Many of the school's ivy-covered buildings were constructed at the turn of the century using Indiana limestone.

There are plenty of grassy areas for spreading out your books and studying on a sunny day. "This is a wonderful place to live," says Michael B. Metzger, one of the B-school's top teachers. "I can go to a dinner and a play on Friday night for chicken feed, go to a football game on Saturday afternoon, and go to the opera Saturday night. And the odds of getting mugged are really small. It's great." A few years ago, Metzger turned down an endowed chair at another university that would have made him the highest-paid professor in business law in the country because he's so smitten by the quality of life here.

Business students call home a seven-story, nondescript limestone building that houses administration, faculty, and classrooms. The B-school also contains the placement office, an MBA lounge, and eight computer-equipped labs. The adjoining business library also serves the School of Public and Environmental Affairs. On a nice day, students brown-bag it to the second-floor patio outside. Some first-year MBAs reside at Eigenmann Hall, a high-rise dorm for graduate students two blocks from the B-school. Because demand outstrips supply, however, most grads move into their own apartments around town. Married students sometimes commute from the south side of Indianapolis because it's difficult for spouses to find work in Bloomington, which has a population of 60,000. IU does hire spouses of some MBAs, but often the work is routine or clerical.

Asked to describe their MBA education, most grads eventually come around to using the word "fun." That's because extracurricular activities assume a large role in student life. The school views its MBA program not as a set of courses, but as a total experience, encompassing both academic and personal development. Almost all of the students join the MBA Association, the umbrella group for 14 special interest groups. Students pay $150 for a two-year MBAA membership. Some of these, such as the Investment Club, help students network by planning field trips and bringing industry speakers to campus. Others handle the MBA newsletter, social events, a teaching evaluation report, and public relations. There are club meetings and functions at the B-school every night. "This building is jammed in the evening with a variety of activities," says Wentworth. "It's one of the advantages of being in a small town with not a whole heck of a lot to do."

One thing they do is congregate every Thursday night at a "designated bar" chosen by the MBAA. Students try to close such popular spots as The Crazy Horse, The Irish Lion, and J. Arthur's. Not to worry. There are no classes on Friday. On other evenings, the association may sponsor theme parties where grads dress up as beach bums, Elvis impersonators, or natives of Wisconsin (for this latter event, MBAs don flannel shirts and Brewers' caps, chatter about bowling, and swill Leinenkugel beer). The best pizza

in town can be had at Nick's English Hut, 10 blocks from the B-school. It's a dark and dingy place, stuffed with basketball memorabilia. Autographed pictures of successful IU alums are hung along the painted dark-brown paneling.

PLACEMENT DETAILS

For years, Indiana boasted a remarkable placement operation, which is why Indiana does so well on BUSINESS WEEK's corporate rankings. However, the latest crop of MBAs are beginning to complain about a lack of geographically diverse recruiters. Students say it's hard for them to find jobs outside of the Midwest. And those complaints contributed to the school's plunge in BUSINESS WEEK's rankings.

That's not to say that Indiana doesn't run a first-class placement office. At Indiana, the search for a job begins before the first class. During orientation week, new MBA students explore career options, polish up their résumés on personal computers, and learn how to find summer internships. Plenty of schools have an assistant dean for alumni relations, but how many have an assistant dean for company relations? At Indiana, that position is held by C. Randall (Randy) Powell. For years, he has made the MBA program here unique—something that has now obviously changed because of the new curriculum.

When corporate recruiters and speakers come to IU, they stay in the Indiana Memorial Union, a stately limestone building that serves as a hotel and conference center. They often have lunch or dinner with faculty members, who tip them off about promising students. Choice football tickets are part of the VIP treatment recruiters get at Indiana. "We treat recruiters like they are customers," Powell says. "You have to provide good service if you want customers to come back year after year."

Last year, Powell and his staff brought 223 companies to Bloomington for recruiting. He helps nearly three-fourths of the school's MBA students find summer internships and more than 85 percent find a job after graduation. Powell's so aggressive that some grads grouse that his office encourages MBAs to forgo salary negotiations with recruiters and immediately to accept any offer—a reason why MBA starting salaries here are not as high as those of other leading business schools. At least, that's what some of Indiana's MBAs maintain.

In any case, the job search is taken very seriously here. After a student types up his or her résumé on a computer during orientation, it is immediately entered into the school's database. Student résumés are made available to employers in both book form and on floppy disk. Like other major B-schools, Indiana students are allocated points that they "bid" to interview with a particular company. The typical MBA here has between 15 and 20 interviews in the second year. These are held in one of 40 interviewing rooms in a $2 million complex built in the early 1980s and dubbed "Powell's Placement Palace."

Indiana may not be known for its placing power on Wall Street, but alums working there are willing to spend time with IU MBAs. The Investment Club visits trading rooms and meets with partners at major securities firms. Goldman, Sachs & Co., Salomon Brothers Inc., Kidder Peabody, and Merrill Lynch Capital Markets recruit on campus. They were among the 230 companies that recruited on campus in 1996, conducting 3402 interviews with Indiana students. Eli Lilly & Co. hauled away the most Indiana MBAs in 1996, hiring 10 grads. Other major employers: Ford Motor (9); Intel (8); Hewlett-Packard (5); Deloitte & Touche (5); Tandem Computers (5); General Motors (5); Citibank (4); and American Airlines (4). Quaker Oats, Sprint, NCR, Coopers & Lybrand, Andersen Consulting, and Boise Cascade each hired three grads.

IU has a truly innovative MBA program and an incredible placement machine. Now it needs a new dean to put it back on track.

OUTSTANDING FACULTY

John Boquist (****—finance); *Wayne Winston* (****—statistics); *Jamie Pratt* (****—accounting); *Mike Metzger* (***—business law); *Scott Smart* (***—finance); *Ronald Stephenson* (***—marketing); *George Hettenhouse* (***—finance); *Arlen Langvardt* (***—business law); *Doug Blocher* (**—operations); *Robert Parry* (**—accounting).

APPLICANT TIPS

Apply early, even though the school maintains only one deadline for applicants. Interviews are "strongly recommended" but are not required. Still, the school interviewed 52 percent of its applicants in 1996. To arrange an interview, call the MBA Office at 812-855-8006 two weeks in advance of a campus visit. Indiana will heavily weigh your GMAT scores and your answers to a trio of mandatory essay questions. It would be wise, as well, to complete the optional essay question to demonstrate your interest in getting into the school. The early deadline for domestic applications is January 6, while all international applicants must apply by February 1.

Contact: James Holmen
Director of Admissions
812-855-8006
Final application deadline: March 1 for fall

INDIANA MBAs SOUND OFF:

My MBA experience at Indiana University was extremely challenging and rewarding. I feel the broad based core curriculum in the first year is very beneficial to both generalists and specialists. I think it allows/forces everyone to consider all functions of business and how they impact one another. This base knowledge was extremely helpful in my internship experience and also resulted in an interest in areas I would have not considered without those introductory/core classes. As for my Finance major, all I can say is John Baquist! He is a superb professor! Faculty are open to and in fact encourage students to stop by or call to discuss class concepts, current topics in industry, or to offer any career guidance. These are relationships which will continue long after graduation.

The quality of teaching in the core classes during the first year is hit and miss. In one class you may have a top quality professor while the professor for the next class may be a real clunker. The quality of the Business Placement office is excellent. I expected a lot when I got here due to the advanced billing the BPO had received and it surpassed my high expectations.

The education I received in Bloomington was excellent. The finance faculty are exceptional. You are not just a "number" in the IU MBA program. The administration listens to the input from the students; changes are made because of our comments. Bloomington is a great place to live; the quality of life here is

excellent. If I had it to do all over again, I'd most definitely return to IU.

Finance is by far the best major in the program. The finance faculty is superior to their counterparts in other disciplines. However, overall the teaching is mediocre. The placement office does an excellent job placing students with Fortune 500 companies. This seems to be Indiana's niche with recruiters, particularly in corporate finance.

Perhaps the most unique aspect about the IU MBA program is the sense of real community and camaraderie amongst the MBAs, the faculty, and the administration. This is no doubt facilitated by the fact that we're all in Bloomington, rather than Chicago or New York or LA. It's rare for MBAs to live farther than 10 minutes from each other, which makes both team projects and social interaction much easier. In the last two years I've been invited to faculty members' homes four times, and it's common to see some faculty out to dinner or at the Thursday Social Club with students. In short, I spent two years of my life and tens of thousands of dollars to receive an education and a career change. But I got so much more.

**16.
WASHINGTON
UNIVERSITY**

WASHINGTON UNIVERSITY

John M. Olin School of Business
Campus Box 1133
One Brookings Drive
St. Louis, Missouri 63130
E-mail address: mba@olin.wustl.edu
Web-site address: http://www.olin.wustl.edu

Corporate ranking: 20	Graduate ranking: 12
Enrollment: 545	Annual tuition & fees: $20,100
Women: 30%	Room and board: $7954
Non-U.S.: 39%	Average GMAT score: 606
Minority: 6%	GMAT range: 470–770
Part-time: 255	Average GPA: 3.2
Average age: 27.7	GPA range: 2.5–3.9
Applicants accepted: 43.5%	Accepted applicants enrolled: 40%
Median starting pay: $62,750	Average starting pay: $61,800

Teaching methods: Lecture, 55% Case study, 30%
Group projects, 15%

Contact:
Deborah Booker
Director of MBA
Admissions
314-935-7301
*Final application
deadline:* March 30

Sitting in the steam bath, naked but for a towel, Stuart Greenbaum learned how to run a business school. Starting in the 1980s, Greenbaum, then a banking professor at Northwestern's Kellogg School, regularly joined Donald P. Jacobs and a few colleagues at a Russian steam bath in Chicago. The sweat-soaked bull sessions covered politics, baseball, and, above all, ways to help Jacobs turn Kellogg into one of the nation's best B-schools.

All that perspiration paid off. Kellogg, as most know, has emerged from the relative obscurity of a top regional school and is now one of a handful of the most high-profile MBA programs in the world. Now, another business school turnaround is beginning—this time, with Greenbaum at the helm. In July, 1995, after two decades at Kellogg, Greenbaum, 59, moved down Interstate 55 to St. Louis to become dean of Washington University's John M. Olin School of Business. In just his first year, he overhauled the curriculum, recruited 20 new professors, and planned a new building. "I wanted to see if I could do it myself," he says.

He's certainly off to a good start. After falling out of the Top 25 in 1994, Olin vaulted to No. 16 in this year's rankings, largely on the strength of massive improvements in student satisfaction. "He has exhibited vast leadership ability with his can-do attitude," says one '96 grad. "I almost envy students who will start the WU MBA program under his leadership." Indeed, no administration gets higher marks for responding to students concerns—and Wharton, which came in at No. 2 in the category, really isn't that close. Recruiters have been impressed, too. "I've noticed a new esprit de corps there," says Sean D. Kenny, a partner at Ernst & Young, the largest recruiter at Olin.

The blueprint sure looks familiar. From the advisory boards of local business people he has set up, to the array of flags from students' home countries he has hung in the lobby, many of Greenbaum's ideas have been modeled after those tried at Kellogg. Thanksgiving with the dean, a faculty orientation program, a remodeled student lounge, an executive manufacturing program—and the center that will house it: They all sprang from Kellogg. About the only thing that's missing is a strip of Northwestern purple paint around the school's faux-Gothic building. "Copy shamelessly," said a grinning Greenbaum, while wearing a Cardinal red "Olin" hat and taking in a St. Louis Cardinals game last summer. "I'll copy anything that works."

Greenbaum's arrival ended a tough time for Olin, which had foundered after the 1992 semi-retirement of longtime Dean Robert L. Virgil. The school went three years without a permanent dean, partly because candidates thought it was trying to run too many programs with its small faculty. "We were rudderless," says Emerson Electric Chairman Charles F. Knight, who heads Olin's advisory council. The school turned down two of its three best teachers for tenure—a remarkable move at a small school allegedly dedicated to teaching.

Looking to Kellogg for a leader made sense. In recent years, the Kellogg philosophy—that universities must shed their arrogance and pay more attention to students—has swept across American B-schools. Certainly, Greenbaum practiced those ideas at Kellogg. He devised some of its best-known programs, including one in which students try to use Total Quality Management techniques to help urban public schools run better.

Yet Greenbaum and Olin weren't an obvious fit. The dean is the son of a New York butcher and has the accent to prove it. When he finishes telling a story, he frequently adds, "Mmm?" just to make sure the listener is with him. He's an opera fan, and, at least for a B-school dean, he is rather liberal. That's not exactly a résumé that would leap out at a Midwestern school surrounded by a conservative business community.

Indeed, it didn't. The search committee offered the job to at least four other people before Greenbaum. When Olin did finally turn to him, he turned it down. "Frankly," he says, "I was a little bit insulted." An appeal from former Dean Virgil helped change his mind, and the marriage has worked quite well since.

Greenbaum's work is made easier by St. Louis's large corporate community. While the disappearance of McDonnell Douglas, which is merging with Boeing, hurts the region, it's still home to almost 10 major companies—including Ralston Purina Co. and Monsanto Co. Already, the dean has lobbied Anheuser Busch Cos. and others to get more involved in the school. Meanwhile, the school's $100 million endowment—larger than that of many other top schools, including Duke's Fuqua and Dartmouth's Tuck—gives it the firepower to try imitating the success of Washington University's nationally respected medical school.

What are Olin's other strengths? The quality of teaching is one of them, having rebounded from the dismissals of a few years past. Indeed, only three rivals get better marks for their electives. Classmates rarely emphasize individual achievement over group work, students say. Combined with an administration that always seems to have its ears open, that creates a terrific atmosphere that resembles the ideal of a small school. While attracting a large number of big-name recruiters is still something of a problem, the career service office gets top marks for helping out MBAs. And Greenbaum—a TQM nut who quotes the late quality guru Edward Deming almost as often as he cites Casey Stengel—has helped boost the school's program in quality concepts to the No. 1 spot, according to the class of '96.

But Wash. U. can't yet be confused with a Tuck or a Darden, small schools that are among the nation's few best. It has yet to attract a sufficiently large cadre of corporate recruiters who aren't based in the Midwest. Greenbaum is still trying to woo some big-name faculty who would help put Olin on the international management education map. The school's information technology program is only mediocre when compared to rivals'. At $61,800, Olin MBAs' average pay package at graduation trails most other Top 25 schools by a wide margin. The school is also alarmingly homogeneous: only 6 percent of the student body is African-American, Latino, or Native American.

When students arrive at Olin, they begin the program with a self-assessment of interpersonal, team, negotiation, and communications skills as well as potential career interests. Based on the results of such tests, MBA candidates design with faculty advisers a proposed course of study. "Our new model says 'measure what each student needs, help the student make an informed decision about a career target, then help him or her choose from Olin's rich offerings the best courses to achieve these objectives,' " says Dean Kropp, a popular manufacturing professor who worked on the MBA curriculum revision. "We focus on the students' learning needs rather than on standardized course offerings." The stripped-down core curriculum covers the business basics: management, economics, accounting, statistics, and business strategy. And then students must choose several courses from what Olin calls a "flexible core": finance, marketing, operations, global issues in management, and public policy. MBAs take an integrative capstone course in business strategy during their last term that requires the creation of a business or strategic

plan for a new or existing business. The rest of the entire program is filled with electives, half of them mini-courses. In any given year, Olin offers MBAs a menu of 69 different elective courses, from those on health services management to leadership.

To appeal to the growing number of companies looking for students with specialized skills—instead of the middle managers of yesterday—Greenbaum wants just 20 percent of a student's credits to come from the core, down from 40 percent in 1996 and 60 percent in 1995. He also wants to drop letter grades in order to focus students more on learning than on competition. That could be risky, though, since recruiters often rely on grades at a school like Olin to pick job prospects.

There are no dorms or graduate housing here, so most students live in apartments and shared homes within about five miles of campus. They commute to a school where the architecture imitates the Gothic style of Oxford and Cambridge and Harvard and Yale. But there's a twist here. These buildings are made of natural red granite, a local resource. The result is a cheerier and newer looking campus that still retains the feel of a tradition-laden school.

It sits on the top of a hill that overlooks a number of St. Louis's neighboring suburbs (though Olin claims to be an urban school). Students typically hang out at Blueberry Hill, which is famous for its burgers, and M.P. O'Reilly's. St. Louis itself is not one of the nation's most dynamic cities, in terms of culture and nightlife, but it's not boring, either. There's the Cental West End, home to O'Reilly's and other restaurants and bars where singles and young couples congregate. A lively blues scene fills the local papers' music listing. The Anheuser Busch brewery tour offers a nice way to spend a day with visitors. And, of course, there's the Mississippi River, which runs right beside the city's most famous landmark: the Jefferson National Expansion Memorial, better known as the Gateway Arch.

PLACEMENT DETAILS

Upon graduation, a good number of MBAs stick around and that could increase as Greenbaum convinces still more corporations in the area to hire his graduates. In 1996, some 125 companies came to campus to conduct 1188 interviews with second-year MBA candidates. Some 754 job opportunities—full-time and summer—were available to students by correspondence. The upshot: Olin grads averaged 3.3 job offers at graduation, a rate better than such schools as Columbia, Virginia, and Dartmouth. Of course, what Olin MBAs pulled down in median starting pay didn't come close to student salaries at those other schools. The median pay was $62,750, compared to $88,850 at Columbia, $85,000 at Virginia, and $105,000 at Dartmouth.

The school's most important recruiters in 1996: Ernst & Young (6); KPMG Peat Marwick (4); Arthur Andersen (4); Price Waterhouse (4); Hewlett-Packard (3); Exxon (3); Anheuser-Busch (3); Andersen Consulting (3); Emerson Electric (2); and Ralston Purina (2).

Olin's best feature these days may be that it's a place on the rise. Most students, professors, and staff members are happy to be part of that and eager to do their part. The result: a thriving community where things get done faster than they do at more established institutions. Its worst feature? Well, if you ask a certain dean, he'll tell you that he hasn't found a good place just to sit and sweat. "I miss it," he says. You know what that means: look for a steam bath to come to Olin soon.

OUTSTANDING FACULTY

Mahendra Gupta (****—accounting); *Dean H. Kropp* (****—operations); *Russell Roberts* (****—economics and entrepreneurship); *Joe Zhongquan Zhou* (***—finance); *Raj Singh* (**—finance); *Srinivasan Maheswaran* (**—finance); *Nick Baloff* (**—organizational

behavior); *Chun-Lun Li* (**—management science); *Rachel Schwartz* (**—accounting); *Stuart Greenbaum* (*—finance).

APPLICANT TIPS

Like other top business schools, Olin looks closely at undergraduate grades as well as at GMAT scores, but also examines an applicant's goals, motivation, experiences, and activities—as well as how well an applicant communicates those to the school in writing. The school says applicants do not require previous course work in business, but they should have "reasonable preparation" in mathematics and be prepared to study calculus in the first semester of the program. Interviews are not required for domestic applicants, but the school "strongly encourages" them. All international applicants must interview by telephone with the director of admissions or with a member of the MBA admissions committee. About 85 percent of applicants were interviewed in 1996. To arrange a visit or an interview, you may contact admissions at 800-MBA-3MBA or via fax at 314-935-6309. Olin begins reviewing applications in January and admits applicants on a rolling basis thereafter.

Contact: Deborah Booker
Director of MBA Admissions
314-935-7301
Final application deadline: March 30

OLIN MBAs SOUND OFF

Since the arrival of our new dean, Stuart Greenbaum, the campus has quickly evolved into a new atmosphere. Dean Greenbaum has provided leadership under which administration, faculty, and students have made proactive changes. The revamping of Olin's curriculum drew on all these resources. The result produced will allow greater flexibility among future students. This is a great example of how the new Olin has been working together to improve the Olin MBA.

I feel very fortunate to be a part of the "new" Olin under the leadership of Stuart Greenbaum. He cares about the students and their MBA experiences. He makes a significant effort to interact regularly with us, either by attending our scheduled parties or through his monthly "Brown Bag Lunches with Dean Greenbaum." A new attitude exists among the students, faculty, staff, and administration that represents Stuart's strive to excellence.

There is exceptional teamwork and camaraderie both in and out of school. There are excellent library facilities. However, too many good and outstanding teachers are let go or not tenured for reasons unrelated to their teaching ability.

The placement office puts in a lot of time helping students. They do a great job of increasing the reputation of Wash. U.

Disappointments include the low numbers of minorities (particularly blacks, who represented perhaps 1 percent of the class) and the difficulties of 1st- and 2nd-year student interaction. On the whole, however, my experience at Olin has been very good. . . .

Olin's relationship with the St. Louis corporate community provides students with numerous opportunities to meet personally with business leaders. Opportunities to apply knowledge to practical projects abound at Olin.

The Management Center Practicum (a student consulting project) gave me great insights on how top managers think. The school facilities are excellent, except for a shortage of parking lots. The current students have complained that the school requires too many core courses, and this will change under the new curriculum starting in 1996.

The nature of the program allows students to get to know the faculty on a highly personal level and to learn about their research. Similarly, it is very easy to get to know every classmate and establish strong personal relationships that will last beyond graduation.

We do most of our work in teams in a very cooperative environment. You often learn as much from each other as from the professors. The professors are all extremely accessible to the students. They are our friends as well as our mentors.

Outside of school, group projects provide a unique opportunity to apply skills to real-life business situations. There are plenty of opportunities to interact with alumni/local businesses. The small size of the class allows an intimate learning opportunity. One knows the professors are always available to students, both in and out of the classroom.

17. CARNEGIE MELLON UNIVERSITY

CARNEGIE MELLON UNIVERSITY

Graduate School of Industrial Administration
Schenley Park
Pittsburgh, Pennsylvania 15213-38990
E-mail address: gsia-admissions@andrew.cmu.edu
Website address: http://www.gsia.cmu.edu

Corporate ranking: 26	Graduate ranking: 5
Enrollment: 738	Annual tuition & fees: $22,200
Women: 19.1%	Room and board: $7080
Non-U.S.: 38.2%	Average GMAT score: 638
Minority: 1.8%	Average GPA: 3.2
Part-time: 200	GPA range: 2.1 to 4.0
Average age: 27	Average years of work exp.: 4.4
Applicants accepted: 31%	Accepted applicants enrolled: 65%
Median starting pay: $81,180	Average starting pay: $85,690

Teaching methods: Lecture, 50%   Case study, 20%   Projects, 30%

Contact:
Susan Motz
Admissions Director
412-268-2272
*Final application
deadline:* March 15
for fall

Tired of all this talk about "managing people"? You know that management is important, but you think you can learn it as you go. You see no need to take semester after semester of courses in "soft skills." Above all, you want to leave business school with identifiable skills you didn't have when you entered. You want to be comfortable with some high-powered number-crunching, never again to be scared by a balance sheet, and to be able to pass as a computer expert.

Sound at all familiar? If it does, you should shift your gaze toward Pittsburgh and consider Carnegie Mellon's School of Industrial Administration. Few places will give you the solid grounding in operations, finance, or analytical skills that GSIA will. Furthermore, the quality of teaching in its core and elective classes get absolutely top marks from students. Faculty are at the leading edge of their fields, they make time for out-of-class chats, and they integrate material across classes, according to recent grads. You'll leave feeling comfortable with computers and new telecommunications tools. And only the University of Virginia's Darden School will give a bigger percentage boost from your pre-MBA salary to your post-degree base pay.

In the summer of 1996, the school for the first time hired a dean from the corporate world: Douglas M. Dunn, who spent 26 years at AT&T. His challenges include maintaining Carnegie's strengths, raising its slipping profile among corporate recruiters, and ensuring that the school's curriculum does not become too focused on quantitative subjects. He'll also need to figure out a way to diversify the student body. Only 19 percent of GSIA students are female, and just 2 percent are

African-American, Latino, or Native American—both easily the lowest percentages for any Top 25 school.

Dunn follows Robert S. Sullivan, who arrived in mid-1991 in the middle of a wicked storm. Students griped about being squeezed out of popular classes, being forced to take courses out of sequence, and a placement office that was, in the words of one graduate, "uncaring, unresponsive, and ineffective." But Sullivan, who had been an associate dean at the University of Texas at Austin, engineered something of a turnaround. In 1996, Carnegie finished 5th in BUSINESS WEEK's poll of B-school graduates—up from 23rd in 1990. Sullivan maintained an open-door policy at his office, held regular brown bag luncheons in the cafeteria, and sponsored monthly student dinners at his home. He placed pervasive emphasis on student satisfaction, quality, and continuous improvement, even sending most of his administrative staff to Total Quality Management training.

Besides being far more user-friendly, GSIA today gives students more flexibility in scheduling required courses and has dramatically improved its ability to meet student demands for the most popular courses. The school also offers collaborative and joint master's programs in computational science, manufacturing management, environmental engineering, and software engineering and management. To encourage more interaction between faculty and students, Sullivan began an advising program in which every faculty member has 8 to 10 MBA candidates assigned to him or her from the first-year class, along with a second-year student mentor.

By nearly all accounts, first-year students badly need the help. The school dumps so much work on them that sheer survival often seems more important than learning. Students routinely describe the experience as grueling and agonizing. Some describe it as an "academic hazing." When they finally graduate, some say the first year is little more than a blur. Said Sulli-

van, while he was still dean: "We're not a party school. We don't bond. But our students are close to each other because they work so hard together."

There's certainly some truth in that. Teamwork is fostered as a means of making it through this boot camp. The quick and daunting pace teaches at least one critical lesson: the interdependence of the group and the need to prioritize everything. It would be tough enough if Carnegie Mellon weren't a quant school, but its emphasis on mathematics and quantitative methods can make the workload even more staggering. The school's own research shows that it requires more than five times the amount of class time on quantitative subjects than Harvard and twice as much as Stanford or Columbia. Even courses that are not usually laden with lots of quant work, such as microeconomics, have a heavily mathematical bent at Carnegie Mellon.

The bent shows in the degree graduates receive and the way that Corporate America views them. You don't get an MBA here. You get a Master's of Science in Industrial Administration, or an MSIA. And while corporate recruiters say that the school is one of their favorite places to find grads with strong operations or analytical skills, they're much less enthusiastic about the Carnegie students who try to enter marketing and general management and the ability of all Carnegie students to work as team players.

But the rigor of this program should not be mistaken for rigidity. In fact, Carnegie Mellon has long been one of the more innovative B-schools over the years, pioneering truly creative courses taught by an eclectic faculty. And though the school is considered a B-school leader in manufacturing, its efforts in both finance and entrepreneurship are significantly stronger. Dunn has said he plans to make entrepreneurship a significantly larger part of the core in coming years.

All of Carnegie's courses fit into an unusual mini-semester that is about seven and one-half weeks long—a format that many other B-schools are only now adopting as they revise their curriculums. The eight minis over the two years allow students to take as many as 18 electives without overloading their schedules. That's almost as many electives as some schools require in total courses to graduate. Five courses per mini add up to 40 courses over the length of this program. Of course, these classes are compressed to fit the mini-semester format, so a few of them extend over two mini-semesters.

On the other hand, within three and one-half weeks of your arrival here, you'll already be sitting down for midterm exams. Study groups convene until 2 or 3 a.m. Students without quant backgrounds often panic because Carnegie profs pack an incredible amount of work in a single mini. "I don't think there's a program in the country that works them harder," says one associate dean. "We work their butts off, and that's one of the comforts they have in going out into the real world. They're used to working hard, and no one can work them harder than we do."

Nearly half of the total courses you'll take are required, versus about 40 percent at many other top schools. The centerpiece of the program is The Management Game. Pioneered by Carnegie Mellon in the 1950s, the game is a computer simulation of the soap industry, originally based on Procter & Gamble. Every second-year student is assigned to a six-person team made up of a president and a host of functional vice presidents who guide their companies through a two-year business cycle over a 15-week period. It's another aspect of the experience here that many other B-schools are only now putting into their revamped programs.

Some older students grouse that the game can become overly repetitive and simpleminded, but most students have good things to say about the experience it gives them. Besides, Carnegie recently added a new, creative wrinkle: While its students play the game, it's also being offered simultaneously at business schools in Japan (Aoyama Gakuin), Sweden (Umea), and Mexico (Monterrey Tech), so Carnegie MBAs find themselves in competition with others outside the school. Students even have to negotiate a labor agreement with local union leaders from the steel industry. Computers also put together multimedia marketing campaigns that are judged by local advertising agencies. And each team has to overcome and survive a crisis—whether charges of price-fixing, employee discrimination, or the dumping of a toxic waste—by, among other things, meeting with local reporters.

Each of the teams reports to a board of directors that actually meets in one of the plush and well-appointed boardrooms of some of Pittsburgh's leading corporations, from H.J. Heinz to the Mellon Bank. On each board sits a faculty member and a handful of senior corporate executives, from the chief financial officer of Texas Instruments to a Hewlett-Packard vice president. The board can be tough and demanding. "You're desperately trying to please your board," recalls one graduate, who reported to an unusually hard-to-please chairman. "He'd look at every move we made with a microscope, and continually say, 'It hasn't been like this in the past. I'm not sure you're sticking to the strategy. We have to crush the competition.' We had the dominant market share, but he still wasn't satisfied. We nicknamed him Mr. Marketshare."

If the game helps to prepare students for general management assignments, Wall Street-bound students gain invaluable insights into today's global financial markets through the school's unique Financial Analysis and Security Trading (FAST) room. It's a multimillion-dollar facility that replicates the computer workstations, live international data feeds, and sophisticated software of Wall Street's top trading firms. GSIA profs steeped in finance, math, technology, and behavioral science use it as a laboratory to explore key issues in computer trading and financial engineering.

As elective offerings, you'll get to pick from among 112 courses in any given academic year.

The catalog lists some novel choices, as well as French, German, and Japanese language courses for business. A new Business Drama elective is taught by the Fine Arts faculty. By far, the most popular elective is Gerald Meyers's Business Leadership in Changing Times. The former chairman of American Motors Corp. invites top executives to class on a regular basis to discuss the trials and tribulations of leadership. In 1993–1994, students heard Alcoa Chairman Paul O'Neill, Chase Manhattan CEO Thomas Labreque, and Emerson Electric Chairman Charles Knight, among others.

The school also numbers among its faculty Jean-Jacques Servan-Schreiber, former French cabinet minister and best-selling author of *The American Challenge.* In his highly rated course, Strategic Thinking, he draws analogies between military and business wars in teaching about global markets. Grads also have good things to say about John R. Thorne, who directs Carnegie Mellon's Center for Entrepreneurship.

For a school known for its "quant jocks," you'd hardly think there would be much happening on the entrepreneurial side. But GSIA boasts a complete entrepreneurship track taught by experienced business hands, and a recent survey showed that more than 28 percent of the school's total alumni base are engaged with entrepreneurial ventures. There's even a project course that has become the springboard for students to launch their own businesses. In both 1989 and 1990, Carnegie Mellon students beat out teams from other top schools in "Moot Corp.," a national entrepreneurship competition sponsored by the University of Texas. Teams of GSIA students also carried away the top prize in the American Marketing Association's graduate Case Competition for three years in a row, and in 1992 won the inaugural Graduate Business Conference case competition.

More than most schools, the faculty members at Carnegie Mellon are at the leading edge of knowledge in their fields. Dunn wants to work with the faculty to focus on the effects that digitalization and deregulation will have on business. Despite the school's research slant, it boasts some superb teachers, and the student-faculty ratio of 5.8 to 1 is one of the lowest at the major schools.

The research emphasis also has allowed the school to pioneer several breakthroughs in management theory and practice over the years, from the rational expectations concept in economics to new fields of cognitive psychology and computer science. There are neither departments nor required majors or concentration areas because the school emphasizes what it calls "interdisciplinary thinking"—yet another supposed innovation at schools redoing their programs these days.

If you're wondering about life in Pittsburgh, don't. Forget the old polluted and smokestacked image of the place. It's an attractive city of ethnic neighborhoods, the intellectual community of which is Oakland, where the university makes its home. There's no dorm life at the school. Instead, students are scattered around the city in different apartments and houses. It's wise to live within walking or bicycling distance because, as one student complained, "Parking is hell!" Once on campus, however, students tend to stay, spending vast amounts of time in Hunt Library, the university library next to the B-school, or walking and studying in neighboring Schenley Park, Pittsburgh's version of Central Park in New York. The school also recently moved to a new, modern building, twice the size of the old, three-story, yellow brick structure that had been home to the business school for 40 years. The $14 million project boasts excellent high-tech classrooms, computing facilities, a comfy student lounge, and social activity areas.

GSIA students tend to gravitate to Doc's in Shadyside and Chiodo's bar featuring a collection of Pittsburgh memorabilia. Adjacent to the old steel works in Homestead in the eastern part of the city, this gathering hole is where students traditionally congregate for a wild celebration after final exams. The Squirrel Hill Cafe and Silky's, both a 15- to 20-minute walk from campus, are other GSIA hot spots. All three joints are favorite stops for the regular Tuesday night bar crawls. (There are no classes on Wednesdays.)

PLACEMENT DETAILS

Even though the school's corporate rankings are somewhat weak, the placement office has worked miracles for graduating students. MBAs averaged 3.3 job offers by graduation—up from 2.7 two years earlier, and better than the 2.8 average for the Top 50 schools. Hiring the largest batches of GSIA grads in 1996 were Deloitte & Touche (13); Ford Motor (8); Intel (8); Ernst & Young (7); Coopers & Lybrand (6); PNC Bank (6); Citibank (5); Hewlett-Packard (5); TRW (5); Bankers Trust (4); Diamond Technologies (4); and Price Waterhouse (4).

OUTSTANDING FACULTY

Fallaw B. Sowell (****—economics), *John Mather* (****—marketing); *Jeffrey R. Williams* (****—strategy); *Richard Green* (***—finance); *Chris Telmer* (**—finance); *Gerald Meyers* (**—management); *Allen Meltzer* (**—capitalism); *Duane J. Seppi* (**—finance); *Ronen Israel* (*—finance); *Sridhar R. Tayur* (*—manufacturing).

APPLICANT TIPS

Here's a school where female and minority applicants are likely to have an important advantage. The reason: Of all the Top 25 business schools, Carnegie Mellon is dead last in the number of minorities and women currently enrolled in its MBA program. Only 2 percent of its full-time MBA students are minorities, while only 19 percent are female. It's possible that the engineering and quantitative aspects of this school make it difficult for Carnegie to attract qualified women and minority candidates for admission. Still, the school will have to tackle these deficiencies aggressively, making it slightly easier for women and minorities to get in over the next few years. On the other hand, Carnegie Mellon boasts the third highest percentage of non-U.S. students of any major business school. That's also worth noting because it may well give a slight advantage to qualified domestic applicants. One critical element is previous coursework and a demonstrated capacity for mathematics, because this program is quantitatively and analytically oriented. Indeed, admissions requires applicants to have completed two semesters of calculus before enrolling—if not by application time.

The school seeks "highly motivated, self-directed, energetic, and innovative" students. Admissions examines the applicant's entire academic record, not just the overall grade point average. The school pays attention to grade trends, the major, the school, extracurricular activities, and work experience.

Interviews are required and can be conducted on- or off-campus, or even by telephone. To arrange for an interview, you may contact the admissions office at 412-268-2272. Carnegie Mellon has four application deadline periods, the first of which ends on November 15 for a decision by December 15. The other deadlines are January 15, March 15, and post-March 15 on a rolling admissions basis. Generally, the school gets back to applicants within one month of receipt of the completed application. Obviously, if you apply beyond the more-or-less final deadline of March 15, your odds of getting into the program are likely to be diminished.

Contact: Susan Motz
Admissions Director
412-268-2272
Final application deadline: March 15 for fall

CARNEGIE MELLON GRADS SOUND OFF

Carnegie isn't for everyone. It emphasizes quantitative skills, and it is hard. There is a lot of work involved. But the education is excellent, the students are very supportive.

There is no conflict between research and teaching because research results are part of the classroom experience. The faculty makes sure students understand how the various functional areas of business interrelate. Graduates are the complete package: They think both strategically and analytically.

The weakness of the school lies in its inability to place people in elite jobs such as McKinsey Consulting and finance jobs on Wall Street. I attribute that more to the employers' unfamiliarity with the school than to our inability to perform the job. On the other hand, anyone coming out of the school possesses highly developed quantitative and analytical skills, and everyone I know has received multiple job offers. The school really prepares you for the real world; you work like crazy but later realize it pays off. Carnegie is on the cutting edge of technology always. The Career Center staff is doing an excellent job.

The professors are extremely accessible and can be found at the local bars buying students pitchers of beer! Due to the small size of the program, everyone knows everyone. Students share knowledge and even interview tips. This is not a cutthroat program. I would call it a "blue-collar" MBA program, where you get a lot of bang for the buck.

The program is structured in such a way as to let each individual pursue what he/she feels is in need of improvement. If "softer skills" need work, there are many classes to improve oneself. Because of the seven-week semesters, I was able to learn about many different fields that I had not been introduced to prior to business school.

The school is very quantitative. I think I am at an advantage over students from less quantitative schools.

I thought I knew a lot about computers before, but now I feel like I know everything. I will know more about computers than everyone else I will work with.

What impressed me was the quality of support for those who needed help on the quant side. Our "math camp" (held just before first-year classes started) was a great program, both academically and socially. Once classes started, tutors and help sessions were plentiful.

The international student body adds a tremendous amount of flavor to classes and social life. Teamwork is emphasized and encouraged, a very important part of the experience. I've made friends here that I have every intention of doing business with for decades to come.

I cannot recall running into a selfish individual. Everyone goes out of their way to give you help if it is needed. The quantitative approach is what brings everything together.

**18.
CORNELL
UNIVERSITY**

CORNELL UNIVERSITY

Johnson Graduate School of Management
Malott Hall
Ithaca, New York 14853-4201
E-mail address: mba@johnson.cornell.edu
Website address: http://www.gsm.cornell.edu

Corporate ranking: 18	Graduate ranking: 20
Enrollment: 513	Annual tuition & fees: $22,450
Women: 32%	Room and board: $7100
Non-U.S.: 28%	Average GMAT score: 634
Minority: 11%	Average GPA: 3.3
Part-time: none	GPA range: 2.3 to 4.0
Average age: 27	Average years of work exp.: 4
Applicants accepted: 25%	Accepted applicants enrolled: 38%
Median starting pay: $70,000	Average starting pay: $54,865

Teaching methods: Lecture, 50% Case study, 50%

Contact:
Daphne Atkinson
Director of Admissions
800-847-2082
*Final application
deadline:* March 15
for fall; January 25 for
12-month program

In the middle of a serene upstate New York town sits an intimate B-school within an Ivy League university. The Johnson School of Management has built strong links to the university's other options, offers a top-flight program in manufacturing, and has established ties with Asia, perhaps the world's most exciting region today. Some of the nation's best-respected experts in labor relations and hotel management call Cornell home. There's a supercomputer on which to test financial models, and a 12-month MBA for scientists who already hold a master's degree.

What could be better, right? Actually, a lot could. Beneath all of Cornell's obvious strengths, some major weaknesses lurk. As of the start of 1997, the school had still not raised all of the $38 million it needs to renovate its new home. No Top 25 school gets lower marks for its program in information technology. The career placement office has had trouble finding the right matches between its students and its corporate clients. Teaching, which once received excellent marks from students, is now in the middle of the Top 25 pack.

While top B-schools around the nation have spent much of the last decade instituting radical reforms, Cornell has largely stood pat. "We stopped to tie our shoes while the rest of the crew caught up," says Thomas Dyckman, the school's acting dean. In fact, it might be more accurate to say that the competition has *passed* Cornell. Ranked 5th when BUSINESS WEEK first started evaluating B-schools in 1988, Cornell has fallen all the way to 18th in 1996. No other school has slipped more.

What happened? In part, Cornell—with about 250 students per class—has always kept its students fairly satisfied. So it never had to institute the wide-scale and successful reforms that, say, Harvard has. The Johnson School now seems to do only a mediocre job of listening to its MBAs, precisely because it has never taken a good, long look in the mirror. At the same time, the school doesn't have nearly the support among corporate recruiters—particularly among major marketers and Wall Street firms—that its rivals enjoy. "We've tried to work at cross purposes," Dyckman says. "We've taken in too many Wall Street types without a big Wall Street network."

All that said, you can get quite an excellent education here, and the quality of life is comparable with that in Hanover, New Hampshire, or Charlottesville, Virginia. Tucked away in New York's Finger Lake region in Ithaca, Johnson's small class size fosters unusually close relationships between students and faculty—whether they're climbing mountains, debating an issue in class, or competing against each other in sports. A productive and caring faculty—who rarely compromise teaching for research, students say—create an intimate and challenging environment. Johnson faculty are among the most approachable and accessible professors in business education. They don't have to post office hours, as one graduate put it, because they are always there.

Indeed, one of the true annual events at the school is the battle between the Frozen Assets, the female MBAs' hockey team, and a group of professors. Faculty and students also compete against each other in the eight-mile Joe Thomas Invitational Run. The Johnson School's high level of faculty involvement and its flexible curriculum also win high marks from students. MBAs who are barely out the door already wax nostalgic about the Cornell experience and the virtues of life in Ithaca, a picturesque village overlooking Cayuga Lake. The school's isolated location fosters a community spirit, and the combination of a small student body and an involved faculty gives Johnson the freedom to be bold and experimental. It often forges links with other Cornell schools to develop unusual programs, encourages team teaching by professors from different disciplines, and creates novel international programs.

One of the most exciting developments has been the creation of the Park Leadership Fellowship. Funded by a foundation named after the late media entrepreneur Roy Park, the program will give $60,000 grants to 30 entering students. That will pay for tuition and still leave them some money as a stipend. The goal: woo top students with identifiable leadership potential away from the Whartons and Harvards of the B-school world. Predicts an optimistic Dyckman: "The Park Leadership Fellows program will eventually become the business world equivalent of the prestigious Rhodes Scholarship. Twenty-five years from now, Park Fellows will be disproportionately represented among the country's most influential leaders."

Johnson grads are less enthusiastic about the school's facilities and its placement office. Although Cornell's pastoral setting is great for studying and enjoying outdoor sports, it's off the beaten path for some recruiters. MBAs here have high expectations, and they should, considering Cornell's hefty price tag—$22,450 a year. The B-school, named after Samuel C. Johnson of Johnson's Wax fame, is no bargain when it comes to tuition. You'll get better bang for the buck at the University of North Carolina, Berkeley, or UCLA. Why? In 1996, the average MBA entered the school earning about $40,000 a year—the 18th highest pre-MBA salary among BUSINESS WEEK's Top 50. She left Johnson with a total pay package of $54,900—the 43rd highest. Meanwhile, she racked up more than $37,000 in debt.

Alan Merten, who served as dean from 1989 to 1996, increased the size of career services and worked on building better alumni support for new graduates, bringing out an alumni directory every two or three years instead of every five or six, producing upgraded monthly job listings for MBAs and an executive search manual, and getting Cornell to join a computer job-matching service. It's a cradle-to-grave approach. The school offers first-years a self-assessment workshop, and the school has hired a full-time staffer dedicated to nothing but counseling services for alumni.

Eventually, the career placement office will take its place in Sage Hall with the rest of the school. Across the street from both the B-school's current home and the famous School of Hotel Management, the historic building is being completely renovated. Construction began in the summer of '96, and, by the end of that year, administrators had $32 million of the $38 million they needed for the project. Even if they have to borrow the final $6 million, they say the building will open in the fall of '98. It should be an impressive mixture of Ivy League charm and state-of-the-art planning.

Cornell's strategy appears to keep its mainstream MBA pretty basic and to tap into the strengths of the rest of the university to make the Johnson degree unique. This has partly occurred through the creation of joint degree programs in Asian studies, engineering, and manufacturing. The newest of the four joint-degree programs is a three-year course of study that's a combined effort of the B-school and the School of Industrial and Labor Relations. Meanwhile, through the Cornell Manufacturing, Engineering, and Productivity Program, students with an undergraduate engineering degree and professional experience can obtain master's degrees in engineering and management in five semesters. The program also allows MBAs who concentrate in manufacturing management to sign up for engineering electives. In the spring of 1994 the school instituted a new 15-unit semester in manufacturing. Of course, there's also the 12-month MBA for those who

already have a master's degree in science or engineering. These quant jocks buzz through the core over the summer and then join the second-year class come September. The drawback: no chance for a summer internship.

Even if you decide you want the good-old straight MBA, there are some twists you can add. The Semester in Manufacturing is a 15-credit immersion class offered jointly by Johnson and the engineering and labor relations schools. Students who sign up take it as their sole course in the spring semester of their second year. Developed with the help of nearby Corning, it's been popular among both manufacturing types and future marketing gurus who want to understand how products are made. The school is now considering developing other immersion courses.

Meanwhile, in 1995 the school started offering a certificate in financial engineering in an attempt to address Wall Street's growing interest in mathematically sophisticated trading instruments. This is where you can find yourself playing with that supercomputer.

The Johnson School has won international recognition for two programs that teach MBAs about Japanese language and culture. The first is a three-year program leading to master's degrees in management and Asian studies. This option includes 12 months of intensive Japanese language classes and often a summer internship in Japan with firms such as Mobil Corp. Japan, Nippon Telegraph and Telephone, and Mitsubishi's chemical unit. The second is a two-year MBA course with a concentration in Japanese business that includes a summer of intensive language classes and Japanese classes throughout the year.

These rigorous Japanese business programs are more than something for Johnson MBAs to put on their résumés or talk about during job interviews. For students with the requisite talent and commitment, they often lead to lucrative management jobs with American companies in

Japan. After earning master's degrees in management and Asian studies, Jim Latimer, a Johnson alum, landed a job with Corning Glass's Japanese subsidiary.

Before he came to Cornell, Latimer had never spoken a word of Japanese. After earning an undergraduate degree from Georgia Tech, he had worked for robotics manufacturer Cincinnati Milacron for several years. "If you decide you want to learn Japanese as an adult, Cornell is one of the few places you can take the language for 12 months straight. The FALCON [Full-Year Asian Language Concentration] program is designed for people starting from scratch," he says. Other B-schools such as Michigan, Berkeley, and Wharton allow MBAs to simultaneously earn a master's in Asian studies, but few offer as innovative a program as Cornell's.

For the run-of-the-mill MBA, there's unusual flexibility and variety, including the choice of 67 electives at the B-school. The greater diversity, however, comes because Johnson MBAs may take more than 15 credits—or about 5 of the 20 courses required for an MBA—in other Cornell top-notch schools, including the College of Architecture, Art and Planning, and the College of Human Ecology, which offers courses in health administration. One 1992 grad boasts that he took 6 courses outside the B-school, including a pair at the law school, 2 in the natural resources program, 1 in agricultural economics, and another in government. "I was able to tailor my degree closely to the environmental concerns I have," he says.

To earn the typical MBA from the Johnson School, you'll need to spend four semesters in Ithaca and earn 60 credits. There are 8 courses equal to 22.5 credits in Johnson's core curriculum, 4 of which are taken in the first semester and 4 in the second semester. These include financial accounting, statistics, microeconomics, marketing, organizational behavior, finance, operations, and strategy.

During the second year, you'll design your own program of elective courses, taking a series of classes as broad or specialized as you like. Johnson provides "road maps" or lists of suggested classes for students pursuing a specific career track, but does not require students to concentrate in any particular area. The choices available to Johnson students through Cornell's Center for International Studies is staggering, including concentrations in international economics and trade, international management, and United States international public policies and issues.

In addition to the two programs in Japanese business, Cornell offers exchange programs with the London Business School, two universities in Belgium, an institute in France, and schools in Switzerland, Norway, Italy, the Netherlands, Venezuela, Hong Kong, and Australia. However, space in these programs is very limited: only two Johnson students can participate in the program with SDA Bocconi in Milan, for example.

Like any Ivy League institution, Cornell puts a lot of emphasis on research. But the Johnson School prides itself on good teaching. *Cornell Business,* the feisty MBA-published B-school newspaper, regularly prints student evaluations of faculty to embarrass the laggards into improving their performance. The weak links in teaching, however, are relatively few. BW's surveys show that teaching in both the core and elective courses is above average among the 50 schools whose graduates are polled by the magazine. Indeed, Johnson puts some of its best teachers into the basic building-block courses, which the seasoned faculty at many other schools prefer not to teach because they are too elementary.

Among the most popular electives here are a pair of courses that simply feature the best of the university's professors: World Geopolitical Environment of Business and Regulatory and Legal Environment of Business, both of which require no more than 10 percent of the B-school profs' time. Instead, these multidisciplinary offerings feature sociologists, political scientists, and historians such as former President Carter adviser Alfred E. Kahn. The B-school's single most popular elective is David BenDaniel's Entrepreneurship and Enterprise class, which has even spawned a few small businesses, including a limousine service started by one MBA that runs between the Syracuse airport and Ithaca.

MBAs don't have to worry about entirely losing touch with the corporate scene while they are up in Ithaca, thanks to visiting executives such as Charles F. Knight of Emerson Electric, Sandy Weill of Primerica, and Lou Noto of Mobil. During breaks in their studies, Johnson MBAs ice skate at the university's rink and play golf on a school course when there's no snow on the ground. Each spring, B-schools from all over the country send teams to Ithaca to participate in an annual Invitational Golf Tournament. Johnson MBAs are dedicated athletes and like to play hockey, lacrosse, and volleyball. There's even a men's hockey team dubbed the Puck Bunnies. You guessed it: Another of the year's big events is the charity matchup pitting the Assets against the Bunnies.

Since many graduates of Cornell's hotel school decide to stay in the area, there is no shortage of excellent restaurants and bars in Ithaca, including the famous Moosewood Restaurant, which has produced several best-selling cookbooks. When it's time to relax, Johnson MBAs often head to Hauncey's or the Chapter House for a few beers. Aladdin's has the best pita sandwiches in town and an impressive selection of homemade soups. Coyote Loco and Mexicali Rose are the favored spots for Mexican fare, while the Nines in Collegetown serves a fantastic deep-dish pizza.

So what's next? First the school will have to hire a permanent dean to replace Merten. Dyckman seems like an ideal interim one: he's been teaching at the school for some 33 years, can be brutally honest, doesn't have an oversized ego, and does have a healthy self-deprecating sense of humor. One of his favorite jokes: Why don't deans look out the window in the morning? If they did, they wouldn't have anything to do in the afternoon. But Dyckman is also 64 years old and an unlikely candidate for the permanent position. Either way, Johnson will need somebody who's mighty good at looking out the window: there's a lot going on out there that the school has missed in recent years.

PLACEMENT DETAILS

While the school's career services office has improved in recent years, students still complain about the quantity and geographical diversity of recruiters. Cornell grads averaged 2.9 job offers each by commencement—above the average of the 50 schools surveyed by BUSINESS WEEK.

In 1996, some 138 companies arrived to conduct more than 2800 interviews. Cornell has also stepped up efforts to bring students to interviews, participating in at least half a dozen job fairs across the United States. In 1996, some 1000 job opportunities were posted via correspondence. The biggest hirers: Hewlett-Packard (nabbed 13); Coopers & Lybrand (10); Procter & Gamble (7); McKinsey & Co. (5); Chase Manhattan Bank (4); Citibank (4); and Salomon Brothers (4).

OUTSTANDING FACULTY

Bhaskar Swaminathan (****—finance); *Maureen O'Hara* (****—finance); *L. Joseph Thomas* (****—operations management); *David Sally* (****—organizational behavior); *Harold Bierman, Jr.* (***—strategy); *David BenDaniel* (***—entrepreneurship); *Roni Michaely* (**—

finance); *Alan McAdams* (**—strategy); *Dick Wittink* (*—marketing).

APPLICANT TIPS

Highly qualified applicants who could get into such elite schools as Wharton, Harvard, Northwestern, and Stanford may want to consider this top quality MBA program. Why? Starting in the fall of 1997, Cornell is awarding full-tuition fellowships to 30 top MBA applicants. The free tuition deal also provides a stipend to cover basic living expenses, books, and supplies. Strong consideration is given to candidates whose academic and work experience demonstrate exceptional leadership, a devotion to public service, and a keen concern for environmental issues.

That said, applicants without work experience may have a better shot at getting into Cornell's business school than into many of the institutions ahead of it on the Top 25 list. Unlike many of its top rivals, the Johnson School doesn't make work experience a requirement for admission. Still, more than 90 percent of its applicants boast some. Obviously, if you lack full-time work experience, you'll probably need high GMAT scores and undergraduate grades to get in.

Interviews are not required but would likely enhance your ability to gain acceptance. To arrange an on-campus interview, you may contact the Office of Admissions at 800-847-2087 or via fax at 607-254-8886 a month in advance of your trip.

Apply early because Johnson begins to make admissions decisions as early as December and continues through May on a rolling basis. If you apply by January 15, the school will respond to you by March 15. Johnson even considers applications beyond the April 15 deadline, but your chances of being admitted are greatly reduced after that date.

There is no financial aid/scholarship deadline, but applicants are encouraged to file as soon after January 1 as possible. Cornell cannot ensure that funds will be available for late filers.

Contact: Daphne Atkinson
Director of Admissions
800-847-2082
Final application deadline: March 15 for fall, January 25 for 12-month program

JOHNSON MBAs SOUND OFF

By the end of my two years, I had developed strong relations with a number of my professors on an academic and personal level. There are excellent courses available on writing and oral communication. I laud the new, outstanding finance professors like Prof. B. Swaminathan. The move to the new building, Sage Hall, should increase much required space.... Lastly, the flexibility and variety of the Cornell University curriculum is a definite plus.

The Johnson School of Business was an excellent experience for myself and for my wife. The Johnson School has approximately 40 percent of its student body composed of married students.... There are weekly happy hours, dinners, play groups for kids, book clubs, and numerous other get-togethers where married students can get to know each other better and form relationships that will last well beyond the two short years spent in Ithaca. Thirteen children were born last year at the Johnson School. The dean knows them all personally!

Hopefully the new dean will clean house in the placement office! BUSINESS WEEK should warn prospective students to be very wary of placement statistics. I know of at least 45 percent of the Class of '96 not having an offer as of May 15—after finals/coursework has been completed! This is very disenchanting!

Career Services continues to be a blight on the face of the school. They do a horrible job of leveraging the quality of the education into recruiting events/opportunities. If you count on the Career Services Office for anything but a 4×4 room to interview in, you will be let down. Except for this, and the size of my student loan, I am very pleased with the Cornell experience.

I came to Cornell for its excellent teaching reputation. The professors exceeded my expectations. Their devotion was evident from the very start, and the culture of going the extra mile extended throughout the two years. . . . It has allowed me to build numerous relationships that I am certain will continue long after I graduate.

I was very disappointed in the students. Too many came across as narrow-minded, selfish, spoiled, and completely oblivious to the plight of people not fortunate enough to attend an Ivy League School. The environment reminds me of a cliquish high school setting. I attribute these shortcomings to the youthfulness of the students.

Being a part of the entire University affords B-school students to be a part of the largest Ivy League alumni network worldwide. On a recent trip to Japan and China, I was stopped four different times by Cornell alums who wanted to buy [me] dinner or have drinks. There are only a handful of other top schools where the alumni network is as loyal and far reaching.

19.
UNIVERSITY OF NORTH CAROLINA

UNIVERSITY OF NORTH CAROLINA

Kenan-Flagler Business School
Carroll Hall, CB#3490
Chapel Hill, North Carolina 27599-3490
E-mail address: howella.bsacdl@mhs.unc.edu
Website address: http://www.bschool.unc.edu

Corporate ranking: 27

Enrollment: 427

Women: 36%
Non-U.S.: 19%
Minority: 16%
Part-time: none
Average age: 27
Average years of work exp.: 4.6
Applicants accepted: 19%
Median starting pay: $77,250

Graduate ranking: 14
Annual tuition & fees:
   resident—$3201
   nonresident—$14,332
Room and board: $8000
Average GMAT score: 630
GMAT range: 500 to 780
Average GPA: 3.3
GPA range: 2.1 to 4.0
Accepted applicants enrolled: 55%
Average starting pay: $80,385

Teaching methods: Lecture, 15%   Case study, 75%   Projects, 10%

Contact:
Aleta Howell
Acting Director of
Admissions
919-962-3236
Application deadlines:
November 15
January 10
March 3

How's this for a problem: when you sit mere hours away from the splendor of the Blue Ridge Parkway, tucked into the quintessential college town of Chapel Hill, how do you convince somebody that the best part of the Kenan-Flagler School is not the setting but the MBA program? For starters, you go out and smash rival schools in case study competitions, just as the school did. Then you carefully maintain your reputation as having one of the most devoted and best teaching faculty in the nation. Finally, you charge just $3201 a year in tuition to residents and lay claim to the title of best MBA bargain in the world.

That's what the University of North Carolina at Chapel Hill has done, and though Corporate America still doesn't view the school as one of the nation's best, it's carved out a pretty strong niche for itself. Dean Paul Fulton, who took over in 1994 after stepping down as president of Sara Lee, has overseen the construction of a $43 million building, increased the school's endowment from $38 million to $66 million, and begun planning for a new executive education center. Construction on the center was scheduled to begin in the summer of 1997. Fulton has since announced he is leaving, by mid-1997, although he will continue to serve in the job until a successor is found.

Chapel Hill's population is dominated by young, bright students whose intellectual conversations carry on in coffee houses, independent bookstores, and vegetarian restaurants. The atmosphere at Kenan-Flagler rivals intellectual centers like Cambridge, Berkeley, or Chicago. Not as well known as some perennial favorites, this business school in a town affectionately known as the "Southern part of heaven" has fashioned a bit of its own heaven in business school terms. On a tree-lined campus boasting brick walkways and Greek revival architecture, Kenan-Flagler Business School offers an up-to-date curriculum taught by a caring faculty. In 1996, it finished in the Top 10 in almost every important teaching category in BUSINESS WEEK's survey: the availability of faculty outside of class; the quality of core and elective teaching; the level to which the curriculum is integrated across courses.

The transformation of North Carolina's B-school from a sleepy, top quality regional school to one of the Top 25 in the United States was largely accomplished by former dean Paul J. Rizzo, whose five-year reign ended in 1992. The former vice chairman of IBM, Rizzo had no problem using his contacts in the corporate world to enhance the national profile of the school substantially. He raised millions of dollars, lured many corporate chieftans to campus for talks, and convinced prestigious recruiters to interview UNC's MBA graduates. His attention to the outside world and the school's external needs put Kenan-Flagler squarely on the map and complemented the painstaking inroads his predecessor, John Evans, made to beef up faculty and curriculum. Not surprisingly, Rizzo now heads up the search committee to seek Fulton's successor.

Whoever takes Fulton's place faces several big challenges: figuring out why top Corporate America views North Carolina MBAs as weaker than those at rivals like Duke and Texas; improving the quality of the school's hard, quantitative-oriented disciplines; and keeping the school affordable for residents and nonresidents. Fulton had been working hard to upgrade information technology where the early returns were solid. In virtually every category, student satisfaction has increased since Fulton's arrival. The biggest gains came in career services, where grads say the office has become much better at helping them with summer internships and preparing for interviews and negotiations. "We've tried to take the Kenan-Flagler experience into career services," Fulton says, noting that the school now has one staff member for every 100 MBAs.

Numbers—specifically, the one that appears at the bottom of the tuition bill—are also a big reason that students flock to the school. At $3201 for North Carolinians, a year at Kenan-Flagler costs as much as many used cars. And at $14,322 a year in tuition and fees for out-of-state residents, it's still one of the best educational values in the B-school world. Unlike Michigan and Virginia, UNC has kept to its mission as a public university and still charges less than half what the top private schools do. Of course, that could change. Explaining that technology and globalization efforts are driving up costs, Fulton is threatening to raise tuition. "You could easily go up another 20 percent from where we are and be O.K. in terms of attracting students," he says. "Low tuition is more important at the undergraduate level than the graduate level."

The low tuition is one reason UNC is so hard to get into and is able to pluck away a few candidates from Wharton, neighboring Duke, and others. In 1996, fewer than one out of every five UNC applicants received an offer of admission—even fewer than the 22 percent who were accepted a mere two years ago. Of those who chose to come to the school, an impressively large number were women or minorities, at least in comparison to other top B-schools. In 1996, more than one in three students were female, and about one in six were Asian, African-American, or Hispanic. But the student body is less international than in many schools: only four Top 25 schools had a smaller percentage of international students than UNC did (19 percent).

At UNC, quality teaching is a must have. Unlike professors at many B-schools, Kenan-Flagler instructors know that their primary job is to teach—scholars interested only in research opportunities need not apply to this students-come-first B-school. The effectiveness of instruction in the core has consistently ranked well above average, according to BUSINESS WEEK's student satisfaction surveys. The magazine's rankings put the overall quality of teaching in the upper echelons of the B-school community. What goes on in the classroom is only part of the formula for success. The unusual level of commitment shown outside of class is a second, all-important ingredient. UNC profs regularly get together with students at brown-bag lunches and early morning coffee breaks with students. It's almost unwritten policy that every professor's door be open to MBAs whether they signed up for their particular courses or not, and professors here even get involved in the job search process.

It can't hurt that these profs teach in a college-town atmosphere that is conducive to business in the real world. Together with Duke and North Carolina State, UNC is part of the Raleigh-Durham Research Triangle, home to such giants as IBM, GE, DEC, Mitsubishi, Northern Telecom, MCI, and Glaxo. Having the state capital just a stone's throw away helps meld government into the Kenan-Flagler education, providing a stimulating, yet pragmatic environment for a B-school.

UNC has traditionally been recognized for its marketing and finance departments, but its operations management area has definitely come on strong. Still, the school boasts strong general management MBAs but loses favor with recruiters who find analysts from the school to be only average. Undoubtedly, the school is still in the ranks of the best, but without careful analysis and a successful upgrade by Dean Fulton, recruiters may go elsewhere slowly. There is no standing still in the B-school world, and the dean knows this better than anyone.

Having major development and manufacturing activities in its backyard and a business man as its dean makes UNC particularly sensitive to the needs of business. Fulton is in constant contact with those on the outside of academia, making sure he knows what big business needs and then developing plans to deliver just that and more. Like many other B-schools, Kenan-Flagler is still struggling to meet those needs on global terms. One way UNC exposes students to international business is through the Kenan Institute of Private Enterprise, which serves as a forum for business, academic, and government leaders.

Frank H. Kenan, whose fortune was made in the oil and transportation businesses and whose family built the research center, is an important donor to the school. Along with the B-school, the institute cosponsors an international executive lecture series and an executives-in-residence program. It also bankrolls five research centers spanning competitiveness and employment growth, international marketing, manufacturing excellence, human resources, and management and financial services. The institute also administers MBA Enterprise Corps, a program modeled after the Peace Corps in which MBAs from Kenan-Flagler and other top schools accept one-to two-year assignments helping entrepreneurs and government officials in Eastern Europe and Southeast Asia to privatize business and start new companies.

Kenan-Flagler isn't all MBA heaven, though. As a state-funded institution, the school may be somewhat limited when it comes to ambition because of dwindling resources and the roll of the political dice. Though by no means poor, the school lacks the deep pockets Northwestern, Harvard, or Wharton have to pay for large staffs in admissions, placement, and alumni offices—the very departments that give many private schools a substantial edge. Things taken for granted at private schools sometimes require bitter fighting at public schools.

The school has not been able to regain ground lost two years ago when an 18-month gap between deans left the school vulnerable. The result: the program's recognition in the corporate world took a surprising tumble that has cost the school eight places in the BUSINESS WEEK survey over the past four years. The business community, wary of the change and the slow transition, have been reluctant to refocus on Kenan-Flagler.

Still, Fulton has won great praise from students for his enthusiasm and energy. He could charm the skin off a snake and convince the slithering beast to get an MBA with his southern drawl and devoted commitment to the school. Fulton had worked hard to restore the corporate links Rizzo began to establish. It seems to be working. Several companies noted that they had recently added UNC to their recruiting lists.

One asset almost four years in the making is soon to arrive at the campus. A new building will house students and faculty much more comfortably. The school's 427 full-time MBAs have been sharing space with nearly 700 undergrads in Carroll Hall, about a block away from Old Well, the historic and geographic center of the university campus. The old Carroll is a classic in academic architecture, in red brick, topped by a white cupola, complete with white columns. The new Carroll will be a glass-and-stone building with more modern classrooms, ample space, and faculty offices. Rizzo led a campaign that raised $24 million toward a new home for the B-school and parlayed a commitment from the state legislature for the remaining loot needed to complete the project. The building—which will be linked to the school's Kenan Center on the very south end of the 729-acre campus—is due for completion in the fall of 1997.

Whether the program moves into this state-of-the-art facility or not, the curriculum at UNC is thorough. Before you arrive on campus, an outside consulting group gathers confidential peer and employer assessments of perceived strengths and weaknesses. Then during the first year Managerial Competence class, the school gives you these evaluations and works with you to identify key growth areas—even preparing a personal mission statement and career plan. If you are a liberal arts major whose heart flutters in fear at the mention of regression analysis, the school puts on an Analytical Skills Workshop over the summer. The intensive four-week boot camp drills you in accounting, statistics, and economics. The class goes a long way toward preparing students for the rigors of the first year of the Kenan-Flagler MBA program. An optional program for international students helps them get a head start, too.

All incoming students have what UNC calls "Intro Week," a seven-day orientation that gets you acquainted with classmates and faculty through a series of workshops, games, and exercises—much like a college orientation. Following Intro Week is a program dubbed Week in the Life of a General Manager, which marks the first official week of classes and serves as an overview of the entire curriculum. Corporate leaders discuss their roles in the context of each day's lessons.

Right from the start, students are assigned to study groups of five to seven members each, and asked to remain together for the entire first year, even if personality conflicts emerge. The idea is to emulate the real world, where people with different levels of knowledge and experience and different personalities must work together on a daily basis. In the real world, you can't just leave a group project because you don't like the person next to you, and Kenan-Flagler wants you to get a taste of life early. This goes hand in hand with UNC's team approach, which relies heavily on case study method and class presentations. A full three-quarters of the program involves rigorous case work. Maybe this explains how North Carolina MBAs are able to win case contest upon case contest, winning out over other top schools like Michigan, Duke, and even Northwestern.

In the first year, all students are required to take the 13 core courses, regardless of previous academic or professional experience. Unfortunately, that means a certified public accountant has to sit through introductory accounting and a Wall Street financial whiz must attend a finance class. And while this sounds like a drawback to students knowledgeable in one area or another, the idea is to guarantee that each student benefits from the others' knowledge. The basic courses in the core—covering accounting to quantitative decision making—meet two or three times a week for 7 of 14 weeks. Underpinning the first year work and taking over the last three 7-week modules is Integrative Management, a course whose purpose is to interweave all the disciplines you've learned on the basis of business decision making.

The second year curriculum features an integrated full-year required course, which brings together international business, regulation, and business policy. There's also a project-based course, requiring that teams apply for projects that companies have submitted for consideration. Sometimes the courses allow the students to create case studies for later use in the school's curriculum. Midway in the second year, student teams engage in a large-scale computer simulation that finds them managing hypothetical companies in an international environment.

Other than this exception, all other electives are taught in 7-week modules. You can continue in a generalized course of study or concentrate on one or more functional areas. Although graduates have complained that the list of electives is somewhat limited, the school is expanding its elective base. Compared to many bigger B-schools with greater resources, the elective base is scrawny, that's true. The shorter modules at North Carolina allow the school to offer more personalized skills to students as well as cutting-edge topics less deserving of full, lengthy treatment.

As a public institution in Chapel Hill, the school is not in a good position to draw large numbers of foreign faculty and students as some rivals on the East and West Coasts do. But don't count Kenan-Flagler out, they have steadily increased the number of international students in the last two years. Today that number is 1 in 5, compared with only 1 in every 8 two years ago. and the B-school is committed to boosting the international content of the program. Whenever possible, international cases are added to the program, and the school is admitting more and more students who can speak one or more foreign languages. North Carolina also boasts

exchange programs with schools in Britain, Belgium, France, Venezuela, and Thailand.

Despite the perception that life in Chapel Hill is laid back, the MBA program is fairly demanding—especially in the first year. But when students take a break from their studies, they often engage in intramural sports and attend Tar Heels' basketball games. After an evening of slam dunking, MBAs tend to find their way to He's Not Here—a bar name that comes close to expressing the fact that women make up 36 percent of the student body. Spankys', on Franklin Street, just two blocks away from the B-school is another popular hangout.

PLACEMENT DETAILS

The school's low tuition, great teachers, and spectacular quality of life win high marks from students. Better than ever is the school's career placement center, headed by Mike Ippolito, who came aboard in 1993, after managing recruitment at three major companies. In 1996 he brought in 124 companies to recruit second-years and they conducted 156 interviews. Some 333 job opportunities were posted via correspondence. On the surface, those numbers seem a bit light, until you realize that Kenan-Flagler graduates fewer than 200 students each year.

Still, grads averaged 3.1 offers each, better than many other major business schools. But, many UNC grads didn't get near the starting pay packages of those elite schools—they also didn't have to mortgage their lives to pay outrageous tuition fees. In 1996, grads were plucked by NationsBank (9); Deloitte & Touche (6); Citibank (6); Intel (5); Sara Lee (5); American Airlines (4); Ernst & Young (4); Goldman, Sachs (3); KPMG Peat Marwick (3); IBM (3); and Eli Lilly (3).

North Carolina students have been more broadly distributed in jobs across the country in the last few years. In the past, more than half of the school's MBAs stayed in the Southeast—a situation that had kept the school from gaining a more prominent national reputation. The number of graduates taking jobs in the Southeast, however, has steadily declined.

Now, a new dean will have to push the school into phase two of the Rizzo/Fulton plan, developing more corporate contacts, and pushing international business into the forefront of the curriculum.

OUTSTANDING FACULTY

David Ravenscraft (****—economics); *Jennifer Conrad* (****—finance); *David Hartzell* (****—finance and real estate); *Ron T. Pannesi* (****—operations); *Kevin Lane Keller* (***—marketing); *Jay Klompmaker* (***—industrial marketing and sales management); *Joe Bylinski* (**—accounting); *Punan Anand-Keller* (**—marketing); *Morgan Jones* (**—operations); *Aleda Roth* (**—operations).

APPLICANT TIPS

On-campus interviews are an essential part of the application process for UNC and are highly recommended for all prospective applicants and required of applicants with no work experience. Because interviews are on a first-come, first-serve basis, you need to schedule a session as early as possible. Call 919-962-3236 to arrange an interview. Alumni interviews off-campus are available after the admissions committee has reviewed your completed application.

Admissions states that "a practical knowledge of the business world through work in a private firm, public organization, or entrepreneurial venture is critical for admission . . . each candidate must exhibit managerial and leadership qualities and have the experience and ability to contribute to the learning of fellow study group members and to the class overall."

Because of the heavy volume of applications UNC receives for relatively few spots, allowing the school to accept only 19 percent of its applicants, early application is recommended. The school's first application deadline is November 15. If you wait until the final March 3 deadline, you may not get a response from the school until May 2.

Contact: Aleta Howell
Acting Director of Admissions
919-962-3236
Application deadlines: November 15, January 10, and March 3

KENAN-FLAGLER MBAs SOUND OFF

The best aspect of the Kenan-Flagler program is the commitment to teaching quality. Professors make an effort to make sure the topics are covered to the best possible degree, even if this means additional tutoring sessions, one-on-one meetings or explanatory handouts. The finance faculty is especially exceptional in that I learned a great deal without being bored despite working on Wall Street for 5 years.

The school strives to orient its students toward cooperative interaction with a real emphasis on end results versus individual distinction. Given my work experience and my upcoming career goals, I think this process and manner of thinking will serve me better than much of the "technical" knowledge taught in school.

The program's overemphasis on teamwork goes overboard at times. Average students benefit greatly, but the most outstanding students have few avenues to display their talents and skills. It's a great program, but if you are a high achiever, you may do better to leverage your skills elsewhere.

I believe that UNC offers the best bang-for-your-buck. You come out of B-school with a solid education and a chance to repay your loans before retirement. Outside of the classroom, you can't beat Chapel Hill. Living here gives you easy access to both the mountains and the ocean. The only draw back at UNC is the facilities. However, with the new building due to open in '97, Carolina will have it all!

While I've enjoyed the program, I believe it will only get better with the opening of the new building and some top notch professors from other schools who are already sharing their energy and knowledge to enhance the school. Three recent faculty additions, all from Stanford, are truly outstanding: Mark Lang in finance; Kevin Keller and Punan Anand-Keller, both in marketing.

Overall, UNC offers a great value in terms of monetary costs vs. educational rewards. The only shortfall comes from major recruiters. For some reason, UNC receives what I would perceive as a less than favorable reputation with respect to analytical tools.

The achievement of Kenan-Flagler students in case competitions nationwide should make it clear that it deserves a place in the Top 10!

Chapel Hill does provide very, very good quality of living (nice atmosphere, mild weather, and tons of outdoor activities), which more or less enhance learning at Kenan-Flagler. Diversity, including the percentage of international students and emphasis on international business, has improved a lot during my two-year stay. Unfortunately, I will not have the chance to use the new business school building which will have much better information technology facility than the one I used.

For me, Carolina has been a spiritual and mental outward bound course. Only in such an environment could a Russian Language major be transformed into an investment banker. The faculty, structure of the program, and quality of the student body are the components that gave me the supportive infrastructure I needed to scale the finance

learning curve. As difficult as the first year was for one not coming from a similar undergraduate background, there was never a professor not willing to spend time explaining, a second year student not available for tutoring, or a team member not enthusiastic about helping, to bring me to a level of financial and quantitative proficiency.

Kenan-Flagler has been an excellent environment for me to build the skill set I will need to succeed as an entrepreneur. These skills (bootstrapping a company, raising venture finance, guerrilla marketing) are often overlooked by many other institutions.

The small size of the class at UNC allows you to really benefit from the experience of fellow classmates, in that you easily get to know a great majority of the class. The professor-student relationships are very helpful, much more of a "partnership" attitude is forged rather than just an institutional one.

The school spends an enormous amount of time and effort to integrate concepts across courses, especially in the first year. Hence, there is little, if any, redundancy of teaching because the faculty is well aware of what's being taught. That causes the learning process to be really efficient. In addition, it is very common to walk into class on the first day and have the professor call you by name or to walk down the hallway and have an administrator say "hi" to you by name (even though you have never previously met). The faculty and administration begin the networking process with the students. I believe that's a rare thing.

The advantage of UNC's MBA program is the very close relationship between professors and students. Most of the professors open their office doors all day and they don't mind students coming in with questions without an appointment.

20.
UNIVERSITY OF TEXAS

UNIVERSITY OF TEXAS

Graduate School of Business
Austin, Texas 78712
E-mail address: texasmba@.bus.utexas.edu
Website address: http://www.bus.utexas.edu

Corporate ranking: 15	Student ranking: 28
Enrollment: 824	Annual tuition:
	resident—$4884
Women: 25%	nonresident—$11,854
Non-U.S.: 17%	Room & board: $7300
Minority: 14%	Average GMAT score: 631
Part-time: None	GMAT range: 440–770
Average age: 28.4	Average GPA: 3.3
Average years of work exp.: 4.4	GPA range: 1.9–4.0
Applicants accepted: 18%	Accepted applicants enrolled: 12%
Median starting pay: $69,000	Average starting pay: $69,300

Teaching methods: Lecture, 40%   Case study, 50%   Projects, 10%

Contact:
Fran Forbes
Director of Admissions
512-471-7612
*Final application
deadline:* April 15

The University of Texas's struggle to build a top B-school reminds one of those cartoons in which a lone character is trying to plug a hole in a dam. He sticks his finger in the void, stopping the rush of water—only to see another hole burst open a few feet away. Every time he solves one problem, another springs up. To be fair, the Graduate School of Business in Austin isn't exactly flooded with troubles. But just as it figured out how to attack its major weakness—the school's reputation among corporations—it found another problem: student satisfaction.

In the early '90s, eager to woo Corporate America to Austin, Texas MBAs produced a slick video on the school and sent it to 2000 companies, including Motorola and 3M. The school started an ambassador program, sending students around the country to spread the word about the changes then Dean Robert Witt had implemented. The idea: show recruiters that UT was more than just a great bargain, that it was a great school which could stand with the nation's best. The result: Texas's corporate rank has risen steadily in BUSINESS WEEK's survey, from 28th in 1990 to 15th in 1996.

Now the school needs to tend to some business closer to home. The Texas class of '96 criticized the school in a number of major areas. No Top 25 B-school received worse marks for the quality of core teaching, and no administration got lower marks for responding to student requests for elective offerings. While more companies have indeed started recruiting at the school, the career services office does a poor job of hooking them up with the right students, according to both

MBAs and human resources executives. The school's programs in international business and ethics both received mediocre marks. "I've basically said for this spring and next fall, we're going to be more aggressive in responding to student feedback," says Dean Robert G. May.

Reform would not be new for the school. In 1992, a team of McKinsey & Co. consultants spent nearly 4000 hours in the MBA marketplace to devise a plan to move Texas into the top B-school tier. Witt carried out most of the changes recommended by the consultants: He made work experience a virtual requirement for admission (the Class of 1998 averages nearly 4.4 years of job experience, up from 2.6 six years ago), created a special information technology program, required applicants to submit multiple essays, placed a greater emphasis on personal interviews in the admissions process, and completely restructured the MBA curriculum to better conform to market demand.

Under the new program, in place since 1993, students are put into teams of 60 students who take all of their first year classes together. The cohorts are further divided into assigned "study teams" of five students. The program's total length of 60 hours (allowing for at least 11 electives out of about 20 courses) has been kept constant, but students now have increased flexibility to explore a "market-driven concentration." That's because the first-year core requirement now consists of 27 hours, down from 36. Based on the highly successful Information Systems Management program offered to 28 students with the highest GMAT scores, the concentrations allow an MBA to explore an area of interest. There are plenty of options, with 133 different elective courses available in an academic year.

Texas has established eight concentrations with the help of Corporate Advisory Councils, or groups of executives, who tailor the program toward the business sector's needs. The areas of concentration are: accounting, entrepreneurship, finance, human resources management, information management, marketing, natural resources and environmental management, and operations management.

But, for now, students say the content of the classes is not always up to snuff. "I thought maybe half of my professors were outstanding and the other half mediocre," says one '96 grad. At no Top 25 school does the faculty get lower marks for being aware of what colleagues are teaching. May, who became interim dean in 1995 and got the job full-time in 1996, says he knows there are problems. "We had a few poor teachers in the MBA core," he says. "By not moving poor teachers out of the core, we told the students that we weren't dedicated enough to teaching." For the fall of 1997, May estimates he and the faculty will replace four or five—or about 20 percent—of teachers in the core. He's also trying to develop a forecasting system so the school can do a better job of figuring out what electives students will want to take in their second year. How? It's pretty simple: he'll ask them.

May has some experience running a top academic program. Since joining the Texas faculty in 1979, he has served two stints as the chairman of the school's highly regarded accounting program. Nearly one-quarter of the school's tenure-track faculty teach in the subject. It's the best program in the nation, according to the *Public Accounting Report*. The info systems program is another major asset. A visiting committee, staffed with managers at such firms as IBM, Ford Motor, Mobil, and Deloitte & Touche, act as top advisers, sponsor internships, and often offer jobs to students. No wonder the program had a 100 percent placement rate in 1994. A 1995 *Computerworld* magazine survey of B-school deans and corporate recruiters ranked Texas's info management program as the third best in the country. And BUSINESS WEEK's student satisfaction survey places the info tech program fifth, behind only Carnegie Mellon's, MIT's, UCLA's, and Berkeley's.

In recent years, the school also has made some inroads in the marketing area, thanks mostly to Marketing Professor Leigh McAlister, a genuine dynamo. McAlister wisely linked up with Procter & Gamble, 3M, and Motorola to offer students both coursework and internships in the emerging field of customer business development. During the summer, MBAs work as interns on interdisciplinary teams solving problems. When students return to campus in the fall, they participate in a symposium with managers and professors. The course draws on the summer experience in discussing manufacturer-distributor relationships. It is also an excellent networking opportunity for MBAs, and, like other summer internships, it can open the doors for permanent positions. Each of the three companies takes about five summer interns.

The school has tried to replicate the successes of its technology and marketing programs by unveiling a Salomon Bros.–type trading room in May of '96 to boost its much-maligned finance department. EDS served as the main sponsor for the three-room complex, and banks and financial firms kicked in another $6 million.

Texas offers a number of extracurricular learning experiences for students. The Quality Management Consortia is sponsored by the Business School and the College of Engineering. The school hosts biweekly seminars for managers of local companies to assist in total quality implementation. About 20 MBAs are hired to work with executives. The companies pay a fee to be included in the program, and MBAs are compensated for their work. MBAs participate in a five-day training session between the fall and spring semesters. "I attribute my successful job search in large part to my considerable efforts and experience gained through QMC," says one recent alum. The school also hosts Moot Corp., an annual event in which teams of MBAs from major schools vie against each other to develop detailed business plans for new companies and present them to a panel of judges.

On the international front, Dean May is hoping to take advantage of the school's southern location by making work in Latin America a priority. A Spanish language track starts students with a five-week intensive class in the summer and continues with a class on commercial Spanish. The school has spent years cultivating close ties to Mexico's Monterrey Tech, a highly regarded business school in a rapidly growing country that is critical to U.S. trade. Texas now has student exchange pacts with schools in Mexico, Brazil, Chile, Venezuela, Canada, the Netherlands, Finland, France, the United Kingdom, Denmark, Germany, Australia, and Japan. It's often possible to earn an MBA (or the equivalent) from both Texas and one of its exchange schools. When you're actually in Austin, though, don't expect one of the more globally sophisticated MBAs: the school's international business program ranks 37th out of the 50 in the book, according to student satisfaction. Only 17 percent of the student body hails from abroad, which puts Texas near the bottom for Top 25 schools.

The school does continue to offer one of the true bargain MBAs available today. You'll find it difficult to get more value for your money, even though Texas's out-of-state tuition has more than doubled in the past four years, to $11,854 a year. That's better than any other Top 25 school, including North Carolina, which charges some $14,000 a year, or Indiana, which is now up to almost $16,000 a year. The charge for Texas residents: a puny $4884 a year. Still, the B-school complex here is in relatively comfortable environs, on the south end of the 300-acre campus in the lively state capital. A modern glass-and-concrete, six-story building, with a mall-like atrium and hallways as wide as those in shopping malls, is home to the graduate school of business.

Austin is a great place to spend two years of your life. Nestled along the Colorado River at the edge of Central Texas Hill Country, it's a lively and dynamic community. From a first glance, you'd never guess that the city boasts a symphony orchestra, 2 ballet troupes, 12 museums, and 11 drama theaters. But it makes sense.

This is the political and intellectual capital of the nation's second most populous state. With a student population of nearly 50,000, there's also plenty of demand for pure fun. Many students unwind on Austin's Sixth Street, home to bars and nightclubs that offer everything from live country music to punk and jazz. And while Stanford and UCLA MBAs often boast of their sun-drenched California climate, Austin offers up some pretty lush, temperate environs. The city averages 300 sunny days a year.

PLACEMENT DETAILS

That welcoming climate can easily offset some of the other drawbacks of attending a public university for an MBA. The school does not have the funds to establish a separate placement office for MBAs and undergrads. The facilities are nothing to brag about, either. "We have some pretty abysmal interview rooms," concedes Dean May. "We don't even have a lounge where recruiters can go and make phone calls." May has gathered $1.5 million to spend and by the end of 1997–1998 school year hopes to have remodeled the area. The goal: close to 40 first-class interview rooms, a conference room, and separate research area for grad students and undergrads. In the admissions realm, applicants shot up 29 percent between 1995 and 1996. The school now admits just 18 percent of those hopefuls, down from 35 percent in 1994. The average GMAT score, after a decline in the early '90s, has rebounded somewhat and stood at 631 for the class of 1998. And on the other end? Texas lured 292 companies to recruit in Austin in 1996. That's up nearly 50 percent from just two years ago. The biggest recruiters: Deloitte & Touche Consulting (14); Intel (13); Hewlett-Packard (11); Procter & Gamble (11); American Airlines (10); Coopers & Lybrand (8); Federal Express (8); and Ford (7). The median starting pay package for the class of '96 was $69,000— well below that at other top public schools, like North Carolina, Michigan, and UCLA. Maybe that's one reason why corporate recruiters are a lot happier with Texas than its students are.

OUTSTANDING FACULTY

Robert Parrino (**** —corporate finance); *Mary Lea MacAnally* (****—accounting); *E. Lee Walker* (***—management); *Steven R. Salbu* (**—business ethics and law); *Anitesh Barua* (***—information technology); *Tasadduq A. Shervani* (***—marketing); *John Dogget* (**—management); *Jeff Sandefer* (**—entrepreneurship); *Edward George* (**—statistics); *Keith Brown* (**—capital markets).

APPLICANT TIPS

For years, the University of Texas business school accepted applicants without any meaningful work experience. That's rarely true today. Indeed, quality full-time work experience is a key to admission now to the point of being as important as your GMAT score. The reason: Texas has repositioned its MBA in the marketplace. Corporate recruiters wanted more experienced grads with quality work backgrounds. So the school has made a significant effort to alter its admissions standards to meet those demands.

Apply early, if you can. The school begins to accept applications as early as September 1 with the deadline for the first application period ending December 1. If you apply by January 15, you'll get an answer no later than March 1. If you apply by February 1, the third deadline, the school will mail you its decision by April 1. Applicants who wait until the final deadline shouldn't expect to hear from the school until May 15.

Interviews are not required. If you'd like one anyway, you can contact the GSB Graduate Student Services office at 512-471-7612 or via fax at 512-471-4243 to arrange for an interview or a campus visit.

Contact: Fran Forbes
Director of Admissions
512-471-7612
Final application deadline: April 15

TEXAS MBAs SOUND OFF

One of the things that is very reassuring is the effort that the administration and faculty are making to improve the school. During the two years I've been here, the information technology has been constantly upgraded. There is a very conscious effort to spend whatever is necessary to ensure that students are exposed to the most recent technologies and resources. My class, I believe, was the second to undergo the "revamped core." The most quantitatively-oriented core courses (i.e., corporate finance, accounting, economics) were generally better taught than the "softs" (i.e., management, marketing, etc.). I think that the administration needs to have some of the more renowned marketing faculty teach at the core level. The entrepreneurship professors are some of the school's best, yet they are almost universally non-tenured.

Being a public school, students are left to fend for themselves in all aspects. The school's administration should take a more active role in admissions and job placement. The size of the program could also be reduced as many facilities are not quite adequate.

My only complaints concern the fact that this is a large, state-run institution and there is a lot of bureaucracy as far as the administration and trying to make changes within the program. The registration system for classes needs to be revised to allow all students to have the opportunity to take some of the better elective classes. I think that UT needs to attract more companies that are not so regionally-based to expand the reputation of the school.

This is truly an excellent program. There are numerous clubs and organizations to join, a diversity of majors from Entrepreneurship to Finance, and caring and committed staff and faculty.

One of the biggest positives for the Marketing Department is that the faculty encourages us to get involved with projects that are sponsored by companies so that we can learn what is happening out in the industry today and apply the concepts that we learned in class. I got several opportunities to consult for several major companies and I was able to see my recommendations being implemented in those companies. We are able to acquire the skills that employers are looking for!

The top teachers and students here are as good as you will find anywhere. However, when looking at about 20 percent of the class, you can't help but wonder how they made it into a "top" MBA program. Maybe UT just needed to reach its breakeven level of students.

**21.
UNIVERSITY
OF
ROCHESTER**

UNIVERSITY OF ROCHESTER

William E. Simon Graduate School of
Business Administration
Rochester, New York 14627-0107
E-mail address: mbaadm@mail.ssb.rochester.edu
Website address: http://www.ssb.rochester.edu

Corporate ranking: 38	Graduate ranking: 18
Enrollment: 686	Annual tuition & fees: $21,240
Women: 26%	Room and board: $6975
Non-U.S.: 46%	Average GMAT score: 630
Minority: 9%	Average GPA: 3.22
Part-time: 274	GPA range: 2.42 to 4.0
Average age: 28	Average years of work exp.: 5
Applicants accepted: 36%	Accepted applicants enrolled: 34%
Median starting pay: $65,000	Average starting pay: $68,440

Teaching methods: Lecture, 50% Case study, 30% Projects, 20%

Contact:
Priscilla E. Gumina
Assistant Dean for
MBA Admissions
716-275-3533
Application deadlines:
November 15
March 1
June 1

When students pour through the doors of Schlegel Hall, they can glimpse him at the end of the long corridor. He's still there when they leave in the afternoon or trek to the library. He always wears a business suit, and he likes to hang a jacket over his shoulder.

The real William E. Simon doesn't spend all his time in Schlegel—it's only the cast-iron statue of the former Treasury Secretary that never leaves. But Simon's spirit and ideas are ubiquitous at the University of Rochester's business school. His notion that free markets provide the best solutions to business problems is taught as gospel here.

When Simon's figure first went up in Dewey Hall—now reserved for the B-school faculty and administrative offices—students used to carry the statue around, sometimes plopping him in the elevator or positioning him so as to stare at a nearby bulletin board. But ever since Simon and the students moved to the 64,000-square-foot, state-of-the-art Schlegel Hall, he has been bolted to the floor.

So has his philosophy. The belief that virtually every business decision, whether it concerns finance, marketing, organizational behavior, or operations, can be explained in terms of microeconomics, permeates the school's curriculum. "All the courses here are taught from a common framework of economics," says Dean Charles I. Plosser.

With the exception of the University of Chicago, there isn't another B-school more strongly committed to the free-market or price-theory approach than Simon. Combine that with a coterie of brilliant scholars, the intimacy of a small program, and one of the best B-school facilities around, and you get a rather unique business school experience. Not that Rochester hasn't had its problems.

The school went through a difficult period in 1992, when a new dean resigned within eight months of taking the job because of a funding dispute with the university president. The crisis, however, mobilized both the faculty and students to work together to improve the program. Plosser, a longtime professor at the school, took over as dean to contain the damage. And a new, more supportive university president arrived.

Under Plosser, appointed dean in 1993, Rochester has certainly undergone a major turnaround. Applications for admission are up nearly 40 percent in the last two years. The number of job offers—according to the school's stats—has risen by 124 percent over the past three years. The school's GMAT average hit a record 630 in 1996. And Rochester popped back up on the BUSINESS WEEK Top 25 list, after having fallen off the shorter Top 20 ranking back in 1992, largely because of lackluster support in the corporate community.

Among the initiatives that came out of the earlier trouble is the school's Vision Program, a newly required leadership component of the curriculum modeled after Chicago's successful LEAD program. Backed by such corporate sponsors as AT&T, Procter & Gamble, Bausch & Lomb, Wells Fargo, and Xerox, it is a series of seminars, group exercises, team building raft trips and simulations that address the "soft" aspects of management long overlooked by this school. For each of the 18 modules there's a student leader, a faculty adviser, and one or more executives from the corporate sponsors. The school itself invests nearly $200,000 in the program each year.

Vision kicks off the MBA experience as part of the orientation program in mid-September. Entering students are assigned to the Blue, Gold, Green, or Purple cohort of 40 MBAs each. During the first three quarters, each cohort takes all the 10 required courses and the management communication sequence together. Students also are assigned to study teams of four or five members for group projects throughout the first year. Simon's initial core courses tend to be more theoretical than those at many other business schools in the 1990s. But the small size of the faculty and the student cohorts also allow for far more integration of coursework across functions.

In the second year, all students take at least one "integrative course," in a subject such as business policy or competitive strategy, which serves as a capstone experience. Grads praise the school for its integration of classwork in BUSINESS WEEK surveys. They also must complete at least one of a dozen concentrations in such areas as public accounting or entrepreneurship. A new health care concentration is being launched in the spring of 1997. The school hired away from Wharton Larry Van Horn, an economics professor and a consultant to many health care institutions, to head up the effort. Simon offers students less program flexibility and fewer choices than many other larger business schools. There are only 48 elective offerings, for example, and in the last three years, the school has launched only 7 new elective courses. As Plosser readily admits, "We're small, and we cannot be all things to all people. We have to carve out our market niche."

Yet for a small school, there's a remarkable degree of diversity here. Indeed, 46 percent of the class of 1998 is international—a record for Simon, and the highest percentage of any Top 25 business school in the United States. The next closest school is Washington University in St. Louis with 39 percent. (Some international students complain that the U.S. students get preferential treatment when it comes to scholarship and fellowship money, but 60 percent of the school's applicant pool is now non-U.S.) The largest single contingent of non-U.S. students is from Japan. Simon gets roughly 180 applications from Japan each year, though students hail from more than 30 countries. "Just when you think you've seen every transcript possible, you get one from Poland," says Priscilla Gumina, assistant dean for MBA admissions.

The school makes good use of this mix. Besides the mandatory teams that mix cultures and backgrounds, students initiated a Broaden your Horizons seminar series that features lunchtime presentations by students from countries around the world. MBAs from Argentina, Australia, Brazil, Hong Kong, India, and other nations will conduct sessions on the economics, culture, politics, and business protocol of their home countries. The school offers exchange programs in partnership with schools in nine foreign countries and executive MBA programs in the Netherlands and Switzerland. Simon students also publish *Simon International,* the only journal of global business written by MBAs for MBAs. An executive seminar series, meantime, attempts to lure senior executives to campus, from the CEOs of Bethlehem Steel to Saatchi. Of course the real Bill Simon— not the statue—is a frequent guest.

Simon's faculty are a powerful and entrenched group at the school. They boast great brainpower in finance and economics, and Simon profs edit several top academic journals—the *Journal of Financial Economics, Journal of Monetary Economics,* and the *Journal of Accounting and Economics*—all virtually unreadable scholarly tracts. Even so, Plosser is happy to remind visitors that recent studies of research productivity have ranked Simon's faculty among the top five in the United States. Perhaps because of the small size of the school, the faculty's pursuit of its research agenda hasn't destroyed its ability to deliver quality teaching rates, above average for the Top 50-plus schools.

Like Cornell's Johnson School, Simon is located in upstate New York, which has more in common with the Midwest than with New York City. In many ways Rochester is a company town, home to Eastman Kodak, Xerox Corp., and Bausch & Lomb—three major supporters of the school and of the arts. And when it comes to the arts, Rochester can boast of the university's world-renowned Eastman School of Music, the Rochester Philharmonic Orchestra, and the International Museum of Photography.

Simon is part of the university's main or River Campus, located on the banks of the Genesee River about three miles from downtown. Most of the MBA action now centers around the attractive Schlegel Hall, a modern four-story building that opened in the fall of 1991. The faculty resides in Dewey Hall, one of four stately, columned buildings on the Eastman Quad. There's no undergraduate business program at Rochester, so most of the resources here can be lavished on the MBAs and the school's Doctor of Philosophy program. The management library on the third floor of the university's Rush Rhees Library, located at the head of the Eastman Quad, is one of the quietest places on campus.

PLACEMENT DETAILS

So how do Simon MBAs fare in the job market? The Class of 1996 averaged 2.6 job offers each— below average for the Top 25 schools but still above such other institutions as New York University, Vanderbilt, and Thunderbird. Simon grads pulled down median starting pay packages of $65,000 each. That's lower than 20 other Top 25 schools. On the other hand, these same students quit jobs that paid median salaries of just $35,000—a sum lower than 19 of the Top 25.

Some 94 companies came to campus to recruit second-years, doing 1128 interviews. Newcomers included such companies as Sun Microsystems and SAP America. The major 1996 employers: Procter & Gamble (6); Citicorp (6); Xerox (6); First Empire State (5); Federal Express (5); Eastman Kodak (4); American Management Systems (3); Arthur Andersen (3); Allied Signal (2); IBM (2); General Motors (2); Deloitte & Touche (2); Nestlé SA (2); and Frontier (2). Recruiters also say that Simon grads have some of the best skills in finance and operations (ranking eighth and sixth, respectively).

Of course, some companies find Rochester a bit too out of the way to make Simon a regular stop on their recruiting tours. And some stay away because Rochester winters are harsh, a fact of life that makes some students wonder why they ventured so far north for an MBA. Humor serves as the best antidote to the cabin fever known to set in after many frigid nights. Students can no longer move William E. Simon around, but that hasn't stopped them from putting a Halloween mask on his face, or slipping a pair of white boxer shorts with little red hearts around his middle.

OUTSTANDING FACULTY

Clifford W. Smith, Jr. (****—finance); *Michael Barclay* (****—corporate finance); *Gregg A. Jarrell* (****—applied economics); *Shailendra Jain* (****—marketing); *Thomas F. Cooley* (***—economics); *K. Ramesh* (**—accounting); *A. Scott Keating* (*—accounting); *Ronald Yeaple* (*—marketing); *Gerald Zimmerman* (*—accounting); *Ray Ball* (*—marketing).

APPLICANT TIPS

If you missed some of the early deadlines for schools in the Top 25, Rochester gives you a little extra time to gain admission to a small school with an excellent program in finance. It admits students in September for the mainstream 22-month MBA program and in January for an accelerated 18-month program. The final deadline for a January start is mid-November. If you hail from the United States, you may have an edge at Rochester. Why? The school has enrolled such a large percentage of international students in recent years that it needs more domestic grads to offer to recruiters.

What does the admissions committee look for? "In selecting students, the committee considers the following criteria: recommendations;

teamwork and communication skills; the nature and scope of prior work experience; undergraduate grade-point average; GMAT score; evidence of leadership and maturity; and the application's career focus." So, in the answers to the essay questions, focus on how well you work in teams and how you played leadership roles in either professional or extracurricular activities.

For applicants whose full-time work experience is three years or less at the start of the program, interviews are required. In 1996, the school interviewed half of its applicants and 75 percent of its domestic MBA candidates. To schedule a session, you may contact admissions at 716-275-3533 or via fax at 716-271-3907. This school still accepts a significant percentage of applicants with little work experience: some 7 percent of the Class of 1998 has less than one year of work experience.

Contact: Priscilla E. Gumina
Assistant Dean for MBA Admissions
716-275-3533
Application deadlines: November 15, March 1, and June 1

SIMON MBAs SOUND OFF

Simon's two fundamental concepts, efficient market theory and agency theory, provide a definitive core to the program. Each course is like another layer on this core and gives you an analytical framework from which to critically examine all business problems. The set of tools that you take away from the program, if applied correctly, will allow you to succeed in your chosen career.

Almost without exception, the teaching is first class: the professors seem very interested in the subjects they teach and provide very good explanations. The facilities are also first rate, and Schlegel Hall is one of the nicest academic buildings I have ever seen. The administration is almost always very quick to respond to any problem. The winter weather is naturally very cold, but shuttle buses and tunnels among buildings make life easier. The group work is a bit overemphasized, especially during the first year in the assigned, socially-engineered study groups. Unlike the faculty, administration, or facilities, the students are not uniformly excellent: there is quite a wide disparity, from very bright students to those who really don't belong in the program.

The Simon School has provided excellent opportunities for learning leading-edge management techniques and philosophies within a friendly environment. The demanding workload was actually enjoyable because of the small school environment and the faculty's dedication to teaching.

Simon has an excellent finance faculty and program. Economics forms the underpinning of the total program. The student-led Vision program has lifted the school to a new level of participatory education. Past administrative problems have been solved in an extremely satisfactory manner, strengthening the school far beyond previous possibilities.

The combination of small class sizes, top faculty, and a state-of-the-art facility made the overall experience very rewarding. In addition, the biotechnology MBA dual master's degree program is ideal for candidates interested in entering the pharmaceutical or biotechnology industries. It combines the resources and faculties of a top business school with those of an excellent medical school.

At Simon, I had plenty of opportunity to take a proactive role in my education. I was involved in numerous organizations and I felt comfortable approaching faculty members to talk about classwork, my job search, or whatever. I have truly enjoyed learning about different cultures, particularly through our Broaden Your Horizons program.

While I believe that going straight from undergraduate school to an MBA program is not right for everyone, it is not necessarily wrong, either. [Student was a '94 undergrad.] Instead of rating schools strictly on the percentage of students without full-time work experience, why not look at the quality of those students? Using myself as an example, I had a good deal of work experience, but it was not full-time, post-bachelor's degree work. My grades and GMATs were strong. I worked hard and got involved in many organizations. In the end, I did well; my offers met or exceeded those of most of my classmates.

The teaching was excellent, the support staff was helpful, and the diverse student body contributed to my depth of knowledge. The computer and classroom facilities were far superior to some of the other top business schools that I had a chance to visit. The small student body made the Simon School a very cozy and cooperative atmosphere in which to learn and operate. (In what other top business school would the career services director know each and every full-time student by name?)

Having such a large proportion of international students is also a disadvantage in doing well in B-school surveys. Because of students' visa status, it is much more difficult for international students to land jobs. Hence, Simon probably boasts fewer offers per students than some schools. But the reason isn't that the recruiting out of Simon is weak. It's just that there are more international students. Also, because a high proportion of students work abroad than at most business schools, this school might do worse than it should in the recruiting survey. A B-school survey conducted only in the United States will understate the quality of Simon.

22.
YALE
UNIVERSITY

YALE UNIVERSITY

School of Management
Box 208200
New Haven, Connecticut 06520-8200
E-mail address: som.admissions@yale.edu
Website address: http://www.yale.edu/som

Corporate ranking: 30	Graduate ranking: 22
Enrollment: 461	Annual tuition & fees: $23,130
Women: 29%	Room and board: $8180
Non-U.S.: 31%	Average GMAT score: 676
Minority: 15%	Average GPA: 3.38
Part-time: none	GPA range: 2.4 to 4.0
Average age: 27.2	Average years of work exp.: 4.3
Applicants accepted: 23%	Accepted applicants enrolled: 54%
Median starting pay: $83,050	Average starting pay: $87,695

Teaching methods: Lecture, 60%   Case study, 35%   Projects, 5%

Contact:
Richard A. Silverman
Executive Director of
Admissions
203-432-5932
Admissions deadlines:
November 25
January 3
February 3
March 24

The Yale School of Management has been waiting a long time for a big boost. In the early 1990s, Dean Michael Levin tried to transform the school into a smaller version of Harvard and Wharton, was roundly hated by alumni, and left New Haven about 10 minutes after his boss, university President Benno C. Schmidt, did. From 1992 to 1995, Professors Paul MacAvoy and Stanley Gartska somewhat grudgingly filled in as interim deans. Most recently, in late 1995, Jefferey Garten, a hotshot former investment banker who had served in the Clinton Administration, agreed to take his turn at the school's helm.

And the school is still waiting for that boost. For starters, Garten inherited a school in which student satisfaction—which had hit a nadir during Levin's term—is actually declining again, largely because of a poor career placement office and an inadequate information technology program. The dean has also had a steep learning curve in making the transition from the world of business to the world of academia. SOM's faculty shot down his first attempt at reform: offering an MBA instead of the school's unique Master's in Public and Private Management. So while students and professors remain generally optimistic about Garten, this is not a school that has left its problems behind.

But there's still plenty of good news in New Haven. SOM does an excellent job of finance, general management, and ethics. For a B-school, SOM is unusually diverse: attracted by the emphasis on public management, its students hail from a wide variety of careers, and 15 percent of the student body is African-American, Latino, or Native American. Applications hit an all-time high of 1805 in 1996, up from a low of

1216 in 1992. Only 23 percent of applicants were accepted, down from an embarrassing 42 percent in the spring of 1993. The percentage of students deciding to enroll rose to 54 percent in 1996. Garten also gets along well with Yale president Richard Levin, an economist and sometime SOM professor himself who admits he has "opened a lot of doors" for Garten to do SOM fund-raising among alumni of all branches of Yale. "I think he has got an important message to communicate," Levin says. While the president has made it clear that he isn't prepared to devote a lot of new resources to the school, raising SOM's status is certainly in his interest. It is one of only two schools in the university not ranked among the very best in the country. (*Note:* The divinity school is the other one.)

Garten arrived at Yale after stints as a banker with Lehman Brothers and as Bill Clinton's Undersecretary of Commerce. He has a Ph.D. in international studies from Johns Hopkins but no administrative experience in the academy. He does have what might be considered a model career for SOM students, having moved among the highest levels of government, Wall Street, and the nonprofit world. His overriding goals: improve ties with the rest of Yale, promote the school to domestic and international businesses, and generally improve its image.

Unlike some of his predecessors, he spends little time with students, leaving the day-to-day operations with deputy dean Stanley J. Gartska, who served as acting dean before Garten came on board. Students aren't thrilled about that but seem to agree with the school line that Garten's main job, for now, is external relations. His first and most visible project has been the career development office, which had the dubious distinction of being ranked dead last among Top 25 schools in the BUSINESS WEEK poll. Shortly before Garten arrived, Mark Case was brought in from the University of Michigan to take over career services. In the fall of 1996, a former student lounge was divided into interview cubicles, each one fitted with a phone and computer hookups

so recruiters can wile away the time between interviewees getting caught up on office work. Previously, recruiters were shuttled in and out of spare classrooms. That's a quick way to turn them off to your school. SOM students had also developed something of a reputation for being cavalier about interviewing. So starting this past fall, each one will participate in a two-year series of career-related workshops called the Professional Strategies Program. Topics include interview etiquette, job search strategies, math review, and computer research skills. Students this year will also be able to participate in career days in Washington, New York, Greenwich, Boston, and San Francisco to accommodate employers not willing to make the trip to New Haven. Students can also sign up for daylong field trips to companies like Lehman Brothers, DuPont, Amtrak, the Ford Foundation, and Xerox. Having worked in the private sector, Garten seems savvier than other recent deans about the world of work in the '90s and has been active in restructuring career development. He tries to talk to alumni and potential employers on every trip he makes and often carries a portfolio of student résumés.

Teaching here consists primarily of lectures (60 percent), with some case studies (35 percent) and "real-world" projects, too. The average number of students in core classes is 70, the average in electives, 30. In the first year, students take eight courses and a two-semester sequence called Perspectives on Organization and Management. The course brings in business executives and consultants. The goal is to spur real-world debate on the more theoretical foundation that is laid down in the core courses. The core includes accounting, economics, statistics, organizational behavior, finance, game theory, and marketing operations. First-year students take a required course called Politics and Control in Business and Government.

Second-year students select from team-taught sessions of a required course called Analysis of Institutions. The sessions' topics reflect the diversity of the school. Among them: mergers and acquisitions, global asset management, and the energy industries. Each class of no more than 35 students is taught by two teachers from different disciplines. That's a throwback to the largely discarded SOM practice. To finish out their requirements, students choose at least seven electives, including two from an area of concentration: finance, marketing, strategy, public management, or nonprofit management. Marketing courses are often blasted in student surveys, and there is talk of hiring a high-profile candidate to beef up the department.

Indeed, Garten wants to increase faculty size by 20 percent, and professors are even saying 30 percent might be more appropriate. But either one could put the school back in the red if the school's $130 million endowment does not increase. "To be truly great requires more resources," Gartska says.

BUSINESS WEEK's most recent B-school surveys show that the class of 1996 is a fairly satisfied bunch, with some significant caveats. Overall satisfaction declined 6 percent from 1994, and teaching scores also dropped slightly. Meanwhile, grads' rating of SOM's aggressiveness in helping them find summer jobs dropped 13 percent to the lowest score of any Top 25 school. But nothing fares as poorly as information technology: here, Yale ranked 50th out of the 51 schools polled in the student satisfaction survey. That should improve somewhat now that students are required to buy their own laptops, which should ease strain on the school's server.

On the plus side, the ethics, diversity, and leadership programs all ranked in the Top 15. Anecdotally, grads say the finance, nonprofit, and consulting strategies professors are topnotch. "I never felt that I was infringing upon a professor when asking for assistance or advice," said one grad. But the administration's decision to play up its high-profile finance department has also led to glitches. In the fall of 1996, so many students signed up to take introductory

finance that, after two days of frantic meetings with angry students, administrators asked Ken French to teach two sections. French, who was brought in from Dartmouth's Tuck School in 1994 to add star luster to the finance department, is one of the most popular professors in the school. His pet project: setting up an emerging markets program with colleagues in the law school and the school of international relations.

Several of Garten's changes are aimed at making Yale into a more traditional business school. When the school was founded in 1976, university officials explicitly said they did not want another Harvard Business School on the Yale campus. Instead, their vision was of a cross between a business school and a school of public policy. One model was Yale Law School, almost always ranked as the best in the country, and the alma mater of Supreme Court Justices, many of the nation's law scholars, and both current adult residents of the White House. Unfortunately, SOM has not yet come close to that ideal. A good number of business leaders don't know Yale even has a business school, and many who do view it as some sort of alternative program.

Garten apparently thought offering the more traditional MBA would help change that image. It's a change students have been requesting for years. Garten now tells students to embrace the MPPM degree and to describe it as an MBA-plus. The core idea: Yale students are prepared to lead in any sector, as Garten is fond of saying, from Ford Motors to the Ford Foundation, from Goldman, Sachs to the Guggenheim. Whatever the degree, the school was one of the first in the country to emphasize teamwork—now in vogue everywhere—and it continues to draw some of the most qualified MBA candidates in the country. Their average GMAT score—675 for the class of 1998—is well above that of other schools ranked near where Yale is, and it has risen almost 20 points in the last two years. What students now find when they come to campus is a more traditional B-school program with a heavy emphasis on economics and finance.

Garten and the faculty have also changed the grading system to make it more closely resemble the A-through-F structure. SOM was originally designed as a noncompetitive culture, with no grading curve, no class ranks, and no honors grade. Starting in the fall of 1996, though, the school grades students on four tiers: Distinction, Proficient, Pass, and Fail.

Despite the change in focus, Yale has not forgotten its dual public-private mission. In almost every class, students gain perspectives in both areas—even though only about 15 percent of graduates end up going into public or nonprofit work directly after graduation. SOM professors believe SOM graduates switch back and forth between sectors more often than MBAs. The school boasts a substantial internship fund to encourage students to forgo lucrative summer job opportunities in investment banking and consulting for work with charities or in Third World countries. Several school fund-raisers stoke the fund, and students who take more traditional jobs donate some of their earnings to it.

The class of 1997's summer internships give a good idea of the variety. The jobs included: speechwriter for Britain's Labour Party, associate in the Zen Center in San Francisco, operations intern in the New York City mayor's office of management consulting, loan officer for the Central Asian-American Enterprise Fund, and production and finance intern for the Vermont Symphony.

"In a lot of [B-schools], the students want to work for Goldman, move up the ladder, get their money and buy their boat," Gartska says. At SOM, "Someone who seems like a rabid investment banker type [who] you'd think would kill their mother to close a deal turns out to be volunteering eight hours a week in a soup kitchen." Indeed, many students seem to have been attracted by the "niceness" of Yale. They contrast themselves with peers at Harvard and Columbia, where Yalies insist that cutthroat competition is rife. SOM "is a special, close-knit community where learning is a priority. Teamwork always comes before personal achievement," says one 1996 graduate who went into investment banking.

A Thursday night keg party—there are no classes on Friday—starts off the weekend for most students. Bars of choice include Bar and Archie Moore's, the latter conveniently located for the majority of students who live in the Grad Student Ghetto. This somewhat yuppified section of New Haven consists of gracious Victorians that have long since split up into grad student apartments. The neighborhood is dotted with gourmet grocery stores and coffee bars and is about a 15-minute walk from the school.

The School of Management buildings are set apart from those of the undergraduate campus, the law school, and the medical school. So there isn't much mixing among schools during the day. One place you'll be sure to find undergrads and other grad students is the SOM cafeteria, widely considered the crown jewel of the university's otherwise grim food offerings. Garten has also expanded cross-listed courses and programs. A handful of students get joint degrees, mostly from the School of Forestry, but also from the medical school, the law school, and even the divinity school.

PLACEMENT DETAILS

The top 10 recruiters in 1996 were: APM, Inc., Ernst & Young, IBM, Monitor Company, Pratt & Whitney, Booz Allen & Hamilton, General Motors, McKinsey & Co., Northwest Airlines, and Price Waterhouse. Each hired three or four students. The average starting salary was $87,700 for the class of 1996, while the median pay stood at $83,050.

That list of recruiters gives you a sense that SOM isn't a traditional B-school—but that it's also got a lot in common with those more conventional programs. Garten's challenge is figuring out a way for the school to benefit from those differences, rather than suffering from them. Too bad he won't have much of a honeymoon in which to get it done.

OUTSTANDING FACULTY

Sharon Oster (****—management); *Barry Nalebuff* (****—management science); *Arthur Swersey* (***—organizational behavior); *Ken French* (***—finance); *Katherine O'Reagan* (***—economics and public policy); *Ed Kaplan* (**—public management); *Roger Ibbotson* (**—finance); *Paul MacAvoy* (**—economics); *Richard Sansing* (*—accounting); *Jon Ingersoll* (*—finance).

APPLICANT TIPS

Yale University's School of Management boasts one of the most mature and diverse student populations of any major business school. If you're older and have a good deal of work experience, you're more apt to gain acceptance into this superb program. Yale also accepts a larger percentage of applicants from the nonprofit and government worlds than do most other business schools.

Admissions says that it evaluates applicants based on three primary criteria: (1) capacity and motivation for academic achievement and intellectual performance; (2) motivation and ability to cope with the complex, practical problems of organizations, to influence the outcome of events, and to work effectively with and lead others; and (3) personal and professional objectives that reflect a commitment to effective management as a socially critical activity.

Yale groups applicants into four separate "rounds," the first of which ends for all applications received by November 25. Round two ends January 3, while round three ends February 3. If you wait until the final deadline of March 24,

you may not get a response to your application until the end of May. Interviews are not required. To arrange a visit to the Yale campus, you may contact the admissions office at 203-432-5932 or via fax at 203-432-9991.

Contact: Richard A. Silverman
Executive Director of Admissions
203-432-5932
Admissions deadlines: November 25, January 3, February 3, and March 24

YALE GRADS SOUND OFF

The environment at Yale SOM is highly collaborative. The noncompetitive grading system enables students to work effectively in groups, to help one another learn, and to take challenging courses in areas we might avoid if we had a GPA or class rank to worry about. The school's small size and the breadth of students' backgrounds mean that a typical course will have students sharing perspectives from the private, public, and nonprofit sectors, from a dozen countries, from numerous industries and functions, and from several political points of view.

The Career Development Office needs a substantial influx of career connected professionals in order to meet the job search demands of the students, especially those students seeking "Wall Street" type jobs. The efforts thus far, as set forth by the Career Development Office, have been inadequate. Looking for a job, without much help from career services, has been the most stressful aspect of my MBA experience.

SOM's professors are among the best in the country, and write the textbooks other B-school students read: Frank Fabozzi, Jon Ingersoll, Ken French, Roger Ibbotson, Steve Ross, Sharon Oster, etc., coming from a finance background, this school has far exceeded my ambitions and has placed me with the job I wanted.

I strongly believe that our new dean, Jeff Garten, will be the one to successfully communicate to the business world the exact character of our school. We are not only a business school, we are a "B-school plus." This "plus" refers to our public and non-profit management concentration.

The Yale School of Management is the best in finance. It's got an outstanding faculty in this area. It's definitely very behind in marketing, however. It's a very small and relatively new school. Therefore, this becomes a problem when companies are seeking to hire people from the school (on campus). Students need to be much more willing and engaged in an independent job search.

I feel that the admissions committee looks at GMAT scores as a criteria too closely. There are many students here with no leadership or personal skills simply because of a high GMAT or GPA. Very few people have both a GPA and good work experience.

I came to this MBA program for a marketing career and was able to sector switch from a government bank examiner to an Assistant Brand Manager with Procter and Gamble! Throughout my job search, I found the alumni network overwhelmingly supportive and helpful, many giving contacts at other organizations.

The alumni connections are tremendous. The Alumni Office is of top quality. I downgrade it because the school is still young and there have only been 18 small graduating classes. The Yale college graduates I have contacted have all also been terrific! For finance, there is an abundance of firms recruiting on campus; general management recruiting is not as prevalent.

23.
SOUTHERN METHODIST UNIVERSITY

SOUTHERN METHODIST UNIVERSITY

Edwin L. Cox School of Business

Dallas, Texas 75275-0333

E-mail address: mbainfo@mail.cox.smu.edu

Website address: http://www.cox.smu.edu/mba/mba.html

Corporate ranking: 43

Enrollment: 672

Women: 29%

Non-U.S.: 22%

Minority: 5%

Part-time: 400

Average age: 27.0

Applicants accepted: 62%

Median starting pay: $62,350

Graduate ranking: 15

Annual tuition & fees: $20,524

Room and board: $5830

Average GMAT score: 601

Average GPA: 3.0

GPA range: 2.1 to 3.8

Average years of work exp.: 3.75

Accepted applicants enrolled: 48%

Average starting pay: $62,900

Teaching methods: Lecture, 40%   Case study, 40%   Projects, 20%

Contact:
Audrey Randuk
Assistant Director of
Admissions
1-800-472-3622
*Final application
deadline:* May 15
for fall

Something rather odd occurred at Southern Methodist University's business school only a few years ago. Not a single MBA graduated in 1992. It wasn't because the faculty flunked an entire class of students. It was because the school ditched its compressed one-year MBA stint in favor of a more traditional two-year program. The upshot: The B-school missed an entire graduating class of MBAs.

Not to worry. The transformation to a two-year program allowed the dean and his faculty the unusual freedom of second-guessing everything the school had ever done. "The calendar change became an excuse for changing the whole program," says David H. Blake, dean of SMU's Cox School of Business. "We opened up everything for change. If we did it any other way, it would have brought out all kinds of resistance here and there. Besides, there wasn't time to engage in the bickering that affects so many faculties."

The result of all that work is one of the most topical and innovative MBA programs in the nation. Unfortunately, however, after leading these dramatic changes at the school, Blake decided to call it quits in early 1997 to run a family business. The school has since named Professor Michael E. McGill as interim dean. One thing's for sure, however. This is a vastly different school than the one that Blake took over in 1990 when he came to SMU after a stint as the dean of the Graduate School of Management at Rutgers University in New Jersey.

The differences begin in September, when local managers and executives who agree to mentor MBAs are invited to campus to mingle with first-years and to chat about their occupations and industries. Following the session, MBA candidates submit a list of who, among the 100 or so volunteers, they would prefer as mentors. Soon after, the pairings take place with professionals from such companies as American Airlines, AT&T, Coopers & Lybrand, EDS, Frito Lay, Goldman Sachs, Neiman-Marcus, Texas Instruments, and Xerox. Each manager, executive, entrepreneur, or venture capitalist is matched with as many as five MBA protégés. Throughout the two-year program, mentors meet with MBA candidates, invite them to their organizations for tours and corporate sessions, and share plenty of advice on business and careers.

All first-year newcomers move through a battery of skill and personality tests to assess their individual strengths and weaknesses. Former supervisors, direct reports, and peers are surveyed—generally nine people in all—to gather a little more insight into each MBA candidate. You're given a report on the results, which become the focus of a four-hour group discussion and an hour's worth of one-on-one counseling. Then, the report offers a host of recommendations to improve your performance. The school's Business Leadership Center sponsors seminars and workshops to cultivate more subtle skills. After your summer internship, the school puts you through another assessment—an effort to measure the impact of the leadership exercises that occur throughout the first year. A final assessment occurs toward the end of your MBA experience. "I can see us handing our graduates work programs along with their diplomas when they graduate," he says. If a corporation sent you through these leadership activities, it would cost as much as $8000 a person. The only other major B-school that has made assessment a fundamental part of its program is Case Western University.

Also in September, MBAs are required to participate in a daylong community-service project rehabilitating the homes of several Dallas-area low-income elderly minorities. The day merely sets the stage for a series of consulting projects students will undertake with local not-for-profit groups—the best student project wins $7500 in cash from Brown Brothers Harriman & Co., which donates the money to the charity. In the first go-round, student teams did studies for 19 community organizations. One group helped to reorganize the production flow of a local food bank. Another established an executive mentoring program in which managers helped disadvantaged teenagers get and keep jobs. In 1996, students worked with 25 nonprofit organizations, ranging from the Dallas Lighthouse for the Blind to the Trinity Ministry to the Poor, dedicating 80 hours to these consulting projects.

So what do community service, personal assessment testing, and mentoring have to do with the real world of business? The school believes these are among the missing elements of traditional MBA education that have led so many schools to produce generations of narrow and insular graduates, quick with a spreadsheet but slow to understand how to motivate and get along with people. The innovations did not end with these new wrinkles. What was once a frenetic 11-month program has been expanded and stretched over 21 months. The 60-hour program features about 33 hours of teaching in core courses. Each required class puts the emphasis on four key issues: international business, ethics, quality management, and workforce diversity. Cox now has four required courses in international business, and every course has been, in the words of former Dean Blake, "globalized." "We want all our people to breathe and think in a global context," he says.

Quality Management, the focus of three electives, has also been infused into several core courses. As much as 25 percent of the work in the core organizational behavior class is devoted to cultural diversity. Once you complete your core courses, the remaining hours of classwork can be chosen from an array of some 50 electives in six functional departments, the lion's share offered in finance. They range from Electronic Commerce and Practicum in Portfolio Management to Energy Economics and Decision Making. Many of these courses are in the evening, combined with the part-time program. Dean Blake teaches a weekly honors integration course that requires students to write a publishable paper in management. Examples: What Leads to Failure in Corporate TQM Efforts? or Why Is Speed a Competitive Advantage? The objective is to synthesize many of the concepts in the core and apply them to topical business problems.

The switch to a two-year schedule also made it easier to take electives outside the Cox School. Owing to its Texas locale, Cox also boasts a bevy of courses in oil and gas. There are study abroad options with five other business schools as well. The school also offers a more typical joint-degree program in law and business and a less typical program in business and the fine arts with the university's Meadows School. The latter experience is an ideal educational background for an administrative job in the art world. In the program's final semester, you're assigned an internship with a museum, orchestra, or zoo. Past graduates have flocked to jobs at such places as the Philadelphia Orchestra, the Dallas Symphony, the Fort Worth Opera, and the Bosch in Germany.

The new two-year MBA program has been well received by students. These changes are a key part of an aggressive campaign by the school to gain greater national recognition. The Leadership Center was created after meetings with executives from such companies as J.C. Penney, AT&T, American Airlines, Xerox, and Federal Express—an attempt to better meet the needs of the school's ultimate customers. In the fall of 1994, the Cox School handed out close to $1 million in student scholarships to lure better MBA candidates into the program, four times the scholarship fund of $250,000 in 1991. The dean was hoping to grow this kitty to $1.4 million.

Of all the Top 25 schools, this one is the smallest, with a full-time enrollment of just 272 students. That makes it an especially cozy and intimate place where students know each other and the faculty of just 69 profs by first names. The average number of students in a core class here is only 50, while the average in an elective is 45.

When you're not in the classroom, the grassy campus is inviting enough to study outdoors. The university's affiliation with the Methodist Church means that virtually all drinking must be done off campus. That's no problem at all for SMU MBAs, who don't have classes on Fridays. One Thursday evening ritual: margaritas on the patio at OTB—short for On the Border, a Mexican restaurant and bar only a short drive from Cox.

The school's tree-lined, 160-acre campus is set in the middle of University Park, an affluent residential neighborhood five miles from downtown Dallas. The $17 million Cox School is a horseshoe-shaped building, built in 1987, with an open courtyard in the center. Undergraduate and graduate business students have separate wings and dedicated classrooms in the three-story brick building. Few SMU grads live on campus. Most make their homes in "the village," a residential area of apartment complexes about a half-mile away from campus.

PLACEMENT DETAILS

Considering that only a few years ago this school didn't graduate a single student because of the change to a two-year program, SMU has been remarkably successful at luring back top corporate recruiters. In 1996, some 105 companies came to recruit second-years on campus, doing 440 interviews. That's pretty good for a program that graduates fewer than 140 MBAs a year. And some 290 job opportunities were posted via correspondence. Grads in the Class of 1996 averaged 2.6 jobs at graduation, though the school reports that one in every four MBAs failed to have a single job offer at commencement. No wonder there were some complaints about the career services office. Where did the luckier grads end up? Sabre (4); Ernst & Young (4); American Airlines (3); IBM (3); Equifax (2); Sun Microsystems (2);

Johnson & Johnson (2); NationsBank (2); Nortel (2); and Andersen Consulting (2).

Cox grads, of course, don't leave the school with the highest starting pay packages in the Top 25. With median salary, bonus, and perks of $62,350, the school ranks 23rd out of 25. But these same students had quit jobs that paid a median $30,000 a year—the least of any Top 25 school with the exception of Vanderbilt and Thunderbird, whose grads had the same pre-MBA salary.

OUTSTANDING FACULTY

Joseph Magliola (****—accounting); *Andrew Chen* (****—finance); *Randolph Beatty* (****—accounting); *Michael Vetsuypens* (****—finance); *Roch Parayre* (***—organizational behavior); *Uday Apte* (**—management information science); *Howard Bunsis* (**—accounting); *William Cron* (**—marketing); *Dileep Hurry* (**—strategy); *Kirk Tennant* (**—accounting).

APPLICANT TIPS

Cox requires personal interviews in the admissions process. After the admissions committee has reviewed your application, the school will call you to schedule an interview. You can complete the interview in person or by telephone. If a Cox faculty or administration member is visiting your city, you can meet for an interview there. Some 62 percent of applicants in 1996 were interviewed.

For a Top 25 school, Cox accepts a large percentage of applicants with little, if any, work experience. Fully 13 percent of the Class of 1998 has less than a year's worth of full-time work experience. If you want to visit the school to sit in on classes and get a feel for what the MBA program is like, you should call the graduate office at 214-768-2630 or fax your request to 214-768-4099.

Contact: Audrey Randuk
Assistant Director of Admissions
1-800-472-3622
Final application deadline: May 15 for fall

COX MBAs SOUND OFF

I am impressed with the quality of the faculty. We went through courses that we would not have been able to take in other programs. The interaction with faculty and peers is an A+ due to the size of the class.

The size of the classes [allows for] personal attention. I cannot say how important the mentors are in learning about prospective industries.

The SMU experience goes far beyond discounted cash flows, five forces modeling, and other general business concepts. We were challenged weekly and in an environment that fostered friendly competition. Students and faculty relate to each other in a helping and encouraging manner. As a result learning goes far beyond classroom discussions and into an open, ongoing forum where ideas are passed back and forth. SMU also offers many informal social activities: weekly socials, club meetings, and intramural competitions.

Why SMU exceeded my expectations: the Business Leadership Center for team-building and soft-skill training; the Mentoring Program, where you select local business leaders as mentors and begin to establish a personal network.

The level of core and elective finance and accounting far exceeded my expectations. The amount of theory and practical application in each discipline was excellent. The breadth of finance classes ranged from extremely quantitative derivative securities to a challenging qualitative/quantitative portfolio class in which 15 students managed $2 million of the school's endowment.

Dallas is a city that lives and dies by commerce. You can feel it everywhere you go. Information technology and computer literacy are stressed. We are kept in constant contact with the community. The small class sizes and informal atmosphere make faculty very accessible.

Even though I rated SMU's Career Services Office somewhat low, I do not feel that this subtracted from the quality of my education. I am very interested in health care and knew I would have to rely on personal networking and other job-search strategies when I chose to pursue an MBA rather than an MHA. The lecturers and course materials at Cox were very good and the networking opportunities simply outstanding. Overall, I have been very pleased with my experience.

I received the knowledge to transfer my skills from an engineering background to finance. However, the lack of popularity of SMU's MBA program among investment banks was a big obstacle for me to overcome. Although I have the skills to work in any investment bank, I was unable to get an offer from any of them. Most of their recruiters are inclined toward the top 5–6 schools. Electives, especially finance courses, were excellent, but not some of the required courses.

The small classes made this a special place. Instructors were always available. Members of the administration knew everyone by name. The small size, however, stopped some companies from recruiting on campus, making it harder to get into those firms. Friends at some of the Top 20 schools are surprised at some of our electives and opportunities.

SMU's relationship with the business community is outstanding, and it's very receptive to the wants and needs of students, in classes and at the Business Leadership Center.

The teaching and camaraderie among students at SMU is outstanding. The administration is very accessible to students who have any concerns or questions. A very challenging and rewarding experience.

The school must attract candidates with more (and higher quality) work experience. I was accepted at Chicago and Vanderbilt but feel that SMU maximized my MBA experience.

I've met some of the most diverse and nicest people. I've lived [in different places] and traveled extensively, so to meet people from areas I've not been to has helped me gain new insights. I'd be better off in Dallas with my degree, at a disadvantage pursuing my interests in Chicago, Philly, or New York.

SMU has generous financial assistance, a good placement office, great availability of professors, [but] average quality of students.

Personal attention received by admissions and all instructors was superior. Classmates contributed to my education greatly. I credit the admissions office for getting high quality and bright individuals into the program. Many of them were sought after by Top 10 schools but chose SMU because of its academic excellence. SMU also attracts high-profile instructors.

The quality of the professors was unbelievably high. The only problem was that 10–20 percent of the students did not put their full effort into their assignments. I had no full-time work experience when I arrived at SMU, but I was still able to beat out top graduates from the "top schools" for my job.

24.
VANDERBILT UNIVERSITY

VANDERBILT UNIVERSITY

Owen Graduate School of Management
Nashville, Tennessee 37203
E-mail address: owenadms@ctrvax.vanderbilt.edu
Website address: http://www.vanderbilt.edu/Owen/

Corporate ranking: 40	Graduate ranking: 19
Enrollment: 427	Annual tuition & fees: $21,800
Women: 24%	Room and board: $7850
Non-U.S.: 23%	Average GMAT score: 615
Minority: 7%	Average GPA: 3.2
Part-time: none	GPA range: 2.0 to 4.0
Average age: 26.1	Average years of work exp.: 3.5
Applicants accepted: 42%	Accepted applicants enrolled: 47%
Median starting pay: $59,000	Average starting pay: $62,900

Teaching methods: Lecture, 50%   Case study, 40%   Projects, 10%

Contact:
Tami Fassinger
Director of Admissions
615-322-6469
Application deadlines:
November 15
January 15
March 14

Vanderbilt University's Owen School is a worthy beneficiary of BUSINESS WEEK's decision to enlarge its ranking of the best business schools to 25 institutions in 1996. The school—which had broken into the BW Top 20 for the first time in 1992, only to fall out two years later—is one of the gems in the world of management education.

Sadly, it lost ground in 1994 when the graduating class was nearly caustic in its criticism of Dean Martin S. Geisel, a big, hulking academic with a Ph.D. from Chicago. Many MBAs believed he had failed to adequately manage a student scandal that erupted in 1994, when a student government officer allegedly embezzled about $3000 out of the treasury. Some grads thought Geisel should have either suspended the individual or withheld his degree. Instead the student was required to return the money and complete 100 hours of community service before gaining his degree.

To be fair, Geisel says his hands were somewhat tied by university policy and a need to keep the specifics of the case confidential. "My first reaction was, 'What a dumb thing [for a student] to have done,' " says Dean Geisel. "But I also was disappointed in why the students couldn't place their trust in the university's established procedures to deal with this. Some students got highly agitated about it and thought the guy wasn't being punished at all."

With that incident behind him, Geisel worked hard to get the school back on track. He has succeeded. After all, Geisel had brought the school national prominence since coming on board in 1987. He hired a slew of new faculty members, recruiting tenured profs with endowed chairs from several universities and real-world practitioners from admired companies such as Hewlett-Packard and Northern Telecom. In the basic curriculum, he placed greater emphasis on communication skills and international business. No less interesting, the school has launched an entire sequence of courses in environmental management, electronic commerce, health care, customer service, service quality measurement, and response time and quality management—relatively new areas where management thinking is rapidly changing. Owen also added a concentration in entrepreneurship.

Owen only recently reached adulthood in the B-school world, having celebrated its twenty-first birthday in 1990. It is a school with a quirky history. The school was founded by local businessmen who wanted a quality regional school to keep Southerners at home and away from Harvard. The school is named after Ralph Owen, a star quarterback at Vanderbilt in the late 1920s and founder of Equitable Securities Corp. In the 1970s, the school became a victim of the counterculture, a place where encounter sessions and sensitivity training assumed more importance than basic accounting and finance. At that time, when international enrollment at B-schools was minuscule, up to 40 percent of the students were foreign. The university's Board of Trust came within one vote of shutting it down in 1975. Instead, Owen found a new dean who began to build a more middle-of-the-road business school. Dean Geisel, who once taught economics at Carnegie Mellon and the University of Rochester, installed his changes on top of what had become a rather basic, but quality, MBA program.

He had a lot going for him. One pleasant surprise is the lack of undergraduate students. The full-time MBA program is not only the flagship program, it's basically the only program, other than an Executive MBA. There are no business undergrads and no part-time students at Owen. So MBAs don't have to share or fight with others for quality time with the faculty or the staff in the computing lab or the library. The

10-to-1 student-faculty ratio, one of the lowest among the top B-schools, assures lots of attention anyway. Everything occurs in Management Hall, a modern red-brick and plate-glass building merged with Old Mechanical, one of the oldest structures on the 300-acre campus.

Owen starts you off in late August with a five-day orientation period, which includes sessions on career planning and an Outward Bound–like group problem-solving and team-building experience. The groups used during orientation are deliberately formed to maximize diversity, and students remain in these groups for various purposes through the first year of the program. First-years are divided into three sections, though the typical cohort system at larger MBA factories does not apply here. The small size of the school does not require it.

The school will march you through 12 core courses, including a required three-credit communications class that stretches over the first two semesters. The course features self-assessment tests, then aims to build a communications program to help address a student's weak points. Owen made the class a requirement after alumni urged the school during a curriculum review to put more emphasis on oral and written presentations and negotiation skills. You can waive out of the lecture-dominated core classes, but must substitute electives in their place. You can pick up to five graduate courses outside the business school, including study of a foreign language. A total of 21 courses are required to graduate.

It's telling that the areas of marketing and operations management boast as many or more electives as finance and accounting—the mainstays of every business school. Some grads grouse that Owen's finance classes tend to lack enough real-world application. Far stronger, they say, are the school's offerings in both marketing and operations. Owen probably offers the most extensive curriculum in service quality at any MBA program. Among its 15 marketing electives is a minisequence in services that begins with Customer Service and the Customer Orientation, taught by Roland Rust. Organized around the Baldrige Award criteria, the course is an intro to service quality and relationship management. The second course is a Services Internship in which students complete work projects for such companies as AT&T, Northern Telecom, Federal Express, NationsBank, and others for academic credit. That's followed by Service Quality Measurement, a seminar-like course taught by Rich Oliver. The course teaches MBAs the nuts and bolts of how to measure service quality and the psychology of customer satisfaction.

Despite the school's small size, with a full-time enrollment of just 427 MBAs, Owen offers students a surprisingly broad selection of elective courses. Among the 105 offerings are such novel courses as Management of Intellectual Assets, Electronic Commerce & the Virtual Organization, and Management of Global Environmental Issues. Another elective standout: the Seminar on Trade and Industrial Competitiveness. The course kicks off with six weeks of classes, then students are divided into teams that go off to a foreign locale during the spring vacation to study some aspect of international business. Over the years, students have trekked to Japan, Europe, Mexico, and Latin America. Other than pocket change, students don't have to pay for these excursions because the costs are underwritten by sponsoring companies. Owen has also recently launched a new international elective on Global Competitiveness taught by the retired CEO of Northern Telecom, Edmund Fitzgerald, and another on current United States-Japan Relations. Owen also has student exchange programs with nine business schools outside the United States in such locales as Chile, Costa Rica, Brazil, Mexico, Venezuela, Germany, France, England, and Sweden.

Just about everyone—students and faculty alike—lives within a five-mile radius of the school. Most graduate students share off-campus apartments that can be rented for $600 a month. The San Antonio Taco Co., across the street from the B-school, is the number-one hangout for MBAs, who go there for buckets of beer on ice and Mexican fare. Only one block away, students converge on Granite Falls, a well-known meeting place for hamburgers, salads, and singles. The campus itself is on the fringe of the inner city, about two and a half miles from downtown Nashville. Of course there's Opryland USA and Graceland, which everyone visits once. A more regular event is the Keg in the Courtyard on Thursdays at 5 p.m. after which it's time for the Larry Tate Society, a diehard group that moves to a local bar once the keg is drained. The "society" takes its name from the advertising exec on the TV show "Bewitched." Thank goodness there are no classes on Friday.

Students, including those from abroad, find Nashville a welcoming locale. In the home of country music you don't have to look hard to find anything, from home-cooked Southern meals to gourmet dining, or from hole-in-the-wall bluegrass joints to slightly pretentious supper clubs. Though the city is hardly a corporate center, it is home base to a few national companies, including Hospital Corporation of America, Genesco, and Aladdin Industries.

As a newcomer among the top schools, however, Vanderbilt's program is still in an improving mode. The alumni base is thin, with some 3650 alums. (Indeed the notes describing the doings of grads cover only four or five pages in *The Owen Manager*, even though the alumni magazine is published only twice a year.) Though there are no MBA alumni clubs, the school hosts receptions and meetings in a dozen cities a year.

PLACEMENT DETAILS

Like most second-tier business schools, which get less traffic from the high-paying consulting and investment banking firms, Vanderbilt's placement record isn't going to make any headlines. About 19 percent of the Class of 1996 failed to have a single job offer at graduation. Those that did walked away with 2.3 job offers each, the lowest of any Top 25 school with the exception of Thunderbird, which posted the same average.

Owen says that 155 companies recruited second-year students on campus in 1996, conducting 2380 interviews. Another 2100 jobs were posted via correspondence. The major employers: Ernst & Young Consulting (8); Arthur Andersen (5); Federal Express (5); Procter & Gamble (3); Deloitte & Touche Consulting (3); Towers Perrin (3); Wheat First Butcher (3); Eastman Chemical (3); Cummins Engine (2); Chase (2); Hallmark (2); Citicorp (2); Continental (2); America West Airlines (2); and Brown & Williamson (2).

That's a broad cross-section of some of the nation's top MBA recruiters. Dean Geisel has gotten the school back on track.

OUTSTANDING FACULTY

William G. Christie (****—finance); *Ronald W. Masulis* (****—finance); *Nancy Lea Hyer* (****—operations); *Roger Huang* (****—finance); *Hans R. Stoll* (***—finance); *William Spitz* (**—finance); *David Rados* (**—marketing); *Cliff Ball* (**—economics); *Gary Scudder* (**—operations management); *Greg Stewart* (**—organizational behavior).

APPLICANT TIPS

Personal interviews are a key part of the admissions process at Vanderbilt, which is one of the few top business schools to interview 100 percent of its applicants. The school uses interviews to "assess your career aspirations and plans and to explore your motivation and clarity of purpose." Obviously, successful applicants need to make a good impression. Vanderbilt prefers to interview applicants when they visit the campus.

If a visit isn't possible, the school's admissions staff conducts interviews in at least 13 major cities, from Atlanta to San Francisco. To arrange a campus visit, you can call 800-288-OWEN and ask for the campus visit coordinator. Admission decisions at Vanderbilt are made on a continuous basis from December 1 through July 1.

Apply as early as possible to enhance the odds of gaining an invite—especially if you lack two or more years of work experience. The school is trying to attract applicants with more work experience and is giving preference to such candidates. About 8 percent of the Class of 1998 has less than one year of full-time work experience. If you boast two or more years of work experience and apply by May 2, the school will mail you its decision by July 2.

Contact: Tami Fassinger
Director of Admissions
615-322-6469
Application deadlines: November 15, January 15, and March 14

OWEN MBAs SOUND OFF

Located in one of the nation's friendlier cities, Owen reflects the best of Nashville. Owen offers a highly accessible faculty that is comprised of nationally recognized leaders in their respective fields. The close interaction among students is unparalleled, allowing unique friendships and teamwork to develop both inside and outside the walls of Owen. The curriculum itself is evolving to reflect Nashville's leadership in the health care industry with respected leaders Doug Smith and Jim Cooper expanding the quality and number of the program's health care offerings. My only regret is that time did not permit me to take all the electives I desired. This singular constraint, however, will be eliminated when Owen moves to a modular system in the fall of 1996.

The Owen School has greatly improved in two years. Student government has been reorganized to provide it with greater influence. The administration has been enhanced with additions (of people) that make the administration more responsive. We had the best lecture series in recent history, a new community group was founded, and our class is going to greatly exceed its class gift goal. I think it's great that the school is changing the core classes and allowing for additional coursework. While I was pleased with my education, the Marketing Dept. needs to be strengthened beyond its customer satisfaction focus. The need for brand management classes continues. Placement was a great resource and I had over 10 on-campus interviews with companies such as: Compaq, FedEx, PPG, Ryder System, Sara Lee, Fruit of the Loom, and Block Financial.

The greatest part about Owen is that you can never get lost in the crowd. The small size promotes a cohesive and active student body. I'm proud to be associated with people who care so much about the school and each other.

Owen does an amazing job of tailoring the curriculum to individual student needs. The beauty of attending a small school is when you ask for something you usually get it. For example, I wanted a course in non-profit marketing; Dean Hyer added it to the schedule even though only three students enrolled. That course was the best I've ever taken. I was also able to complete three concentrations, including a custom concentration. That would have been impossible at most schools. Finally, Owen students can take courses at other colleges within Vanderbilt. I've taken Management of Technology at the Graduate School of Engineering. My roommate's taken Employment Law at the Law School. You get the best of both worlds here.

Falling out of the Top 20 during my first year turned out to be a blessing in disguise. The administration became much more receptive to student concerns, the students also dedicated themselves to improving the school. These efforts resulted in improved communication with the administration, restructuring of the student government, formation of a unique community service group, and student participation in a comprehensive curriculum review. These changes and the recent large gift from the Owen estate should serve Owen well for years to come.

The enthusiasm for the school can be proven by looking at the Class of '96's class gift: $123,000 over 5 years—the largest in Owen's history. The money will be used to remodel the placement and admissions offices to make them more friendly and comfortable to students and corporate recruiters.

In order to meet student desires to be able to take more elective courses, the administration undertook the enormous task of revamping the curriculum. As a result, next year, the school will be using an overlapping schedule of courses, instead of the traditional semester framework. Some of the core courses have been shortened to half-semester courses to allow students to take more electives and focus their studies more. Congratulations must go to the administration for responding quickly and efficiently to this matter.

As 1 of 14 students selected to travel with the Dean to Chile during Spring Break, I spent a great deal of time discussing his vision of the program. While I found the Dean to be very business-like at school, similar to my exposure to CEOs in the business world, my one-on-one contact exposed a focused and caring leader. He has built an undistinguished program into one of the top programs in the country. He seems to pride himself on hiring the best personnel to handle routine matters, yet is available for big picture, strategic matters. In my time here, he has recognized the need to: bring in outside consultants to objectively analyze the program; modernize the curriculum, which will become effective in the fall; continually attract new teaching talent; and bring in an experienced MBA Director. I applaud his efforts and this school's direction.

I was part of a team that secured the bid for the 1997 Graduate Business Conference and traveled to Canada and Barcelona, Spain to promote that effort. I also was on the start-up committee of the revamped community service organization, co-named "100% Owen," that gained national recognition in a matter of months. My acknowledgment of these two experiences is not to pat myself on the back,

but to demonstrate the support of the students and especially the administration in making Owen a better place.

I was especially pleased by the amount of real-world experience I gained while enrolled at Owen. Like many professionals returning to school for an MBA, I wanted to make a career change (in my case, from computer systems integration to service marketing). During my two years at Owen, I completed seven major projects for outside companies: five in marketing, one in finance, and one in human resources. The hands-on experience I gained through these class projects was extremely valuable. These experiences not only helped me better define my career objectives within the field of marketing, but they also gave me tangible results to discuss during job interviews.

**25.
AMERICAN
GRADUATE
SCHOOL OF
INTERNA-
TIONAL
MANAGEMENT**

AMERICAN GRADUATE SCHOOL OF INTERNATIONAL MANAGEMENT

Thunderbird
15249 N. 59th Avenue
Glendale, Arizona 85306-6003
E-mail address: tbird@t-bird.edu
Web-site address: http://www.t-bird.edu

Corporate ranking: 23	Graduate ranking: 26
Enrollment: 1420	Annual tuition & fees: $18,950
Women: 35%	Room and board: $4800
Non-U.S.: 33%	Average GMAT score: 572
Minority: 10%	Average GPA: 3.41
Part-time: none	GPA range: 2.51 to 4.0
Average age: 27	Average years of work exp.: 3.38
Applicants accepted: 75%	Accepted applicants enrolled: 64%
Median starting pay: $57,000	Average starting pay: $56,585

Teaching methods: Lecture, 32% Case study, 32% Projects, 36%

Contact:
Judy Johnson
Director of Admissions
800-848-9084 or
602-978-7100
*Final application
deadline:*
January 31 for
summer and fall
entrance;
July 31 for
Winterim and
spring entrance

At graduation every year, the Thunderbird grads do more than don mortarboards and gowns: Many of them carry the flags of their home countries in a colorful parade of bright reds, whites, yellows, and blues. The accents are as varied as the visitors from as many as 60 different countries around the world. "In a lot of ways, this place is like the United Nations," says David A. Ricks, vice president for academic affairs.

Indeed, it is. If you can imagine a business school version of the UN, it might well be the American Graduate School of International Management. The global nature of the school can be seen everywhere on the 160-acre campus. The United Nations flag flies outside the administration building, while a "flag of the day" flaps in the dry Arizona wind in front of Founders Hall.

The uniqueness of the program, of course, goes well beyond these mere symbols. Students here complete not one but three areas of study: culture, language, and business. An internship program offers opportunities to gain experience in multinational corporations and trade agencies. At any one time, a fifth of the enrollment is overseas in internships and exchange or study abroad programs. Every graduate leaves the program with fluency in a foreign language.

Yet, it is not unusual for snobby academics to turn up their noses when you mention Thunderbird to them. Roy Herberger says that some of his academic colleagues expressed surprise when he told them he had agreed in 1989 to become president of the Thunderbird program. They warned him that he would never be able to return to the world of academia.

Phooey on them. Anyone seriously interested in international business cannot fail to consider going to this school for a Master's in business. Thunderbird, which takes its nickname from its location on a deactivated army air training base just outside Phoenix, was offering a global slant to business education when most B-school deans never thought it was important. Indeed, for 30 years, the school had the only international business program in the United States. The school was founded by Lt. General Barton Kyle Yount in 1946 to help Americans enter the emerging international business environment.

Now that nearly every executive chatters on about global-this and global-that, Thunderbird is sitting pretty. One recent study proclaimed it the No. 1 international MBA program in the country. Even after increasing tuition by 25 percent in 1990, enrollment zoomed to an all-time high of over 1500. Some students were sitting on the floors in classes. Those growing pains were relieved after President Herberger sank nearly $15 million into four new Southwestern-styled buildings, with red tiled roofs and white stucco trim. In the past two years he has cut ribbons outside a new classroom and lecture hall, a building for his international studies faculty, a world business/administration building, and yet another dormitory (in addition to the dozen or so he already dedicated). (The school houses more than 500 students on campus.) In June 1994, Thunderbird opened a new library that offers state-of-the-art electronic retrieval systems. Behind Harvard and Wharton, it now boasts the third largest full-time enrollment of any B-school in the United States, with 1420 students.

Thunderbird offers about 45 international business courses and just as many classes in the cultural, political, legal, and religious aspects of countries. Students tend to major in or focus on regions of the world instead of narrow discipli-nary functions. "So a student wanting to study Arabic will start with the Arabic language," says Herberger, who left Southern Methodist University's B-school for the presidency at Thunderbird. "Then they'll also, alongside of it, start studying the politics of Islam. They'll look at the cultural influence of the Saudis and royal families. There are a lot of different things that go into the shaping of business practices of an area."

The school offers plenty of flexibility. Students can enter this program at four different points in any year: January, February, June, or September. To graduate, you must be proficient in a foreign language. If you're already fluent in another language when you enter the program, you'll be required to complete 54 hours of coursework in international studies, world business, and electives. If not, you'll have to add nine extra hours of work—mainly in 1 of 10 modern languages from Arabic to Russian. You can waive out of the core courses in the business basics if you've already covered the material in undergraduate or graduate classes, which can reduce the program to its minimum of 42 semester hours. If you haven't been trained in business and a language, expect to stay at Thunderbird for close to two years. There are 75 electives in the catalog, 25 percent of which are new in the past three years.

Among the school's most unusual features is Winterim every January. It's a three-week period when the school serves up an unusual menu of courses taught by prominent international experts who travel from around the globe to Arizona to teach. The courses have ranged from Marketing to U.S. Hispanics Seminar to Privatization, and from Countertrade/Offset to Doing Business in Eastern Europe and Russia. A Winterim CEO seminar in 1994 featured the chairmen and presidents of ARCO International, Harley Davidson, CNN International-Turner Broadcasting, McDonnell Douglas Helicopter, and Honeywell International.

Most business schools offer just a few study-abroad programs. Thunderbird has a slew of them. You can go to the school's own facility in Japan to study a select range of regular courses or regionally specific offerings. You can take a 10-week session in Guadalajara during the summer for courses taught by Thunderbird profs and Mexican scholars. If you're proficient in German, you can take off for the European Business School at Schloss Reichartshausen in Germany, which offers a two-month internship with a German or U.S. multinational corporation. Or you might want to try the 9-week summer program in France. There are more options in the People's Republic of China, Finland, Norway, and Spain. In early 1993, Thunderbird also opened a campus in Archamps, France, on the outskirts of Geneva, Switzerland, its second satellite after the one established in Tokyo in 1991. It's also training Russian managers in Western business practices at three locations in the former Soviet Union.

Many students come here to pursue careers outside of the conventional business world. "It's more than a business school," says Ricks. "A lot of the things we are doing in international studies are not offered in regular schools." Foreign ambassadors regularly come to the campus to speak with students, and one of every five graduates goes to work for such not-for-profit places as the CIA, World Health Organization, the Peace Corps, and, of course, the United Nations.

At Thunderbird, only recently accredited by the AACSB, grads earn a MIM (Master in International Management) instead of the MBA. The core curriculum differs from the typical MBA fare. Although the average GMAT scores here have risen by more than 50 points since 1986, they're still on the low side—at 572 for the Class of 1998, they're the lowest of any BUSINESS WEEK Top 25 school.

Still, there's no shortage of recruiters wanting the grads. More than 20,000 Thunderbird graduates populate the ranks of such companies as General Motors, American Express, IBM, and General Electric. Thunderbird's top employers are the U.S. Department of State, where 93 alums work; Citibank (88); Chase Manhattan Bank (88); Merrill Lynch (66); Bank of America (64); U.S. Department of Commerce (45); IBM (44); U.S. Agency for International Development (44); Electronic Data Systems (42); Motorola (42); Chemical Bank (37); and Ford Motor (31). Many graduates have foreign postings, or U.S. jobs with international responsibilities. The alumni network is large and strong. On the first Tuesday of every month, alumni gather in local pubs and bars in 157 cities around the world, from Mexico City to Taipei. T-Birds, as they call themselves, live in more than 130 countries and in every state of the United States.

PLACEMENT DETAILS

Don't expect big money after graduating with a Thunderbird degree. In 1996, grads of the school earned median starting pay packages of $57,000—dead last among the Top 25 schools. The MBAs of 10 Runners-up schools earned more than Thunderbird grads in 1996. That sum still has to be viewed in perspective: these same grads earned only $30,000 a year before attending the school—also dead last among the Top 25.

In 1996, 271 companies came to campus to recruit students, conducting 3504 interviews. Some 2005 job opportunities were posted by correspondence. The major employers: Citibank (16); Ernst & Young (11); Zenith (7); Cargill (6); EDS (5); General Motors (5); Intel (5); Coca-Cola (5); AT&T (4); and Scherling-Plough (4).

OUTSTANDING FACULTY

Robert Howell (****—accounting); *Michael Moffett* (****—international finance); *Frank Tuzolino* (***—finance); *John Zerio* (***—marketing); *Kenneth Ferris* (**—accounting); *Caren Siehl* (**—human resources); *Dale Davison* (**—accounting); *Sundaresan Ram* (**—marketing); *Glen Fong* (**—international studies); *Paul Kinsinger* (**—international studies).

APPLICANT TIPS

As a Top 25 school, Thunderbird, is something of an oddity: it accepts 75 percent of its applicants, a number which makes it hardly selective amidst the company of some of the world's choosiest schools. That said, however, Thunderbird's global bent means that applicants with international experience and exposure are likely to have an advantage over others with similar GMAT scores and undergraduate grade point averages. If your professional work experience is international in scope, you stand an even greater chance of getting through the door. Indeed, the application process requires an essay describing "international motivation and accomplishments." Thunderbird allows students to enter the program at any one of four times: summer, fall, spring, and Winterim, an intensive three-week term held every January. The final deadline for fall or summer entrance is January 31. For Winterim and the spring term, the final deadline is July 31. Admission decisions are made within eight weeks of the deadline. Interviews are not required for admission.

Walking tours of the campus are scheduled every Monday, Thursday, and Friday of the school year. Tours begin at noon and include a complimentary lunch in the student dining hall followed by information sessions. To arrange a visit or gain other admission details, contact the admissions office at 800-848-9084 or via fax at 602-439-5432.

Contact: Judy Johnson
Director of Admissions
800-848-9084 or 602-978-7100

Final application deadline: January 31 for summer and fall entrance; July 31 for Winterim and spring entrance

THUNDERBIRD GRADS SOUND OFF

The number and diversity of the students makes Thunderbird a very challenging institution. However, because there are so many students, there is a lot of competition for the jobs and interviews on campus.

There is not a day in which we could not talk about or actually see the changes the school is experiencing: new outstanding faculty were hired; a senior vice-president for academic affairs joined the administration; new dorms and pool were constructed; a new information technology building is under construction; a new dining hall is expected to be ready this year. All in just one year and six months! All without large endowments or government money! All of this while receiving superb teaching in languages, international studies, and business!

Thunderbird is not in the "hiring loop." Companies usually begin reviewing résumés in the fall and interviewing in the spring. Thunderbird students graduate at the end of fall, spring, or summer. Therefore, only a third or so are in the "loop" of U.S. corporate hiring of MBAs. This explains our low percentage of hired graduates.

T-Bird provides a unique alternative to the generic MBA program, with a tripartite curriculum. This is what makes Thunderbird stand out from the rest. Although the quality of teaching in core courses is not at the level of a Top 10 MBA program, there are "5000-level" elective courses offered by the school which do meet the high quality standard.

I loved the flexibility a student has when choosing courses. Instead of being forced to follow a rigid structure, I was free to choose classes that allowed me to strengthen my weaknesses and apply my previous work experience."

Thunderbird is not the typical MBA—that is why I love the MIM Program. The unusual curriculum (languages, international studies, and international business) and the student international diversity attracted me the most to T-Bird. Also, I like the fact that the program is not rigid. You have up to five years to complete the program, allowing one to take internships and adhere to your own schedule. Also, you can finish the program in two or three semesters (less than a year). There is room for leadership and for getting involved at T-Bird. There are many clubs organized by the students (i.e., Wine Tasting, International Business Women, Adventure, etc.). We believe in party hard and study hard.

In a day and age where the only way to do business is globally, Thunderbird provides an excellent education to future global business leaders. Not only does this school teach the basics of all the other MBA schools, but provides understanding of cultures, languages, and customs. Even the core courses have a global component. Students leave Thunderbird with an understanding of how to do business in every area of the world. You can't say that for a typical MBA program.

Thunderbird is not well known domestically so many firms are missing the wealth of talent here. Students at Thunderbird exceed MBA standards in my opinion because critical leadership/team building skills that cross-cultural business requires are emphasized.

Additionally, the low GMAT average does not indicate the quantitative abilities of T-Birds—there are really excellent students!

The school is outstanding in terms of its "international" spin, i.e., guest speakers, diverse students, and faculty, symposia, and course offerings. The school is very weak, however, in general management and traditional MBA-style courses such as information technology, economics, finance, and accounting, which need to be further integrated with the International Studies Department in order to be effective. More money needs to be dedicated to arming students with a core set of skills, and less on the visual appearance of the school (i.e., landscaping).

The administration does not respond to the students (but the faculty almost always does). I have three job offers but it is because I did my job search entirely on my own and that's the way Career Services prefers it. They don't want to lift a finger to help a student. All of their advice is outdated. This will not change because the administration has too much invested in career services to change it.

I have had the opportunity to choose from an unbeatable selection of timely and interesting international business courses (e.g., International Finance and Trade and Legal Environment of International Business), core-business courses (e.g., Finance, Accounting), and language courses tailored to the international business environment (e.g., Commercial Spanish: Documentation and Operations). This "triumvirate" of business, international studies, and language creates, in my opinion, the most valuable and well-rounded curriculum possible. Not only is the school's curriculum strong, but it offers significant and unique practical experience. I have participated in a simulated futures trading game, I have worked directly with companies like Mattel Inc. and Sensormatic Inc. as both a consultant and as a strategic international marketing planner. I have also spent a semester abroad in Guadalajara, Mexico where I was exposed firsthand to Mexican society and business practices.

If there is one thing that is truly unique about Thunderbird, it is the general openness of alumni (and students) to assisting one another in any way possible, particularly when confronted with personal or commercial challenges abroad. The experience of connecting with fellow T-Birds overseas is unlike what happens when other MBA grads meet, at least from what I can tell. It is almost a spiritual experience of meeting a like-minded, kindred member of the international community. T-Birds seem to automatically go into action to support and assist each other, as if they were family.

One of the most positive aspects of my T-Bird experience was the opportunity to study at the Thunderbird Europe campus, outside of Geneva, Switzerland. My classes were small, the teaching quality excellent, and we had several opportunities to go on company visits, both in the Geneva area and in London (we took an investment banking trip). These opportunities were extremely practical, as we met professionals and had networking opportunities.

THE RUNNERS-UP

Just about everyone who considers going to get an MBA wants the degree stamped by the most prestigious university brand possible. It's easy to understand why. Just look at the starting pay packages earned by graduates of those schools and imagine the well-connected networks of their alums. But not everyone can pass through the tight admission screens of the elite schools.

Some people believe that if you can't get into a Top 25 school, it's not worth the bother. That's not true at all. Truth is, you don't have to go to a Top 25 school to get a good graduate business education. This next group of 25 schools, dubbed Runners-Up to our best list, generally deliver the same basic body of knowledge and quality of education you'll find in the more prominent institutions. In some cases, the quality of education may even exceed some of the schools in the top list, especially in certain niche areas. Babson College, for example, is widely recognized as the best business school in the world in entrepreneurship. The University of Tennessee can rightly boast of having the best program in total quality management. Few Top 25 schools, moreover, can offer a better program in management information systems than the University of Minnesota, just as few schools on the best list can top Purdue University in the field of production and operations management. Ohio State's real estate program is no slouch, either.

So what's the difference? Overall, these schools often lack the breadth of quality offered at the Top 25. Not only will you find fewer superb teachers and scholars at these schools, you'll also discover that these schools are more likely to lack the infrastructure in support of demanding, discerning students. Graduates of these programs may also find it a little more difficult to connect with the job market, particularly the prestige employers. And they will also discover that the alumni networks of these schools are far less cohesive and valuable than those in the Top 25.

Still, some of the Runners-Up schools are just as selective as their elite counterparts. Some even boast better records of placing their students. And some boast professors in certain niche areas that can put teachers in the Top 25 to shame.

BUSINESS WEEK lists this group alphabetically, without an actual ranking.

> The quality of education may exceed some of the Top 25 schools.

BABSON COLLEGE

F.W. Olin Graduate School of Business
Babson Park, Massachusetts 02157-0310
E-mail address: mbaadmissions@babson.edu
Website address: http://www.babson.edu/mba

Enrollment: 1674	Annual tuition & fees: $20,800
Women: 35%	Room and board: $9225
Non-U.S.: 31%	Average GMAT score: 599
Minority: 14%	Average GPA: 3.0
Part-time: 1315	GPA range: 2.0 to 3.8
Average age: 28	Average years of work exp.: 5.1
Applicants accepted: 48%	Accepted applicants enrolled: 40%
Median starting pay: $60,000	Average starting pay: $57,288

Teaching methods: Lecture, 10%   Case study, 70%
                           Field programs, 20%

Contact:
Rita S. Edmunds
Director of MBA
Admissions
617-239-5124
Application deadlines:
January 15
March 1
April 15

A decade ago, when William F. Glavin, the vice chairman of Xerox Corp. and a member of the Wharton School's board of trustees, was giving a speech to the faculty there, he hinted that management education was ripe for a revolution. With Corporate America about to undergo wrenching changes, the world of B-schools would have to follow suit, he told them. "Wharton was doing a spectacular job of educating people for jobs that didn't exist," Glavin says now.

But as one trustee at a venerated, tradition-bound institution, he wasn't in a position to do very much. Two years later, and 300 miles to the northeast, that changed. On July 1, 1989, Glavin became president of Babson College in Wellesley, Massachusetts, beginning an eight-year tenure filled with radical change during which the school became known for its leadership in entrepreneurship. Babson scrapped its entire core curriculum in 1993, replacing it with a first year unlike virtually anything else in MBA education today. Students don't take traditional courses in marketing, finance, or operations. Instead, they're led through four modules that are supposed to mimic the life of a business. They may see a marketing expert one day and a finance jock the next. "We're trying to teach an entrepreneurial way of thinking," says Allan R. Cohen, dean of Babson's management school.

As the technology revolution pulls down the barriers between industries and continents, managers need to learn to be more flexible, Babson profs argue. It is, in some ways, the mantra of the '90s: Be lean, act quickly, think like an entrepreneur—no matter how big your company is. "Graduate business education should have changed a long time ago," Glavin says. Even amidst all the changes that have happened at B-schools in the last decade, Babson, for better or worse, stands out. Indeed, Glavin says that when Harvard administrators were visiting more than two dozen other B-schools as preparation for their own curriculum reform, they listed Babson as the only school that has changed "radically."

Has it worked? Largely yes—though the school still has some major weaknesses. They will be left to Leo I. Higdon, the dean of the University of Virginia's Darden School, who is succeeding Glavin. Higdon comes with an impressive B-school reputation. In his four years in Thomas Jefferson country, the former investment banker reached out to companies, meeting with more than 150, to find out what they wanted in MBAs. He didn't exactly ignore students, either. Ninety-four percent of U-Va's class of '96 gave donations to the school, and it grabbed the top spot in BUSINESS WEEK's student satisfaction survey. The school's overall rank shot up seven places, from 12th to 5th.

Now he comes north to try to vault Babson into the first tier of U.S. B-schools. The first piece of good news is financial. Babson's endowment has more than quadrupled since Glavin's arrival and now stands at $96 million. Alumni participation in fund-raising has doubled since 1993 to 34 percent. The results: in the last five years, the faculty has grown by 30 percent to 148, and the $15 million Olin Hall that sits at the center of campus opened in September, 1996.

Nothing is more important to the school than the unusual first year. It begins with a monthlong module on creative management that's similar to many of the teamwork exercises used at other schools. Students work together in outdoor exercises and community service projects. They review writing, math, economics, and computer skills. There's even a "creativity" seminar which is rather different from what you'll find on most campuses: students take a five-week class in fiction, sculpture, poetry, theater, or another art to get their mental juices flowing. It's part of the school's heavy emphasis on entrepreneurship—the field in which it's long been known as a national leader.

They spend the rest of the fall learning the analytical skills needed to assess business opportunities and companies' competitive positions. Here, they begin working in groups of six with a mentor company in the Boston area. Two examples: State Street Bank and Digital Equipment. First, the team compiles an industry profile that looks at the competition. Then, during the second half of the year, the students work more closely with executives and analyze a specific part of the company. Large chunks of time are set aside during weekdays for students to work on the project.

At the same time, they spend the spring split between modules three and four: managing the delivery system and expanding the business. The former focuses largely on operations and Total Quality Management. The latter attempts to integrate the entire curriculum and teach students how to deal with a changing global environment. It also includes segments on law and communication.

The class of '96 gives the first year a big thumbs-up. Indeed, of the schools in BUSINESS WEEK's second group of 25, only Southern California and Rice get higher marks for the core. Meanwhile, no second-tier school gets better marks for teaching an integrated curriculum, and Babson finishes higher than most Top 25 schools—including Wharton and Dartmouth—on this measure. "The first year included tightly integrated materials, challenging work, and a strong team environment," says one recent grad. "The second year is spotty."

That may be generous. After a first-year curriculum unlike almost anything else, Babson students find themselves with a rather typical schedule for their year of electives. It's a poor fit with the first year, and the quality of teaching is inconsistent. Only three schools—Penn State, Minnesota, and Michigan State—got worse marks for their electives. And while students say the administration does a good job on the whole in responding to their concerns, it does a poor job of offering the electives that MBAs want. "From an academic standpoint, we need to make the second year as strong as the first," Glavin says.

On the whole, though, Babson students praise their professors as committed teachers who rarely compromise classroom work for research. "We don't, for example, have a 25-person marketing department offering 40 electives," Cohen says. "If you want to go very deep in one of these areas, we're not the place for you." Indeed, Babson receives some of the worst marks for the freshness of its coursework—probably a result of the lack of research power on campus. The school's other weaknesses: its efforts to teach ethics, information technology, and quality concepts all finished in the bottom 10 of the Top 50 schools.

At an average of 29 years and 2 months, students here are older than at any Top 50 business school other than Southern California. They spend their two years on a 450-acre campus dotted with hills and wooded areas. Wellesley College, the all-female liberal arts school where Hillary Rodham Clinton got her B.A., is two miles away, and Boston is 14 miles away. Students either drive there or take the commuter railroad. There's a stop one mile from campus, and shuttle buses run from it to Babson and Wellesley. The advantages of Boston are well-known. It's a small New England city that doubles as a cultural and intellectual center. It is home to the Museum of Fine Arts (MFA, if you want to sound like a native), the Boston Pops, a slew of Revolutionary War stops, and Fenway Park, which many argue is the best single place to watch a baseball game. Cape Cod is only an hour-and-a-half from campus, traffic permitting. And if you want to listen to Bill Glavin talk about B-school reform, you'll have to make the two-hour drive to New Hampshire. That's where he's retiring to.

PLACEMENT DETAILS

Babson is also not a great financial deal when compared to its competition. Students graduate, on average, with $42,100 in loans—a bigger debt than you'll rack up at any other Runners-Up school, and larger even than the ones you'll find at Duke, Yale, or Columbia. Meanwhile, students enter with the 29th largest salary out of BUSINESS WEEK's Top 50—but leave with the 34th highest. One reason: the large numbers of entrepreneurs at the school, who don't make a big salary during their first post-MBA years. Another reason: the best-paying MBA companies just don't recruit at Babson. In 1996, 68 companies came on campus to recruit second-year students. The major employers: Arthur Andersen (4); Bose Corp. (3); Fleet Financial (3); GTE Corp. (3); Harvard Pilgrim Health Care (3); Vitol Gas/Electric (2); Johnson & Johnson (2); Reebok (2); Bronner Slosberg Humphrey (2); and Baybank Systems (2).

OUTSTANDING FACULTY

Daniel H. Gray (****—strategy); *Michael L. Fetters* (****—accounting); *Kathleen T. Hevert* (***—finance); *John E. Martinson* (***—finance); *Eric Sirri* (***—finance); *Douglas Tigert* (***—marketing); *William Bygrave* (**—entrepreneurship).

APPLICANT TIPS

Campus visits are a critical part of the admissions process at Babson. The school holds a general information session monthly for applicants as well as a morning visitors program, with a campus tour and class visit. You can schedule a trip with admissions at 617-239-5591. Candidates also are encouraged to arrange personal interviews, and in 1996, 100 percent of the applicants were interviewed—usually while on campus for a morning visit.

In your visits and essays, you'll need to play up your appreciation for living and working in a diverse world and how you value differences among people—an important part of the school's culture. Babson requires applicants to boast a minimum of two years of full-time work experience. Besides the two-year MBA program, Babson also offers a one-year MBA for candidates who boast an undergrad degree in business. The application deadlines for the abbreviated degree are earlier: December 15 and January 15.

Contact: Rita S. Edmunds
Director of MBA Admissions
617-239-5124
Application deadlines: January 15, March 1, and April 15

OLIN MBAs SOUND OFF

The first year of the Babson program, which was overhauled three years ago, is a tremendous experience—challenging, superbly integrated, and well-coordinated. The second year was slightly disappointing. Clearly the emphasis and resources are on the first year.

Babson's first year of the two-year MBA was dynamic and fully integrated. A lot of skills and tools were quickly identified and utilized. There was an ongoing effort within 30 days to get you placed in an overseas assignment. The school fell short in terms of information technology (state-of-the-art industry equipment), certain electives, and overall quality of electives and career placement choices. Additionally, the school lacked financial scholarships for African-Americans. The program model, however, was excellent.

I was very satisfied with Babson's entrepreneurship program and the school's ability to integrate the curriculum. Problems: job placement is poor, and payoff is long-term.

Babson's redesigned curriculum does a superb job in integrating the different functional aspects of the business environment. This integration has allowed me to look at the issues from all aspects and functional areas and to easily understand how decisions affect each part of the business.

The classroom size ranged from 15 to 44 students, so one learned very much from the classroom discussions. The professors were always available to discuss subjects relating not only to the courses they taught, but also business subjects in general. Many professors also gave students good contacts at companies to aid in the job search process. Many even gave out their home phone numbers so that students could contact them in the evening and on weekends.

BRIGHAM
YOUNG
UNIVERSITY

BRIGHAM YOUNG UNIVERSITY

Marriott School of Management
640 Tanner Building
Provo, Utah 84602
E-mail address: mba@byu.edu
Website address:
http://www.msmonline.byu.edu/programs/grad/mba

Enrollment: 136	Annual tuition & fees:
	LDS member—$4760
Women: 19%	non-member—$7140
Non-U.S.: 17%	Room and board: $8050
Minority: 0%	Average GMAT score: 621
Part-time: None	GMAT range: 480 to 770
Average age: 27	Average GPA: 3.47
Average years of work exp.: 3.46	GPA range: 2.39 to 3.99
Applicants accepted: 51%	Accepted applicants enrolled: 31%
Median starting pay: $56,500	Average starting pay: $54,755

Teaching methods:　Lecture, 20%　Case study, 80%

Contact:
Brent D. Wilson
Chairman of MBA
Admissions Committee
801-378-3500
*Final application
deadline:*
March 1 for fall

The students at Brigham Young University quip that the Tanner Building, where Marriott students take classes, was the box that the famous Mormon Temple in Salt Lake City was shipped in. Its business school building is a huge granite-and-glass rectangle that looks like a boxy corporate headquarters.

While obviously a joke, the connection between the business school and the Church of Jesus Christ of Latter-Day Saints is very real. The school, named after the Mormon founder of Marriott Corp., boasts a strong honor code. Students aren't supposed to drink coffee, tea, or alcohol, and they're advised against viewing R-rated movies. More than 90 percent of the students are Mormons, who get a tuition break to come to this campus at the foot of picturesque Mount Timpanogas.

If you're not a Mormon, this school can be a difficult place to earn an MBA. As a Class of 1996 graduate puts it: "The social life is run by the church; Mormon girls usually only date Mormon guys. There is no other place I think you can feel so socially isolated, but if you survive, it's going to be a unique experience for your lifetime!" Indeed, many grads say one of the most valuable aspects of this program is that it plugs you into the formidable worldwide network of Mormon business people.

The religious affiliation, however, isn't the only thing that makes the Marriott School unique. Eighty-five percent of its students are bilingual, and most have spent two years in foreign countries serving as Mormon missionaries. Six-person study groups are also assembled around foreign-language competence, including Spanish, Portuguese, Japanese, French, German, and Korean. Foreign languages are also being taught at the business school, with an emphasis on business vocabulary and current events. As for diversity, don't expect all that much: Marriott ranks dead last for the percentage of women (19 percent) enrolled in its MBA program and has virtually no minorities at all.

All students enter in the fall, then take all their classes together during the first year. You'll be assigned to a study group throughout your first-year management core. In your second year, you'll get to select from a menu of 50 elective courses, allowing you to focus on one of a dozen specialties, from entrepreneurship to international management. Marriott has recently added such concentrations as strategic planning, community service, and engineering management. The school also offers three dual-degree programs in international studies, law, and engineering.

Another unusual aspect of the two-year program is a team-taught course that brings together the MBA basics for strategic decision making. There is a high level of integration between the functional courses. When the class recently took apart a marketing case study, for example, faculty from four disciplines (economics, quantitative methods, strategic planning, and marketing) were all involved.

PLACEMENT DETAILS

In 1996, 142 companies came to campus to recruit MBA students, doing 515 interviews of second-years. Among the leading recruiters are: Intel (8); Ford Motor Co. (6); Procter & Gamble (3); Ryder (3); Pizza Hut (2); Otis/United Technologies (2); Microsoft Corp. (2); Tektronix (2); Payless (2); and Northwest Airlines (2).

OUTSTANDING FACULTY

Hal Heaton (****—entrepreneurship); *Ned Hill* (****—finance); *Robert Daines* (***—management); *Ray Nelson* (**—management); *Bill Giauque* (**—operations); *Burke Jackson* (**—management); *Bill Sawaya* (**—operations); *Ron Schill* (**—marketing); *Monty Swain* (**—accounting); *Mike Swenson* (**—marketing).

APPLICANT TIPS

The hurdle rates for getting into this program are a bit higher for non-Mormons. So don't just look at the GMAT and GPA averages and figure you're a shoo-in if you're well above them. The acceptance rate of 51 percent—second highest after the University of Pittsburgh for a Runners-Up school—doesn't really apply to non-Mormons. The school looks especially closely at your math score on the GMAT, the last two years of your undergraduate grades, and evidence of "managerial or leadership skills in your application letter, letters of recommendation, and your work."

Don't bother applying early to this program. Admissions doesn't even begin to make any decisions until after the final March 1 deadline. It takes several weeks to process all the applications so you're unlikely to hear from Marriott until April or May. Some 65 percent of the school's 349 applicants were interviewed in 1996. Financial aid is integrated into the application and will be considered after the admissions have been determined. No further financial aid application is required beyond what you submit with the application for admission. About a third of the first-year MBA students are given financial aid. Scholarships average $2500 a year.

Contact: Brent D. Wilson
Chairman of MBA Admissions Committee
801-378-3500
Final application deadline: March 1 for fall

MARRIOTT MBAs SOUND OFF

In the past, BYU has been quite poor in utilizing the language skills and international experience that most students have. Over the course of my two years here, the program has improved greatly in this aspect. Not only has the core program integrated global management into the curriculum, but business language courses and other international electives have been added. The international management faculty is also growing rapidly, bringing in younger professors whose work experience did not end in the 1950s and 60s.

BYU excels in the finance area, but is weak in marketing. The caliber of students is outstanding—very hard working team players, technologically skilled. The lack of emphasis on research for professors is a dilemma as it gives a focus on teaching but can result in some professors relying primarily on the work they did for their Ph.D.s 20 years ago.

I would classify BYU's MBA program as very religiously homogenous. Some people may think that this homogeneity is good, and others might think ill of it. I just state it as fact. However, despite the religious similarity amongst the student body, the program is very diversified ethnically, taking into account all of the international students. I am inclined to defend BYU because I know that the administration is genuinely striving to achieve greater diversity. One problem that members of the administration are having is finding non-LDS (Latter-Day Saints) students (minorities included) who are willing to live according to BYU's standards of dress, grooming, and conduct. I don't see BYU ever sacrificing its standards for the sake of diversity.

Coming back to school full time after years of work experience and with children represented some interesting challenges—particu-larly since we wanted to get through without taking on any debt. After a great deal of research we concluded that BYU made the most sense for us. We have not been disappointed. I ended up with multiple job offers and a salary well in line with my expectations—and we came out debt-free, without my wife ever having to work outside the home.

I feel that the relatively large number of foreign students contributed greatly to the class's understanding of international issues in an increasingly global economy. The fact that many students in the program also spent two years in a foreign country doing volunteer work for the Church of Jesus Christ of Latter-Day Saints also added flavor to the program.

I think that BYU is a real bargain. We did not have to incur any debt for my education because the tuition is so low and the cost of living is inexpensive. At the same time, I was able to secure a starting salary that compares well with many average 'A' school starting salaries.

While BYU grads may receive lower starting salaries in absolute terms, most end up in Utah which has a lower cost of living than elsewhere in the nation. Nevertheless, they (BYU grads) do quite well financially.

Last year's placement was down (1995) because we increased the size of our class and had a new Career Services Director. This year the placement should be much better. Many companies such as Ford increased their offers 20 percent over last year. Most of my classmates have job offers, and have had them for months. My education has been outstanding! The quality of my professors is high, but you have to choose the right ones.

**CASE
WESTERN
RESERVE
UNIVERSITY**

CASE WESTERN RESERVE UNIVERSITY

Weatherhead School of Management
Cleveland, Ohio 44106-7235
E-mail address: lxg@po.cwru.edu
Website address: http://www.weatherhead.cwru.edu

Enrollment: 1085	Annual tuition: $19,300
Women: 33%	Room & board: $8900
Non-U.S.: 31%	Average GMAT score: 603
Minority: 12%	Average GPA: 3.2
Part-time: 775	GPA range: 2.2–4.0
Average age: 28	Average years of work exp: 5.5
Applicants accepted: 39%	Accepted applicants enrolled: 52%
Median starting pay: $60,500	Average starting pay: $59,725

Teaching methods: Lecture, 20%   Case study, 40%
                            Group projects, 40%

Contact:
Linda Gaston
Admissions Office
800-723-0203
or 216-368-2031
*Final application
deadline:* April 15 for
four-semester program;
April 1 for
accelerated program

When someone eventually tallies up the foibles and fumbles among the massive efforts by business schools to revitalize their MBA programs, there's one innovative school you're not going to find on the list. It's a school that shunned marketing gimmicks, business fads, and quick fixes. It's a school that pioneered, rather than followed, many of the more meaningful curriculum revisions of the early 1990s. Chalk it up next to the building of the Rock & Roll Hall of Fame and the recent success of baseball's Cleveland Indians as another sign that the city everybody liked to mock is on the rebound.

The smallish Weatherhead School at Case Western Reserve University has proven that it's one of the more creative business institutions in America. As Dean Scott S. Cowen puts it, "Innovation in management education isn't really occurring at the Top 25 schools. It's happening at the next level of schools because things like this can rapidly propel you into the Top 25."

It's hard to think of a school that has more dramatically changed its curriculum in more creative ways than Weatherhead, which takes its name from a local entrepreneur. With an entering class of only 150 full-timers, the school promises a small, intimate learning experience and dedicated teachers who use the city's business community as a laboratory for students. It's also promising one of the most distinctive MBA programs. Cowen organizes core courses around broad themes, tying courses overall to skill development, and tailors the MBA program to take best advantage of the strengths and weaknesses of individual students.

First-year MBA candidates will immediately find themselves in a required course dubbed Management Assessment and Development. It has as dull a ring to it as many core courses do, but in this class each student will be evaluated for strengths, weaknesses, and personal skills. Professors will test for leadership potential, for entrepreneurship, and for decision making. Students take sit-down tests, but their presentations will also be videotaped to see how they can be improved. Then the student, consulting with faculty, will develop a tailor-made learning plan for the remainder of the two-year program.

The approach is getting good reviews. "The Management Assessment and Development program provided me with important feedback on a host of management skills," says Robert L. Kraber, a 1992 alum. "The program forced me to take a hard introspective look at the areas in which I needed the most improvement, and helped shape my graduate studies." On the whole, core teaching receives better marks than it does at most second-tier schools. Electives do even better, outpacing virtually all schools not in the Top 25.

Every course at the school has been audited, not for just the discipline-based knowledge it may impart in such fields as finance or marketing but more importantly for the skills it attempts to develop in students. If you're weak in quantitative methods, you'll be steered to courses that teach those skills better—whether they are in marketing, finance, or operations. If you're weak in communication skills, you'll pick courses that will emphasize that area regardless of their subject matter. It's far more refined that this, of course, since the faculty at Weatherhead has broken down skill development into 72 separate categories, from your ability to sell ideas to your skill in using computer modeling.

That's not all. In the second year, you'll take a pair of what Cowen is calling "perspective courses" that cover material that transcends the traditional B-school disciplines. Example: Technology and Society, which doesn't really belong in any single department, is team-taught by professors from different disciplines. You'll also become a member of an Executive Action Team of 12 students who will work with a host executive in the area. Students will be paired by common interests, weaknesses, and experience. The mentor may bring the team into his or her organization to meet with managers in marketing and production. How does this differ from the typical study group? Team members won't be studying for a particular course. Instead, they'll be sharing their own different learning programs, figuring out how to work together, and exploring the sponsoring organization's way of business life.

Besides these three required courses and the team assignment, you'll have 11 more typical courses. But even here there's a big difference. Weatherhead faculty have been redesigning these core courses to overlay certain intellectual themes. "When you take accounting," says Cowen, "you are not going to just learn accounting, you're going to learn it in the context of several underlying themes." They include: the global economy, understanding the cultural settings in which managers function, social responsibility, and how to adapt to change and technology. With an undergraduate business degree, you could waive 6 of these 11 classes and graduate in 11 months. Otherwise, you typically choose 6 electives from nearly 100 courses offered by a full-time tenure-track faculty of about 80.

A summer program allows MBA students to earn six credits by combining international management research with a three-week, multi-country study tour in such European countries as England, Belgium, the Czech Republic, Austria, and Germany. In 1996, Weatherhead signed a partnership with the International Management Center in Budapest, Hungary, to offer Case Western's MBA degree in Europe. Students on both campuses may spend one or two semesters at the other to complete their work. For budding global managers, the school also signed a deal with the well-known Thunderbird school in Arizona to offer a joint MBA/Master of International Management degree. Students can complete their studies at both schools in two years by working through the summer. There's also a Master of Nonprofit Organizations granted through Weatherhead with the university's Mandel Center.

Another Weatherhead strength: its executive mentor program. Like SMU's B-school, Weatherhead matches students with executives from such companies as AT&T, TRW, Eaton, and McKinsey, who serve as mentors throughout the length of the program. And in virtually every course here students are organized to do projects for companies in the Cleveland area. More than 400 managers and executives annually volunteer their time in class projects, lectures, clubs, or mentorships. The school also boasts student internships tied directly into the MBA program.

What about Cleveland? You obviously won't find an intellectual climate such as in Ann Arbor or Berkeley, or a setting with the dynamics of a Chicago or New York. But Cleveland can surprise. As a Weatherhead professor says on the school's video for applicants: "Cleveland has what every city ought to have, but in more manageable terms." For $10 a seat, students can hear a symphony performed by the first-class Cleveland Orchestra at Severance Hall on campus. Forget about getting a seat at Jacobs Field, the Indians' new home, though. In 1996, the team became the first in baseball history to sell out all of its games before the season had begun. Closer to home, the B-school took over a new, modern building in 1989. It sits in a park-like campus in Cleveland's University Circle on the eastern edge of the city. Once a rough, high-crime area, it has gone through major gentrification.

University Circle is home to the city museums of art and natural history. For drinking and eating, MBAs favor Minnillo's Italian Garden, a restaurant and bar on Murray Hill Drive, just a five-minute walk from campus, and the Euclid Tavern, also within walking distance. Students get together for two school-wide picnics a year and frequent faculty and student softball games. And on the last Thursday afternoon of each month students meet for the latest party in a "survival series" where beer, pizza, and subs help attract a good crowd to the atrium of the building.

PLACEMENT DETAILS

Weatherhead obviously isn't on the tip of everyone's tongue. There's little brand-name identity to the program and not much national recognition. In a recessionary year, those disadvantages can clearly be felt by the graduating class. But in 1996, roughly 78 percent of grads had job offers by commencement. Those that did averaged 2.7 offers each, just a tad below the average for the Top 50 schools. That's a big improvement over Weatherhead's recession-plagued stats four years earlier, when 34 percent of the class was without a single offer by graduation and MBAs average only 1.4 offers each.

The change occurred because Cowen installed a new placement director and doubled the placement staff to four persons. He also worked overtime to cultivate local corporations. Some 115 companies came to recruit on campus in 1996, conducting 910 interviews. Another 508 job opportunities arrived via the mails. The leading recruiters: Ernst & Young (11); National City Bank (9); Citibank (4); Deloitte & Touche (3); Signet Bank (3); American Greetings (3); Intel (2); A.T. Kearney (2); Andersen Consulting (2); and OfficeMax (2).

OUTSTANDING FACULTY

Sam Thomas (****—finance); *Jonlee Andrews* (****—marketing); *Julia E.S. Grant* (****—accounting); *Richard L. Osborne* (****—entrepreneurship); *N. Mohan Reddy* (***—marketing); *J.B. Silvers* (***—finance); *Paul Laux* (**—finance).

APPLICANT TIPS

You can complete the Weatherhead MBA program in one year (42 credits) or two years (60 credits). The accelerated program is open only to people who hold an undergraduate business degree from an AACSB-accredited school or a school approved by the admissions committee. Students in the 42-hour program start in the summer and finish the following spring. Weatherhead says students who apply for the accelerated program should have well-focused career goals, because the program is intensive and there isn't an option to do a summer internship. The school also gives preference for the short course to applicants with at least two years of work experience. The final deadline for the accelerated program is April 14. If you want to be considered for a scholarship you must apply by January 18.

If you don't have an undergraduate business degree or if you choose to complete the program in two years, you must apply by April 14, or by March 14 if you wish to be considered for a scholarship. Admissions and merit scholarship decisions are made on a rolling basis, so candidates are encouraged to submit their applications as early as possible. You can usually expect a decision within six weeks of applying.

No matter which program you choose, your entire portfolio will be examined, including your academic achievements, professional experience, GMAT score, career goals, written recommendations, and responses to interview questions and application essays. Weatherhead stresses diversity in admitting students: "Incoming classes will be composed of highly qualified individuals representing a diversity of academic, professional, and cultural backgrounds and accomplishments."

So you should focus on what makes you unique. Although interviews are optional, the school saw only three out of every four applicants last year. Interviews are required for merit-based scholarships. For more information call the admissions office at 216-368-2030 or 800-723-0203. You can fax requests for information to 216-368-5548.

Contact: Linda Gaston
Admissions Office
800-723-0203, or 216-368-2031
Final application deadline: April 15 for four-semester program; April 1 for accelerated program

WEATHERHEAD MBAs SOUND OFF

Case Western Reserve University is paving the way for all future MBA programs. The program allows you to interact with the leaders of some of the top Fortune 500 companies and find out how they achieved their present position, what their current concerns are, and where they expect to be in the next five years. Case offers an experience where your teachers have powerful community networks and teach skills that will make us (the students) the leaders of tomorrow.

The infrastructure is ready to be ranked in the Top 20. . . . The notorious library will be greatly improved in three years. However, WSOM lacks a mission or vision that differentiates the school from others. This problem leaves WSOM behind as a local MBA school. Indeed the tie with local companies and leaders is important, but the school fails to attract non-local students. The great majority of American students come from northeastern Ohio.

Overall, I was extremely impressed by all aspects of the MBA program, especially the personalized attention of the placement office, the quality of teaching, the diversity of the students, the accessibility of faculty and administration, and the innovative structure of the program itself.

EMORY
UNIVERSITY

EMORY UNIVERSITY

Goizueta Business School
Atlanta, Georgia 30322
E-mail address: admissions@bus.emory.edu
Website address: http://www.emory.edu/BUS/

Enrollment: 460	Annual tuition & fees: $21,430
Women: 28%	Room and board: $9000
Non-U.S.: 21%	Average GMAT score: 626
Minority: 11%	Average GPA: 3.3
Part-time: 190	GPA range: 2.0 to 4.0
Average age: 26	Average years of work exp.: 4.5
Applicants accepted: 33%	Accepted applicants enrolled: 38%
Median starting pay: $65,000	Average starting pay: $64,510

Teaching methods: Lecture, 25% Case study, 60%
                   Group projects, 15%

Contact:
Julie Barefoot
Assistant Dean of
Admissions
404-727-6311
*Final application
deadline:*
April 15 for fall

It's been eight years since Ronald E. Frank came to lead Emory University's business school as dean. When he quit as dean of the business school at Purdue University in 1989, Frank viewed Emory as a school on the verge of breaking out into the national limelight. The business school, to his mind, had great upside potential. The good news: it still does. The bad: it's still far from realized.

Emory still boasts a small, intimate MBA program, with just 270 full-time students, and a remarkable student/faculty ratio of six to one. Some of its professors are among the best teachers in management education. The school is named for one of the most admired chief executives of the current generation—Coca-Cola's Roberto Goizueta. And it will get a big boost in mid-1997 when the business school moves into a new five-story, state-of-the-art home on Clifton and Fishburne Roads.

Somehow, though, Emory isn't delivering the goods to its graduates. When the Class of 1996 was asked if the MBA program was worth the time and the expense, only one other school—Michigan State—among 51 surveyed by BUSINESS WEEK scored lower than Emory. Goizueta, in fact, scored among the bottom 20th percentile on 15 of 36 questions asked of the most recent graduating classes. Graduate satisfaction with Emory's placement operations was especially abysmal: only two other schools got worse scores when MBAs were asked how helpful placement was in getting them a job before graduation and in supporting independent job searches.

Though Dean Frank clearly has his work cut out for him, there's still much to applaud about the program. Like Duke, Emory is known as an excellent liberal arts university with Methodist roots. For eight years now, Emory has been trying to duplicate Duke's success in making a run at the Top 25. No MBA program can aspire to great quality without strong faculty, and Emory has lured teachers from such schools as Harvard, Wharton, MIT, and Northwestern. Three out of four professors are new to the school since 1987—which means that Frank not only recruited new, more qualified people, but also cleaned house. "We've really redefined the faculty in an incredibly short period of time," he says.

The Center for Leadership and Career Studies, directed by leadership guru Jeffrey Sonnenfeld, has attracted more than 4000 executives since 1989. The center, which has been dubbed "CEO College," brings CEOs and other top executives together in a noncompetitive atmosphere to attend brief leadership conferences—and provides a great networking opportunity for students. The center also leads to interesting learning opportunities. After attending a seminar at the center, entrepreneurs Ben & Jerry came to talk to second-year MBAs, even supplying ice cream samples for 150 students. The Dean's Speaker Series also brings more than half a dozen senior executives to campus. Some recent guests: former President Jimmy Carter; Warren Buffett; Roberto C. Goizueta, CEO of Coca-Cola; and Stephen Schwartz Sr., an IBM vice president.

The basic Emory program isn't very different from what most B-schools offer. In your first year, there's virtually no flexibility—unless you're able to waive out of some core courses by exam and replace them with electives. Otherwise, 30 out of the 33 credits you're expected to rack up in the first year are in required core courses. After the first-year grind, the program opens up. Some 9 of the 15 credits in your second fall semester are electives and all 15 of the expected credits in the final semester are consumed by courses of your own choosing.

Emory's small size naturally limits the choice (Emory has about 56 electives), but you can also develop an area of concentration in marketing, finance, accounting, organization and management, and decision and information analysis. Moreover, the school allows you to take classes offered by other departments at Emory. Students with undergraduate business backgrounds can complete the program in one year. They take an accelerated core in the summer and then jump into class with second-year MBAs.

The school has made an effort to offer students more of an international perspective on business in recent years. Emory boasts semester study abroad programs with 13 non-U.S. schools. Remarkably, nearly one in every five MBA students here enrolls in these programs. Emory also offers a trio of programs that allow MBAs to earn two separate master's degrees in five semesters, with business schools in France, Austria, and the Netherlands. The university's language courses also are available at no extra charge to MBA candidates.

A major plus is the school's location in Atlanta, a dynamic community and headquarters to such corporate giants as Coca-Cola, Delta Airlines, and, more recently, UPS, which just moved into the area from Connecticut. The university campus sits between Virginia Highlands, the artsy, village-like area in midtown, and Buckhead, a section loaded with clubs and discos. For drinks and conversation, MBAs head toward the Highland Tap or the Euclid Avenue Yacht Club, which serves up extra spicy "nuclear wings." Moe's & Joe's is a favorite for hamburgers.

PLACEMENT DETAILS

Despite student complaints about Emory's placement office, the school says that only 11 percent of its graduates in 1996 failed to have a single job offer at commencement. That's not too good if you were among the 11 percent, but as things go, that's not terribly bad, either. Only a few years ago, however, some administrators believed it was a strategic necessity to increase the number of on-campus recruiters to 100. The school has embarrassingly lost ground in this area. In 1996, only 58 companies recruited on campus, down from 82 just two years earlier. Emory attempts to fill the gap by bringing students to job consortiums in Atlanta and New York where they are exposed to more than 100 additional companies. But it doesn't help that 68 percent of its grads stay in the southeast, with 55 percent in Atlanta alone. In 1996, the leading recruiters were BellSouth (6); KPMG Peat Marwick (5); Deloitte & Touche (4); Procter & Gamble (4); MCI (3); SmithKline Beecham (3); Airtouch Cellular (3); Coca-Cola (2); Johnson & Johnson (2); and GE Capital.

OUTSTANDING FACULTY

Patrick Noonan (****—information analysis); *L.G. Thomas* (****—organization); *Al Hartgraves* (***—accounting); *Omesh Kini* (***—finance); *Shehzad Mian* (***—finance); *Jeffrey Rosensweig* (**—finance); *C.B. Bhattacharya* (**—marketing); *Rob Kajaizian* (**—organization); *Jagdish Sheth* (**—marketing); *Nicholas Valerio* (**—finance).

APPLICANT TIPS

Though clearly a second-tier school, Emory prefers candidates with good work experience. "Full-time business experience is viewed as a means of gaining a realistic view of the corporate world and enables students to enter the program with directed, focused goals, equipped to participate actively in the classroom," says the school. The upshot: less than 1 percent of the Class of 1998 lacked at least one full year of work experience.

Who has an edge here? Emory says that "applicants who are able to exhibit both a high level of academic ability and a breadth of interests, as well as a focused orientation toward business, will be most competitive for admission." Though Emory doesn't require admission interviews, it encourages them. And some 75

percent of the school's 980 applicants were interviewed in 1996. So it would be wise to schedule a session while visiting the campus.

You'll receive a decision by January 31 if you send in your application before the end of December. After that, applicants are notified on a rolling basis. If you want to be considered for fellowships, scholarships, or need-based loans, the school must receive your application by March 1.

Contact: Julie Barefoot
Assistant Dean of Admissions
404-727-6311
Final application deadline: April 15 for fall

GOIZUETA MBAs SOUND OFF

My experience at Emory far exceeded even what I expected to gain from an MBA. The quantitative, analytical skills and the marketing and strategy tools I take from Emory fully met what I expected from an MBA program.

Emory was a decent program; however, there were two first-time teachers that were teaching second-year MBA's. Totally unacceptable!!! Career services office personnel were incompetent.

I have had only three professors who academically and intellectually are worthy of respect. This is out of a universe of 20 professors. I would further argue that 15 of these 20 are not qualified to teach graduate students.

The professors are truly outstanding. They initiate/facilitate meaningful class discussions; were always available to help with coursework, give career advice, and job search information; are leaders in their chosen field; and work together to develop classes that enhance the objective of the students.

GEORGETOWN UNIVERSITY

School of Business
Washington, D.C. 20057
E-mail address: MBA@GUNET.Georgetown.edu
Website address: http://www.georgetown.edu/gsb.home.html

Enrollment: 465

Women: 35%

Non-U.S.: 26%

Minority: 7%

Part-time: None

Average age: 27

Applicants accepted: 30%

Median starting pay: $70,000

Annual tuition & fees: $22,000

Room and board: $10,000

Average GMAT score: 634

Average GPA: 3.26

GPA range: 2.78 to 3.73

Average years of work exp.: 4.4

Accepted applicants enrolled: 46%

Average starting pay: $73,120

Teaching methods: Lecture, 40%   Case study, 40%   Discussion, 10%

Contact:
Nancy D. Moncrief
Director of Admissions
202-687-4200
*Final application
deadline:*
April 15 for fall

Little more than a decade ago, Georgetown University's business faculty met every Friday at 7:30 a.m. in "dawn patrol" meetings for six months straight to invent an MBA curriculum. "It was really an exciting time to be here because it was a big deal to launch an MBA program," says William G. Droms, founding director of the program. Even then, sitting in a temporary building on 36th Street, which is now a dorm, the school's objective was to become a national player. "From the beginning, we have taken advantage of what the world thought were Georgetown's strengths, international and government business," he says.

Just 15 years after the first 37 MBA students entered the program and 8 years after the school gained accreditation, Georgetown is already making a name for itself in international business under the leadership of Dean Robert S. Parker, a former McKinsey & Company partner. His mission: to catapult Georgetown to Top 25 stature and carve a niche as the nation's premier school for international management.

He faces tough competition from resource-rich schools with better reputations. But Parker also benefits greatly from the halo effect of an excellent university and from having established high admission standards. The average GMAT scores here are up 42 points since 1986, and the typical first-year student arrives with 4.4 years of work experience.

International business is more than just a fad at Georgetown. Each course, whether it's accounting, marketing, or production, is taught from a global perspective. The core curriculum includes Global Environment of Business. One of every four MBAs here is from outside the United States, and nearly three-fourths of students speak a second language or have lived abroad. "We offer a general program that focuses on working with and managing people of all cultures not just Americans,"

Parker says. "We don't want anyone without a global perspective."

The urbane dean's focus seems a natural. Georgetown is home of the elite School of Foreign Service that trains diplomats from all over the world. The school offers an International Business Diplomacy Certificate and a joint MBA/MFS degree. MBAs apply for the program during their first year, and need to use all six of their elective classes toward earning the honors certificate. Business types can also earn an area studies certificate in Russian, German, Latin American, African, Arabian, or Asian studies. Students study the culture, history, and social and economic development of their region. In the regular MBA program, there's one major complaint about the school's international focus: Noncredit languages can be studied, but only on top of the required five courses per semester.

Georgetown's location in the nation's capital obviously provides MBAs with a window on the relationship between business and government—another major theme that runs through the program. Just as NYU students study securities analysis with and under people who do it for a living on Wall Street, Georgetown MBAs have the advantage of learning how government and business interests collide from adjunct faculty working at the U.S. Treasury, the Federal Reserve Board, the Small Business Administration, and the U.S. Senate Banking Committee. "One of the great things about being in Washington is that you can run down to the SEC to do research on a company," says an MBA alum. The constant interaction with these kinds of agencies, the people who work for them, and the visitors that Washington attracts is a major advantage. To promote greater understanding between private and public sector leaders, Georgetown has established a center for Business-Government Relations.

"Quant jocks" need not apply here. About half of the class majored in social sciences as undergrads and another 15 percent have undergraduate degrees in humanities. "The focus is general and not particularly quantitative," says a recent grad. "It's good for liberal arts undergrads." In keeping with the university's liberal arts bent, MBAs are trained as generalists and must take a communications course. Georgetown loads 13 courses into the core, 10 of which are in the first year.

In the second year, students select 6 electives from only 39 within the business school or from a variety throughout the university. An interesting footnote: 45 percent of the school's electives are new in the past three years, including such courses as African Trade and Investment and Marketing Ethics. Georgetown recently began offering half-semester elective modules on topics such as Japanese Management and International Operations. The school is also adding electives taught in French and Spanish. But students complain that there aren't enough electives to choose from within the B-school, and that also limits the number of areas they can specialize in. Although MBAs are not required to concentrate in an area, students do typically develop an area of specialty. The school is adding to its elective offerings each year.

You're also required to take a yearlong ethics course that benefits from this institution's tradition of emphasizing morals. Like Notre Dame, Georgetown did not jump on the recent ethics bandwagon. "Ethics was a big deal from the first day of this program," says John G. Onto, associate dean of graduate business programs. "For Jesuits, ethics is not a flavor-of-the-month issue." Students are actively involved in tons of community service activities through the MBA Volunteers, a student-run organization that coordinates volunteer projects. MBAs volunteer locally at such places as Joshua House, a halfway house for men. The Volunteers also plan national events like the MBA Ultimate Four Basketball Competition with top U.S. business schools, to benefit the "I Have a Dream" Foundation.

Like the curriculum, Georgetown's extracurricular activities are internationally flavored. With choices like Students for Eastern European Development, Students for Latin American Development, Alliance for Cultural Awareness, and the International Business Forum, it's easy for students to supplement the global focus they receive in the classroom. For instance, Students for Eastern European Development has provided internship opportunities for 50 students since 1992. Graduates can also find opportunities abroad through the MBA Enterprise Corp., a group of schools that sends grads to work in Central European companies for one year.

The building that houses the B-school unites history with modern ideas. Built in 1795, Old North is the oldest surviving university building. "People take great delight in the fact that the youngest school on campus is in the oldest building," says Droms. Old North has a long history of attracting distinguished speakers, including many U.S. presidents. George Washington started the ball rolling when he spoke in 1797. Bill Clinton, the most recent presidential attraction, was preceded by former presidents Andrew Jackson, John Tyler, and Ulysses S. Grant. Old North might be old, but it's certainly not falling apart. The building was renovated several years ago and contains three case-style classrooms and a state-of-the-art computer lab. Students now benefit from a refurbished career management office, which includes a role-playing room with audio, library, and interviewing rooms. Not too long ago company interviews were conducted in faculty offices. Georgetown itself is a wonderful playground for young adults. Most students live off-campus in townhouses in the cosmopolitan neighborhood filled with trendy bars, foreign restaurants, and tiny boutiques. The private homes are quite expensive, but less luxurious townhouses are shared by groups of students just starting out on the Hill. There are cocktail parties in the MBA lounge in Old North and groups of students often head over to The

Tombs for thick, crusty pizza and beer after an exam. There's no shortage of things to do in D.C., which is why students tend not to hang around Old North when classes are over.

Despite the small size of the program, the B-school still splits incoming students into more intimate groups of 40 each. Parker wants to increase the graduating class to 200 during the next few years while at the same time boosting admissions standards. He believes he can do that without sacrificing the personalized attention MBAs get here.

PLACEMENT DETAILS

In keeping with the global slant, career management helps find international jobs for U.S. graduates—whether they want to work here or go overseas—as well as for foreign students who want to return to their home countries or work abroad or in the United States for an American corporation. But this is a young program with a tiny alumni base. So far only around 1000 students have received Georgetown MBAs.

In 1996, only 55 organizations came on campus to recruit, down by 12 in the past two years. It didn't seem to hurt their prospects all that much: grads left with median starting pay packages of $70,000—tying with Southern California for the highest for a Runners-Up school and more than the grads got at seven Top 25 schools. That may be because students also had the opportunity to interview with around 100 companies at consortiums. About 16 percent of the Class of 1996 graduated without job offers. While the B-school did not attract many companies to its campus, it did manage to lure some top-drawer concerns. Major recruiters included AT&T Global Solutions (6); Ernst & Young (4); Chase Manhattan Bank (3); Tidewater Inc. (3); American Management Systems (3); Bain & Co. (2); Continental Airlines (2); Marriott (2); Procter & Gamble (2); and Prudential Securities (2).

OUTSTANDING FACULTY

John Dealy (****—strategy); *Robert Thomas* (****—marketing); *Susan Dugan* (****—management); *Bardia Kamrad* (****—accounting); *Richard Ernst* (***—logistics); *Robert Bies* (***—organizational behavior); *Tom Donaldson* (**—ethics); *Eugene M. Salorio* (**—international trade); *Ali Fekrat* (**—accounting); *Annette Shelby* (**—business communication).

APPLICANT TIPS

Georgetown is more selective than several competing business schools with higher ratings, including Carnegie Mellon, Rochester, and Washington University in St. Louis. So you'll need to position yourself smartly to put the odds in your favor. In addition to academic background, Georgetown looks for a variety of skills and accomplishments. "Selection also depends upon an applicant's distinctive and useful achievements, ideas, talents, and motivation for graduate business education. Professional experience, while not required, strengthens an application. Applicants who have completed an undergraduate business degree are particularly encouraged to obtain professional experience before applying to the Georgetown MBA program." Only 4 percent of the Class of 1998 failed to have at least one year of full-time work experience on their résumés. You should also emphasize international experience, foreign languages, writing ability, interpersonal skills, leadership ability, and entrepreneurship. Admission interviews are not required, but the school interviewed 46 percent of the 1831 applicants in 1996. Although the final deadline is April 15, Georgetown encourages applicants to apply as early as possible. The dead-line for international applications and for those applying for financial aid is February 1.

Contact: Nancy D. Moncrief
Director of Admissions
202-687-4200
Final application deadline: April 15 for fall

GEORGETOWN MBAs SOUND OFF

The quality of teaching is outstanding. Each course has a global and ethical component. The student body is over one-third international. The greatest downfall is the administration. The dean is invisible. A school that teaches leadership should demonstrate it!

Overall, classes were excellent, though there was a lack of integration between them. Strengths of the school: location, professors, and broad-based management skills. Weaknesses: job placement and information technology.

The quality of classroom instruction was outstanding. I had one instructor who was extremely disappointing, a few who were average, and most were among the best I've ever had. The disappointment, an adjunct who was a last-minute fill-in, was counseled on ways to improve by other faculty members during the semester. It was ultimately decided he should not come back.

Over the last three years, Georgetown has been saving money to purchase a new building for the business school. The current facilities are pathetic. The computers are antiquated, the classrooms run down, and the meeting space nonexistent. On the upside, in two years Georgetown's facilities will be quite impressive.

GEORGIA INSTITUTE OF TECHNOLOGY

GEORGIA INSTITUTE OF TECHNOLOGY

DuPree School of Management
Atlanta, Georgia 30332
E-mail address: msm@mgt.gatech.edu
Website address: http://www.iac.gatech.edu/mgt

Enrollment: 220	Annual tuition & fees:
	  resident—$2790
	  non-resident—$9363

Women: 26%	
Non-U.S.: 31%	Room and board: $6000
Minority: 23%	Average GMAT score: 633
Part-time: None	GMAT range: 470 to 780
Average age: 27	Average GPA: 3.2
Average years of work exp.: 4	GPA range: 2.0 to 4.0
Applicants accepted: 40%	Accepted applicants enrolled: 52%
Median starting pay: $56,050	Average starting pay: $51,200

Teaching methods: Lecture, 30%   Case study, 30%   Projects, 40%

Contact:
Ann Johnson Scott
Director of the MSM
Program
404-894-2623
*Final application
deadline:*
May 1 for fall,
April 1 for
assistantships

You can easily think of this place as the MIT of the South. Like its more prestigious counterpart in Cambridge, Georgia Tech doesn't merely hand out typical MBAs to everyone. Its diplomas are stamped with the initials MSM, Master's of Science in Management. A science-math culture premeates the program, from the type of students who come here to the heavily quantitative curriculum the school offers. Technology is infused throughout the curriculum and employed, in the words of Dean Arthur Kraft, as a "building block" for both core and elective courses.

Since arriving from Rutgers University School of Business in 1994, Kraft has been the beneficiary of a $20 million naming gift from Tom E. DuPree Jr. An alumnus, DuPree hopes the money will move the school into the country's Top 10 business programs by attracting well-known professors and expanding the curriculum. That isn't likely. The competition is simply too severe. But the gift allows Kraft a lot of flexibility to make significant changes that can vastly improve this school.

Right now, it's a fairly basic nuts-and-bolts program. In the first year, every one of your 15 courses is required as part of the core curriculum—though three of them are called "core electives." There are even separate computer lab courses. In the first quarter you work on the Macintoshes; in the second, on IBMs. In Classroom 2000, where accounting, finance, and other courses are taught, professors can take control of students' computers and project their screens for the entire class to review. First-year classes typically meet on Mondays and Wednesdays or Tuesdays and Thursdays. Incoming students are broken into two groups of 60 each and put through the paces of the core.

In the second year, there's only one required course: Managerial Policy in the spring quarter. Otherwise, you can choose 11 electives. For a very small graduate business program, this school offers a wonderful selection of elective courses. Among the 80 offerings are Compensation and Jobs, Cross-Cultural Management, and Buyer Behavior—not especially course titles you might have expected to find at a Tech school that hands grads a master of science degree. You can choose your course work in one of nine concentrations or you can simply take electives at random. The school grants a trio of interdisciplinary certificates in entrepreneurship, management of technology, and computer integrated manufacturing systems. The entrepreneur certificate requires 15 hours of coursework, while the technology certificate demands 21 hours.

PLACEMENT DETAILS

Georgia Tech, a campus spread over 330 acres and 143 buildings near midtown Atlanta, also has a reputation for aggressively getting its B-school students summer internships with such firms as UPS, Federal Express, NCR, and AT&T Global Information Systems. The school claims a 90 percent placement rate for its internship program. By virtue of the school's technology bent, about one out of every five graduates here takes a job in information systems or operations management. More than a quarter of the students become management consultants, often with more technical firms. Only 30 percent of the class land jobs outside of the Southeast.

Some 65 companies came to recruit second-years on campus in 1996, conducing 350 interviews. That's about two grads per company, not a bad ratio, allowing each grad to average 2.93 job offers—better than some of the schools in the Top 25. About 16 percent of the Class of 1996, however, failed to have a single job offer by commencement. More than 300 job opportunities were posted via correspondence. The major

employers: Coopers & Lybrand (11); Ernst & Young (8); Andersen Consulting (7); Federal Express (6); Procter & Gamble (5); Deloitte & Touche (5); Arthur Andersen (5); International Paper (4); Entergy Services (4); and Ford Motor Co. (3).

OUTSTANDING FACULTY

Charles Mulford (****—accounting); *Ajay Khorana* (****—finance); *Edward Nelling* (****—finance); *Rich Daniels* (***—operations management); *Guatam Challagalla* (***—marketing); *Deborah H. Turner* (**—accounting); *Narayanan Jayaraman* (*—finance); *Marilu McCarty* (*—economics); *Jeffrey Covin* (*—strategic management); *Soumen Ghoush* (*—operations management).

APPLICANT TIPS

DuPree says it looks for "creative, intelligent, and focused individuals. Successful candidates must demonstrate leadership potential, high motivation, and excellent academic promise." Sounds familiar, huh? This school heavily weighs GMAT scores and your undergraduate transcript, especially eyeing grades in tougher, more rigorous courses. Indeed, applicants must have completed at least one course of college-level calculus.

Work experience, while not mandatory, is preferred. Only 7 percent of the Class of 1998 had less than a year's worth of experience in a full-time job. Interviews are not required, but prospective applicants are encouraged to visit the campus. In 1996, the school interviewed 30 percent of its 585 applicants. You can schedule a visit by calling 404-894-8722.

Contact: Ann Johnson Scott
Director of the MSM Program
404-894-2623

Final application deadline: May 1 for fall, April 1 for assistantships

DUPREE GRADS SOUND OFF

The analytical skills taught here are much better than any tier I school. I worked on a team project (at Coke) with other interns (from Emory, Duke, Virginia, Michigan, Northwestern, and Wake Forest) and was able to easily assess their talents. It made it difficult for me to understand how those schools could be rated higher.

Georgia Tech's DuPree School of Management is not well known for its finance program, but I found the finance program especially strong! I came into the program with a strong finance background, and the courses at Tech broadened my skills and deepened my understanding of issues. Also, the professors are very accessible. Comparing notes with others I feel that our finance program is as strong as any of the programs at the Top 10 schools.

The placement office has made great strides over the past year due to personnel changes. I believe it will become one of the strengths of the program.

Georgia Tech offers some of the best financial aid in the country by offering Graduate Research Assistantships (GRAs). I received it in the Computer Integrated Manufacturing Systems (CIMS) Program. Because of my GRA, my out-of-state tuition was waived, and my only remaining fees were $179 per quarter. In addition, I worked in a lab 13 hours a week and made $1000 a month. All in all, my GRA was a great financial aid package plus a great manufacturing education.

I feel that Georgia Tech has an excellent operations management program. I would have preferred a higher level of experience among my classmates.

I was basically paid to go to the DuPree School of Management by my graduate research assistantship in computer integrated manufacturing—it was a heck of a bargain. Tech's alumni networking in the Southeast, where I want to live, is outstanding.

I think Tech is very good considering the low cost; it is one of the top "best buys." Atlanta is great to live in as well. I'm very satisfied with what I learned. I got a great job, working with people from the Top 10 schools.

We just received a $20 million endowment gift from Mr. Tom DuPree, president and CEO of Applesouth, the nation's largest franchisee of Applebee's restaurants. I am confident that this endowment will significantly boost the quality of the program; attract better students, teachers, and company recruiters; and enhance the reputation of the program nationwide and internationally. I was my class's president and consider myself to have been very active in the program and to have made a positive contribution.

Great opportunities to take classes in other schools at Tech to help customize individual curriculum. The program offers great value with lots of individual attention from professors. I started at NYU's Stern and transferred to Tech because they provided individualized attention at a fraction of the cost.

The administrative staff at GA Tech's DuPree School of Management, headed by Ms. Ann Scott, is notably outstanding. I was working on an engineering degree concurrently with my business degree, creating tricky tailoring, timing, and scheduling problems.

MICHIGAN STATE UNIVERSITY

MICHIGAN STATE UNIVERSITY

The Eli Broad Graduate School of Management
215 Eppley Center
East Lansing, Michigan 40024-1121
E-mail address: mba@pilot.msu.edu
Website address: http://www.bus.msu.edu/grad/home.htm

Enrollment: 264

Women: 33%
Non-U.S.: 27%
Minority: 10%
Part-time: None
Average age: 26
Average years of work exp.: 3.0
Applicants accepted: 41%
Median starting pay: $53,500

Annual tuition & fees:
   resident—$8716
   non-resident—$15,167
Room and board: $6290
Average GMAT score: 610
GMAT range: 500 to 730
Average GPA: 3.3
GPA range: 2.2 to 4.0
Accepted applicants enrolled: 40%
Average starting pay: $62,750

Teaching methods: Lecture, 40%   Case study, 35%   Projects, 25%

Contact:
Jennifer Chizuk
Director of MBA
Admissions
517-355-7604
or 800-4MSU-MBA
*Final application
deadline:*
March 31 for fall
November 1 for spring

In 1991, an alumnus who has made a fortune as an entrepreneur reached into his pockets to give Michigan State University's business school $20 million. The goal of Eli Broad, a 1954 accounting grad who built a hugely successful financial services firm in California, was to transform the business school in every way. Instead of putting Broad's money into bricks and mortar, the school was to put the vast majority of the cash into revamping and upgrading the MBA program. The objective: to push the newly named Broad Graduate School of Management into the top tier of B-schools in the country.

After having six years to fulfill the promise of that gift, the school and its faculty have failed miserably. When BUSINESS WEEK asked the graduates of 51 top business schools whether they thought the program they attended was worth the time and expense, no school scored lower than Michigan State. The school also got the lowest marks possible for the quality of teaching in elective courses, for teaching students how to use computers and other analytical tools, and for the teaching of corporate ethics. Moreover, Broad scored in the bottom 10th percentile on 21 of 36 dimensions of quality and customer satisfaction measured by BUSINESS WEEK. Even worse, Broad graduates were the least likely to urge friends or colleagues to take this MBA program.

So why would anyone want to come here to study to get an MBA? First off, when you're aiming to pick the Top 50 MBA schools in the nation, someone has to finish last on at least some measures. But being near the bottom of 50 of the best still places the school above 750 of the

800 or so schools that offer an MBA in the United States. Second, the results fail to reflect the outcome of a long-overdue overhaul of the MBA curriculum, which is expected to be installed in the fall of 1997.

Though the new supposedly "innovative" curriculum will sound awfully familiar to most deans who have updated their MBA programs years ago, it is a step in the right direction. It will offer more integration of the business basics as well as team teaching to show how business concepts fit together. The school also will put much more emphasis on business applications through corporate sponsorship of MBA study teams and what the school is calling a "live integrative case competition." The program will put more focus on international business through increased coursework, language programs, and overseas study opportunities.

It's about time. This is a school that decided to get a new $21.5 million building before putting something new in it. The modern home of the business school—erected in late 1993—is connected by a covered walkway to Eppley Center, the B-school's old home. The addition was sorely needed. The brick-and-sandstone Eppley Center opened in 1961 to 3000 students and eventually served 8000, until the addition of the new 59,000-square-foot building. The Business College Complex now houses all departments except for economics, which has alleviated the crowding problems. And the school recently opened a new MBA-only computer lab along with the first of several "high-tech" classrooms that allow each student to have a computer in class and provide the professor with a master control podium. A new state-of-the-art business library, three times the size of the current one, is expected to open in the fall of 1997.

This is the industrial heartland, and it's in need of some kind of revitalization. East Lansing, Michigan, is a short strip of storefronts eight blocks long and one block wide. The main drag, Grand River Avenue, was the old Indian trail from Grand Rapids to Detroit. Neighboring Lansing is the state capital and home to looming smokestacks and red-brick factories, from tiny tool-and-die shops to GM's expansive Buick-Oldsmobile-Cadillac complex.

Yet the huge campus is, as *The Chicago Tribune* once described it, "shockingly beautiful." The Red Cedar River flows through the handsomely landscaped and tree-lined grounds. The buildings may be a bit of a hodgepodge, from classic red-clay brick and slate roofs to rectangular slabs of concrete that look like old IBM punch cards. And if the old factory areas can sometimes look shockingly desolate these days, there's lots of activity on the 5000-acre campus that overflows with 40,000 students. More than 24,000 bicycles are registered on campus.

Indeed, incoming MBAs tend to gripe about the difficulty of just knowing how to get around the place in the first few weeks. The MBA program with fewer than 300 full-time students, is vastly overshadowed by a mammoth undergraduate business program with more than 4500 students. Michigan State has the fifth-largest undergraduate business school in the nation. The program imposes a huge demand upon faculty time, so that some MBAs find it difficult to meet with teachers outside the classroom.

To be fair, Broad's gift did lead to numerous changes. The school phased out its part-time MBA program so that it could focus more of its efforts on the full-time, two-year MBA program. James Henry, former dean of Louisiana State's B-school, was recruited to take over the deanship in mid-1994. Besides finally getting the new curriculum approved, he's also pushing several other new initiatives. They include two concentrations (a major of sorts requiring four courses): Business Information Systems and Food and Packaged Goods Marketing. The school's two strongest areas of study are clearly finance and supply chain management. Other concentrations include professional accounting, general management, hospital business, human resources management, and marketing.

A good number of students here not only haven't given up on American manufacturing, but have truly embraced it by getting a master's degree in materials and logistics. The program spans both the management and marketing departments in covering what former Dean Lewis called a "complete systems approach" from procurement of materials to manufacturing and shipment to the final consumer. Some 50 students are signed up for this unusual program, which gets financial support from such companies as IBM, Kellogg, Steelcase, and Procter & Gamble, which offer internships and hire from the program.

As a Big Ten school, Michigan State also offers an all-encompassing campus lifestyle for those who want it. Sure, there's the annual MBA picnic at Lake Lansing Park, and every Thursday afternoon business grads pick a local bar to drink and chat in (the Land Shark on Abbot Road or Olga's downtown are the favorites). Crunchies is great for its burger-and-beer special, while Cafe Venezia has become the hangout for MBA fans of espresso drinks. But one of the key social events evolves around the Michigan State Spartans, the school's football squad. For pre-game tailgate parties, MBAs get together across the street from Eppley Center and then walk to Spartan Stadium where they have a block of choice tickets.

The Broad gift has helped to energize the students to become more active in the school. The MBA Association was instrumental in expanding the school's orientation program from one day in 1991 to nearly a full week of group activities, including the launch of a student mentor system. It has also organized students to serve meals at a local soup kitchen, donate food and clothing to local charities, adopt a highway, and raise money for Big Brothers and Big Sisters. The MBA Association also sponsors an annual international symposium and an Excellence in Business lecture series.

PLACEMENT DETAILS

The school's younger graduates (the school still accepts applicants with no job experience, though it prefers more seasoned candidates) make the median starting pay packages of Michigan State MBAs look worse than average. The Class of 1996, for instance, pulled down $53,500. Still, Broad reports that 94 percent of its class had job offers at graduation, and some 153 companies came to recruit on campus in 1996, conducting 808 interviews. Another 215 jobs were posted by correspondence. The top hiring firms: Ford Motor Company (8); Price Waterhouse (5); Hewlett-Packard (4); IBM (4); Ernst & Young (4); Selectron (2); CSX Transportation (2); DSC Logistics (2).

When Broad handed over his generous gift, he said he intended to watch closely how his money was being spent. "I want to make certain the money just doesn't plug the state deficit," he said. That hasn't happened. But neither has Michigan State made much of a difference in the world of business education. The well-intentioned Eli Broad should demand his money back.

OUTSTANDING FACULTY

Donald Bowersox (****—management); *Mike Mazzeo* (****—finance); *Glen Omura* (****—marketing); *Naveen Khana* (***—finance); *Jack Bain* (**—communications); *David Closs* (**—marketing and logistics); *John Gilster* (**—finance); *Steven Melnyk* (**—management); *Anil Shivdasani* (*—finance); *Jack Allen* (*—marketing).

APPLICANT TIPS

Average GMAT scores at Broad hit a new record in 1996, reaching 600. That's a vast improvement from 10 years ago when the average was just 561. So the school puts a lot of emphasis on

GMATs as well as your undergraduate transcript. Yet, this school is admitting higher numbers of applicants than it once did. Broad now accepts 41 percent of applicants, compared to just 23 percent back in 1992.

Broad wants its full-time MBA applicants to have at least one year of full-time work experience "that demonstrates dedication and commitment." But nearly 10 percent of the Class of 1998 lacked a full year's worth of job experience. For the school's 17-month fast-track alternative MBA, the school requires at least two years of quality work experience.

Though personal interviews are not required, Broad strongly encourages them. Yet, in 1996, only 26 percent of its 659 applicants were interviewed.

Contact: Jennifer Chizuk
Director of MBA Admissions
517-355-7604 or 800-4MSU-MBA
Final application deadline: March 31 for fall; November 1 for spring

BROAD MBAs SOUND OFF

The MSU MBA experience was an enlightening one. The program provided me the opportunity to gain important skills that have enabled me to secure a position with an organization that would not have considered me prior to pursuing my MBA. Overall, I rate the experience very highly. The faculty for the most part was phenomenal, the curriculum solid, and the student body was high caliber.

MSU provides a superb business education that is strongly focused on the "basics." MSU's MBA provides ample training in core subjects such as Accounting, Finance, Marketing, and Operations. Moreover, the program is an excellent value based on the quality of the MBA curriculum. In-state tuition in my last year was under $7000 and housing was very affordable ($200–$350/month) in East Lansing. MSU's MBA "core" strengths are in accounting and materials logistics management. The finance program is solid, however the marketing department is very mediocre. The program would probably not add much value to an individual seeking "esoteric" courses dealing with finance and/or marketing theory.

I am disgruntled by the quality of education provided in this program. I felt this would be a university on the cutting edge—it is just the opposite. In one class, the professor informed us that the best way to invest internationally is through a mutual fund. Is this the advice finance majors should be given in an investments course? In another course, a professor did not arrive for an exam or have a representative on hand to administer the exam. In yet another class, when the professor was asked if he would be available the Friday prior to a Monday exam to answer questions he informed us we were on our own and to have a good weekend. If this is a cutting edge school, I would hate to witness a school that is not.

I regularly use the skills acquired in the MBA program for my job. I've noticed that people I deal with in business take me a little more seriously since having received my MBA. I encounter age discrimination regularly, however. I'm making million dollar deals at age 29 and it is hard to get over the age thing with some people. When I tell them about my education, I believe that it provides me with additional credibility.

The MBA office was highly responsive to improving the MBA experience. All of the MBA office staff were very concerned with improving the overall MBA curriculum.

OHIO STATE UNIVERSITY

OHIO STATE UNIVERSITY

Max M. Fisher College of Business
Columbus, Ohio 43210
E-mail address: cobgrd@cob.ohio-state.edu
Website address: http://www.cob.ohio-state.edu

Enrollment: 425	Annual tuition & fees: resident—$5301
Women: 33%	non-resident—$13,191
Non-U.S.: 32%	Room and board: $4332
Minority: 11%	Average GMAT score: 612
Part-time: 155	GMAT range: 440 to 770
Average age: 27	Average GPA: 3.29
Average years of work exp.: 4	GPA range: 2.24 to 4.0
Applicants accepted: 31%	Accepted applicants enrolled: 44%
Median starting pay: $56,000	Average starting pay: $55,870

Teaching methods: Lecture, 40%   Case study, 40%
                    Group projects, 20%

Contact:
Susie Cinadr
Coordinator for
Recruitment and
Admissions
614-292-8530
*Final application
deadline:*
April 30 for fall

Ohio State University's Fisher College of Business proudly promotes itself as a business school "where theory meets practice." The school says it attempts to provide students with as much experiential learning as it does scholarly thinking. Unlike a lot of B-schools which make all sorts of marketing promises about their programs, Fisher pretty much delivers the goods.

It puts more than $5 million of endowment money into the hands of MBA students so they can manage a real investment portfolio. It teams students up with client companies to work on 20-week-long consulting projects. It sends MBA candidates into the local community to do good deeds. And it invites in senior executives to debate students who have analyzed case studies about their companies.

Oh sure, at a public Runners-Up institution, you'll find no shortage of complaints. The Class of 1996, for example, thought the program could have done a better job with international business, corporate ethics, and leadership topics. They also expressed some dissatisfaction with the school's career services center because of its lackluster efforts to help students gain summer internships and find a job before graduation. Otherwise, though, Ohio State falls nicely among the averages for a top business school.

What's more, the business school will soon be moving into a new $80.7 million six-building complex, the largest multi-building project ever undertaken in Ohio State University's 125-year history. The complex—which will include a hotel with 121 rooms for visiting executives—will provide the school with nearly 700,000 square feet of new, modern space. All this, for a business program that boasts just 270 full-time MBA students. Of course, it also will house a fairly large undergraduate business program as well as an aggressive effort in executive education.

So what's the MBA program like? In early September, Fisher College offers optional pre-enrollment classes for incoming students to allow MBA candidates to bone up on their skills in computing, accounting, economics, and statistics. These classes immediately precede what the school calls "Super September Start-Up," an orientation segment designed to jump start the MBA program. Not merely a feast of social events, start-up puts newbies through case simulations, case studies, tours of local businesses, and lectures from senior executives. A recent group did a one and a half day case analysis of Ford Motor's acquisition of Jaguar with an executive team from Ford. There's also a community service project in which students have built a Habitat for Humanity Home or have gone into local elementary schools to read books, plant trees, paint classrooms, and build playgrounds.

In your first year of studies, Fisher puts students through the business basics, providing flexibility for two electives or courses in a major area. A key feature of the program is Business Solutions Teams, small groups of students who spend 20 weeks on a consulting project for a local corporation. At project's end, each team presents its recommendations to the client firm's senior executives. In recent years, BSTs, as they are called, have worked with Banc One Financial Card Services and the Rickenbacker Port Authority.

During year two, students develop expertise in a major area and can pick up a minor as well. Fisher offers six majors: corporate financial management, investment management, marketing management, operations and logistics management, consulting, or interdisciplinary studies in which you'll combine three minor areas to form a major. Overall, the school boasts a menu of 54 elective courses, the most popular of which are Human Resource Negotiation, Analysis and Design of Logistics Systems, and Marketing Strategy. The required 16 core classes and 9 electives can be completed in six quarters. The school has recently added two new requirements: a management communications sequence, in which MBAs practice and try to improve their written and oral presentation skills, and a yearlong teamwork and leadership laboratory, which focuses on management style.

Operations and logistics are a key strength of the school. So are accounting and finance. No wonder Ohio State allows student teams to invest millions of dollars in the stock market. The risk has produced big profits for the university and hands-on investing experience for students. In recent years, students participating in the Student Investment Management Program (SIM) have consistently outperformed the Standard & Poor's 500 index.

Columbus, Ohio, is a fairly hospitable place to live for a couple of years, if not a major financial or business center. The Limited, Wendy's, and Worthington Industries started as small businesses in Columbus. The sprawling campus is just two miles from downtown, which boasts a major art museum and a new convention center. Nearby are restaurants, night spots, galleries, and shops in Short North, Brewery District, and German Village.

For a campus with 55,000 students, the MBA class size is minuscule—about 135 full-timers graduate each year. While the small number helps to provide an intimate learning experience, it also hurts Ohio State in the placement area. Some companies are not willing to make the trip to Columbus because they can't fill more than a day of interviews. The B-school is likely to increase the size of the program to 240 students a year once it moves into its state-of-the-art complex and out of overcrowded Hagerty Hall.

PLACEMENT DETAILS

Though grads grouse about the placement office here, the school maintains that only 10 percent of its graduates in 1996 failed to have a single job offer at graduation. In that year, Ohio State attracted 152 companies to recruit at its campus, up from 106 in 1994. Those firms conducted 1025 job interviews with second-year students. Some 2600 job opportunities were posted via correspondence. The biggest recruiters: Ford Motor Co. (11); Andersen Consulting (6); General Electric (4); Northwest Airlines (4); Bank One (3); Borden (3); CSX Transport (3); Intel (3); Price Waterhouse (3); and Kimberly Clark (2).

OUTSTANDING FACULTY

Rakesh Vohra (****—statistics); *Greg Allenby* (****—marketing); *James Ginter* (****—management); *Paul Schultz* (****—finance); *Roy Lewicki* (***—organizational behavior); *Andrew Karolyi* (***—finance); *Anil Arya* (*—accounting); *Bernard La Londe* (*—marketing); *Robert Leone* (*—marketing).

APPLICANT TIPS

Applications for the full-time MBA program have been steadily growing at Ohio State, hitting a record 1038 in 1996 from just 772 in 1994. So this program is pretty competitive. Indeed, it is the fourth most selective Runners-Up school along with Georgetown. GMAT scores loom large in the admissions process here and have increased to 612 from just 586 in 1990. About 16 percent of the Class of 1998 was without a year's worth of full-time work experience.

Personal interviews are not required, but prospective students are encouraged to visit the campus. Call the MBA Office at 614-292-8511 to arrange an appointment.

Contact: Susie Cinadr
Coordinator for Recruitment and Admissions
614-292-8530
Final application deadline: April 30 for fall

FISHER MBAs SOUND OFF

My goals of moving into a high growth industry, rounding out my educational background, and repositioning my career were all exceeded by attending OSU's Fisher College of Business.

Just recently, a couple of incidents involving international students collaborating on assignments and turning in identical work have made me aware of different ethical standards among countries. This event demonstrates the need to make all students aware of the ethical standards this country abides by in order to create a level academic playing field. Also, I think the quality of the program is undermined by the administration filling up slots with underqualified applicants (i.e., GMAT < 600) when a sufficient number of qualified applicants fail to enroll. The administration knows this but needs the additional tuition money to continue to improve the program. It is indeed improving every year.

The unspoken rule that nobody was to fail, or be given a failing grade, undermined the program because without the fear of failing, some students did the bare minimum, and became a disruptive group in a classroom setting.

OSU has an excellent MBA program, which is unfortunately undervalued by the business community. The fact that the MBA class consists of only 100 students enhances learning experience, since the faculty has more time for each individual student and the relations between students are almost "family-like." Overall, it was a stressful but pleasant experience; an excellent investment of my time and money.

PENNSYLVANIA
STATE
UNIVERSITY

PENNSYLVANIA STATE UNIVERSITY

The Mary Jean and Frank P. Smeal College of Business
Administration
106 University Administration Building
University Park, Pennsylvania 16802
E-mail address: szm6@psu.edu
Website address: http://www.smeal.psu.edu

Enrollment: 277

Women: 26%
Non-U.S.: 26%
Minority: 17%
Part-time: None
Average age: 27
Average years of work exp.: 2.8
Applicants accepted: 30%
Median starting pay: $52,000

Annual tuition & fees:
  resident—$6078
  non-resident—$12,516
Room and board: $4500
Average GMAT score: 616
GMAT range: 470 to 760
Average GPA: 3.15
GPA range: 2.0 to 3.98
Accepted applicants enrolled: 11%
Average starting pay: $55,360

Teaching methods: Lecture, 30% Case study, 40%
Group projects, 30%

Contact:
James H. Hoy
Director of MBA
Admissions
814-863-0474
*Final application
deadline:*
May 31 for fall

It was a typical entrepreneurial dilemma: Your company comes up with a new product. Should you develop a partnership to more aggressively market the item, or should you try to go it alone? Either way, exactly how should you proceed? Bruce R. Robinson, a recent Penn State MBA, and four of his classmates had all of 72 hours to come up with the answers. Then the team had to present their ideas to a faculty board and possibly a panel of major company presidents.

Sounds like a bad dream. But the assignment is the culmination of a yearlong Managerial Communications course in the first year. Taught by a team of profs, students are assigned to write business memos and letters, and to make individual and group proposals. "After the communications course, making a presentation becomes second nature, and you actually begin to enjoy it," says Robinson.

Penn State's communications program is one of the strongest and oldest in the country. And it's a distinctive feature of the MBA program here that draws raves from students and alums alike. The school has received a similar reaction to the revamped curriculum that it put in place for the 1993 fall semester. "We have thrown away the book that we used to be bound to," says Roger A. Dagen, who directed the MBA Program through the changes.

The book discarded by the school contained the outlines of a highly rigid program with little flexibility or much linkage among courses. For years, Penn State loaded up its core curriculum with so much coursework that MBAs could only enroll in five electives. The new, integrated model rips apart the traditional three-credit courses in 15-week semesters and replaces them with courses of varying length that start and stop at different intervals. Students get their first dose of the capstone course on strategic management, for instance, in the first quarter. Then they pass through two quarters without a single class in the subject, only to pick it up again in the final quarter of the first year. The upshot of all the juggling? Students have to pile up 50 credits to graduate, 4 credits fewer than before, yet they can select 3 more electives. All told, MBAs now get to pick 8 elective offerings out of the school's menu of 66 per year.

Graduates of the Smeal College of Business Administration welcome the revised program. But many still complain that a palpable tension exists between the student body and the administration.

Several graduates also bemoan the inconsistent teaching in the program. There are obvious exceptions, but BUSINESS WEEK's 1996 customer satisfaction surveys show teaching quality in both the core and elective offerings to be below average. (In fact, the teaching was so bad in one management information systems core class a few years ago that the school gave students the option of dropping the course—with credit—six weeks into the semester.) That's not too surprising, however, because the school has put far more emphasis on academic research than teaching. More surprising, perhaps, is that some students maintain that some of their colleagues are admitted into the program without significant work experience, even though Smeal claims its grads average 2.8 years on the job prior to B-school. "It's hard to discuss sexual harassment and discrimination in the workplace with guys fresh out of frat houses," says Danielle R. O'Donohue, a recent alum.

For better or for worse, the small size of the program—no more than 160 in each graduating class, allows just about everyone to know one another. Penn State's MBA program requires total immersion. Students are accepted only in the fall and must spend two academic years in the program. Each incoming class is divided into four sections of 40 (instead of the giant classes of 90 that typify the Harvard experience) that take core courses together. The average class size in elective courses shrinks to about 20. The intimacy in such small classes creates long, enduring friendships among many of the students. A mentoring program also matches students with successful alums, creating opportunities for helpful friendships with established business leaders. The school even schedules two formal mentoring days in its academic calendar, though many students develop relationships that last throughout their careers.

One thing that hasn't changed since the curriculum's revamping is the school's strength in business logistics—the procurement of raw materials and the distribution of products after they are manufactured. Few other B-schools can beat the course offerings of Penn State in this area. A few years ago, some students expressed concern that Penn State's strength in business logistics may erode in the future, because the administration cut 2 of its 11 logistics positions through attrition. But the school's reputation in this area has been built over many years and it remains a strategic strength at Smeal.

Thanks to the marketing department's Institute for the Study of Business Markets, Smeal also is renowned for its expertise in business-to-business marketing, an area many other schools are only beginning to discover. Penn State has recently taken advantage of the university's strength in engineering by adding a manufacturing option, or major, for MBAs with undergraduate degrees in engineering. This latter program is a full-time, two-year option, requiring 15 credits in operations management and industrial engineering.

All students live within five miles of the B-school. Penn State likes to say that it is equidistant from everywhere, but it's also in the middle of nowhere. The school is smack in the center of Pennsylvania, off Interstate 80. Pittsburgh is 120 miles west and Philadelphia 150 miles east. Other than Penn State's sprawling 5032-acre University Park campus with 30,000 students, there's nothing much else here.

That means that there are few opportunities for internships or part-time jobs during the school year. It also makes it difficult for students to conduct independent job searches. Indeed, the school's location may deter some recruiters, no matter how good they think the program is. "The problem with Penn State is that they are in the middle of nowhere," says Thomas E. Wagner, director of human resources at Ernst & Young. "That would be a more popular program if it were easier to get to."

Yet, the school's locale isn't a turnoff to everyone. Students give favorable reviews to the lifestyle in what is known as "Happy Valley." The campus, surrounded by mountains, is great for mountain biking, hiking, and other outdoor activities. MBA tailgating parties outside Beaver Stadium feature kegs, hamburgers, and hot dogs every Saturday during the football season. The MBA Association also sponsors a series of get-togethers, from Halloween and Toga parties to semiformal holiday bashes and picnics.

When the MBAA isn't providing students with entertainment, they are good at organizing it themselves. The bulletin board in the MBA lounge, located in "BAB" where students take most of their classes, lists the latest happenings. To unwind, MBAs favor the G Man, a Houlihans-type bar and restaurant that is a popular hangout on Thursday nights. Also favored is a downright dive, The Skeller, famous for selling cases of Rolling Rock. Some of the best entertainment in town can be heard at The Saloon, a blues club, and at Tatoo, an alternative dance club.

Like many B-schools, Penn State is attempting to improve its placement efforts. The school added two databases to help MBAs link up with alumni, and changed the name of its placement center to the Office of Professional Development to better manage the expectations of its students. Smeal participates with other Big Ten MBA schools in job fairs held in New York, Atlanta, and Chicago. In addition, PSU offers two career fairs held on campus: the Smeal College Career Fair, open to both graduate and undergraduate business students, and the Minority Center Awareness Days, open to all MBAs.

The number of companies recruiting at Smeal has dwindled in recent years. In 1996, 127 corporations visited Penn State. Still, 85 percent of grads reported job offers by graduation. Recruiters luring the most MBAs included Ernst & Young LLP (5); AMP (5); IBM (4); Andersen Consulting (3); GTE (3); Texas Instrument (3); AT&T (2); Ford Motor Co. (2); Pfizer (2); Johnson & Johnson (2); PNC Bank (2); and General Electric (2).

OUTSTANDING FACULTY

Stewart Bither (****—marketing); *Chris Muscarella* (****—finance); *Rocki-Lee Dewitt* (****—strategic management); *Dave Butt* (***—business communications); *Fariborz Ghadar* (***—strategy and international finance); *Sean O'Keefe* (**—public finance and technology management); *Judith Bogert* (*—business communications); *Joseph Cavinato* (*—logistics); *Kofi Nti* (*—management science).

APPLICANT TIPS

If you're off to a late start on the application process you probably have a shot at Penn State, which accepts applications until May 31. However, since it has a rolling application process, the school suggests that you apply as early as possible. And if you're an international applicant, you'll need to apply by April 30. Interviews aren't required, but the school interviewed 99 percent of its applicants in 1996, so it's probably a good idea to interview if you think it could add to your appeal. What is the school looking for? "The MBA program admissions policy assures that incoming classes will comprise highly qualified individuals representing a diversity of backgrounds in terms of prior education, undergraduate institutions, significant work experience, and other academic and professional accomplishments." That said, a full third of Smeal's Class of 1998 lacks even a single year of full-time work experience. So if you have racked up job experience, that will certainly give you an edge.

Contact: James H. Hoy
Director of MBA Admissions
814-863-0474
Final application deadline: May 31 for fall

SMEAL MBAs SOUND OFF

I feel like one of the strongest parts of our MBA program is the communications class. The emphasis on written, oral, and visual presentations throughout the year gave me an edge over other MBA students during interviews, internships, and case competitions. Penn State is a great value. I look at the fact that my outstanding loans are much smaller than other friends at other MBA programs with our starting salaries being equal.

Penn State provides you with an excellent marketing program where cooperation and teamwork are highly emphasized. The relationship between students, faculty, and staff is very personal, and students' concerns are promptly addressed with the utmost respect. The diversity in the program, in terms of ethnic and cultural backgrounds, is superb and provides students with perspective.

This is an outstanding program for the tuition cost. While it may not have the reputation of a Harvard or Wharton, this program delivers great value. The placement office is outstanding. The numerous Penn State alumni in business are always willing to help in job searches or offer general advice. The companies recruiting from the program are topflight and recognize the potential of Penn State grads. The number of companies recruiting on campus is increasing as a direct result of the placement office efforts and also the performance of recent hires.

Penn State is excellent in terms of value (cost of program in relation to salary potential), quality of life (great athletics, college life), job opportunities (there are good companies recruiting here), and alumni base. I came here especially for the Logistics Program. My one concern involves the quality of students. In my opinion, some students received preferential treatment in admissions (and in terms of grades) based upon ethnic information/background. We had a diverse class—over 30 percent international students—which was great for cultural learning.

PURDUE UNIVERSITY

Krannert Graduate School of Management
1310 Krannert Building
West Lafayette, Indiana 47907-1310
E-mail address: krannert-ms@mgmt.purdue.edu
Website address: http://www.mgmt.purdue.edu

Enrollment: 298	Annual tuition & fees:
	resident—$5708
Women: 21%	non-resident—$13,136
Non-U.S.: 27%	Room and board: $5000
Minority: 10%	Average GMAT score: 602
Part-time: None	GMAT range: 410 to 730
Average age: 27.3	Average GPA: 3.21
Average years of work exp.: 4.2	GPA range: 2.1 to 4.0
Applicants accepted: 23%	Accepted applicants enrolled: 51%
Median starting pay: $65,000	Average starting pay: $66,940

Teaching methods: Lecture, 30%   Case study, 45%   Projects, 25%

Contact:
Ward D. Snearly
Associate Director
Master's Programs
765-494-4365
Applications deadline:
Rolling admissions
January 1
February 1

If someone planted you smack dab in the middle of nowhere, 70 miles from any substantial city, hundreds of miles from Wall Street, and thousands from Sillicon Valley, and then said you'd be getting a top-drawer MBA experience, you might laugh at them. You'd be wrong.

Purdue University's Krannert Graduate School of Management is a favorite hunting ground for industrial companies and turns out grads with rock-solid quantitative skills. At about $13,000 a year, Krannert offers a bargain-priced MBA—and an amazing deal if you're an Indiana resident, paying only $5700. In short, it's one of the Midwest's best B-schools.

But it's slipping. Ranked 20th in 1994, Purdue fell off the Top 25 list entirely in 1996. Why? The class of 1994 criticized the school for uneven teaching quality and a "mental bootcamp" atmosphere that they said overwhelmed them. The administration vowed to respond. In 1996, however, students said the problems had worsened. Krannert received significantly lower marks for the freshness of classroom material and the responsiveness of the administration, for example. Among the 50 schools in BUSINESS WEEK's survey, it finished in the bottom 10 for the quality of second-year electives, the international business program, and overall teaching.

Though recruiters still consider it a top school for operations and anaytical skills, even they gave the school lower marks in '96 than in '94. So what's going on at the West Lafayette, Indiana school that was long considered a diamond in the corn field, as it were? Administrators and professors still haven't figured out how best to serve their customers, the students—though they've certainly tried.

Aware of the complaints about coursework overload, Dean Dennis J. Weidenaar trimmed back core requirements to offer students more flexibility in choosing electives, while keeping the workload strenuous. He instituted mandatory teaching evaluations to give instructors feedback and determine which ones should be referred to workshops. He set up town forums in which students can offer praise or criticism. And he changed his faculty recruiting process so that he now interviews every candidate and says he no longer recruits rookies.

All this comes in addition to an overhaul of the curriculum that happened in 1992. Modeled on a total quality initiative at Motorola University, where 100 Purdue faculty members studied in '92, the new Krannert program is designed to give softer management skills a bigger place in the curriculum. Krannert has developed a cohort system in which students are preassigned to teams for eight-week exercises to help them understand teamwork and to develop problem-solving skills. During orientation, students are given a Myers-Brigg test to determine strengths and weaknesses in their leadership ability. Students also now attend four 8-week modules instead of two semesters yearly. One result: they take one class each in both organizational behavior and human resources management and two classes in communications. Another result: they're free to choose one elective their first year and at least nine electives during their second.

In addition, students are no longer required to pick an "option"—the equivalent of a major—to gain a degree. Many still do, though. They choose among accounting, finance, marketing, strategic management, operations management, management of information systems, and human resources management. There are also three new interdisciplinary options: manufacturing management, international management, and general management.

What's the end result of all this work? Not quite what you'd think. Instead of an MBA, graduates receive a Master of Science degree in one of three areas: industrial administration (an 11-month sprint), management, or human resources management. Above all, the difference reflects the program's emphasis on technical and analytical training. After all, some 30 of the 31 graduates of Krannert's first class in 1957 were engineers. In 1996, 27 percent of grads landed jobs in operations management. Fifty percent of Krannert students still boast undergraduate degrees in science or engineering. But the hidden gem of the program may be the finance option. A little more than one-third of the students select this program, and 36 percent of the class of '96 landed in a finance-related field. Where? Intel, Hewlett-Packard, Procter & Gamble, Ford Motor, IBM, Allied Signal, and others.

Beyond the quantitative influence that seeps into virtually every nook of the curriculum, the most important thing to know about academic life in West Lafayette is that it's hard. That's probably one reason why students here aren't always happy during their two-year stay, but corporate recruiters like the product that walks out the door. One break in the schedule: there are no Friday classes. Instead, students participate in Forum Days, which allow time for experiential activities. For example, all students participate in an outward bound–type program one Friday. Outside speakers also visit campus on Fridays and discuss hot business topics like technology, the environment, and diversity. These things "don't fit very neatly into a 90-minute forum," says G. Logan Jordan, an assistant dean at Krannert.

Another less obvious asset is the unpretentious, down-home culture of this small, conservative university town. West Lafeyette is the kind of place where you can walk down the street and strangers will say hello and talk to you about the weather. You can spot the seven-story Krannert Building, named after the founder of the Inland

Container Corporation, on the southeast edge of the university's 1565-acre campus. In a sea of red-brick buildings, it is a massive block of white concrete with narrow strip windows that run up and down. Computer equipment fills the top floor, while the ground floor is home to a French Provincial drawing room that serves as a student lounge. As part of a Krannert ritual, graduate students and faculty gather in this room at 9:30 a.m. for coffee after first-period class.

The B-school is also a block away from the Chauncey Village Mall, where grads sometimes meet at the Wabash Yacht Club for drinks or get a cone at Ben & Jerry's. Another favorite spot: Harry's Chocolate Shop, an old, weathered place with scribblings on the walls, where students migrate after exams. Many grads live off campus, where you can get a one-bedroom apartment for as little as $400 a month. You can park in the Grant Street garage just across from the B-school for $30 a year.

But West Lafeyette isn't the most exciting place in the world. If you've ever driven down I-65 from Chicago, you may have stopped off at the exit—one of only a handful in the area. There's a McDonalds, a gas station—and corn fields. It's easy to feel isolated with Chicago 120 miles to the north and Indianapolis 70 miles to the south. Big Ten football and basketball games are the highlight of the fall and winter seasons. The school also holds a talent show, a charity ball, and different seasonal parties to remind students that they can have fun.

But while Lafeyette may lack the easy-going charm and diversity of a Chapel Hill or Austin, it's hardly a wasteland. It's a perfect microcosm of life in the Midwest—matter-of-fact and friendlier than the urban northeast. *Money* magazine, in fact, ranked it 30th on its list of the Top 300 places to live in 1996. The community has its own civic orchestra and theater as well as a nationally accredited art museum. In the spring, there's the Around-the-Fountain Art Fair next to Lafeyette's Neoclassical courthouse. In the summer, bluegrass and mountain musicians gravitate to the city for the Indiana Fiddler's Gathering. And in the fall, the Feast of the Hunter's Moon draws thousands of visitors to Fort Ouiatenon where the area's French and Indian history is re-created on the banks of the Wabash River.

PLACEMENT DETAILS

In 1996, a total of 98 companies recruited on campus, up from 72 in 1994 and 54 in 1992. The top ones: Hewlett-Packard (9); Intel (9); United Technologies (5); General Motors (5); Ford Motor (4); Allied Signal (4); Ernst & Young (3); Procter & Gamble (2); International Paper (2); and Price Waterhouse (2). Over the years, Purdue grads have been most likely to end up at General Motors, where 161 have landed jobs. After GM comes IBM (97), United Technologies (96), Hewlett-Packard (86), and Ford (82).

That list gives you a good idea of the respect that Corporate America holds for Krannert. Now the administration just needs to figure out how to satisfy its students.

OUTSTANDING FACULTY

Gerald Lynch (****—economics); *John McConnell* (****—finance); *Arnold Cooper* (***—strategy); *Charlene Sullivan* (***—finance); *Catherine Daily* (**—management); *Douglas Bowman* (**—marketing)

APPLICANT TIPS

Krannert is one of the most selective schools in the Runners-Up group, accepting only 23 percent of the total applicants—the second stingiest percentage, behind only Maryland. In deciding whom to admit, Krannert heavily weighs GMAT scores, undergraduate grades, and work experience. The essay portion of the application is comparatively small. Interviews are not required, although the school may ask you to come to campus for an interview if it believes additional information is necessary to make a final decision on your application. Only 10 percent of the school's 1607 applicants in 1996 were interviewed.

Although calculus is recommended, there is no specific mathematical preparation for admission to either the Master of Science in Management, Purdue's two-year, full-time MBA equivalent, or the Master of Science in Industrial Administration, an accelerated program that can be completed in just 11 months. Applicants with little or no mathematical training, however, must be able to show that they have an aptitude for developing quantitative skills. That means the school will look especially hard at your math score on the GMAT. For additional info, you may contact admissions at 765-494-4365 or via fax at 765-494-9658.

Contact: Ward D. Snearly
Associate Director Master's Programs
765-494-4365
Applications deadline: Rolling admissions January 1, February 1, and April 15

KRANNERT GRADS SOUND OFF

I think the cohort system, which emphasized a diversified team environment, was excellent. It encourages sharing of information, clean competition, hard work, and peer development. Krannert should (also) be noted for having a good overall placement center and a friendly learning environment. But, homework assignments and exams in quantitative methods, and operations management are a little too extreme for a core class—especially for students with non-engineering backgrounds.

We have a motto at Krannert—"Krannert Means Business"—which really exemplifies the education. I am so pleased by having been educated alongside so many no-nonsense type individuals. We all work hard and appreciate each other's abilities. If you want to work hard and develop a solid foundation for a future role as a business leader, Krannert is the place to be.

Purdue has a misguided effort with its graduate management program. All things considered, Krannert is a good school: it loads you up with work to teach work ethic, it exposes you to tremendous amounts of team experience, and it demands good time management. However, the dean is a poor leader. He is not personable, not active with the students, and not very good at resolving conflict. Also, the faculty and administration tend to politics a little much.

RICE
UNIVERSITY

Contact:
D. Richard Trask
Director of Admissions
713-527-4918
*Final application
deadline:*
March 1 for fall

RICE UNIVERSITY

Jesse H. Jones Graduate School of Administration
Houston, Texas 77251-1892
E-mail address: enterjgs@rice.edu
Website address: http://www.ruf.rice.edu/~jgs

Enrollment: 262	Annual tuition & fees: $13,300
Women: 24%	Room and board: $8500
Non-U.S.: 14%	Average GMAT score: 613
Minority: 16%	Average GPA: 3.21
Part-time: None	GPA range: 2.20 to 4.18
Average age: 27.8	Average years of work exp.: 4.8
Applicants accepted: 27.8%	Accepted applicants enrolled: 54%
Median starting pay: $63,000	Average starting pay: $66,920

Teaching methods: Lecture, 45%   Case study, 45%
                       Field projects, 10%

It would be easy to mistake Rice University's B-school for a modern museum. Nestled in a grove of oak trees, the red brick and white limestone building is topped by terra-cotta roof tiles. Its sleek design is worthy of the pages of top architectural reviews. In fact, Herring Hall, the home of Jesse H. Jones Graduate School of Administration, has been featured in *Progressive Architecture* and *Domus* of Milan.

A museum, however, it is not. The B-school, named after a Houston entrepreneur and financier, offers one of the best MBA programs in the Southwest. By design the classes are small and personal. Of the 1300 graduate students on this 300-acre campus in a Houston residential area, roughly 15 percent go to the business school. And the academic standards are high. That's why the school is commanding greater attention these days.

One odd fact about Jones: It lacks official accreditation because of an undergraduate "managerial studies" major that the school does not control. The AACSB believes it should run the program. Another sticking point could be that the part-time faculty of about 30 teachers outnumbers the 27 full-time professors on the tenure track. Still, it doesn't seem to bother the recruiters or the students, many of whom could easily get into far more prestigious programs.

The core curriculum is a real grind, just as it is at most other top B-schools—you need 64 credits to earn a degree. The most unusual feature of the core is a yearlong study of "legal and governmental processes" that explores the government's impact on business. The course reflects the program's early roots in initially granting not an MBA but a Master

240

of Business and Public Management degree, like Yale University's B-school. Jones's diplomas are now stamped with the MBA. Another new feature: in 1996, the school became one of the first to require all students to take a semester-long class in entrepreneurship. Though Rice doesn't pop up on most lists of the best programs in entrepreneurship, it might be helpful to know that the school boasts one teacher—Edward Williams—who is one of the top five teachers in the subject in the world. Williams is a Wharton grad who serves on the board of a Texas funeral home company he helped to expand to $7 billion in market capitalization.

In the second year, the required coursework includes a case-method seminar, Strategy and Operations I, focusing on global business, and a field project in which you'll be assigned to a student team to work on a strategic management issue for an area company. The second year also features the dean's seminar and programs in career management. One drawback to anyone interested in global management: Although international business is one of 10 areas of concentration for MBAs, Rice is one of the very few business schools without a single exchange program with a foreign business school.

This is a very small program. The advantages are obvious in the low student-faculty ratio and the intimacy of the program. The school enrolls about 135 full-time students a year, boasts just 25 full-time professors. In BUSINESS WEEK's graduate surveys, Rice scores among the leaders for having faculty who are accessible to students outside the classroom. The average number of students in elective classes is just 15. With only 55 electives, however, there are far fewer courses from which to pick and choose. And because many of these are taught by adjuncts, it's not always easy to arrange time to see professors outside of class.

The school's size, of course, also has an impact on its alumni network. There are only 1235 alums of the business school. That's less than two graduating classes from Harvard, Wharton, or Northwestern. So don't expect all that much from alumni networking. Instead, you'll have to appeal to the broader alumni of the entire university.

PLACEMENT DETAILS

Grads aren't very enthusiastic about the school's placement operation. They gave the school among the lowest grades of the Top 50 in several key placement categories, criticizing Rice for its help in finding them jobs before graduation, in supporting independent searches for employment, and for helping students with résumés and interviews. Yet, Rice claims that only 10 percent of the Class of 1996 was without a single job offer by commencement. And grads pulled down median starting pay packages of $63,000—fifth highest among the 25 Runners-Up and more than the grads got at four Top 25 schools.

In 1996, 70 companies recruited on campus, conducting some 800 interviews with second-years. About 50 job opportunities were posted via correspondence. The major hiring firms in 1996: Andersen Consulting (5); Enron (4); AA/Sabre (4); Amoco (3); Oracle (3); FMC (3); Compaq (3); Coca-Cola (3); IBM (3); and Continental Airlines (3). Not a bad group of companies for a school that looks like a museum.

OUTSTANDING FACULTY

David L. Ikenberry (****—finance); *Ed Williams* (****—entrepreneurship); *Jeff Fleming* (****—finance); *Barbara Ostdiek* (***—international finance); *Karen E. Schnietz* (***—international trade); *Douglas A. Schuler* (**—international trade); *Randy Batsell* (**—marketing); *Steven C. Currall* (**—organizational behavior); *David Ross* (*—strategy).

APPLICANT TIPS

For some nearly unexplainable reason, Rice has suffered a significant falloff in applicants in recent years—making this a very good time to get into a superb graduate business program. Back in 1992, the school had 858 applicants. In 1996, it received applications from just 571 people.

So how do you get an edge? Rice, of course, looks at GMAT and GPA scores. But the admissions folks go out of their way to explain that "quantifiable data alone do not present us with the full picture of an applicant." The school says it also weighs such factors as your choice of major, selection of courses outside your major, course load, and grade patterns. "In other words, if you were involved in extracurricular activities, did they affect your GPA? Can you explain any major inconsistencies in your academic record?" About 11 percent of the Class of 1998 has less than one year of job experience. Personal interviews are not required, but the school strongly urges applicants to do them anyway. Some 35 percent of the school's 571 applicants were interviewed in 1996.

Contact: D. Richard Trask
Director of Admissions
713-527-4918
Final application deadline: March 1 for fall

JONES MBAs SOUND OFF

Good emphasis on the instruction and importance/influence of public policy (on business). Program needs to interject teachings in business law. Program respected locally, but it needs more national exposure. School gets "bad rap" on the accreditation issue.

My experience at Rice is one that I will cherish not necessarily for the coursework (it was demanding and challenging) but more for the network of friends and colleagues that I established. This network was made possible through an atmosphere of cooperation and teamwork not competition, as with most professional grad programs. I firmly believe that the vast majority of my colleagues will do what is necessary to aid and support each other even at the cost of putting oneself at a disadvantage.

Overall, I've been more than pleased with my experiences in B-school. In all fairness to the placement center, they underwent massive changes during my time here. My school stresses more teamwork and cooperative effort rather than pushing leadership which is important considering many of the more successful companies are exploring the benefits of cross-functional teams and systems/organizational learning.

I believe there are three components to a B-school program: the students, teachers, and the administration. Rice's students and teachers are great, the administration needs help. Our class size is around 100/year, yet the Dean probably only knows five of our names. I've asked the Dean of Students why we don't market our school more and his reply was that ". . . I don't want to spend $100,000 on PR. We just need to get more quality students out there and companies will learn about us." He was not receptive to my explanation of the role of marketing (and I'm a finance guy). The bottom line is . . . I think the program is great, but it could be improved.

The most significant characteristic of the program is the high value and quality of education for the amount you pay. It is the highest ratio. Tuition cost for the entire program is $22,000 (very cheap), and the education you get is the best. Another important quality of Rice is that because the school is so small (100 students per class), you have personal attention by all professors. They all know who you are and how you're doing.

TEXAS A&M
UNIVERSITY

Contact:
Elissa L. Ellis
Assistant Director of
MBA Program
409-845-4714
*Final application
deadline:
May 1 for fall*

TEXAS A&M UNIVERSITY

Lowry Mays Graduate School of Business
College Station, Texas 77843
E-mail address: inquiries@mba-lab.tamu.edu
Website address: http://www.mba-grad.tamu.edu

Enrollment: 229	Annual tuition & fees:
	resident—$3000
Women: 27.5%	non-resident—$8800
Non-U.S.: 28.5%	Room and board: $8200
Minority: 11.8%	Average GMAT score: 608
Part-time: None	GMAT range: 480 to 750
Average age: 25.6	Average GPA: 3.14
Average years of work exp.: 2.4	GPA range: 2.46 to 4.0
Applicants accepted: 46%	Accepted applicants enrolled: 50%
Median starting pay: $47,000	Average starting pay: $47,890

Teaching methods: Lecture, 50%   Case study, 50%

Texas A&M University's MBA brochure is a celebration of the Lone Star State and feel-good college days. The state flag graces the cover of the MBA program booklet over a subtle white star. Inside, pages go on and on about the "Aggie Attitude," the "Aggie Network," and how "Aggies Help Aggies." There's even a picture of a big, old class ring, the kind you failed to order during your high school days.

You wouldn't expect to find anything but a rather ordinary MBA program at this adolescent business school which began producing MBAs in 1960. But you'd be dead wrong. While most new MBA candidates are climbing ropes and juggling five courses, incoming students at A&M spend their first week in an intensive course called The MBA Challenge. The class explores the foundations of business behavior and its interactions with such key stakeholders as customers and suppliers. It also simulates a business environment by requiring students to make decisions under stress.

The unusual course provides the framework for the entire MBA program. Then, first-years roll up their sleeves for three "highly integrated" classes in accounting, info systems, and quantitative methods. In the second semester, Texas A&M splits the program into a pair of seven-and-a-half week terms, putting MBAs through only two core courses at a time. To reach the second year, students must also complete a mandatory cross-discipline project and attend executive skills development workshops held every Friday. While your colleagues at other schools may head for the beach in the early summer months, A&M encourages you to pick up a pair of electives. You can do this by studying abroad, taking a corporate internship, or signing up for the school's Washington, D.C. campus program. You also must take a course in international business.

In the second year, students plunge into the capstone course on Corporate Strategies and Public Policy as well as two remaining core courses. That doesn't leave much flexibility to choose many electives. In fact, if you picked up a pair over the summer, you only need 4 more to complete the program requirements. Finance and accounting are the school's strongest departments. All told, students have to tally up 53 hours' worth of work: 35 hours of the new core curriculum and 18 through 6 elective courses. A&M offers students a dozen different concentrations, including entrepreneurship and family business management and consulting and strategic management.

This is one of the smaller graduate schools of business so elective pickings are slim. There are 48 possibilities, ranging from Strategy Formulation to Product Innovation. Among the electives is also an innovative Wall Street Seminar, during which students spend a summer session in New York, live in the dorms of New York University, and are taught Financial Markets by an A&M finance prof who also coordinates visits to 15 financial firms. A similarly structured elective, Doing Business in Southeast Asia, is a summer session in Japan, Korea, China, and Hong Kong. Like most other business schools, A&M boasts semester abroad programs with nine non-U.S. B-schools in Europe, Mexico, and Japan.

College Station, about an hour and a half drive from Houston, is a comfy, inexpensive place to spend a couple of years. The B-school and all of its students—including a rather overwhelming 5600 undergrads—are housed in a modern, six-story building. The university plays up its Aggie reputation as "the friendliest school on earth." "You'll be repeatedly greeted with a warm smile and a hearty howdy," says the school's brochure. That is likely an exaggeration, but students here are friendly if a bit more competitive than you might expect—and they are few. The average core class has just 40 students in it, while the average elective has about 30 students. With only 229 full-time MBAs and no part-timers, it's one of the easiest places to get to know all the MBAs and their brothers and sisters by their first names. The same is true of the faculty: there are only 25 full-time profs at the business school.

PLACEMENT DETAILS

An MBA from this school probably isn't going to get you one of those really plum MBA jobs that pay lots of money. In fact, the median starting pay for Aggie grads in 1996 was just $47,000—the lowest of any Runners-Up school with the exception of the University of Wisconsin, whose grads made just $200 less. The average of $47,891 was dead last. Part of the reason is because 65 percent of the grads stay in Texas where incomes aren't what they are in either the Northeast or the West.

Still, A&M MBAs came in third among the Runners-Up for most job offers, with 2.93 per student at commencement. Some 105 companies recruited on campus in 1996, conducting 630 interviews with second-years. Another 250 job opportunities were posted via correspondence. The top employers of the Class of 1996 included some top-notch firms, even prestigious consulting outfit McKinsey & Co., which tends to recruit only at the very best and most elite schools. The major hirers: Andersen Consulting (5); Arthur Andersen (4); IBM (4); Koch Industries (3); NationsBank (3); General Mills (2); Procter & Gamble (2); McKinsey (2); KMPG Peat Marwick (2); and Compaq Computer (2). Pretty good company for Aggies from the Lone Star State.

OUTSTANDING FACULTY

Gerald Keim (****—management); *Michael Abelson* (***—management); *David Dubofsky*

(***—finance); *Robert Hoskisson* (***—management); *Winston T. Shearon, Jr.* (**—accounting); *Neeli Bendapudi* (*—marketing); *Tina Dacin* (*—management); *Donald Frasier* (*—finance); *Stephen McDaniel* (*—marketing); *Powell Robinson* (*—business analysis).

APPLICANT TIPS

Among the Runners-Up schools, Texas A&M enrolls a pretty young crowd. In fact, it's the second youngest class, with an average age of 25.6 years, with the lowest amount of full-time work experience, at an average 2.4 years. Though the school says it prefers applicants with a minimum of two years of work experience, one of every four students in the Class of 1998 had less than a year's worth of experience on the job. That makes this graduate school a place that certainly welcomes a good number of candidates direct from their undergraduate studies.

The school says it looks for "demonstrated leadership and academic potential" as well as verbal and quant GMAT scores that are above the 50th percentile. Personal interviews also are recommended, but the admissions office could not report how many of its 528 applicants in 1996 did an interview. Apply by February 1 if you would like priority admission or want to seek scholarship money or an assistantship.

Contact: Elissa L. Ellis
Assistant Director of MBA Program
409-845-4714
Final application deadline: May 1 for fall

MAYS MBAs SOUND OFF

The first year Lock Step Program is extremely challenging and very team oriented. A student entering this program should expect 20 class presentations at least. Texas A&M's MBA program far exceeds the costs. The computing and research facilities are state of the art, and are continuously being updated. The College of Business has its own library. First-year professors communicate well with one another and are extremely aware of what is being taught in each other's courses. Likewise, they make themselves very accessible. Perhaps the thing I like best about the program is the value placed on students' input. The program is continuously being improved based on this input. Roundtable discussions are held with the dean and with the program office.

Strengths: quality and dedication of MBA core faculty, alumni network, coordination of class schedules during the first year of the program (Lock-Step Program), self-determination/drive of students (we hold our own career conference each Fall), computer resources, "bang for the buck," and a diverse student body (in MBA program). Weaknesses: lack of electives to choose from (especially in operation management area), too many students without any work experience, study abroad programs are just parties on wheels, and the lack of structure during the second year of the program.

The Lock-Step Program in the first year is an excellent one. It really helps team-building and stresses the student's abilities to its extremes. All the courses are interlinked with each other and all projects are done with the same group. The first-year experiences make the other semesters in the program relatively simpler. For me it's been quite a learning experience.

The program is always improving itself in terms of courses offered, job search methods, and available tools (upgrading computers, etc.). It has been a challenge to compare each graduating class: the chemistry of one class appears totally different from another as a result of curriculum design, new tools, etc.

Study Abroad experience was the highlight of the program. Texas A&M's computer library resources are excellent. Unfortunately, the program recruits too many inexperienced and very young students.

I do owe my technical skills to A&M. The computer facilities are absolutely outstanding—state-of-the-art PCs. I challenge any other B-school to match our facilities (as far as computers go).

Great teamwork experiences, very international atmosphere (large percentage of foreign students), very "real world" oriented, and a lot of interaction between students and administration/faculty.

Texas A&M is an incredible value. The professors are also very flexible and helpful in allowing you to pursue projects outside of class. We took a field trip to the border with Mexico in Laredo where we visited U.S. customs, a customs broker, a bank, and a Mexican factory. It was so successful we took another field trip the next semester to Houston to visit the Houston ship channel and several other companies.

TULANE UNIVERSITY

TULANE UNIVERSITY

A.B. Freeman School of Business
Goldring/Woldenberg Hall
New Orleans, Louisiana 70118
E-mail address: admissions@office.sob.tulane.edu
Website address: http://freeman.sob.tulane.edu/
freeman/freeman.htm

Enrollment: 405
Women: 29%
Non-U.S.: 31%
Minority: 11%
Part-time: 193
Average age: 27
Applicants accepted: 37%
Median starting pay: $48,450

Annual tuition & fees: $21,236
Room and board: $6820
Average GMAT score: 621
Average GPA: 3.3
GPA range: 2.31 to 4.0
Average years of work exp.: 4
Accepted applicants enrolled: 40%
Average starting pay: $52,525

Teaching methods: Lecture, 40%   Case study, 60%

Contact:
John C. Silbernagel
Director of Admissions
504-865-5410
or 800-223-5402
Application deadlines:
April 1
May 1

The A.B. Freeman School had a reputation as a sleepy business school within a fine university—until Dean Meyer Feldberg came along. He raised $22 million, increased enrollment by 50 percent, hired new faculty, and built a $7 million home for the school. So successful was Feldberg that top schools started dangling job offers before him. He's now dean of Columbia University's School of Business.

What Feldberg left behind in 1986 was a solid business school, housed in a modern seven-story building on a beautiful 110-acre campus in a residential area of grand Victorian homes in uptown New Orleans. Dean James W. McFarland has built upon that strong foundation largely through strengthening the school's international program. He has set up a summer-abroad program with four weeks of coursework. Meanwhile, he continues to build a worldwide network of universities and corporations that trade students, faculty, and internships with Tulane. And 31 percent of the entering class of 1998 hail from outside the United States. The consequence of all this: no second-tier B-school gets better marks from students for its international business program.

But that's just the beginning. From the career placement office to the quality of teaching in electives to the overall responsiveness of the administration, few schools have improved as much as Tulane during the last two years. It's now starting to live up to its promise as a small school, with an accessible faculty and an integrated curriculum. It's a school that can now compete with places like Emory and Georgetown. Like those other private B-schools, this is a program for people who want to study for an MBA with classmates and faculty they know by name. Of course, one downside that tends to go hand-in-hand with being quaint is a partial snubbing by the corporate world.

Not that Freeman doesn't have some big-name recruiters, but with such a small class each year, many corporations find it unprofitable to send a recruiter to New Orleans. They also remain skeptical of the school. None of the 50 MBA programs reviewed in this book gets an overall lower score from recruiters than Tulane.

Administrators and faculty hope the students' new confidence in the program will eventually spread to Corporate America. The school's goal is to produce well-rounded managers who can operate in an international context. That's why one-third of Freeman students participate in study-abroad programs and summer internships overseas. In 1996, Freeman offered study-abroad programs in Europe, Asia, and nearby Mexico (where McFarland has made particular efforts). The international focus is also evident from the new curriculum implemented four years ago. The revamping injected more international business material throughout the core courseload, and there's now a required first-year class on the economic environment of global business.

The Freeman experience begins with an intensive nine-day series of modules designed to set the stage for the academic program to follow and to establish relationships among the school, students, faculty, and staff. The first exercise, dubbed "the job of the executive," features case studies. Another module hones students' computer skills, and a third includes an outdoor challenge. The point is to develop self-awareness and skills in problem solving, communication, and team building. Then there's the annual Freeman Games, a friendly competition between first-year and second-year MBAs.

After the modules, the first semester begins with a typical group of courses: accounting, economics, communications, statistics, and organizational behavior. Prior to the second semester comes a two-day speaker series intended to sharpen students' understanding of the social and political context in which businesses function. Executives participate in talks on ethics, regulation, the environmental, and diversity. (At Freeman, 11 percent of the MBAs are African-American, Latino, or Native American.)

Semester two features finance, operations, and marketing, along with the required class in global economics—and one elective. Augmenting traditional courses during the first year is a career development strategy series. One highlight of the series: a luncheon on business etiquette/protocol at Commander's Palace, often named as one of the best restaurants in the United States.

In year two, there's only one required course—in business strategy and policy—allowing students to take nine electives. At least one of them must be chosen from a set of nine other international courses. The other requirement is that students choose one elective from each of seven different fields. It's a rule that hammers home Tulane's general management philosophy. Freeman lists accounting and taxation, economic analysis, finance, human resources, management, marketing, and decision information and operations as its fields of study.

Tulane boasts one of the oldest MBA programs in the country. Since 1940, when Tulane's MBA program was founded, the business school has churned out 4358 MBAs. But it wasn't until a decade or so ago that the university significantly upgraded the quality of the school under Dean Feldberg. The changes of the early 1980s were sweeping, and Freeman watchers agree that Feldberg made all the difference.

Following Northwestern's example, Tulane started interviewing most domestic applicants. Those who gain admission will study in a red-brick building with a three-story atrium. MBAs share the place with 300 undergrads, but there's plenty of room. The B-school's new home even boasts a television studio to tape students for a required course in management communications. An elective class on negotiations also puts students on film for evaluation.

The campus sits near one of the most culturally rich areas in the country: the French Quarter, only 20 minutes away by streetcar. Such a short ride to a world of wonderfully spicy cuisine from jambalaya and gumbo to red beans and rice. And don't forget the music. It follows you everywhere. If you're visiting and looking to get a taste of Tulane life, stop by Philips, a popular spot on Cherokee Street, or Waldo's Restaurant and Bar, which serves up a Greek-Cajun mix of grub about a block away from the B-school. For something more unusual, try Mid-City Bowling Lanes featured Rock 'n' Bowl, where some of the hottest bands in town play. Don't be surprised if some of the twenty-somethings around you are Freeman students. In general, local bars offer cheap drinks, and they're easy to get to. Most students walk everywhere. You won't have to shell out a huge chunk of change for an apartment either; most students live in and around campus in apartments that rent for between $400 and $600 a month.

PLACEMENT DETAILS

Thanks to the success of Mary Rose O'Neill in the placement department, Freeman MBAs have been finding it easier and easier to get jobs. Asked to evaluate the school's overall agressiveness in helping them find jobs before graduation, the class of '96 gave Tulane marks that were an astonishing 49 percent higher than two years earlier. The school's grades for assisting MBAs with summer internships jumped 54 percent.

No wonder. In 1992, 39 percent of the class lacked job offers at graduation. In 1994, that number dropped to 19 percent, and for the class of 1996, only 12 percent lacked a single offer by commencement. The school claims that 195 companies recruited second-years on campus in 1996, but they did only 554 interviews. Top hirers: Entergy (7); Arthur Andersen (3); Merrill Lynch (2); Deloitte & Touche (2); AT&T (2); and American Management Systems (2).

Not bad, though the school clearly has work to do with its corporate customers. Still, with student satisfaction up dramatically and New Orleans as enticing as ever, the real question now seems to be why anybody would want to leave Tulane.

OUTSTANDING FACULTY

Russell P. Robins (****—economics); *James T. Murphy* (****—finance); *Prem Jain* (****—accounting); *Ken Boudreaux* (**—finance and economics); *Arthur P. Brief* (**—organizational behavior); *Beau Parent* (**—accounting); *James Biteman* (*—management); *Victor Cook* (*—marketing); *John Elstrott* (*—entrepreneurship [in management area]); *Chitru Fernando* (*—finance).

APPLICANT TIPS

Tulane states that "diversity among the student body is an integral part of the Freeman experience. The Admissions Committee actively seeks applicants from all over the world and encourages candidates with degrees from accredited institutions in all major fields of study." Tulane says 90 percent of the entering class has at least one full-time year of work experience, but it is not required: "While the committee strongly encourages full-time work experience in terms of practical educations, candidates with outstanding undergraduate records are encouraged to apply." Candidates are reviewed on a rolling basis so Tulane suggests that you apply as early as possible.

The admissions committee starts reviewing applications in September, and the final deadline is May 1. Approximately half of the full-time entering class receives merit-based fellowship awards, and about half of the full-time MBAs hold assistantships in the Freeman School. All full-time applicants are automatically considered for fellowships during the application process, and the school advises applicants who are interested in such aid to apply by April 1. All applicants who live in the United States or Canada must complete an interview with an admissions staff member, and in 1996, 78 percent of all applicants were interviewed. You can fulfill this 30- to 45-minute requirement by visiting the campus, by telephone, or you can schedule an off-campus interview if an admissions officer is visiting your area.

To schedule an interview, you should call the admissions office at 504-865-5410 or 800-223-5402 between 8:30 a.m. and 5:00 p.m. central time.

Contact: John C. Silbernagel
Director of Admissions
504-865-5410 or 800-223-5402
Application deadlines: April 1, May 1

FREEMAN MBAs SOUND OFF

You pay a great deal financially, but what you get at Freeman is a relatively small class size that is team oriented and extremely close-knit. Freeman's emphasis on teaching business from an international perspective is enhanced by the fact that more than one-third of its students are from abroad. Seventeen of the 20 courses I took involved group projects—a strong testament to Freeman's dedication to integrate teamwork and leadership into the curriculum.

The school's placement center is in a difficult position. New Orleans is far from industrial bases and other quality schools. As such, not many firms find it economical to recruit on campus. The placement center does an excellent job setting up opportunities at consortiums in other cities and assisting on location. They are able to bring some good firms to campus. They do an outstanding job with the position they are in.

Smaller class sizes make for more intense and comprehensive learning. Professors know students by name and spend extra time outside the classroom with students. Each professor tries to help with your job search. The school is able to overcome not being located in the Northeast with a job fair in New York City and an extensive alumni network.

I have had a great experience at Tulane. The teachers and the courses were top-notch. The quality of the student body was also very high. Many students came from other countries, giving a fantastic international point of view. In a global economy this is important. I can't think of a better location than New Orleans—this town is full of fun and adventure. There is always a festival going on and Mardi Gras is one of the most unique experiences that I have ever had.

UNIVERSITY
OF GEORGIA

UNIVERSITY OF GEORGIA

Terry College of Business Administration
Athens, Georgia 30602
E-mail address: ugamba@cba.uga.edu
Website address: http://www.cba.uga.edu

Enrollment: 172

Women: 27.9%
Non-U.S.: 20.9%
Minority: 9.3%
Part-time: None
Average age: 27
Average years of work exp.: 4
Applicants accepted: 23.1%
Median starting pay: $48,750

Annual tuition & fees:
 resident—$2799
 non-resident—$8238
Room and board: $5850
Average GMAT score: 630
GMAT range: 450 to 750
Average GPA: 3.14
GPA range: 2.14 to 3.97
Accepted applicants enrolled: 58.6%
Average starting pay: $47,688

Teaching methods: Lecture, 40%   Case study, 30%   Projects, 30%

At the University of Georgia's Terry College of Business, the old South meets the new. On a campus that could have been the setting for *Gone with the Wind,* MBAs study finance, accounting, insurance, real estate, and management information systems—all growth areas in Georgia's dynamic service-based economy. At the same time, Rhett and Scarlett would feel right at home on UGA's 532-acre campus, with its antebellum architecture, tree-lined walkways, and fiery-colored azalea bushes.

Located 70 miles northeast of Atlanta, Athens calls itself Georgia's Classic City—and with good reason. People joke that there are probably more Greek columns here than anyplace else except the original Athens. One thing Georgia's Athens has that the Greek one doesn't is a progressive music scene: REM and The B52's originated here.

This is a very small program, where personalized attention is a key attribute of the culture. The class size is not much more than 110 students. Core classes have no more than 65 students in them, while electives average about 30 students. At 109 profs, the full-time faculty is rather large given the tiny size of the MBA program, but that's because they also teach in a fairly good-sized undergraduate business program.

Georgia offers two versions of its MBA: a two-year program for students without undergraduate business degrees, and a one-year program for those who have undergraduate degrees from AACSB-accredited schools. The two-year students are expected to complete 50 credit hours of core in the three quarters of the first year. Georgia's faculty has recently revised the core curriculum. The changes, including a new course in negotiation and a required international class, were put into place in the

Contact:
Donald R. Perry
Director of MBA
Admissions
706-542-5671
*Final application
deadline:*
March 15 for fall

fall of 1995. The school's best areas of study are entrepreneurship, finance, management information systems, and real estate. A new human resources curriculum was installed in 1996.

In addition to the core curriculum, students are required to pick 2 "sequences" out of a possible 21 to follow in many differing fields, ranging from accounting to strategic marketing. The school offers 60 elective courses in an academic year. You can pursue investment management in the finance department or strategic management of innovation in the management group. You can also pick one of three novel paths offered by other areas of the university: media organization management, textile management, or pharmacy care administration.

Accounting, finance, and management are among the strongest departments at Georgia in terms of faculty research. But the innovation and entrepreneurship, insurance, and real estate areas attract strong student followings. About half of the students receive assistantships. In return for two years' worth of tuition, students work around 13 hours a week for a professor. Not a bad deal for a school where the tuition is already pretty low.

PLACEMENT DETAILS

Grads of this program came out with median starting pay packages of $48,750 in 1996—next to the bottom for the 51 schools whose graduates were surveyed by BUSINESS WEEK. MBAs with job offers at commencement averaged two each—also at the bottom. And roughly 20 percent of the Class of 1996 failed to have a single job offer at graduation.

Some 40 companies recruited in Athens last year, about one for every two grads. They conducted 278 interviews of second-years on campus. About 40 job opportunities were posted via correspondence. The major employers: Wachovia Bank (7); Arthur Andersen (4); Federal Express (4); Union Camp (2); Kimberly-Clark (2). Coca-Cola, NationsBank,

Coopers & Lybrand, Andersen Consulting, and Burlington Northern each hired one graduate from Terry in 1996.

OUTSTANDING FACULTY

Warren French (****—business ethics); *James Verbrugge* (****—finance); *Jeff Netter* (***—finance); *Peter Shedd* (**—legal studies); *Melvin Crask* (**—marketing); *Kay L. Keck* (**—marketing); *Annette Poulsen* (**—finance); *Robert Bostrom* (*—information systems); *J. Don Edwards* (*—accounting); *Charles DeLorme* (*—economics).

APPLICANT TIPS

Terry is a highly selective business school, accepting only 23 percent of its applicants. That makes it the second hardest Runners-Up school to get into after the University of Maryland. One reason is the small nature of the program. With only 172 full-time MBA students, Terry is the smallest of all the Runners-Up schools. Its median GMAT score has been edging higher in recent years, hitting a record 630 in 1996, up from 575 ten years ago.

Apply early. Most applications are received by February 15 for the school's one-year program for those with undergraduate business degrees and by March 15 for the two-year MBA program. Applications sent in after those dates are likely to be at a competitive disadvantage and will be considered only on a space available basis.

While on-campus interviews are not mandatory, they are strongly encouraged. In 1996, Terry interviewed 50 percent of its 824 applicants. About 14 percent of the Class of 1998 did not have a year's worth of full-time job experience. Applicants are required to demonstrate knowledge of calculus prior to enrollment.

Contact: Donald R. Perry
Director of MBA Admissions
706-542-5671
Final application deadline: March 15 for fall

TERRY MBAs SOUND OFF

Ninety percent of the faculty was excellent—as good or better than my economics professors at UVA. The students on the whole were equally impressive. However, the facilities were weak. This should be remedied when the new building is complete.

UGA was an excellent school at which to get an MBA. The faculty was superb; they were very knowledgeable in their subject matter and cared a great deal about the students. UGA has outstanding financial support for its students. Between teaching assistantships, grants, and scholarships, most students I knew graduated with few if any loans. You definitely get the most for your money at UGA!

This is the best value for the money out of any school—this fact is coupled with a very attentive and responsive administration. The program is small, which affords many advantages. UGA needs to improve on tapping alumni resources and increasing quality of career services, however.

The student body was excellent. My classmates were exceptional in intelligence, motivation, and diversity. The quality of companies recruiting on campus was generally good but was weak in some areas, such as investments.

The faculty, having the utmost confidence in the students, expected and demanded the best from them. They created many opportunities for the students to succeed together, as a group.

This is a fantastic program for the money—50 percent of the students have assistantships. Between my assistantship and UGA scholarships, I received full tuition plus $8000 per year stipend. I was paid to go to a great MBA school! The quality of the students is a huge asset. With a very few exceptions, it was a very cooperative, noncompetitive experience.

The best part about the UGA MBA is the personal touch that comes with a smaller program. Every student had an opportunity to get to know at least one faculty member very well. Also, the faculty was always accessible, and the small size of the class lent to a team environment rather than one of competition.

This program is held back only by a lackluster career placement/services office.

The program lacks an active alumni base. It always amazed me how close we were to Atlanta and how few alumni participated in pushing the program forward. Facilities are antiquated, but this is made up for by a faculty that is ever accessible and always willing to change for the betterment of the students' needs. The small size of the program coupled with the quality of the teaching truly enhanced my learning experience.

Athens is a wonderful place to live while working hard. The program stresses positive competition; never a zero-sum game.

The class size (approximately 50/class) makes the program very flexible and personable. Students get to know each other well, and faculty and students build rapport quickly (the class size allows the faculty to know students by name/face). Dr. Kay Keck, Director of Graduate Studies, forms the foundation for the business school. She is constantly soliciting comments from students and faculty on ways to improve the program. She literally knows each student's name. She takes students out to lunch to gain insight on their thoughts, perceptions, and feelings. Dr. Kleck's door is always open and she will stop what she is doing to talk with you. She is a great listener who provides timely feedback.

UNIVERSITY OF ILLINOIS AT URBANA-CHAMPAIGN

UNIVERSITY OF ILLINOIS AT URBANA-CHAMPAIGN

College of Commerce and Business Administration
1206 South Sixth St.
Champaign, Illinois 61820
E-mail address: jwhite@commerce.cba.uiuc.edu
Website address: http://www.mba.uiuc.edu

Enrollment: 566

Women: 32%
Non-U.S.: 35%
Minority: 19%
Part-time: None
Average age: 26+
Average years of work exp.: 3.5
Applicants accepted: 39%
Median starting pay: $50,000

Annual tuition & fees:
   resident—$10,130
   non-resident—$15,475
Room and board: $8000
Average GMAT score: 605
GMAT range: 420 to 760
Average GPA: 3.25
GPA range: 2.5 to 4.0
Accepted applicants enrolled: 52%
Average starting pay: $51,390

Teaching methods: Lecture, 50%   Case study, 30%
                      Group projects, 20%

Contact:
Jane White
Director of Admissions
and Financial Aid
217-244-2953
or 800-MBA-UIUC
*Final application
deadline:*
April 1 for fall

You can think of this school as a farm team for Chicago's business community. If you've ever wanted to work for Arthur Andersen, Leo Burnett, Kraft, or Price Waterhouse, there's a well-worn path along Interstate 57 from Champaign to Chicago. The only more direct route to a job in the Windy City is to attend The University of Chicago or Northwestern's top-rated Kellogg School of Management in Evanston. And those two schools are harder to gain admission to and much more expensive.

Along with other state universities such as Indiana and North Carolina, Illinois offers a lot of bang for the buck. But in the past, Illinois's MBA program has always trailed those other institutions in stature because it was a stepchild to a far larger undergraduate program in business. This has changed with the appointment of Dean Howard Thomas, who views the MBA program as the B-school's flagship program. And Thomas, a management professor who took over the deanship in mid-1992, has been putting the finishing touches on a dramatic overhaul.

The B-school has boosted the size of its student body, faculty, administration, and staff. The changes reflect a desire to become a bigger player on the MBA scene as well as a chance to develop a more innovative curriculum, which was implemented in the fall of 1995. MBAs are now required to take eight core business foundations courses in the first year. The courses are taught by a faculty team in an effort to assure integration among finance, economics, marketing, accounting, and other disciplines. The school still has some work to do here, though. Illinois's curriculum is one of the 10 least integrated among the Top 50, according to graduate surveys.

MBAs also are required to choose three business environment courses in a variety of topics, including leadership styles, environmental issues, international business, and applied management techniques. You'll need to complete seven courses for a specialization to graduate. The central idea behind the changes: making the curriculum more practical and more standardized so that its focus isn't on individual faculty research. Here, the school is making some progress. In BUSINESS WEEK's customer satisfaction survey, the Illinois class of '96 gave the school noticably better marks for the curriculum's practicality than the class of '94 did.

Incoming students now enter a one-week orientation where they are assigned to four- or five-person teams they will work with throughout the first semester. Then, they go through a lockstep program that begins with Foundations of Business, which, among other things, teaches them how to write a business plan and form a business. There's a weeklong extended case study after that first eight-week course before they take Designing and Managing Business Processes. After a break for the Christmas holidays, they'll return to school in late January for Managing Stakeholder Relationships in a Changing Environment and Topics in Management. The latter requires students to select five 7-week courses that match their interests, ranging from Critical Thinking in Business to Managing Interfirm Relationships in the Food and Agribusiness Sector. By the middle of the second semester, students are put through a computer simulation called Super Tycoon. The first year is finished off with Managing Change, a course taught by Dean Thomas.

The second year offers students three options: study abroad at one of a dozen business schools, adopting a "professional track" in one of nearly 20 topics, or pursuing a joint degree in one of a dozen programs. Believe it or not, 150 of the school's 600 MBA students are working in dual-degree programs. Generally, though, the professional track—ranging from information systems to tax accounting—consumes the second year of most students' study. There's also Corporate Strategy and Global Issues in Management, the one mandatory capstone course that builds on the first-year work.

For anyone interested in accounting, a look at Illinois is a must. The school's undergraduate and graduate accounting programs were ranked number one in the country by *The Public Accounting Report* in both 1992 and 1993 and continue to score well today. Indeed, recruiters judged *no* school—including those in the Top 25—a better hunting ground for accounting grads in 1996, according to BUSINESS WEEK's survey. The school considers this its best area of study, along with finance, marketing, agribusiness, and its joint-degree programs with engineering and computer science. Other telling tidbits: With more than one in three students from abroad, Illinois has the third-largest international student body for a Runners-Up school. It also has the largest full-time MBA enrollment for a school in the second tier.

MBA students share space with undergrads in Commerce West and David Kinley Hall. Illinois has set aside tiered classrooms with state-of-the-art technology for MBAs and has scheduled daily coffee breaks that allow grad students to mingle with faculty. "We're trying to send the message that this is a pre-professional program," says Jane Nathan, director of international programs. "We hope the feeling of the MBA program will be closer to an executive workshop than an undergraduate class."

Illinois alumni show lots of loyalty to their alma mater, often helping new grads to find jobs. A group of alums at advertising agency Leo Burnett even contributes artwork, photos, and graphics for the alumni magazine, *Commerce,* making it among the slickest B-school mags in the country. The same is true of *Illinois MBA Today,* a publication sent to applicants. And an annual event is the MBA trip to Evanston for the Northwestern-Illinois basketball game, an outing that includes sessions with alumni, tours of the Chicago futures and options exchanges, shopping along Michigan Avenue's Miracle Mile, and drinking and dancing at jazz bars and rock clubs until the wee hours. Closer to home, MBAs favor Gully's Riverview Inn for drinks—especially on Thursday nights because no classes are scheduled on Fridays. For the best burgers in town, students go to Murphy's. In between classes, MBAs will often grab a bite at the cafeteria in Newman Hall.

The campus is an oasis of culture surrounded by miles of farmland. The Krannert Center for the Performing Arts pulls in the likes of violinist Itzhak Perlman and the rock group Dire Straits. Across from the center is Espresso Royale, which has become an after-concert institution for coffee lovers. The campus also is home to the World Heritage Museum's extensive collection of ancient art. Even so, you'll find more sports lovers than museum goers. The MBA Association sponsors tailgate barbecues before football games that bring the faithful out to watch the Fightin' Illini and its mascot, Chief Illiniwek, replete with warpaint and feathered headgear. When they can't watch athletic events at Illinois, MBAs vigorously compete in intramural sports. They work on their curve ball in the hopes that next summer they'll be playing on Arthur Andersen's softball team in Chicago's Lincoln Park.

PLACEMENT DETAILS

The MBA career services office continues to come under criticism from MBAs—but it's improved a ton in the last two years. The school separated MBA placement from undergraduate services. In 1996, 99 companies arrived, conducting 1140 interviews with students. Nearly 25 percent of the Class of 1996 failed to have a job offer at commencement. Those that did averaged 2.3 each—well below the average for the 50 schools whose grads were surveyed by BUSINESS WEEK. The major recruiters were: Ford Motor (11); Andersen Consulting (10); Procter & Gamble (4); Hyundai (3); Navistar International (3); Samsung (3); Allied Signal (3); Arthur Andersen (2); AT&T (2); Bank of America (2); Deloitte & Touche (2); General Electric (2); KPMG Peat Marwick (2); Sears (2); State Farm (2); and Computer Sciences Corp. (2).

OUTSTANDING FACULTY

Larry DeBrock (****—managerial economics); *J. Richard Dietrich* (****—accounting); *James Gentry* (****—finance); *Anzu Seth* (***—business strategy); *David Gardner* (***—marketing); *Joe Mahoney* (**—strategic management).

APPLICANT TIPS

Illinois has a rolling admissions policy and begins making decisions in late January. The school advises applicants to apply as early as possible. This is a program that continues to accept a good number of students with little or no experience in the work world. In 1996, about 17 percent of the Class of 1998 had less than one year of work experience.

Personal interviews aren't required, and the school interviewed only 65 percent of its 1507 applicants in 1996. But if you are interested in visiting the school to meet students or attend classes, you should call the Graduate Studies Office at 217-333-4555.

The school offers merit-based financial assistance through its MBA Student Management Grant. It says it identifies outstanding MBA candidates by looking at GMAT scores, grade point averages, prior work experience, and other evidence of leadership potential. Illinois also says "consideration is given to historically underrepresented groups." MBAs must provide research, teaching, or administrative support in exchange for the $3000 to $10,000 grants. Recipients are informed beginning in March until aid is exhausted. You can call the financial aid office at 217-333-0100 for more information.

Contact: Jane White
Director of Admissions and Financial Aid
217-244-2953 or 800-MBA-UIUC
Final application deadline: April 1 for fall

ILLINOIS MBAs SOUND OFF

There is no better "bang for the buck." I got accepted to Indiana, but Illinois was much less expensive, and I got a better finance education here. There is absolutely no reason not to have a job (or good prospects) by graduation, given all the work Career Services does to help you with placement. My only regret is that Champaign isn't a suburb of San Francisco.

I was really disappointed with the Illinois MBA Program. I had no interviews on-campus for a summer internship or permanent placement this year. The interviews I had were set up on my own. As of today, a week after graduation, I am still looking for a job. I have sent out over 350 resumes. . . . Finding alumni was another problem. The database they have hasn't been updated in quite some time. I had to go through an alumni book from 1990 to find names, and many of those people weren't at those jobs, so the trail went dead.

The only area in which my expectations were not met was in the Career Placement Office. Several seminars were conducted to work on résumé, interviewing, and negotiating skills, however the overall emphasis on actually getting the class placed into full-time positions seemed lacking.

Last year, the MBA curriculum was changed (didn't affect my class though) to a more integrated one with lots of bells and whistles attached to it. These changes are in the right direction and I believe have improved the quality of MBA education.

As with anything, you end up getting out what you put in. I took this education seriously and feel like I grew tremendously. It was obvious that not all of my classmates put in the same effort. The opportunities are certainly there if you seek them out and take advantage of them.

We need to make interviews a mandatory part of the application process in order to select better students. We have too many "good students" who look good on paper. "Good students" need to be good leaders with aggressiveness and appropriate work experience as well.

I see the need for a more cooperative attitude among the administration. Leadership needs to come from the people who make and implement changes. I sincerely appreciate the efforts to help students financially through grants and core faculty associate positions. The program is also largely student-run.

THE UNIVERSITY OF IOWA

THE UNIVERSITY OF IOWA

School of Management
108 Pappajohn Business Administration Building
Iowa City, Iowa 52242
E-mail address: iowamba@uiowa.edu
Website address: http://www.biz.uiowa.edu/mba

Enrollment: 721	Annual tuition & fees:
	resident—$3826
Women: 50%	non-resident—$10,418
Non-U.S.: 49%	Room and board: $5120
Minority: 7%	Average GMAT score: 589
Part-time: 520	GMAT range: 370 to 720
Average age: 27	Average GPA: 3.38
Average years of work exp.: 3.4	GPA range: 2.2 to 3.98
Applicants accepted: 47%	Accepted applicants enrolled: 30%
Median starting pay: $52,950	Average starting pay: $53,780

Teaching methods: Lecture, 20%   Case study, 50%
                    Projects, videos 30%

Contact:
Mary Spreen
Director of
MBA Admissions and
Financial Aid
319-335-3604
or 800-622-4692
*Final application
deadline:*
July 15 for fall

There's a memorable line in the hit movie *Field of Dreams* that rings true for those who come to the Hawkeye State. At one point in the film, baseball legend Shoeless Joe Jackson asks, "Is this heaven?" "No," comes the reply, "it's Iowa!"

"People make Iowa what it is," says Willis R. Greer Jr., a former accounting professor here who recently left to become dean at the University of Northern Iowa. "It's a good place to live and a good place to study. The students are straightforward, and the faculty members reflect those values."

It's fair to call Iowa's B-school a good place that's getting better. The school has been a well-kept secret except to those who read scholarly journals. The faculty's expertise in finance and economics has led to some influential government appointments. Susan M. Phillips left Iowa in 1992 to serve on the Board Governors of the Federal Reserve System, and William P. Albrecht spent time on the Commodity Futures Trading Commission before returning to Iowa City.

Now, though, word is slowly slipping out about the rest of the school. Over the last two years, it has made the curriculum more flexible, and students say teaching has improved with it. No school made more progress in integrating subject matter across classes, according to BUSINESS WEEK's student survey. The administration became more responsive to student concerns and the information technology program grew stronger. "The University of Iowa MBA Program far exceeded most every expectation I had," says one recent MBA, using words you'd have been hard-pressed to hear a few years ago.

In short, an already-solid school listened to what its students asked for and is better because of it. That said, Iowa's B-school still has a long way to go to catch up to the nation's top tier of schools. Out of the 50 schools profiled in this book, the school ranks among the bottom 10 of the 50 profiled for virtually every measure of teaching. The quality of the core is decidedly average, receiving better marks than only Penn State. Electives don't score much better. Faculty members could do a better job of staying on the leading edge of their fields, and they should be more aware of what their colleagues at Iowa are teaching, students say.

But the fact is, for better *and* worse, Iowa does not have ambitions to compete with the Michigans, Harvards, and Stanfords of the B-school world. "We are not a large program, and we don't have plans to become large," says Dean Gary Fethke. "We see ourselves as a regionally dominant, nationally visible school. We know that our students are going to be interested primarily in jobs in the extended Midwest."

Those students will find themselves in one of the nation's most charming university towns and at a B-school where they'll be able to get involved in virtually anything. "Students here have extraordinary opportunities for participation," Fethke says. They can consult with companies around the world or work closely with ones around the state. They can participate to an unusual degree in the school's workings, since there's a student on every faculty committee save the one that handles promotions and tenure. And they help run the Iowa Electronic Markets, the only Commodity Futures Trading Commission-regulated, Internet-based real-money futures market designed to predict election outcomes.

They'll spend most of their time, however, in a curriculum that remains fairly rigid. The two years begin with a week of orientation called IMPACT, when students participate in an

Outward Bound session, attend workshops on diversity and communication, meet the faculty, and listen to a case study.

To graduate, students must complete 60 credit-hours of classes. The core entirely consumes the first year, while 27 of the 30 credits in the second year can go toward electives. Students choose from one of eight concentration tracks, including accounting, entrepreneurship, finance, human resources, management information systems, operations management, and product development. If those options don't sound enticing, then you can design your own concentration. A student interested in international business may want to take finance, language, and cultural courses. You can select from the B-school's 25 to 30 elective classes, or go outside of the school. Iowa is trying to put more electives in the catalog, but don't expect miracles at a state school with limited resources. "The evolution of the program has been somewhat sporadic," says Finance Professor W. Bruce Johnson. "But we have essentially opened up the entire second year to electives and that has encouraged faculty members to bring on line classes that develop experience in industry, business, and job functions."

Iowa's B-school moved into a new facility, the Pappajohn Business Administration Building, in 1993. The $36 million structure sits right in the heart of campus and houses the entire business school, with a wing dedicated to MBAs. Placement and career advising services are located in the building, along with an impressive library, computer lab, and real-time "trading room," which is linked by high-speed phone lines to more than 130 exchanges around the world. It's the result of an alliance between the school and Dow Jones Co.

You may have to rely on it, however, for much of your contact with Corporate America since big-name CEOs seldom trek to Iowa to address students. A good number of presidents do come through the school's visiting speaker programs, though. In recent years, Iowa City has played host to leaders of Baxter International, the Federal Reserve, Mid-American Energy, Deere and Co, and Maytag Corp., among others.

One thing that needs little improvement is the campus environment. Unless you've visited Iowa City, it's hard to imagine how enchanting this college town is. With a population approaching 80,000, including 30,000 students, Iowa City is the state's answer to Wisconsin's Madison or Texas's Austin. It's also home to one of the premier writing programs in the nation, Iowa Writers Workshop. By Iowa standards, housing here is pricey, about $500 for a one-bedroom apartment. Ninety percent of MBAs live off-campus, either in apartment complexes or Victorian homes that have been divided into apartments. One thing to keep in mind: the student body has a good number of international students but otherwise is rather homogeneous. The class of '96, for example, included just two African-American students.

The campus sits on a bluff overlooking the Iowa River and intermingles with the downtown area. During fall and spring evenings, musicians play guitars and portable keyboards along a downtown pedestrian mall—a favorite place for MBA students to stroll. On Thursday nights, the MBA Association holds parties at Fitzpatrick's, the B-school's unofficial student union. When the weather is warm, students sit at the outdoor bar and eat grilled ribs, burgers, and chicken. Throughout the year, U of I MBAs experience a high quality of life in an environment that's safe, down-to-earth, and vibrant. Is it heaven? No, it's Iowa.

PLACEMENT DETAILS

A regular source of student criticism, career services has become a priority in recent years. There have been some major improvements. One hundred and eight companies recruited on campus in 1996, up 34 from 1992. Most of the firms, however, are from the Midwest. "We don't

have significant campus contact with the national business community," concedes Johnson, "so our strategy has been to move recruiting off campus." They take students to companies and also work aggressively to match current students with openings in the corporate world. The extra effort has paid off with some improved placement numbers. The school says 96 percent of its first-year students were placed in internships for the summer of 1996, and seven companies—including Ernst & Young, John Deere Credit, Deloitte & Touche, Pillsbury Co., and Frontier Cooperative Herbs—hired two or more grads in '96.

Still, placement is not a strength of the school. "The weak link in the program is placement, but a lot of the problem has to do with the location and class size," says one '96 grad. "Not too many employers will want to lose a whole day of travel to interview four students." Says another: "The program has greatly increased the work experience of the students in the last three years, but the placement office has not caught up. The firms that came on campus were looking for inexperienced students and were not good matches for those of us with experience." Indeed, about 20 percent of 1996 grads were without a job offer at graduation, according to BUSINESS WEEK's survey. And, despite the efforts at improvement, students didn't give the placement office much better marks than they did in '94.

OUTSTANDING FACULTY

Kurt Anstreicher (****—management); *Bruce Johnson* (****—finance); *Bill Burns* (***—marketing); *James Cotter* (***—finance); *Doug Foster* (***—finance).

APPLICANT TIPS

The Iowa School of Management stresses that there is no need for previous business training, although it says some employment experience is desirable. About 20 percent of the Class of 1998 have less than one year of full-time work experience. You needn't worry about an interview, either. Only 15 percent of the applicants in 1996 went through an admissions interview.

What does the admissions committee look for? "We consider many factors in weighing your application; there is no admissions formula, and no predetermined cutoff point for grades and test scores." So you should not be intimidated if your GMATs or grade point average are subpar if you have good work experience. Indeed, in 1996, the school accepted one applicant with a 370 GMAT score.

Iowa also gives you plenty of time to apply. You have until July 1 for the fall semester, and you should send in your application by November 15 if you want to begin classes in January. However, if you want to be considered for fellowships or graduate assistantships, you should apply by March 1.

Contact: Mary Spreen
Director of MBA Admissions and
Financial Aid

319-335-3604 or 800-622-4692
Final application deadline: July 15 for fall

IOWA MBAs SOUND OFF

The MBA experience at Iowa was outstanding. The one glaring weakness is the placement department.

The University of Iowa MBA Program far exceeded most every expectation I had. The brand new, state-of-the-art facility and advance technologies are superior to every other MBA school I visited before accepting at Iowa. The faculty's care and desire to teach the most applicable real world material in the best manner possible truly aided my learning.

The program must improve the quality of incoming students. I feel it sacrifices the caliber of students to accomplish other objectives. The placement office is average. It appears they encourage firms that come to recruit undergrads to also interview MBA students. This is frustrating.

UNIVERSITY
OF
MARYLAND AT
COLLEGE
PARK

UNIVERSITY OF MARYLAND AT COLLEGE PARK

Maryland Business School
College Park, Maryland 20742
E-mail address: bmgtgrad@deans.umd.edu
Website address: http://www.bmgt.umd.edu/

Enrollment: 778

Annual tuition & fees:
    resident—$8384
    non-resident—$12,223

Women: 35%
Non-U.S.: 35%
Minority: 12%
Part-time: 398
Average age: 27
Applicants accepted: 19%
Median starting pay: $55,000

Room and board: $10,500
Average GMAT score: 640
Average GPA: 3.41
GPA range: 2.7 to 4.0
Average years of work exp.: 4.5
Accepted applicants enrolled: 53%
Average starting pay: $56,880

Teaching methods: Lecture, 40%   Case study, 40%   Projects, 20%

Ever been in prison? If you're an MBA candidate at the University of Maryland, you couldn't help but serve some time. It's not that the admissions committee requires every applicant to have been behind bars. It's just that visiting a jail is part of the unusual experience that every MBA student enjoys at this excellent business school.

The trip to Allenwood Federal Prison occurs during the second year of this program as part of the school's business ethics Experiential Learning Module. While behind the walls, students chat with inmates whose crimes involve violations of business ethics. It's a novel invention that leaves a strong imprint on Maryland MBAs. But so does this highly innovative program that has improved by leaps and bounds in recent years.

This school has come a long way under William E. Mayer, the Wall Street whiz kid and former CEO of First Boston, who returned to campus in 1992 for a four-year stint as dean. He left to go back to the business world in 1996, but he left behind major improvements. Since 1992, average GMAT scores here jumped 35 points to 640. Applications rose by 65 percent to 1711. And Maryland's acceptance rate—now the lowest of the Runners-Up schools, reached an incredible 18.7 percent in 1996, up from 23 percent two years earlier and 34 percent back in 1988. And that was after the school increased its full-time class to more than 200 students from just 135 the year before.

While dean, Mayer had the pleasure of moving this school into a new four-story building in early 1993—the handsome structure fea-

Contact:
Hayden Estrada
Director of Admissions
301-405-2280
*Final application
deadline:*
May 15 for fall

tures a huge skylighted roof that floods the building's cherry-wood interior with sunlight. It's equipped with state-of-the-art classrooms and labs, as well as more comfortable interviewing rooms for recruiters. It's loaded with the most modern technology you'll find—which is why graduates rate the school very highly in the area of information systems. It's also easily one of the most attractive buildings on this pretty 1580-acre campus, an oddly secluded oasis amidst the suburban sprawl and dizzying network of highways outside Washington, D.C.

More importantly, though, the new plant houses an overhauled MBA program with some fairly innovative elements in it. The school's new academic program incorporates seven required mini-courses, called Experiential Learning Modules (ELMs), into the core curriculum, including the one featuring the trip to prison. The intensive, one-week-long ELMs have been designed to introduce the "softer skills" of management to students. For example, in one ELM, called The Washington Experience, Maryland grads learn the importance of government and public policy to the business community. The group meets with Capitol Hill staffers, participates in practice committee hearings, and questions lobbyists at a mock Ways and Means Committee hearing. They also attend EPA and SEC briefings and hear from lobbyists who represent business associations and labor unions. And there are ELMs on leadership, Total Quality Management, and career development. Other features of the revised curriculum include a mandatory group field project and a required course in business communications.

In the second year, Maryland students get to apply their theoretical learning in the real world through group field projects that bring MBA candidates in touch with such companies as AT&T, Bell Atlantic, Black & Decker, Electronic Data Systems, Hewlett-Packard, and Lockheed Martin. In the past, students have installed management information systems, up-

dated accounting procedures, developed marketing plans, and implemented quality control programs for client firms. A case competition, also held in the second year, puts students to the test in analyzing complex strategic problems, writing persuasive reports, and making savvy oral presentations.

There are 75 elective offerings at Maryland, ranging from Electronic Commerce to Fixed Income Securities. The school's best areas of study are information systems, finance, and entrepreneurship. That last one occurs under the province of the Michael Dingman Center. It provides mentoring for emerging growth companies, an investment network, seminars, and international programs. While only a handful of students specialize in logistics and transportation, the school is known for having a pretty strong faculty in this area.

There are also a panoply of joint programs: an MBA/MS in science, an MBA/JD in law, an MBA/MPM in public affairs, and an MBA/MSW in nonprofits. Besides a concentration in international business, an area in which Maryland boasts 17 electives, there's also the opportunity to crossregister at John Hopkins's Paul H. Nitze School of Advanced International Studies. That gives MBA candidates access to more than 125 additional international courses. And there are exchange programs with seven non-U.S. business schools in Australia, Norway, Belgium, France, Hong Kong, Venezuela, and Ireland.

PLACEMENT DETAILS

The one area that former Dean Mayer found hardest to improve substantially was placement. The career services office is much better than it was before he got to campus. In 1996, only 14 percent of the graduating class lacked a single job offer at commencement, down from 29 percent two years earlier. Those with job offers averaged 2.03, a tad below average for the Top 50 schools. And in 1996, Mayer lured only 50 companies on campus to recruit second-years. With job fairs in Washington and Chicago, the school was able to expose its students to another 57 companies. All told, graduating MBAs had 1030 interviews by prospective employers. Another 550 job opportunities were posted via correspondence.

The major employers of the Class of 1996: Coopers & Lybrand (4); MCI (4); Arthur Andersen (3); Ernst & Young (3); Fannie Mae (2); Fidelity Investments (2); First Union (2); General Electric (2); Intel (2); and Marriott (2).

OUTSTANDING FACULTY

Frank Alt (****—statistics); *Haluk Unal* (****—finance); *Ken Smith* (***—entrepreneurship); *Kathleen Hanley* (***—finance); *George Marakas* (***—information systems); *Anil Gupta* (*—management); *Robert Hauswald* (*—finance); *Robert Krapfell* (*—marketing); *Dan Sheinin* (*—marketing).

APPLICANT TIPS

Maryland has become a very selective school of late. You'll need strong GMAT scores to get through the gate. Apply early. The first deadline is December 15, and if you're an international applicant, the school recommends that you apply by February 1. Calculus and computer literacy are prerequisites to the MBA program, although a prospective student can apply to Maryland before completing these requirements.

Personal interviews are becoming an important part of the admissions process, but interviews are not required. In 1996, the school interviewed 31 percent of its 1711 applicants. The same is true of full-time work experience, which gives applicants an important edge. Just 7 percent of the Class of 1998 lacked a year's worth of experience in a full-time job.

Contact:
Hayden Estrada
Director of Admissions
301-405-2280
Final application deadline: May 15 for fall

MARYLAND MBAs SOUND OFF

The best part of the Maryland MBA experience for me has been the practical, outside-of-the-class activities that I have participated in. For example, last semester, I had the opportunity to work on a student team that consulted for Chase Manhattan Bank in New York. In addition, I worked on the Terrapin Fund (as a technology analyst), a student run fund with assets under management of over $300,000. This experience has been valuable in my interviews with firms on Wall Street.

Maryland is an excellent value for the tuition dollar. They have an excellent graduate assistant program which further reduces tuition costs. The MBA program continues to become more nationally recognized, which enhances the value of my degree. The facility is modern and more than adequate for our student body's needs.

I'm impressed by the faculty/staff's responsiveness to student needs. The new dean, new building (both about 4–5 years into the program) and high-tech, fully loaded classrooms are very impressive. We are also privileged to take advantage of a high quality computer science department on campus. I do have to say that sometimes the team work spirit was pushed too much. The students are very cooperative, and I made some very good friends. The location of the school is great. I especially enjoyed an experimental learning module (ELM) called The Washington Week, which blended politics and business quite well.

The Experiential Learning Modules (ELM's) were right on target with their selection of topics.

The value of the education in terms of quality of schooling for the price paid was exceptional. In addition, the faculty and staff did a commendable job trying to tailor the program to fit the needs of both students and future employers. The biggest weakness came from a lack of certain resources (e.g., no library in building) which can be expected from a state institution.

The close vicinity to Washington, D.C. and Baltimore is a definite advantage in that the school can invite many practitioners as adjunct professors to teach special topics (e.g., Asset-Based Securitization). It also helps when job hunting—we are close to many headquarters. The professors who teach the elective courses are great. They really motivated us to grasp the concepts and apply them.

One of the big benefits of getting an MBA at Maryland Business School was the small size of the program. It created a less competitive, more friendly environment, and enabled me to get to know my peer students and teachers very well. I also enjoyed the exposure to information technology issues, which helped me to really take a new direction in my career and to work in the high-tech industry. The diversity of the class, in terms of national and racial origins and in terms of background of people (education, geography), was another major experience for me.

THE UNIVERSITY OF MINNESOTA

THE UNIVERSITY OF MINNESOTA

Curtis L. Carlson School of Management
271 19th Avenue South
Minneapolis, Minnesota 55455
E-mail address: mbaoffice@csom.umn.edu
Website address: http://www.csom.umn.edu

Enrollment: 1120

Women: 27%
Non-U.S.: 17%
Minority: 8%
Part-time: 850
Average age: 28.5
Average years of work exp: 4.8
Applicants accepted: 36%
Median starting pay: $60,000

Annual tuition & fees:
   resident—$9621
   non-resident—$13,842
Room and board: $6400
Average GMAT score: 602
GMAT range: 420–740
Average GPA: 3.2
GPA range: 2.1–3.9
Accepted applicants enrolled: 19%
Average starting pay: $60,000

Teaching methods: Lecture, 45% Case study, 40%
Field projects, 15%

Contact:
Sandra Kelzenberg
Associate Director
of MBA programs
612-624-0006
*Final application
deadline:*
April 1 for fall

The Carlson School of Management claims to have completed a long-overdue revolution. In his five years as the school's ninth dean, Dean David S. Kidwell has overhauled the curriculum, boosted the international studies program, cultivated close ties with the Twin Cities business community, and raised $45 million for a new building.

Here's what he hasn't done: figured out a way to improve mediocre teaching at the school. Kidwell has long talked about putting teaching and research into better balance, and he launched an initiative to improve teaching at the start of the 1995–1996 school year. So far, it's shown few results. Teaching scores were actually lower in 1996 than in 1994. Indeed, not a single school in the Top 50 received worse marks for the overall quality of teaching than Minnesota.

The results are particularly troublesome when you consider the small size of this program: core classes average 50 students, while electives typically enroll about 35. That should provide a better chance for substantive contact between professors and students. Instead, says one '96 grad, "The major problem with the program is the significant variability of teaching. Some [professors] are excellent, while others are the worst instructors I have ever had." Too bad there's such a thing as tenure.

Not everything here has been stagnant, though. Since 1991, when Kidwell became dean, the number of opportunities to study abroad has doubled. There are now 13 exchange programs with schools around the world. Carlson MBAs can also enroll in summer study at the Université Jean Moulin-Lyon in France or the Vienna School of Economics and Business Administration. The Carlson faculty, meanwhile, has begun to focus on the struggling economies of Eastern and Central Europe. No wonder that students now give the program much better marks for international study than they did two years ago. Yet, the school is most recognized for its program in management information systems. Carlson faculty serve as editors to the top journals in this field, including *MIS Quarterly.*

The first year of Carlson's MBA program explores basic business concepts, the function of firms, and the topic of leadership. The fall quarter features four foundational core courses, in data analysis, managerial economics, behavioral science, and financial accounting. The winter quarter centers arounds "the functions of the firm," including marketing, finance, human resources, operations, and information systems. And the spring and final quarters of the year are devoted to leadership and other "soft" topics such as ethics, international business, quality, and managing change.

Minnesota also offers a 12-month advanced placement program for students who have an undergraduate degree in business or management. They waive out of several core courses during the summer—when they are required to start—take the leadership core in the fall, the field project in the winter, and the top management perspectives course in the spring. During the last two quarters, they need to get at least seven electives out of the way before graduating in June with an MBA. "It's intense and indeed accelerated," says one happy customer, "but it certainly is well worth the time and hard work."

In the traditional two-year version, the school has lumped all the core courses, with the exception of its innovative and well-received 14-week field project with local corporations, into the first year. That frees up virtually the entire second year of study for nothing but electives. Carlson offers 82 electives in any given academic year, and MBAs can take up to 12 credits outside the business school.

One of the better electives is Top Management Perspectives, which brings in six CEOs to interact with second-year students in their last quarter. The guests in 1996 included the chief executives of Northwest Airlines, 3M, First Bank, Cargill, Best Buy, and H.B. Fuller. Another effort to connect students with the real word, the executive mentor program, pairs groups of students with top local managers. Those two programs are a big reason why Carlson's class of '96 gave it much better marks than previous classes did for connecting students with outside professionals. No Top 50 school improved more in the area over the last two years, according to student surveys.

Typical of urban schools, Carlson MBAs are scattered around the Twin Cities area and tend to have their own lives away from the school. The school has tried to bring its students together more often with volleyball tournaments, pub crawls, picnics, and a "Thank God It's Thursday" in the MBA Lounge. But the big improvement in student esprit de corps should come in 1998, when Carlson plans to open its new building. It will house all classes and students services and should help the school do a better job of living up to its rhetoric about integrating life and coursework across disciplines.

The weather won't change, however, and that may scare away some applicants. Minnesota is cold enough in the winter to make people wish for the warmer climate of, say, Chicago. But just as the air conditioning is never turned off during the summer in Houston, heating is nearly ubiquitous in the Twin Cities. Even the parking garages are heated, and virtually all campus buildings are linked by tunnels or skyways.

PLACEMENT DETAILS

Local corporations recruit heavily here, accounting for many of the 89 companies that interviewed MBAs in 1996. Like many schools outside of California, Illinois, and the Northeast, the school takes students to companies, rather than waiting for recruiters to come to Minneapolis. It's already clear that Kidwell has dramatically improved the school's career placement operations. Carlson MBAs received 2.4 job offers on average in 1996, still below the median for Top 50 schools but well above the school's 1.5 average two years earlier. Starting pay packages typically came in at $60,000, putting Minnesota in the same league as Midwest rivals like Washington University, Michigan State, and Case Western. The top hirers at the school in 1996: Andersen Consulting (14); First Bank (11); Pillsbury (7); General Mills (5); Medtronic (5); Northwest Airlines (3); 3M (3); Cargill (3); Guidant (3); and Deloitte & Touche (2).

But the momentum in career services may be slipping a bit. The class of '96 was considerably less satisfied than its 1994 predecessors with the placement office's effort at helping students find summer internships, write résumés, and prepare to negotiate with companies. Dean Kidwell may want to give those areas a place on his to-do list—right after teaching quality.

OUTSTANDING FACULTY

Tim Nantell (****—finance); *David Runkle* (****—finance); *Akbar Zaheer* (***—strategic management); *Akshay Rao* (***—marketing); *Ed Joyce* (**—accounting); *James Gahlon* (**—finance).

APPLICANT TIPS

Carlson looks closely at a candidate's overall academic record, but places greater weight on the last two years of his or her undergraduate program. The school also says that it weighs work experience heavily: "Although academic ability is a principal criterion, we also give major consideration to work experience, extracurricular activities, and/or community service, especially if the student has been away from the academic environment for several years."

So if you lack a high GPA, you can often offset it with strong work experience. You'll want to emphasize your non-academic achievements on the required personal statement of goals, challenges, and experience. Though the school encourages personal interviews with admissions, it couldn't tell BUSINESS WEEK what percentage of its 708 applicants in 1996 were interviewed. In order to enroll in the MBA program, you need to earn a "B" grade or higher in a college-level calculus course. International applicants must apply by January 15 for the one-year MBA program, and by March 15 for the two-year MBA. U.S. applicants need to apply by February 1 for the accelerated one-year program.

Contact: Sandra Kelzenberg
Associate Director of MBA programs
612-624-0006
Final application deadline: April 1 for fall

CARLSON MBAs SOUND OFF

There was an overwhelming emphasis on research as opposed to teaching quality. This emphasis needs to change before the school can be ranked in the Top 25. Also, the administration would listen to concerns, but would never act on those concerns.

There are a lot of older professors who seem mediocre at teaching—maybe because they are lame ducks and/or close to retirement.

The kinks of the new curriculum have not been worked out, but the new building may help. I was never conscious of the school being a place of intellectual ferment.

Carlson has made tremendous strides in becoming a top MBA school. The integrated core curriculum, the field consulting project, and speeches by CEOs . . . all provided exceptional exposure to the top management positions and the skills it takes to get there and succeed.

This has been an unbelievable experience. This year alone, I've met over 20 CEOs including Bob Galvin of Motorola, Desi Desimone of 3M, John Dasburg of Northwest Airlines, and the list goes on. This program can stand toe to toe with any of them!

The level of camaraderie in this program was a high point. The Carlson community is a very tight-knit, cooperative environment. The "team" concept is taken very seriously here.

UNIVERSITY
OF
NOTRE DAME

UNIVERSITY OF NOTRE DAME

College of Business Administration
109 Hurley Center, Room 109
Notre Dame, Indiana 46556
E-mail address: j.c.crane.9@nd.edu
Website address: http://www.nd.edu:80/~mbawww

Enrollment: 261	Annual tuition & fees: $19,400
Women: 28%	Room and board: $4250
Non-U.S.: 25%	Average GMAT score: 611
Minority: 9%	Average GPA: 3.09
Part-time: None	GPA range: 2.12 to 4.0
Average age: 25.3	Average years of work exp.: 2.98
Applicants accepted: 44.62%	Accepted applicants enrolled: 42%
Median starting pay: $56,100	Average starting pay: $58,855

Teaching methods: Lecture, 10% Case study, 45% Discussion, 45%

Most people wouldn't even want to imagine themselves within the 40-foot concrete walls of Indiana State Prison. Not Notre Dame's MBAs. They toured death row, interviewed inmates, and took turns sitting in the electric chair. Notre Dame's efforts to prevent white-collar crime? Not at all. The visit to the state's forbidding maximum security prison was just one aspect of Notre Dame's annual Urban Plunge program, which also includes visits to South Bend's Welfare Center and its Homeless Shelter.

Notre Dame's interest in the community is one result of its Catholic heritage. Founded by the congregation of the Holy Cross in 1842, Notre Dame still retains its religious identity. That doesn't mean that MBAs are required to start their days with Mass, but you're not apt to forget you're attending a Roman Catholic university. There is a chapel in every dorm. Murals cover the walls and ceilings of the university's elaborate cathedral, which is situated in the center of the campus. Adjacent to the church is Notre Dame's administration building, with its huge, golden dome topped by a statue of the Virgin Mary.

Amidst this environment, you'll find a fairly nuts-and-bolts MBA that comes in two flavors: a regular two-year program and a three-semester version for students with undergraduate degrees in business. The abbreviated MBA program consists of 44 credits, begins with the summer semester, and allows students to gain the degree in 12 months. Two-year MBAs are required to take 12 core courses and 10 free electives for a total of 62 credits, with admission only during the fall semester.

The biggest news on the B-school campus is the College of Business Administration building, a $23 million facility which opened in the fall of '96. The four-story building houses both MBA and executive

Contact:
Lee Cunningham
MBA Admissions
Coordinator
219-631-8671
*Final application
deadline:
May 9 for fall*

development classes, faculty offices, a two-story MBA lounge, and a new center for career development. Until the fall of 1992, MBAs used the university's centralized office, and the placement office still receives some of the worst marks from students of any of the Top 50 B-schools.

In the curriculum, there are no "modules," integrated theme courses, or experiential projects in the core curriculum—just the plain, old-fashioned business basics, with two mild exceptions. In the fall of 1993 the school added an international business class in the first year, in addition to a currently required second-year course. And for the last three years, students have taken a pair of one-credit management communications classes. One focuses on speaking, the other on writing.

In year two, MBAs will find some pretty basic electives, too. The small size of the school prevents it from offering more than 44 choices in any given year. There is some recent good news on this front, though: the class of '96 gave the administration significantly better marks for responding to its electives demands, and Notre Dame no longer ranks at the very bottom in the area. By taking 3 to 5 courses in one of six areas, you can gain a specialization, such as finance or marketing. It is not required, though. Given the basic structure and limits of this program, Notre Dame attempts to differentiate itself on the basis of its ethics slant.

The B-school's ethics program is one of the oldest in the country, and the program ranked third nationwide in BUSINESS WEEK's most recent student satisfaction survey. Second-year MBAs examine such things as labor relations, environmental issues, and equal opportunity for women and minorities. The school has also tried to integrate ethics throughout the core by getting professors to pinpoint ethical dilemmas in marketing, finance, accounting, and other functional areas.

As the trip to a prison suggests, ethics and community service are already critical elements in the school's overall culture. "Urban Plunge really opens students' minds to other people's lot in life, especially for the stereotypical MBA who is all caught up in wealth," says Paul Kucera, a '92 grad, who was president of the MBA Association. While Urban Plunge is aimed at broadening the minds of MBAs, Christmas in April provides students with the opportunity to get out there and actually do something. The annual university-wide event brings teams of students together to rehabilitate run-down houses in South Bend. Students aren't the only ones repairing dilapidated houses. Notre Dame's tradition of community service is carried on even after MBAs receive their degrees. The Michigan chapter of the Notre Dame Alumni Association recently went to downtown Detroit to participate in "Paint the Town." That is not surprising to Larry Ballinger, director of Notre Dame's MBA program. "It is inherent in the Notre Dame tradition to look toward other individuals who may not be as fortunate as we are," he says.

The school's small size provides a family-like atmosphere—with the exception of the dean, whom students have criticized for being aloof and unavailable. The program ranks 47th—out of the 50 in this book—for administrative and faculty responsiveness to students. (In August, 1997, Carolyn Woo will become dean. She has been a vice president and management professor at Purdue. In South Bend, she'll succeed John Keane, who's held the deanship for seven years.) MBA students number about 260, including 60 in the three-semester program, and about 45 of the 100 B-school faculty members teach MBAs regularly. That assures an intimate learning experience. Classes are so small that when MBAs walk into the Huddle, the campus food court where students often study in small teams, it's rare not to see a group of familiar faces. "It is the type of school where a professor sees you in the hall and says, 'Hello Gail, how are your studies going?' " says Gail Boyden, a recent alum.

While many students find Notre Dame a welcoming environment, some still take advantage of the school's London Program, which is located in its own Law/MBA Centre in the heart of London's financial district. A Notre Dame professor acts as resident director, teaching one course for the semester-abroad experience. The remainder of the coursework is taught by professors from British schools. Through academics and field trips, MBAs get a feel for the European Economic Community. A similar program in Santiago, Chile, began in the fall of 1993, and several students have also taken to studying in Lille, France.

Located 90 miles east of Chicago, South Bend's population is about 110,000. The campus is located on the northern edge of the town, and students tend not to stray too far. There's a slew of school-sponsored gatherings, ranging from the annual Halloween Costume Party to the Spring Formal, where students mix with faculty and administrators. The stadium parking lot bar run by the alumni association is a hangout on Thursday nights. Popular spots include Coach's and The Linebacker, both just a few blocks off campus. Coach's, for pizza and beer, boasts a pair of big-screened TVs and is crammed with jocks and fans. A block away, the Linebacker is tiny, jam-packed and smoke-filled.

With names like Coach's and The Linebacker, it's easy to guess that football is popular here. What an understatement. "You never miss a football game at Notre Dame," says Rachelle Carrier, a '93 grad. "When you walk into that stadium, you're in awe." In addition to going as a group to tailgate and watch the Fightin' Irish play football, MBAs participate in several intramural sports. Some MBAs spend the whole year practicing for "bookstore basketball," a tournament held on courts outside the bookstore.

PLACEMENT DETAILS

In 1996, 92 companies came to recruit MBAs here—not so bad for a graduating class of 160 students. Most of the firms, however, are from the Midwest. The B-school counts on local alumni associations to help MBAs get interviews with companies in California, Texas, and Florida. The strong sense of loyalty alums feel toward their alma mater is definitely a plus. The big hirers of the Class of 1996: Ford Motor (8); Deloitte & Touche (6); Andersen Consulting (5); Whirlpool (4); Towers Perrin (3); and KPMG Peat Marwick (3).

OUTSTANDING FACULTY

John Affleck-Graves (****—finance); *Frank Reilly* (****—finance); *Jim Peterson* (****—financial management); *Jeff Bergstrand* (**—finance); *James Davis* (**—strategy); *Tom Frecka* (**—finance); *Steve Dee* (**—marketing).

APPLICANT TIPS

Although Notre Dame doesn't require work experience, the school says it prefers applicants who have tallied up at least two years in a job, and slightly over 20 percent of the Class of 1998 has less than a year of full-time work experience. "Experience is a compelling factor when combined with strong undergraduate performance and upward career progress," says admissions. The school also tries to gain a sense of the personality of its applicants. "We value an upbeat, optimistic attitude and a well-rounded personality; we prize students with high levels of energy and intellectual curiosity."

It's sometimes harder to convey enthusiasm and curiosity on paper than in person, so you might want to make a trip to the school to show those qualities in person. Admissions strongly encourages applicants to interview, and in 1996 the school interviewed 52 percent of its 594 applicants to the full-time MBA program. There are no classes on Friday, so go Monday through

Thursday if you want to sit in on one. Call the MBA office at 219-631-5206 to schedule an interview.

You need to apply by May 9 for the two-year program and by March 7 for the accelerated program for those with a business undergraduate. If you boast GMAT scores of 600 or above and at leat two years of professional experience, you'll get priority attention for a scholarship. But you must apply by February 24 if you need the money.

Contact: Lee Cunningham
MBA Admissions Coordinator
219-631-8671
Final application deadline: May 9 for fall

NOTRE DAME MBAs SOUND OFF

More scholarships are attracting a more diverse student body, a large number of international internships (25 percent of our class), and a new and improving placement office.

The administration's promises are a lot like nonalcoholic beer—NO SUBSTANCE. The school offers few MBA accounting classes and almost no information technology classes. Those who intended on majoring in information technology are enrolled in undergraduate classes under the heading of directed readings.

The problem with the Notre Dame MBA Program is the quality of students. There is a high percentage of students without work experience. There is also an easy grading system. The material covered in class is too superficial because students don't have the work experience or undergraduate business knowledge to critically evaluate issues. Career placement is poor.

The program lacks a truly international focus. This is evident in the few international elective courses offered and in the small number of companies recruiting on campus for international positions.

The quality of teaching at Notre Dame is unmatched! The top professors are in the classrooms actively engaged with students, rather than dedicating all of their energies to research. . . . The school is reaching out to minorities in an attempt to increase the diversity of the program. This will not only enhance what is already an energetic and enthusiastic classroom environment, but will also improve the program's position with companies for career placement.

UNIVERSITY OF PITTSBURGH

The Joseph M. Katz Graduate School of Business
Pittsburgh, Pennsylvania 15260
E-mail address: mba-admissions@katz.business.pitt.edu
Website address: http://www.pitt.edu/~business/

Enrollment: 920

Women: 31%
Non-U.S.: 37%
Minority: 6%
Part-time: 624
Average age: 27
Average years of work exp.: 4.5
Applicants accepted: 67%
Median starting pay: $57,650

Annual tuition & fees:
  resident—$16,553
  non-resident—$26,663
Room and board: $12,000
Average GMAT score: *585
GMAT range: 450 to 750
Average GPA: 3.2
GPA range: 2.4 to 4.0
Accepted applicants enrolled: 45%
Average starting pay: $59,720

Teaching methods: Lecture, 50% Case study, 30% Workshops, 20%

Contact:
Kathleen R. Valentine
Director of Admissions
412-648-1700
*Final application
deadline:* April 15

Which MBA program guarantees you the quickest payback on your investment? Surprisingly, it's not Wharton or Northwestern, Harvard or Michigan. It's the Katz School of Business, housed in a striking glass and steel building in Pittsburgh. The reason: it's the only U.S. school offering a first-rate MBA program that lasts just one year. That alone cuts both tuition and lost earnings of MBA candidates in half, while Katz's graduates see a 63 percent boost in pay over their pre-MBA income.

This is no experience for the mild or the meek. When AT&T Chairman Robert E. Allen once came to campus to deliver the graduation address, he called the program "the intellectual equivalent of swimming the English Channel underwater." At times, that's exactly how students feel. Potential students should think carefully before attending, warns a recent alum, because "the intensity and the pace are not for everyone." While your friends are still on the beach, you're showing up at Katz for five days' worth of orientation at the beginning of August. The first of six 7-week terms begins about August 15. The last one doesn't end until June 16.

That's a torturous schedule that for years had been made a little more palatable by the school's long-term dean, H.J. "Jerry" Zoffer. A dynamic and enthusiastic leader, Zoffer helped make the school a major success during a 27-year stint that ended in 1996. Professor Andrew R. Blair, an expert in international business, has been named interim dean. Now, he'll have to deal with the ongoing complaints about the fast-paced nature of this program.

Twice a week at 7:30 a.m., small groups of students gather on the third floor of Mervis Hall for the breakfast with the dean. In the first term, nearly everyone complains about the pressure and the difficulty of managing their time. Soon after, most students are wondering if they made a mistake. Scheduling is a common gripe among students. They complain that it's easy to get blocked out of popular electives. Because they have only 11 months of classes, it's common for students to leave without taking the more popular classes they badly wanted.

The school revised its curriculum in the fall of 1994. Instead of 14-week courses tucked into three terms, Katz now offers 7-week courses split up into six different modules. This should allow students more options to pursue their interests. Packed into those six modules is a whirlwind of activity: 14 required courses in the core curriculum and 14 electives. The main drawback to the program is that you lose the opportunity of a summer internship. For the career switcher or someone with little work experience, that is a considerable negative. If you're trying to convince H.J. Heinz to hire you for a marketing job despite your financial background, a summer job at Procter & Gamble makes the task a lot easier.

Pittsburgh also boasts an extremely active speakers' program. Two or three times each month, the school hosts an Executive Briefing, in which CEOs from major Pittsburgh corporations talk for 40 minutes on the challenges and frustrations of the job and then field student questions. After each session, a handful of students heads for the University Club for a private lunch with the chairman of Westinghouse Electric Corp., Bell Atlantic, or Alcoa.

Each spring, over a dozen corporate executives also come to campus for the American Assembly Dialogue. Pitt MBAs set the agenda for the off-the-record discussions that have attracted the likes of a varied group of big-time chieftains from Ted Turner of Turner Broadcasting System Inc. to Richard A. Zimmerman, chairman of Hershey Foods Corporation. The real-world thoughts of visiting CEOs provide a good balance to all the learning in Pitt's tiered, horseshoe-shaped classrooms. Katz offers students about 90 electives. A key part of the program is its emphasis on how to use information as a strategic resource. Katz boasts an impressive computer lab filled with $6 million worth of hardware and software. Electives in management information systems outnumber those in finance, marketing, human resources, and international business. No wonder *Computerworld* magazine recently singled out Pitt as one of the top 10 "Techno MBA" schools. If you're not interested in computer languages, you might be interested in knowing that students can take Japanese, French, German, and Spanish for credit in the business school.

Some of the most rewarding electives are "project courses" that allow students to consult with corporations on actual problems. Pitt MBAs have helped to forecast trends in entertainment behavior for Eastman Kodak Company and helped to build a computer-simulated model of an operating room for a local hospital. Special programs? If you're really an academic masochist, Pitt offers the MBA in double-degree programs with a master's in the management of information systems (21 months), international business (2 years), international affairs (21 months), area studies (21 months), or health administration (2 years), and even a Master of Divinity with the Pittsburgh Theological Seminary.

Most students, of course, find one 11-month degree program tough enough to handle. The B-school doesn't schedule classes on Fridays. Pitt loads up that day with optional workshops and executive briefings. There's also a Significant Film Series, in which such famous flicks as *All Quiet on the Western Front* and *Caine Mutiny* are shown to students on Friday afternoons. Each film comes with a lecture on how the movie portrays relevant business issues.

Although Katz's average student boasts four years of work experience, many grads fault the school for admitting too many students with little or no experience. About 15 percent of the Class of 1997 lacked a year's worth of work experience. The upshot: Class discussions aren't always as dynamic as they should be.

Students gravitate to the basement of Mervis Hall for lunch at Clara's Cafe. As you might have guessed, Clara runs the joint, even reprimanding the dean for grabbing too big a piece of cake for lunch. For drinks, the MBAs favor Zelda's, which serves up pizza and is only one block from the school, and Doc's Place, the yuppie watering hole in Shadyside some two miles away. Most students choose private housing near campus, in the culturally diverse Oakland section of Pittsburgh.

PLACEMENT DETAILS

Some 110 companies came to Pitt in 1996 to conduct 1112 interviews. Federal Express, which recruited for the first time at Pitt in 1996, carted away 8 of 10 students who were offered jobs. The other major recruiters: Ford Motor Co. (8); PNC Financial Corp. (6); Ernst & Young (6); Arthur Andersen (4); Kimberly Clark (3); Deloitte & Touche (3); Andersen Consulting (2); Intel (2); and Price Waterhouse (2). About 16 percent of the Class of 1996 did not have a job offer by commencement.

But when you crunch the numbers on payback, Pitt comes out on top thanks to its one-year program. Students can usually pay back their investment in the MBA in 3.9 years. That's much better than Wharton at 5.5 years or Columbia at 7 years.

OUTSTANDING FACULTY

Ken Lehn (****—finance); *Dan Smith* (****—marketing); *Daniel Fogel* (***—organizational behavior); *Madeleine Carlin* (***—accounting); *Prakash Mirchandani* (**—operations); *Don*

Moser (**—accounting); *Nandu Nagarajan* (**—accounting); *Robert Atkin* (**—human resources); *Tim Heath* (**—marketing); *Craig Dunbar* (*—finance).

APPLICANT TIPS

With applications down by more than 12 percent in the past two years, the acceptance rate for Pitt has risen to 67 percent, highest for a Runners-Up school. So the hurdle rates on this program aren't what they were just a couple of years ago. Still, this 11-month MBA program is intense, so you should demonstrate that you have the motivation and perseverance to hack it. Katz encourages applicants to apply early. The school says it reviews applications about every six weeks from November through April, and it won't consider your application after April 15 unless there is space in the program. The early admission deadline is January 15. If you want scholarship aid or are an international applicant, you should apply by February 15.

Katz encourages interviews, but in 1996, the school interviewed only 42 percent of its 879 applicants. If you think you make favorable impressions in person, you should request an interview.

Contact: Kathleen Riehle Valentine
Director of Admissions
412-648-1700
Final application deadline: April 15

KATZ MBAs SOUND OFF

I believe the pace and challenge of this 11-month program is excellent preparation for students entering the 1990s business environment. The program was a lot of work and very intense. The faculty is of the highest caliber and the team experiences are very "real world." As far as placement, Joan Craig, our Director of Placement, is quite possibly the best in the business. She brought in many great companies and she (and her staff) helped us put our best foot forward during the interview process.

There is no better value for the MBA experience than the Katz Graduate School of Business at Pitt. The class of '96 was made up of 35 percent international students and everyone was high caliber, interesting, and professional. The one-year program includes excellent required and elective courses in strategy, operations management, finance, and marketing. Then, using a "learning organization" framework across all classes, students work in both static and changing teams—giving them the opportunity to really apply team-building, project management, and conflict management skills. The local, national, and international corporate community is very involved with our program, giving students hands-on experience and frequent CEO-level perspective.

Kudos are most certainly due Katz. While many other MBA programs only accept applicants possessing a minimum of two years of work experience, Katz on average, maintains classes with approximately 15 percent of the student body coming straight from their undergraduate institutions. I firmly believe that this diversity allows for a rich learning experience by all.

Katz offers outstanding opportunity to understand group dynamics through participation in MBA-Learning Organizations (MLOs). It is great for leadership development and confidence-building. The program is high intensity because of the condensed time frame. It forces students to maximize time-management and efficiency skills. There is a very large international student body and strong faculty ties to Eastern Europe give courses a global feeling. Participation in "American Assembly Dialogue and Executive Briefings" gives excellent opportunity to converse with CEOs.

The school utilizes MBA or Management Learning Organizations (MLOs) to expose students to the use of teams in decision making. There were 23 MLOs during this past academic year and each team is comprised of 9 to 11 full-time students. Each student team will have at least 2–3 international students (which makes up approximately one third of the incoming class this year). Three MLO-based classes were required: Competing in a Global Environment (CGE), Organizational Transformation (OT), and Managing Strategic Performance (MSP). In addition, each MLO is assigned to an actual company. My MLO team had the privilege of working with Rubbermaid Inc. in developing and recommending a strategy in their requested area. I think that the curriculum at Katz is very well globally integrated. There are 14 core courses which count as about 60 percent of the total requirement. Those 14 courses are well-braided together. More than 50 percent of the class materials are case study. Each core class requires a team report which is in addition to the original MLO. Those 14 core courses cover all areas including finance, marketing, strategy, management information systems, accounting, organizational behavior, operations, and ethics.

Katz is a great school that provides great value for your time and money. However the program needs more faculty! The administration has come far in getting the program to this stage, but the system has not been completely tweaked. Library and computer lab resources need updating. General and broad based business skills have been stressed rather than specific technologies, which works out in my favor since I'm going to be a general manager.

UNIVERSITY
OF
SOUTHERN
CALIFORNIA

UNIVERSITY OF SOUTHERN CALIFORNIA

Graduate School of Business Administration
University Park
Los Angeles, California 90089
E-mail address: uscmba@sba.usc.edu
Website address: http://www.usc.edu/dept/sba

Enrollment: 1290
Women: 30%
Non-U.S.: 23%
Minority: 33%
Part-time: 830
Average age: 27.1
Applicants accepted: 38%
Median starting pay: $70,000

Annual tuition & fees: $19,516
Room and board: $11,000
Average GMAT score: 630
Average GPA: 3.2
GPA range: 2.0 to 3.98
Average years of work exp.: 4.0
Accepted applicants enrolled: 47%
Average starting pay: $69,457

Teaching methods: Lecture, 40%   Case study, 50%
Field projects, 10%

Contact:
Annette Loschert
Director of Admissions
213-740-7846
Application deadlines:
December 2
January 20
February 17
March 25
April 15

The hustle and bustle of tinsel town dominates most of the Los Angeles area with movies being made, famous actors on display, and pop culture galore. Show business types always seem to find a way to make a buck off of everything in sight. And now the B-school at USC has figured out how to capitalize on Hollywood itself with California's glitzy appeal and an MBA in the business of entertainment. Say it ain't so, sweetheart!

This entertainment track, along with the school's well-established programs in entrepreneurship and real estate management make up three of the school's most notable MBA concentrations. These niche programs and the school's new focus on becoming a powerhouse in the Pacific Rim market make for an interesting MBA experience. And as they say, location, location, location—it's hard to beat two years in Southern California.

For years, USC has been home to some of the sharpest and most articulate management thinkers in America. Leadership guru Warren Bennis, one of the world's best-known B-school profs for his work on leadership, heads the pack. He's among great company—Edward Lawler, who runs the school's Center for Effective Organizations, and Morgan McCall, who has developed some of the leading management simulation exercises on the market today.

The school has been going through a constant curriculum change under Dean Randolph W. Westerfield, who is attempting to carve a niche for USC in Pacific Rim business. The B-school has focused its marketing efforts toward companies in the Pacific Rim and has instituted new recruiting strategies in those countries as well. The inherent risk of a curriculum like this is that it doesn't fit everyone's needs. With this changing tide at USC, the school could fall into the trap it has seen before.

For example, the strength of the school's organizational behavior group, among the best in the world, had often overwhelmed other departments, making recruiters believe USC was a "soft" school. But in the past five years, the school has picked off superior teachers in finance, accounting, and marketing from Wharton, Michigan, Stanford, and Northwestern. One of those master teachers, Westerfield, the former chairman of Wharton's finance department, took over as dean of USC's B-school in 1993. He's made a lot of changes, but with this new push to become a leader in a Pacific Rim business curriculum, the school might make its newly solid ground a little shaky again.

The school had revamped its program in 1991 in an attempt to emphasize fundamental skills in business, economics, statistics, accounting, finance, and communication in the first semester; a cross-functional approach to process innovation in the second; and the freedom to pursue a concentration of one's own making in the second year. These efforts seem to be working, and students seem happier with the curriculum. This change also did something else—it made the school's first year curriculum tougher. The program kicks off with a two-and-a-half day retreat aimed at teaching the skills needed for working in project teams and at building a collaborative learning environment. The entire first year is taught by a dedicated faculty team featuring some of the school's best professors. An interesting downside to this strategy is that many of the electives are taught by weaker faculty.

Core courses are integrated through a "key cases" program, in which groups of faculty share a single classroom to present business cases from different perspectives. MBA candidates take a required business presentations and writing class, taught in small groups, and are graded for their communications skills in every first-year class. Case competitions with executive judges, business simulations, and field-study projects keep the focus on real world applications.

In the second year, you can choose from an array of 19 concentrations by taking at least four courses in an area of specialty, ranging from consulting services to venture management. The school's contingent of 171 full-time profs offers students many options. Of the nearly 110 electives offered to MBAs, the lion's share is in accounting and finance. As many as 10 courses each are taught in the school's programs in entrepreneurship and real estate. And MBAs can also take courses outside the B-school in law, public administration, urban planning, music, communications, and international relations. The newest program, entertainment management, is offered in cooperation with the university's School of Cinema-Television. It provides the chance to explore such key areas of the entertainment biz as motion pictures and TV, entertainment technology, and sports management. The school has been able to lure into the classroom top Hollywood executives to teach some of these courses. The president of worldwide marketing for MCA Recreation, for example, honchos the two-semester elective on Motion Picture Marketing.

Many electives, however, are offered only at night, requiring full-time students to enroll in them with USC's 830 part-timers. Most of the complaints about the quality of teaching seem directed at these night courses. Westerfield has tried to change this, but he has a long way to go. The school has set up a Teaching Excellence Center to encourage better teaching, but students say it's still tough to find a good professor in one of the evening courses.

Located on a 150-acre campus, the B-school occupies three buildings, including the I.M. Pei-designed Hoffman Hall. Currently in the midst of a capital campaign, the school plans to add a new $23 million building to its existing facilities by 1998. The reason: MBAs are packed in with some 2000 business undergraduates. To make life a little more comfortable, the school opened a dedicated MBA lounge and information center, as well as a 20-unit Macintosh computer lab in 1992—hardly enough computers for the school's huge class, but certainly a start in Westerfield's campaign to upgrade technology at USC.

The campus, about two and a half miles from L.A.'s central business district, is next to Exposition Park, site of the 1984 Olympics and home to the L.A. Raiders and the L.A. Clippers. It's not the greatest of neighborhoods, although many students rent nearby apartments because they come cheaper that the more desirable spots closer to Santa Monica beach. A limited number of on-campus dorms are available, but you have to apply early to get in.

Lights? Camera? Action?

PLACEMENT DETAILS

Even though on-campus recruiting was up 17 percent in 1996, students still complain that there aren't enough interviews or jobs to go around. Even so, only 12 percent of the Class of 1996 failed to have a single job offer by commencement. Those that did fared pretty well, pulling down median starting pay packages of $70,000 each—tops for a Runners-Up school and better than seven schools on BUSINESS WEEK's Top 25 list.

Some 144 companies came to recruit students on campus in 1996, conducting 2592 interviews. Another 1119 job opportunities were posted via correspondence. The major employers: Hewlett Packard (7); Deloitte & Touche (6); Arthur Andersen (5); Ernst & Young (5); IBM (4); Allied Signal (3); Andersen Consulting (3); Avery Dennison (3); Walt Disney (3); and McKinsey & Co. (2).

OUTSTANDING FACULTY

Dennis Draper (****—finance); *William Davidson* (****—management); *Arvind Bhambri* (***—management); *Sam Hariharan* (**—management); *Dennis Rook* (**—marketing); *Linda DeAngelo* (*—finance); *Mark Defond* (*—accounting); *Randolph Westerfield* (*—finance); *Jerry Arnold* (*—accounting); and *Harry DeAngelo* (*—finance).

APPLICANT TIPS

USC says there is no "formula" or minimum GMAT score it uses to determine admissions. The school says it pays "significant attention" to personal essays and recommendations, and that a minimum of two years of "full-time work experience" also counts significantly. Indeed, only 7 percent of the Class of 1998 lacks at least one year of job experience. In recent years, the school has begun to require admission interviews for all U.S. applicants and to encourage them for international students. The school interviewed 100 percent of its domestic candidates in 1996 and 6 percent of its international applicants. Applications hit a record 1471 in 1996, up from 1266 two years earlier. You should call the admissions office at 213-740-7846 at least three weeks in advance to schedule a campus interview or a meeting with a local alum.

Apply early. If you get your application in by December 2, the school guarantees you a decision by January 24. If you wait until April 16, the last deadline, when most seats in the entering class will be filled, you may not hear until June 6.

Contact: Annette Loschert
Director of Admissions
213-740-7846
Application deadlines: December 2, January 20, February 17, March 25, and April 15

USC MBAs SOUND OFF

AT USC there was a coherent emphasis on process. We were taught to think carefully about how best to implement goals and visions throughout our program. Every effort was also made to learn from high performance rather than mistakes. These two facets of the program made for an unexpectedly enriching experience.

I feel the B-school program suffers for being one of the university's cash cows. As such, resources which could be used toward new facilities, career resources, or additional technology are spent on salvaging marginal programs elsewhere in the university.

The openness of the faculty and good-natured temperment of the student body were two major factors in my choice of MBA programs. I could not have chosen a better environment in which to have to do too much work. Unfortunately, staff members in career services caused my evaluation of the school to be so low.

Both the Entrepreneur Program and the Finance Department were outstanding. The new building should solve most of the concerns about the program. The class size, professors' availability, the number of international students, and the rigorous workload make USC one of the premier programs in the country. Most of the students want to stay on the West Coast. I was incredibly surprised by the overall quality of the program.

USC offers a superior MBA program. This is true for the following reasons: (1) The quality of the professors. Every professor I have come in contact with at USC demonstrated outstanding levels of "real world" experience, academic knowledge, and communication coherence. With respect to finance, I do not think I could have been taught by a better group of professors. (2) The Career Resource Center. I was offered several jobs both for an internship and full-time position. They also helped me perfect my interviewing skills, résumé preparation, etc., more so than I ever would have expected. (3) The alumni network. USC has an alumni network which reaches world-wide. Literally, I can at anytime make a connection whether for a job lead, business assistance, or just to make a friend with alumni located anywhere in the world.

UNIVERSITY
OF
TENNESSEE
AT KNOXVILLE

UNIVERSITY OF TENNESSEE AT KNOXVILLE

College of Business Administration
Knoxville, Tennessee 37996-0552
E-mail address: dpotts@u+k.edu
Website address: http://funnelweb.utcc.utk.edu/~gbpadmin

Enrollment: 181

Women: 51%
Non-U.S.: 29%
Minority: 8%
Part-time: None
Average age: 27
Average years of work exp.: 4.5
Applicants accepted: 31%
Median starting pay: $56,080

Annual tuition & fees:
   resident—$2654
   non-resident—$7094
Room and board: $5000
Average GMAT score: 600
GMAT range: 460 to 730
Average GPA: 3.3
GPA range: 2.33 to 3.97
Accepted applicants enrolled: 50%
Average starting pay: $58,615

Teaching methods: Lecture, 25%   Case study, 25%   Simulation, 50%

Contact:
Donna Potts
Director of MBA
Admissions
615-974-5033
*Final application
deadline:*
March 1 for fall

When it comes to teaching business, most MBA programs come in two flavors. There are the case-study champions led by Harvard, and there are the quant schools led by MIT. Then there's the University of Tennessee.

Who? Relatively unknown until recently, this innovative B-school has made a name for itself by embracing one of the most influential movements in contemporary business: Total Quality Management. It did so largely in the executive education arena. Now it's trying to pull off a similar feat by overhauling its MBA curriculum.

By many accounts, little Tennessee is among the B-school pioneers in developing a program for the 1990s. First-years no longer take the traditional core courses, with marketing, finance, and other disciplines taught separately by one specialist in each area. Instead, students are thrown into just one class each semester combining all of the functional areas. They're divided into five-to-seven-person teams, taught by groups of faculty, and sometimes awarded team grades. The entire first year of work is based on a complex case written by the core faculty. Memos are sent to the students via mailboxes or E-mail, notifying them of their grandfather's death and their subsequent inheritance of his company, Volunteer Vegetables. The fictional company is managed by MBAs who face a series of problems called "milestones," which build throughout the year to include new-product launches and international expansion.

Moreover, the class is team-taught by 14 core faculty members. Some days 4 or 5 of them will lead the class, while on the other days only 1 or 2 are at the helm. Not only do the core professors teach together, they all prepare test questions and agree on a final semester grade for each of the 80 first-year students. MBAs are given only one grade at the end of each semester, but they receive extensive comments on their work throughout. The second year of the program is more traditional, and pretty flexible. Students have to complete 24 credits of electives. A minimum of three classes (9 credits) are needed for a concentration. The pickings are slim, however, Tennessee only offers 38 electives a year. They range from New Paradigms in Management to Strategic Issues in Health Care. In the last three years, the school has added concentrations in global business and environmental management.

The school says its best areas of study are marketing, finance, entrepreneurship, and transportation logistics. It would like to improve its economics department. If you're keenly interested in international business, Knoxville isn't exactly the place to be. Tennessee has just one semester abroad program with a business school in France.

This is yet another small and intimate program, with a full-time enrollment of only 181 students. It's also one of only two schools (Iowa is the other) to have a full half of its MBA population comprised of women. Indeed, no school in the Top 50 boasts a higher percentage of women enrolled in an MBA program. MBA students are not just outnumbered by business undergraduates here. With 2900 undergrads, MBAs are overwhelmed, a reason why the full-time faculty here numbers 103.

PLACEMENT DETAILS

Tennessee grads certainly appeal to many of the corporations that have adopted widescale quality efforts in recent years. Problem is, there aren't as many of them these days and they aren't as fervently impassioned about quality as they once were. So about one in every four members of the Class of 1996 failed to have a single job offer by graduation. Those that did averaged 2.85 offers each—right on the average for the Top 50 schools.

Frankly, it's surprising that more MBAs here don't have jobs by commencement because the hiring companies outnumber the graduates. In 1996, some 177 companies came to campus to recruit second-years, conducting 743 interviews. Other jobs were posted via correspondence. The major employers were dominated by quality advocates: IBM (4); Diesel Recon (3); Frito-Lay (3); Milliken & Co. (3); Phillips Consumer Electronics (3); Procter & Gamble (3); Federal Express (2); Fleetguard (2); Mercer Capital (2); and Andersen Consulting (2).

OUTSTANDING FACULTY

Jim Reeve (****—accounting); *Sarah Gardial* (****—marketing); *Joyce Russell* (***—management); *John Wachowicz* (***—finance); *Jim Wansley* (***—finance); *Alex Miller* (***—strategy); *Ken Gilbert* (**—management science); *Ray Mundy* (**—logistics); *Cary Collins* (*—finance); *Deborah Gunthorpe* (*—finance).

APPLICANT TIPS

Tennessee is a fairly selective school, accepting only 31 percent of its applicant pool. That ties it with Ohio State for being the fourth most selective B-school among the Runners-Up group. To enhance your odds of getting into this school, apply early. Personal admission interviews are not required, although it may give you an edge in the admissions process. In 1996, about 50 percent of the school's 600 applicants were interviewed.

Work experience is also a plus. One successful candidate for admission in 1996 had 22.6 years of experience. Still, 13 percent of the entering class had less than one year's worth of experience on a full-time job.

Contact: Donna Potts
Director of MBA Admissions
615-974-5033
Final application deadline: March 1 for fall

TENNESSEE MBAs SOUND OFF

The best aspects of the Tennessee MBA include: the structure of the first-year program; the diversity of ideas and schools of thought; the tolerance of alternate views (other than those of the professors); the surprising lack of prejudice and bigotry for a southern university (open acceptance and complete inclusion of African-Americans, gays, students with less experience/knowledge, etc.); TOMBA social events; the *Vol Street Journal;* and the ability to select electives from the entire university. The worst aspects of the Tennessee MBA: the university placement office; the lack of PR for the school; and the size of the alumni network.

This is an integrated program that gives exposure to all the sides of business. It is highly intense and demanding. The program is taught by a team of 15 professors who work together to ensure the meshing of topics. I believe that some of the best professors are located at UT. Special mention needs to be made of the following core team: Dr. Gardial, Marketing; Dr. Reeve, Accounting; Dr. Erhardt, Finance; Dr. Miller, Strategy; Dr. Gilbert, Supply Chain Management; Dr. Massingale, Business Law and Ethics; Dr. Russell, Leadership and Team Building; and Dr. Judge, Management.

One of the most positive aspects of our program is the interest the core faculty has in student input. Through my mentoring experience with the first-year students, I can see how our suggestions have been implemented and how they have impacted our program.

The grading system needs to reflect the objective of the program (i.e., teamwork) and the amount of effort devoted to coursework. A select few seemed to get the highest grades regardless of the quality of their work or how well they actually performed in a team environment.

The small class size (80 per class) allows for much faculty interaction. Both in the first and second year our projects are modeled on real companies. In the second year we spent a year on a "marketing consulting" project for MasterCraft boats. What we learned and did for this project has mirrored what I will be doing with my job at Philips Consumer Electronics (I have interned for Philips all year, so I am very aware of what my job will entail). I have been very happy with my experience at UT. The three problems the program faces are: an antiquated building for conducting classes; poor placement services (although they are working to improve this); and a class with little work experience who can't understand why they are not getting high salaries when they want to stay in the Southeast and have no work experience.

The first-year core integrates everything a top business school should have: teamwork, computer learning, leadership, situation analysis, as well as traditional courses. The second year provided opportunities to meet top executives from around the country as well as the opportunity to do real projects for industry leaders.

Faculty connections for jobs are far superior to the university's services. Candidly, this state institution is far too dependent on appropriations. It should develop (aggressively!) its alumni network and develop an endowment, especially for the College of Business. The alumni network will help both job placement prospects and support the college's reputation in the workplace. The Logistics and Transportation School is deservedly the best in the nation (according to Foster Partners report 2/20/96). The course of study continues to improve with regular quantitative additions. In addition, the staff seeks good job placement for every candidate. Many of the best companies are now coming with specific openings instead of for general recruiting—Frito Lay, Diesel, Motorola, and Milliken among them.

I feel that the Logistics and Transportation Department is probably the best in the country in terms of reputation of professors and helping students find jobs. This department should be the benchmark for all departments across the campus. I am not even seeking L+T as a concentration, but I have received numerous job contacts via professors in the department who do outside consulting. At times I have been frustrated with the caliber of my classmates—and extremely upset with the competence of the Director of Graduate Business programs and his staff—but I have to remind myself that I'm only paying $2500 a year in tuition. The UTK is a really good program for the money, but you really do get what you pay for. The Finance Department has also been a benefit to my experience at UTK. The courses are very rigorous and force students to know the material. The professors have won many awards for excellence in teaching and really know how to separate academia from the real world. I'm glad I decided to get a finance concentration because all of the other departments really pale by comparison.

UNIVERSITY OF WASHINGTON

UNIVERSITY OF WASHINGTON

Graduate School of Business Administration
110 Mackenzie Hall
Seattle, Washington 98195
E-mail address: mba@u.washington.edu
Website address: http://www.weber.u.washington.edu/
~bschool/mba

Enrollment: 404	Annual tuition & fees:
	resident—$5044
Women: 35%	non-resident—$12,475
Non-U.S.: 20%	Room and board: $7458
Minority: 15%	Average GMAT score: 634
Part-time: 46	GMAT range: 500 to 780
Average age: 28	Average GPA: 3.26
Average years of work exp.: 4.9	GPA range: 2.05 to 3.99
Applicants accepted: 38%	Accepted applicants enrolled: 52%
Median starting pay: $62,150	Average starting pay: $60,750

Teaching methods: Lecture, 40% Case study, 55%
Independent study, 5%

Contact:
James Danko
Director of
MBA Program
and Admissions
206-616-4966
Application deadlines:
December 1
February 1
March 1
April 15

Few schools have experienced the kind of upheavals that the University of Washington's business school has undergone in recent years. The school has a new dean, a new director of its MBA program, and a new core curriculum. To enroll better students with higher GMAT scores and more work experience, it also has reduced the size of the entering class.

The changes are being put in place by Dean William D. Bradford, who took over the helm in late 1994. Bradford, who had been at the University of Maryland, has made the school's MBA program its number one priority. He has given it more support and resources to improve recruiting, enhance student services, and raise overall student satisfaction with the quality of the program. Perhaps the single most important move was to recruit James M. Danko, the former director for program innovations at the University of Michigan's business school. Danko came aboard in late 1995 so his dedication to customer service has yet to show up in BUSINESS WEEK's surveys of graduates.

Finally, though, this school may well benefit from some long overdue attention. For years, the natural beauty of Seattle and its environs has been a powerful draw. Mount Rainier and other nearby recreational spots allow for a lifestyle that lures quality students and faculty. Skiing, biking, and kayaking are obsessions for many and the reason why this school has long attracted an outdoorsy, and rather diverse and mature crowd, for a Runners-Up school.

Now, for the first time, the school seems to be listening to its students. Dean Bradford has created an environment in which faculty and students are encouraged to voice their comments and suggestions for making the MBA program more responsive to their needs. One recent change pushed by students: Orientation Week, once a series of social events, has now become a goal-oriented, leadership-development program that includes academic and team-building exercises.

The first-year core integrates the different disciplines of business and places a greater emphasis on international business and ethics. Students are assigned to multidisciplinary teams which are used throughout the curriculum. MBAs also attend several sessions on professional skills, many taught by consultants who specialize in business training. Executives come to campus to share their expertise with students through Washington's new Conversations with Executives program.

In the second year, MBAs design their own programs. In addition to the typical specialties, new programs include Environmental Management, International Management, Entrepreneurship and Innovation, and Manufacturing Management. The Environmental Management Program has attracted the most attention and the most students—just what you'd expect from a business school in environmentally conscious Washington State.

In the first year, expect to be in class roughly four hours a day, Monday through Friday. Grads say you need to do about two hours of prep work before a class, plus another two hours of homework after it. Students are grouped into cores of 45 each and attend the required courses together. Washington uses a mix of lecture, case study, and seminars to deliver the business basics. The teaching quality in the core courses is nicely above the average in BUSINESS WEEK's ratings—possibly because a core curriculum committee of faculty now teaches first-year MBAs. These profs have responsibility for inte-

grating case studies and group projects so that each successive module builds on material that has been previously introduced. The school also has eliminated its pass/no pass grading system in favor of a numeric grade for each of the three courses in the core to increase student accountability, recognize superior performance, and promote healthy competition.

Most of the workload in the first year falls on the individual, while the second year tends to be dominated by group work. The school offers a menu of 71 electives, 22 percent of which are new in the past three years. They include such offerings as Leadership and the Board of Directors and Trade with China. The school also added a new concentration, Management of Technology. Washington believes its strongest areas of study are finance, accounting, and marketing.

Washington claims that its environmental program, begun in 1991, is the first of its kind in the country. The program gives MBAs the chance to gain a certificate in environmental management by taking a sequence of three core courses in the subject as well as a pair of environmental or natural resource electives from the B-school and other university programs. Students work in small groups on actual management consulting projects dealing with environmental issues.

The international management fellows program provides students the chance to combine an MBA degree with advanced language study, in-depth area study, and an overseas business internship. The school requires a minimum of two years of college-level instruction in Chinese, German, Japanese, or Spanish for applicants. After admission to the 24-month program, you'll show up for a brief orientation in June, then travel abroad for a crash language course covering business terms. Fellows return to Washington in the fall to begin the full-time MBA program. The summer and fall quarters of the second year are devoted to the overseas internship and study at a foreign university.

That's only for students who can tear themselves away from this beautiful locale. The University of Washington itself is in a park-like setting with a combination of classic old buildings and nicely styled new ones. Everywhere it's green. In the spring, cherry trees bloom along the main campus corridor. Around the east perimeter of the grounds are the shores of Lake Washington, the residence of the graduate sailing club. Looming in the background are the majestic Olympic and Cascade Mountains. Balmer Hall, a four-story stucco building housing the library and classrooms, and Mackenzie Hall, the faculty and administrative center, form the focus of the B-school on the upper campus. Lewis Hall, one of the two oldest historic buildings, houses the MBA career center.

Outdoor activities are a major attraction. MBAs hike through the rain forest on the Olympic Peninsula or climb Mount Rainier. A fixture of MBA life here is the salmon bake—an event that has seen just 100 grads wolf down 40 pounds of fresh salmon barbecued on grills beside the shores of Lake Washington. The Thursday evening ritual, dubbed TGIT (Thank God It's Thursday), sees most MBAs pick one of the several microbreweries in town in which to swill such tavern-brewed beers as Ballard Bitter, Pyramid, and Red Hook. Nearly as popular as the local brew is the local espresso. MBAs like the outdoor porch of the Burke Museum for its potent coffee drinks. They also like to travel into Vancouver, British Columbia, for weekends, or to Portland. When in Seattle, you might live in the university's graduate housing, but most students reside off campus.

MBAs created what they call a Business Diagnostic Center in 1991 to volunteer their services to local businesses. Student teams solicit proposals from small companies and nonprofit organizations in and around Seattle, roll up their sleeves, and go to work. An example: MBAs drafted a new marketing plan for a nearby resort. It's been so successful that students can't meet the demand for their services, and in the fall of 1992 the school incorporated the center into the MBA program with credit and faculty supervision. One surprise outcome: Many internships and jobs are now coming out of what was once a voluntary initiative.

PLACEMENT DETAILS

In 1996, only 53 companies came to recruit on campus. Not very many, but then again that's an improvement on just 38 companies who recruited here two years earlier. Those firms conducted 545 interviews with second-year students. Washington also brought grads to job fairs in Chicago and Los Angeles. Still, the school reported that 24 percent of the Class of 1996 failed to have a single job offer at commencement at a time when MBA hiring was setting new records. No wonder Washington's placement operations got amongst the worst scores by graduates in BUSINESS WEEK's survey. In fact, the school scored in the bottom 10 percentile of 51 schools on four of five placement questions.

In 1996, the major employers of Washington grads were Deloitte & Touche (13); Intel (8); Ernst & Young (4); Aris (3); Paratechnology (3); Arthur Andersen (2); AT&T Wireless (2); Sequent Computer (2); Tektronix (2); and the Walter Group (2).

Whether the school's new changes and customer focus have a real impact is yet to be seen.

OUTSTANDING FACULTY

Gary Biddle (****—accounting); *Steve Sefcik* (****—accounting); *Karma Hadjimichalakis* (****—finance); *Rocky Higgins* (****—finance); *Steven J. Rice* (***—accounting); *June Morita* (***—management science); *Judy Edwards* (**—marketing and international business); *Julie Ruth* (**—marketing); *Kathryn Dewenter* (*—finance); *Charles Hill* (*—management).

APPLICANT TIPS

While GPAs and GMAT scores are of continuing importance in the school's screening process, it is putting more emphasis than ever on applicant responses to essay questions, recommendations from former employers and professors, and on personal interviews with each candidate. Applicants are strongly encouraged to attend one of the weekly information sessions held at the University of Washington on Thursdays at 3:30 p.m. Once your application is complete, you can call the admissions office at 206-543-4661 to schedule an interview. If you can't travel to the campus, you can interview by phone or with an alum in your area. In 1996, only 22 percent of the school's 852 applicants interviewed. The recommended date for financial aid qualification is February 28, 1997.

Contact: James Danko
Director of MBA Program and Admissions
206-616-4966
Application deadlines: December 1, February 1, March 1, and April 15

WASHINGTON MBAs SOUND OFF

The information technology emphasis has the potential to lead UW to the top as a B-school that offers the best IS program in the world due to its close relationships with top high-tech companies as well as its B-school/engineering faculty. The school needs to expand the IS elective selection, International business selection, expand finance class size, and respond to students' study interests. UW has renowned accounting and finance programs that need to be marketed more strongly, along with the IS program.

The MBA program has improved tremendously during my two years here—largely due to the new Dean. Three aspects of the program of most value to me: the quality of students; the emphasis on teamwork; the finance/accounting/business economics. Three most needed improvements: facilities for meeting and computing; system of faculty advisors; structured opportunities for finance students to apply skills in the private sector. (Marketing students have many opportunities.)

My total compensation my first year out will be about 65–75 percent higher than before I entered. In addition, I won't have $50,000+ in outstanding loans afterward, which allows me a lot more flexibility in choosing from employment opportunities going forward ad infinitum.

For the price, UW is quite a bargain! It's the students and most of the faculty that make this MBA Program so valuable. Students are cooperative, creative, good team players, competent, and ambitious. The program itself emphasizes and promotes these characteristics. The Puget Sound area is hopping with high tech, entrepreneurial firms, and this spirit catches on early with most UW students, as reflected by their career choices. Many positive changes are being made with the core curriculum. This means things will only get better because I already think the core integrates all the subjects well and effectively teaches the importance of teamwork.

This program has an enormous amount of potential. The new dean is very focused and motivated. It is going through a certain amount of transition, and is being very open to student opinions. Unfortunately, implementing change in academia is difficult. There are a few dinosaur faculty members (like any school) but for the most part, professors are motivated and interested in students' learning.

UNIVERSITY
OF
WISCONSIN
—MADISON

UNIVERSITY OF WISCONSIN—MADISON

School of Business
Grainger Hall
975 University Avenue
Madison, Wisconsin 53706
E-mail address: uwmadmba@bus.wisc.edu
Website address: http://www.wisc.edu/bschool

Enrollment: 574

Women: 36%
Non-U.S.: 28%
Minority: 12%
Part-time: 18
Average age: 26.6
Average years of work exp.: 3.3
Applicants accepted: 33.6%
Median starting pay: $46,800

Annual tuition & fees:
  resident—$5278
  non-resident—$14,204
Room and board: $6756
Average GMAT score: 597
GMAT range: 340 to 760
Average GPA: 3.38
GPA range: 2.1 to 3.96
Accepted applicants enrolled: 54%
Average starting pay: $50,850

Teaching methods: Lecture, 65%   Case study, 30%   Projects, 5%

Contact:
Randall Dunham
Director of Admissions
608-262-1556
*Final application
deadline:*
June 1 for fall
October 1 for spring

Have you ever heard the Bible verse: "The first shall be last and the last shall be first"? Well, the B-school at Wisconsin stays true to this concept, being one of the best technologically equipped schools and the first business school to use videoconferencing for interviews, but barely gaining any recognition from recruiters.

Several years ago, Dean Andrew Policano threw out the school's entire curriculum and started over, with feedback from business leaders as his guide. He created a more innovative, integrated, and techno-business style curriculum, incorporating multimedia presentations into coursework and a further emphasis to the school's biggest strength—its niche programs. The three-phase curriculum debuted last fall and the final phase will be implemented in Fall 1997. In the meantime, this B-school isn't standing still.

The school moved into a new $40 million facility in 1993. Grainger Hall doubled the capacity of the B-school's computer labs, tripled the size of its library, and vastly expanded the technological capabilities of the school. Students are immersed in technology at Wisconsin, trained not only to use and manage it, but doubly exposed to it in classrooms with Internet access, coursework on the Web, multimedia classrooms, and a new videoconferencing room. Even with this technological advancement and marked improvement in admission standards, the school still can't break into BW's Top 25.

The reasons are simple. Even though Wisconsin strives to be the best—which it is in many of its niche programs—the general management program and the quality of applicants can't compete with schools like UCLA, North Carolina, or Texas. Nearly 20 percent of this B-school's students come in with less than a year's worth of work experience, and the average time on a job is only 3.3 years. The GMAT average, moreover, has fallen to 597, a slight drop from 603 in 1994—but at a time when average scores have been going up at most of the best schools. Wisconsin, in fact, is one of only five schools in BUSINESS WEEK's Top 50 with average GMATs that fail to break 600.

Still, you have to give Policano some credit. He is pushing to break away from the limits on Wisconsin's success by expanding and marketing the school domestically and internationally. Despite this, it remains largely a regional school. Policano, a former economics professor who had been a dean at State University of New York at Stony Brook, arrived here in 1991. He wants to make Wisconsin one of the top five public university business schools in the country. That won't be easy by BUSINESS WEEK's standards. He'll have to compete with the likes of UCLA and Indiana and the B-schools at the universities of Washington, Minnesota, and Texas at Austin. Even with the new curriculum, the fact is that Wisconsin remains a niche school.

Don't be misled, though: Wisconsin's niches are some of the tops in their fields, with its risk management and insurance program and its real estate program ranked in the top five in some surveys. Other nationally recognized niche programs at Wisconsin: arts administration, applied security analysis, manufacturing and technology management, and the new distribution management program. Wisconsin boasts 100 percent placement out of these niche programs, but with only 7 to 15 students in each of the school's eight niches, a majority of the students are left out of lucrative placement opportunities.

If one of these specialty programs interests you, though, Wisconsin may be the place for you. The new distribution management program is geared to teach MBAs the distribution process all the way from the inception of an idea to the shelves—or wherever the product may be going. Thirty companies recruited the 10 1996 graduates of this program and each had several offers from which to choose. The situation is similar in other niches. The school basically offers four master's degrees: the MBA, the Master of Science in Business, the Master of Accountancy, and a Master of Arts in Business. To allow for lots of program flexibility, the school even has three different graduate dates: in May, August, and September.

Unfortunately, students occasionally speak poorly about the general management courses and the lack of experience of some of their colleagues. In past years, students have complained about the teaching quality at the school, and Policano has tried to fix this. Students seem to think it's working. Complaints about the dean are few. Policano's open-door policy appeals to students. Once, a student approached the dean about a problem with an adjunct professor. The dean picked up on the problem immediately and replaced the prof that week.

The new curriculum for the management program runs in 7-week modules. In the first semester you'll take financial accounting, marketing, and finance for 14 weeks, one optional course, and managerial economics and data analysis for 7 weeks each. In the second semester, six course are taken, all on 7-week modules, with one additional class in your chosen concentration and one elective. The second-year curriculum is a little more flexible, combining required classes in strategies, information technology and management, and ethics with four elective concentration units and two more optional courses.

The curriculum does have a few kinks, though. You could end up hearing the same thing twice since classes aren't closely integrated. One plus with the new curriculum: since the information in classes is presented in a multimedia format, you'll get more true-to-life exposure and the dean says the new techniques allow profs to teach more—faster and to a new comprehension level. Another thing, all the course materials—even test dates and assignments—are on the Web. Students can check out a course before, during, and after they've taken it. You'll always know what's expected of you at Wisconsin.

Life in Madison isn't any kind of punishment either. You'll be surrounded by picturesque landscapes, lakes, farmland, and rolling terrain. Madison is full of parks, eclectic cafes, and shops. It is a liberal, cosmopolitan community. But there's no denying that Wisconsin is also the land of beer, brats, and Badgers (the name of the school's sports teams). If you don't mind winter temperatures that regularly reach 40 below zero, then it won't be so bad. When the weather warms, MBAs trek to the Memorial Union to drink beer and wine on the terrace overlooking Lake Mendota, a favorite spot for canoeing. Wisconsin is no UCLA, but a resort mentality prevails here during late spring and summer when temperature climbs to the eighties and nineties.

PLACEMENT DETAILS

About 10 percent of the Class of 1996 failed to have a single job offer at commencement, a drop from 19 percent in 1994. Some 189 companies recruited Wisconsin MBAs in 1996, up from 160 a year earlier and just 115 in 1994.

Despite that notable increase, though, not many recruiters brought their silver platters with them. At $46,800, median starting pay packages for Wisconsin MBAs in 1996 were dead last among the Top 50 schools—despite the fact that graduates of eight other schools made less money when they began their MBA programs. Top employers: Ernst & Young (6); Oscar Mayer Foods (5); Coopers & Lybrand (3); Deloitte & Touche (3); General Mills (3); Strong Capital Management (3); Andersen Consulting (2); Hallmark Cards (2); IBM (2); and Kimberly-Clark (2). Rather than wait for the recruiters to come to Madison, placement director Karen Stauffacher is trying to bring more MBAs to them. The school annually carts students to job fairs in Chicago, New York, Atlanta, and San Francisco. That strategy won't allow Wisconsin to leap from last to first in the Top 50, but it should pay off in the future and win grads better offers.

OUTSTANDING FACULTY

Denis Collins (****—ethics); *Ella Mae Matsumura* (****—accounting and information systems); *Robert Pricer* (***—entrepreneurship); *Jan Heide* (**—marketing); *Pete Frischman* (**—accounting and information systems); *Rafael Lazimy* (**—operations and information management); *Michael Rothschild* (**—marketing); *Howard Thompson* (**—finance); *Gilbert Churchill* (*—marketing).

APPLICANT TIPS

To gain admission to Wisconsin's MBA program you need to apply to two different offices—the Graduate School of Business and the Graduate School of the University of Wisconsin at Madison. The B-school's admissions requirements are more rigorous than the Graduate School's requirements, but the Graduate School does make the final decision. The B-school notifies the Graduate School of its decision, and if the two schools are in agreement you will be notified immediately.

The B-school says it seeks two years of full-time work experience, even though 19.2 percent of the Class of 1998 had less than a single year. It also says it seeks a GPA of between 3.0 and 4.0, though in 1996 it accepted at least one or more candidates with undergraduate grades as low as 2.1. Interviews are not required for admission, but visits to the campus are encouraged.

Contact: Randall Dunham
Director of Admissions
608-262-1556
Final application deadline: June 1 for fall, October 1 for spring

MADISON MBAs SOUND OFF

I loved my MBA experience at Wisconsin. Everyone worked together to create a positive working environment. Networking was a key. Never did I feel that I was competing with someone for a job—that is a unique and rare attribute of any MBA program.

While the work load made the program very difficult, I felt that many of the concepts we were taught were very simple and that too much time was spent trying to make things appear more complicated than they are. Overall, I am very satisfied with my education and would choose UW—Madison again if I could do it over. Madison is the best city in the country!

Biggest gaps were: linkages between courses and department need for more systemic approach; practical applications and practices (teams, leadership, problem solving). Biggest plusses: Madison is a wonderful community; committed, energetic student base who focus primarily on coordination and collaboration instead of competition.

I am really disappointed with my 2-year experience in this business school. Most of my colleagues are fresh undergrads who have no experience. They are very local-minded, arrogant, and stupid. The MBA curriculum itself is out of fashion, at least 5 out of 12 MBA classes are totally useless. Above all, I wish I could get a full tuition refund and am ashamed to be among the school's alumni.

WAKE FOREST
UNIVERSITY

WAKE FOREST UNIVERSITY

Babcock Graduate School of Management
Winston-Salem, North Carolina 27109
E-mail address: edwina_groves@mail.mba.wfu.edu
Website address: http://www.mba.wfu.edu

Enrollment: 203	Annual tuition & fees: $18,400
Women: 29%	Room and board: $4700
Non-U.S.: 15%	Average GMAT score: 609
Minority: 7%	Average GPA: 3.2
Part-time: None	GPA range: 2.2 to 4.0
Average age: 26	Average years of work exp.: 4
Applicants accepted: 41%	Accepted applicants enrolled: 20%
Median starting pay: $56,000	Average starting pay: $56,630

Teaching methods: Lecture, 20% Case study, 35%
Field studies, 45%

Contact:
Mary C. Goss
Assistant Dean of
Admissions
910-759-5422
or 800-722-1622
*Final application
deadline:*
April 1 for fall

Nestled in the gently rolling hills of North Carolina's Piedmont region, Wake Forest University's business school is a southern version of Dartmouth's Amos Tuck School. Like Tuck, the Babcock School of Management promises students a general management MBA in a cozy and intimate setting where personal attention is a hallmark.

Winston-Salem may not be Boston or Los Angeles, but it's North Carolina's fourth largest city. Halfway between Washington, D.C., and Atlanta, it's a comfortable place to spend two years. Just 90 minutes away by car are the majestic Blue Ridge Mountains, while Carolina's sandy beaches are close enough for weekend trips when the weather turns warm. The Wake Forest campus is a beautiful oasis of red brick buildings surrounded by manicured lawns and gorgeous trees. Not exactly New England-styled Tuck, but a smaller Southern version to be sure.

With just 110 entering students in a class, the emphasis at Babcock is on a close educational encounter. All students know each other by their first names. And they also know the faculty who work closely together to deliver what Babcock maintains is a highly integrated business program. Like Tuck, this school heavily employs group study and team-based learning throughout the two years of study.

You'd be hard-pressed to find a more modern or appealing place to study business. Babcock moved into a 178,000-square-foot professional building in 1993 along with the university's School of Law. The three-story center is U-shaped with separate wings and distinctive entrances for each school. Both schools share a library that occupies 40,000 square feet on four floors.

Babcock is also like Tuck in another way. With only 7 percent of the students minorities and just 15 percent from outside the United States, the school rates poorly in cultural diversity. Indeed, no school among the 51 whose graduates were surveyed by BUSINESS WEEK ranked lower on diversity than Wake Forest. It doesn't help that 45 percent of the student body is from the South.

Wake Forest, of course, isn't Dartmouth, and Babcock isn't really Tuck. You're not going to find the very best professors on this campus. Nor are you going to find the very best students since one in five lack even a year's worth of work experience. That's one reason why 1996 graduates rated the caliber of their classmates fifth from the bottom of 51 schools surveyed by BUSINESS WEEK. Only Penn State, Florida, Texas A&M, and Iowa scored lower. Dartmouth, by the way, was second only to Harvard on this measure. Yet, Babcock has lots of the flavor of the Tuck experience.

In the first year, students are marched through a lockstep program of required courses and integrative exercises. Although nearly 55 percent of the students already have undergraduate degrees in either business or economics, Babcock does not allow any waivers out of core classes. The same is true at Dartmouth and Harvard. Graduates rate the school very highly for both the analytical and interpersonal skill content in the curriculum. In the second year, there are another four required courses, including a field study project in which student teams act as consultants to local businesses and non-profits. Students also get to choose as many as 13 half-semester electives during the second year. But with a full-time faculty of 27 professors, the elective offerings are slim: 42 courses in an academic year. The school claims its best areas of study are finance, marketing, and operations.

Though Wake Forest's slick promotional brochures play up its international focus, graduates fail to place the school anywhere among the leaders in global business. Even so, Babcock offers students three interesting study trips abroad every summer. From mid-May to early June, student teams can travel to Japan for corporate visits and home stays with Japanese families. A second Asian trip focuses on company visits in China and Hong Kong. A third trip features a two-week course in July on business developments in Europe at England's tony Oxford University. Babcock also offers semester abroad programs in England, France, and Germany. More interestingly, the school boasts an international internship program under which 10 percent of the class goes to Japan and Europe to work for such companies as Ford Motor Co. Ltd., the Kellogg Co. of Great Britain, and the London Kensington Hilton.

If grads don't necessarily praise these efforts all that much, they are impressed with the school's emphasis on information technology. All full-time MBAs are given IBM ThinkPad laptop computers as part of their tuition. Every learning space—from study rooms to lecture halls to the library—are equipped with ports to link up to the university's network. Students also can dial into the network from home to check electronic mail or access a professor's class notes.

There's also a mentoring program that matches students with nearby professionals who have agreed to offer advice and career guidance to MBA candidates—a reason why graduate satisfaction was the second highest after Dartmouth itself for putting students into contact with successful professionals. The school also offers two joint programs: a four-year track for an MBA and a law degree, and a five-year track for an MBA and an MD with the School of Medicine.

PLACEMENT DETAILS

It will come as no surprise to learn that the career services office took something of a beating from recent graduates who rate the number and quality of recruiting firms here lower than any of the 51 schools surveyed by BW with the exception of Florida and Babson. After all, Winston-Salem is no business metropolis.

That said, however, only 12 percent of the graduates in 1996 failed to have a single job offer at commencement. Some 50 companies recruited second-years on campus, doing 832 interviews. Most of the recruiters here are companies headquartered in the South or the nearby branch offices of other corporations. The top employers: Sara Lee (6); Delta Airlines (5); Wachovia (5); KPMG Peat Marwick (4); RJR/Nabisco (3); Johnson & Johnson (3); Burlington Industries (2); Duke Power (2); IBM (2); and First Union (2).

OUTSTANDING FACULTY

Ram Baliga (****—statistics); *Charles Moyer* (****—finance); *Frederick Harris* (***—marketing); *Jon Pinder* (**—operations); *Bruce Resnick* (**—finance); *Ken Middaugh* (**—accounting); *Jack Ferner* (*—management); *Chuck Kennedy* (*—international business).

APPLICANT TIPS

Babcock is one of the very few schools that actually invites applicants to call up its admissions director and even its dean. As the school puts it: "Personal attention in the admissions process distinguishes Wake Forest from other MBA programs. . . ." Besides examining your undergraduate transcript and GMAT score, the school closely looks at "character qualities, evidence of leadership, motivation, and managerial potential." So it would be a good idea to play up those attributes in your application.

Babcock does not require work experience, and 20 percent of the Class of 1998 has less than one year's worth of full-time work. Still, experience on a job will improve your chance of gaining admission. And if you have none, admissions will evaluate the quality of your summer work experience and leadership ability.

Personal interviews are not required, but they are strongly recommended and Babcock says they can give an applicant an advantage over someone who has not interviewed. In 1996, the school interviewed 34 percent of its 532 applicants. You should have an application on file before you schedule an interview. Another option: on Saturdays in early December and February, the school hosts open houses that give prospective applicants a chance to tour the campus; meet Dean Gary E. Costley; and have lunch with faculty, staff, and students.

Applicants who get their materials in early have a better chance of admission and of receiving scholarship awards. The school begins reviewing applications on December 1, and will consider applicants who file after the final deadline on a space-available basis.

Contact: Mary C. Goss
Assistant Dean of Admissions
910-759-5422 or 800-722-1622
Final application deadline: April 1 for fall

BABCOCK MBAs SOUND OFF

The small size of the entering class enables one to meet most classmates and develop many close friendships. It also allows for strong personal relationships with the faculty to form. The faculty are very approachable and enjoy getting to know the students outside of class. The new dean and the faculty are making concerted efforts to upgrade the quality and depth of the tenured faculty.

Overall, I believe my MBA experience was very positive. The key success of this MBA program is based on its class size. I believe this allowed for tremendous interaction within the classrooms, and allowed me to develop relationships which will last a long time. This program was a lot of hard work, but I am very pleased with the skills I have developed at Wake Forest.

During the interviewing process most of the companies interviewing were regional. I wish more companies came from the West Coast and Midwest. Because Wake Forest is a private school, the tuition is quite high. I sometimes wondered if the education was worth the $17K/year.

I had the choice of attending schools that were ranked higher than Wake. I am glad I went to Wake. I would choose Wake again. Wake is on the cutting edge of business and the use of technology, something Wharton, Harvard, Duke, and Kellogg lack.

THE BEST BUSINESS SCHOOLS OUTSIDE THE UNITED STATES

It's hard to have a chat with either a senior executive or a business school dean these days without at least a mention of *the* word: *global.* We routinely speak about the global economy and the global corporation. What about the global business school? Is an international gloss on an MBA an asset or a liability with corporate recruiters?

American business schools are feverishly pumping more "international" material into their programs, creating more opportunities for students and faculty to study abroad. But they also face growing competition from non-U.S. institutions that are aggressively expanding as interest in all things international widens. Many of these B-schools located abroad are truly global, with a more diverse mix of cultures and nationalities among faculty and students. As a prospective business school student shopping for the right place to collect the MBA, you might ask: Should I go to a business school outside of the United States?

Already, some of these institutions are attracting foreign MBA students who in an earlier era flocked to the United States. And some observers believe that they could begin to grab their fair share of quality American MBA applicants. If you're interested in getting an MBA outside the United States, there's a staggering range of business schools from which to choose. The programs they offer vary as greatly as their geographic locations. You can get an advanced degree in business at schools in Nigeria, Thailand, or Bangladesh. At INSEAD, based in Fontainebleau, France, you can pick up an MBA in just 10½ months at what is the best non-U.S. business school in the world. At England's classy Cambridge University, it would take you as long as three years.

All told, more than 250 institutions outside the United States offer a master's degree in business. In Canada alone, more than two dozen institutions compete with Ontario's Western Business School and the University of Toronto's B-school for the honor of offering the best in that country. About 24 MBA factories have sprouted up

> These schools offer a diverse mix of cultures and nationalities.

in Australia, while over two dozen are scattered throughout Asia. They include Tokyo's International University of Japan, the National University of Singapore, or Bangkok's SASIN Graduate Institute of Business Administration in Thailand. A number have also blossomed where communism has failed in Budapest, Warsaw, and Prague.

By far, however, Europe boasts the greatest concentration of business schools outside the United States. For many years, the American MBA degree had been derided as crass in Europe. In recent years, a shift in attitude has rippled through the European continent: Management education has become respected as a way to train managers and accelerate careers. The supply of MBAs stamped in Europe has more than doubled since 1987 to more than 7000 annually. Though that's only one-tenth of the MBAs produced by the United States, the increase in recent years demonstrates how popular the degree has become.

To satisfy the high demand, European schools have been opening up the gates of enrollment. INSEAD, for example, has boosted enrollment by 50 percent, to 486 students in recent years. London Business School has also upped its enrollment, and now has 432 part-time MBA students, up from just 237 in 1994. And new business schools have been popping up all over the world at both world-famous universities and obscure institutes. The number of MBA programs in the United Kingdom has doubled in five years. Cambridge University's three-year MBA program only debuted in October 1991. Oxford University has gotten into the game with a two-year program.

Ironically, American business schools are contributing to the boom abroad. The deans of many U.S. B-schools have been jetting around the world, inking cooperative pacts to help fledgling institutions get off the ground. They've also been anxious to sign agreements to allow for faculty and student exchanges. Indeed, such exchange deals have been touted by many American deans as proof that they are working hard to internationalize their MBA programs. New York University's Stern School of Business now boasts exchange programs with 25 non-U.S. schools, 14 in Europe and 5 in Asia. London Business School alone has exchange agreements with 29 institutions, many of them in the United States.

> New B-schools have been popping up all over the world.

U.S. B-SCHOOLS VERSUS EUROPEAN B-SCHOOLS

Besides the obvious differences in location and culture, there are less obvious disparities between the American pioneers in business education and the relatively new upstarts overseas. U.S. business schools, for example, have traditionally been stronger in nuts-and-bolts technical skills, while their European counterparts have tended to emphasize softer skills. "The European curriculum has never been as quantitative as North America," says George Bain, principal of the London School of Business.

That's certainly true from the students' point of view. Stefanie Lynn Smith, a Wharton MBA who went to LBS for a term on an exchange program, says that London paid far more attention to strategic issues than technical skills. She also believes that London devoted more class time to integrating the various business disciplines, from accounting to marketing. "It was perfectly normal to discuss management issues during a marketing class or operational issues during a class on international corporations," says Smith, who now works as a consultant at Grant Thornton in New York.

Another key difference: European schools have long had close ties with business. Lacking the huge endowments of many American institutions, the Europeans were forced to put greater emphasis on executive education. "We had to be much closer to our customer," Bain insists. Because senior executives are likely to be more demanding than MBA students, he also believes that European schools had to put more weight on teaching excellence than most U.S. schools. Still, the vast number of curriculum overhauls in the United States is narrowing such differences. These days, one U.S. business school after another is emphasizing softer skills at the same time that many European schools are urging their faculties to do more academic research.

Some even argue that INSEAD may very well be the ideal model of a modern business school, on the verge of replacing the best American institutions at the cutting edge. "That bodes ill for U.S. schools," says Terry Williams, senior partner and former director of recruiting at McKinsey & Co., the world's most prestigious management consulting firm. He notes that from his firm's perspective, European business schools are highly competitive with American ones. The "dirty little secret" of business schools, adds Williams, is that their quality depends more on the students than the faculty. "Harvard Business School has proven able to attract very good students, and INSEAD is attracting the best and brightest in Europe. I see no difference in the quality of students at these two institutions." McKinsey hired 58 members of INSEAD's Class of 1996.

THINGS TO
CONSIDER
BEFORE
APPLYING
ABROAD

So what are the pros and cons for prospective MBA students? If you live in the United States and strongly desire an international experience, then schooling abroad is the right choice. The chance to fully immerse yourself in another culture is the chief advantage. No American business school, no matter what it contends in a marketing brochure about being global or international, can duplicate the wonderful experience of living in a different country where Americans are a minority. It enhances your ability to handle cultural differences, a soft skill that may be useful in management. It broadens your perspective in ways that will make you more mature and more experienced. It will significantly add to your ability to speak a different language. And it will give you an appreciation for all things different and foreign. As Bain of the London Business School puts it, "You get two learning experiences: business and culture. The second is almost free. It's something you experience. It's always a useful experience to do one or two degrees in your own country and to go do another degree elsewhere."

If you badly want to work abroad, a non-U.S. school again may be the right choice. Even though there are no guarantees, an MBA from a prestigious school located abroad will enhance your opportunities to get hired by a foreign company or one of the overseas outposts of an American multinational. At INSEAD, about 36 percent of its MBA graduates get a job in a country different from the one they worked in before joining the school. Some 32 percent work in a country other than their nation of origin. But non-European Community members must remember that their employers have to get them work permits before they can work in any country in Europe. In some cases, that can pose a formidable barrier.

From an American perspective, the allure of a non-U.S. degree may have a down side. You'll probably pay more for the MBA. Your job search will be far more complicated. And if you return to the United States, you'll likely find that the degree could lose much of its cachet. After all, how many American companies have heard about the International Institute for Management Development in Lausanne, Switzerland? Yet, it's one of the more established, prestige institutions granting the MBA. Alumni networks at most of these schools are limited at best. You're not going to find too many alums from the Copenhagen Business School in Chicago or L.A.

Choosing a foreign setting for your degree may also be quite a luxury. The cost of tuition, room and board, and travel is likely to be substantially higher than in the United States. Fewer loans and other financial aid are available. Just 10 months at INSEAD runs $30,000, not including the sizable expense of living in Fontainebleau, France, or the airplane tickets to get you there and back a couple of times. You can get a two-year MBA from Northwestern University's Kellogg School for $16,000 more.

What you gain in the "international" diversity of the student population at a non-U.S. business school is often lost by the paucity of minority students in these schools. Many of the prestige foreign institutions are far more class-conscious and overtly elitist than their U.S. rivals. Some of them don't even grasp the concept of minority representation. And what's truly international to some, of course, isn't terribly global to others. By many standards, some of the top American business schools are far more international than they are given credit for. Consider MIT's Sloan School. Roughly one-third of the full-time faculty hails from abroad, and 37 percent of the students are non-U.S., from nearly 50 different countries. By either faculty or student standards, that's far more global than you'd get at the London Business School, where 7 out of every 10 professors are British and about 1 out of every 4 students is from Great Britain alone. The American Graduate School of International Management, known simply as Thunderbird, in a suburb of Phoenix, Arizona, has established a strong reputation as a global school. In any given class, you'll find students from more than 60 countries, and every graduate of the school must be proficient in a second language.

YET ANOTHER OPTION FOR AN INTER-NATIONAL EXPERIENCE

Another option tries to capture the best of both worlds: Go to an American business school that offers exchange programs with foreign institutions. This route can get you the clout of an American MBA while giving you a taste of living abroad. You won't get the chance to really soak up a foreign culture in a single semester, but you also won't need to scramble feverishly for a job. And few people in the United States or elsewhere will question your decision to get an MBA from Northwestern, Chicago, Michigan, or Wharton.

Smith, who went to LBS for 10 weeks while pursuing her Wharton MBA, has no regrets about her decision. Indeed, she enjoyed her experience so much that she thought, "Maybe I should have gone here the whole time." Wharton seemed more obvious, however. She was 24 years old with public-sector experience when she enrolled at the University of Pennsylvania's B-school. "I went to business school to learn about business," says Smith. "If I had worked in an American corporation for six years, I would have gone abroad."

With the sole exception of the Harvard Business School, every Top 25 B-school in the United States has at least one exchange program. New York University leads the pack with 25 options, while Stanford offers only one—its own program in Kyoto at the Center for Technology and Innovation in Japan. The latter offering for the spring term of second-year students is followed by a summer internship with a Japanese firm. Georgetown University boasts 10 semester-abroad programs, as well as five summer-study-abroad opportunities with such places as Oxford University, Japan's Waseda University in Tokyo, and the Czech Management Center in Prague. These options will increase the cost of your degree, but not nearly as much as a full program abroad.

There's also another route you could select if you decide to link up with a U.S. B-school. Many of the best schools now offer joint-degree programs in both business and Asian or European studies. One of the best is Wharton's Joseph H. Lauder Institute. An alliance between the business school and the university's School of Arts and Sciences, the 24-month program is an innovative way to capture an international experience. After spending the month of May on the Philadelphia campus, students ship overseas to countries in which their chosen foreign language is spoken. (A second language is required for admission to the program.) While there, they tour the facilities of a dozen corporations and take in lots of cultural activities. Students return for the traditional start of the school year in September, only to go back for 12-week internships with both foreign companies and the overseas affiliates of U.S. firms. They then return to campus to complete their studies.

Despite the program's quality, Laura Lee Garner who recently graduated from London Business turned down a place at Wharton's Lauder Institute for the opportunity to study full-time abroad. Looking for an international experience, Garner concluded that "Europe seemed to offer more" than an American

> Almost all B-schools offer exchange programs.

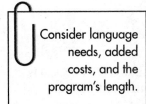

Consider language needs, added costs, and the program's length.

MBA program could. At LBS, Garner believes she has learned as much from her fellow students from all over the world as she did from her professors. She recalled a classroom debate on the South American debt crisis. Brazilians, Chileans, Venezuelans, Americans, Britons, and Europeans were going at it with a vigor that wouldn't be found in a predominantly American classroom.

If you do decide to take the plunge, full-time or through an exchange option, the next question is: Which school? Factors to consider include the language requirements, the additional cost, and the program's length, in addition to the overall quality of the institution. INSEAD requires three languages in its 10-month program. IESE in Barcelona demands two languages by graduation from their two-year curriculums. IMD's one-year stint requires English only, although a second language is recommended as being attractive to recruiters.

Whatever your choice, your experience will certainly be memorable. You'll learn as much about business as you will about another country and culture. You'll make very different friends with different people. And you'll probably return a different person yourself. As Garner puts it, "You'll break down barriers you may not realize you have, especially for an American. We come in with frameworks. It takes a challenge to recognize that."

THE EUROPEAN INSTITUTE OF BUSINESS ADMINI- STRATION (INSEAD)

THE EUROPEAN INSTITUTE OF BUSINESS ADMINISTRATION (INSEAD)

Boulevard de Constance
77305 Fontainebleau Cedex France
E-mail address: admissions@insead.fr
Website address: http://www.insead.fr

Enrollment: 1674	Annual tuition & fees: $30,000
Women: 21%	Room and board: $19,000
U.S.: 10%	Average GMAT score: 654
Minority: 0%	GMAT range: 530 to 800
Part-time: None	Average GPA: NA
Average age: 28.3	Average years of work exp.: 4.5
Applicants accepted: 29%	Accepted applicants enrolled: 74%
Median starting pay: NA	Average starting salary: $80,000

Teaching methods: Lecture, 20%   Case study, 45%
Projects & simulations, 35%

Contact:
Carol Giraud
Director of Admissions
33 1 60 72 4245
*Final application
deadlines:* April 28
for September start
August 11 for
January start

Located on what was once the private hunting grounds of French kings, INSEAD is Europe's preeminent business school. In the picturesque town of Fontainebleau, at the edge of the Fontainebleau forest, the school is just a 40-minute drive from Paris. But faculty and students here would cringe if you called the Institut Europeen d'Administration des Affaires a French business school. Rather, they insist on calling the school "international," emphasizing its diversity and the global character of the many case studies they dissect and debate. "INSEAD isn't even European," claims Lawrence Freedman, a recent graduate from Ithaca, New York. "It has its own culture."

Founded in 1959, INSEAD has long enjoyed a reputation as the best graduate school of business in Europe. Even though its program is only 10 and a half months long, many companies believe an MBA from INSEAD is as prestigious as one from Northwestern or Harvard. Privately funded and not affiliated with any university, the school underwent a major expansion in 1986 that led to a 40 percent rise in enrollment, to 460 MBA students a year. Increasing interest in global affairs allowed the school the luxury of expanding without lowering its admission standards. "Demand grew by leaps and bounds and we tried to meet it," says a spokesman.

The increase also allowed INSEAD to support another goal: enlarging the faculty and the amount of research generated by the school. The number of professors more than doubled, to 82. Hailing from 22 nationalities, the faculty is highly individualistic. Many of the new faculty recruits, moreover, are research-oriented professors, reflecting the school's efforts to improve its reputation among academics. MBA Director Herwig Langohr, a finance professor from Belgium, views academic research as relevant to actual business operations. "Nothing is so good for practice as a good theory," he says. However, Langohr envisions the school moving toward more project work in the long run. The combination of research and practical experience should lead to a "more insight-oriented" program.

Although 6 of every 10 students at INSEAD are European (compared to only 47 percent at the London Business School), Langohr believes his school is "international in all dimensions." The largest single group of students, about 17 percent, come from France, while some 16 percent of the students hail from the United Kingdom. Roughly one in every four students here is from some other European country. North Americans account for about 10 percent of the student population, outnumbering those from Asia (6 percent) and the Middle East (4 percent). "No one nationality or culture dominates," says Herwig.

The interaction among diverse students and faculty creates a mindset that is impossible to duplicate in a program dominated by one nationality. To successfully avoid cultural clashes, Americans must learn "a style, a grace" in working with others, says Kristin Allen, a U.S. student who graduated in 1993. The differences are readily apparent in the classroom, where an array of accents and languages are spoken. For one thing, students here must speak both French and English to gain entrance to the program. Allen says she met the French requirement by taking a two-month, $3000 intensive French course before the school year began. By the time they graduate, students must be able to at least maintain a business conversation in a third language. INSEAD offers German and Spanish for four and a half hours a week for 30 weeks, which is added to the regular MBA courseload.

The program runs at two different times of the year: from August to June and from January to December, with a six-week break in the summer. The odd schedule may make it difficult for some students to land summer internships, but many still gain summer employment to tack onto their résumés. The program is divided into five eight-week periods, the first pair of which is crammed with the business basics of the core curriculum.

The workload is heavy. "Time pressure is pretty hairy here," Freedman says, citing days from 7 a.m. to 2 a.m. as typical. Although he prefers eight hours of sleep a night, he says "I get six if I'm lucky." But it's also not as highly competitive as some U.S. schools. With class participation accounting for only 10 to 30 percent of your grade in any given course, class discussions tend to be more constructive.

The school's blend of hard work and play seems to pay off: Top recruiters, including McKinsey, Boston Consulting Group, Citicorp, and IBM routinely make on-campus rounds here to woo grads. In 1996, 201 organizations recruited on campus, conducting 6500 interviews. Another 300 job opportunities arrived via correspondence. Major employers in 1996: McKinsey (58); Boston Consulting Group (28); Bain & Co. (21); Booz Allen & Hamilton (10); Mercer Management (8); Eli Lilly (7); Marakon (7); Gemini Consulting (6); L'Oreal (5); and the Lek Partnership (5).

The school's exalted reputation tends to be larger than its actual influence in business. That's because INSEAD has produced a smallish alumni base, especially compared to any of the major U.S. business schools. Its presence in the United States is minimal: A little over 500 of its MBAs now work in the United States. About 500 alums are American, though more than half of them live outside the country. INSEAD boasts 30 alumni clubs around the world, each in a different country. Most are in Europe, but there are also groups in Hong Kong, India, Japan, and Singapore. The school also has a North American office in New York City.

Contact: Carol Giraud
Director of Admissions
33 1 60 72 4245
Final application deadlines: April 28 for September start; August 11 for January start

LONDON
BUSINESS
SCHOOL

Contact:
Julia Tyler
Director of Admissions
44 0 171 262 5050
*Final application
deadline:*
June 1 for fall

LONDON BUSINESS SCHOOL

Sussex Place
Regent's Park
London NW1 4SA
United Kingdom
E-mail address: mba-info@lbs.lon.ac.uk
Website address: http://www.lbs.lon.ac.uk

Enrollment: 648	Annual tuition & fees: $16,485
Women: 22%	Room and board: $6000
Non-British: 82.5%	Average GMAT score: 630
Minority: 0%	GMAT range: 510 to 770
Part-time: 432	GPA range: NA
Average age: 28.5	Average years of work exp.: 5.5
Applicants accepted: 47%	Accepted applicants enrolled: 30%
Average median pay: NA	Average starting salary: $74,804

Teaching methods: Lecture, 33.3%   Case study, 33.3%
Projects, 33.3%

Set upon the lovely green grounds of Regent's Park, the Sussex Building of London Business School is a magnificent greeting to a new student. Inside the grand Georgian walls, you can sip tea while gazing through huge windows at swans and geese gliding on a lake. Once a week, the Queen's Cavalry parades across the park. The scene is postcard-perfect England.

These days, it's a postcard that includes greater numbers of American MBAs than ever before. Calling the school "a bridge between North America and Europe," Principal George Bain recommends that North Americans ease their way into careers in continental Europe by picking up their MBAs in England first. "I see us as an aircraft carrier off the coast of Europe," he says, "a place where students can perfect a language and get sensitized to a new culture. After that immersion, students can 'take off' from the carrier to land anywhere in Europe."

True enough, London is a welcoming place, particularly for Americans who don't have to overcome a language barrier to get around the country or the school. Unlike INSEAD, which requires applicants to speak both English and French and graduates to pick up a third language, London Business School only requires English. Proficiency in another language isn't required until you graduate. Students can take French, Spanish, German, or Japanese through language courses offered at London University.

Like other European business schools, cultural sensitization is inevitable in an environment where no one nationality dominates the student body. In the Class of 1998, about one in five students hails from

North America (the highest of any non-U.S. school). Still, an equal number are non-British European, while 19 percent are Asian, 7 percent are from Australia and New Zealand, and about 4 percent are from South and Central America. The largest single chunk of the class is British.

That truly international mix leads to stimulating discussions in and out of the classroom. You not only debate the substantive issues of business and economics, you feel the passion and the heat those issues often stir. Laura Lee Garner, an American in a recent class, recalls how on one occasion tempers flared when Japanese and American students debated trade barriers between their home countries. When the word *rice* was mentioned, "the room just exploded," says Garner.

The 21-month course for full-time students adopts an American-style approach, with the core courses set up front and all the electives in the back. The program is divided into six terms, with the basics of business hogging the first three terms. At year's end, students must pass a two-day qualifying exam, each a grueling four hours long. Then, in the second year, the school piles on the electives. You can choose from among 75 different courses that range from New Venture Development, one of the most popular, to The Art & Science of the Long View.

Each year and in the summer, students also complete a team project generated by corporate sponsors who ante up cash for each student in return for the work. The opportunity to work on real business problems attracts many students. "It is the reason why I came to BS," says William E. Northfield, Jr., a Boston native and recent graduate. The projects range from an analysis of the pharmaceutical industry in both the United Kingdom and the United States to a feasibility study for a luxury Spanish restaurant.

London's longer full-time program, two years versus the one-year length at either INSEAD or IMD, allows for both a summer internship and a semester abroad in what may well be the largest MBA exchange program offered by any business school in the world.

London boasts exchange pacts with 29 other schools, many of them in the United States. (American students, of course, cannot spend a semester abroad in a U.S. program.)

The first-year workload, just as it is at most U.S. schools, is tough: 12- to 16-hour days are typical. But Northfield says he manages to get 7 hours of sleep per night and to take off one weekend evening for fun. The Windsor Castle Pub, attached to the school, is a convenient stop for pints and also serves up traditional English pub grub from bangers and mash (sausages and potatoes) to cottage pie (ground beef layered under mashed potatoes). The school also boasts numerous clubs, including wine and performing arts societies.

London, of course, offers many diversions and historical sites that are easily accessible from centrally located Regents Park. A small museum, Sherlock Holmes's home, is a mere three-minute walk away. The financial district, called The City, is about 15 minutes away on the subway. Students themselves live throughout London and get to campus by bus or subway (the school is just a block from the Baker Street underground stop). Study bedrooms on campus are reserved for executive education programs and for international exchange students.

LBS's Career Management Centre says that in recent years more American companies are recruiting for their head European offices. German companies have also increased their recruiting at LBS for non-German managers. In total, 62 companies recruit at LBS each year, conducting about 1382 interviews in 1996. The big hirers: Andersen Consulting (9), McKinsey (5), Gemini Consulting (5), CSC Index (4), AT Kearney (3), JP Morgan (2), Lehman Bros (2), Perot Systems (2), Fidelity (2), and Marakon Associates (2).

Contact: Julia Tyler
Director of Admissions
44 0 171 262 5050
Final application deadline: June 1 for fall

WESTERN BUSINESS SCHOOL

The University of Western Ontario
London, Ontario
Canada, N6A 3K7
E-mail address: admiss@ivey.uwo.ca
Website address: http://www.ivey.uwo.ca

Enrollment: 450

Women: 28%
Non-Canadian: NA
Minority: NA
Part-time: None
Average age: 28
Applicants accepted: 45%
Accepted applicants enrolled: 60%

Annual tuition & fees:
  resident—$3000
  non-resident—$11,000
Room and board: $4000
Average GMAT score: 630
Average GPA: 3.7
GPA range: 2.5 to 4.0
Average years of work exp.: 4.8
Average starting salary: $49,000

Teaching Methods: Lecture, 10% Case study, 70%
                   Group projects, 20%

Contact:
Larysa Gamula
Admissions Director
519-661-3212
*Final application
deadline:*
April 1 for fall

If you're looking for value with cachet in your MBA program search, then Western Business School in London, Ontario, may be an unusual answer. With annual tuition of about $11,000 for non-Canadians, the two-year degree is substantially cheaper than many American programs, including some offered by public universities. And as one of Canada's top business schools, it offers quality with clout. Of the more than two dozen graduate schools of business in Canada, Western is held in high esteem by corporate recruiters, executives, and deans, who have repeatedly ranked it No. 1 in the country, according to *Canadian Business* magazine.

"The value I'm getting for my education is really second to none," believes Tony Cianca, a Nashville native and recent graduate. Formerly a college textbook salesman, Cianca chose WBS over American schools like Vanderbilt in part because the price was right. "Vanderbilt is $25,000 a year. Here it's maybe a third of that."

But that isn't the only reason why he and many others are selecting the school. The quality of the teaching faculty is another draw. Many of the professors in Western's classrooms got their educational credentials stamped at Harvard and Stanford. So they bring high expectations and high-level experience to their courses. They're also known for their close contact with students. Cianca, for instance, recalls that on Thanksgiving, which Canadians do not celebrate, one professor awarded him a ham and some cranberry sauce, recognizing him as the section's only American. "It really made me feel good. It's a personal type thing." And unlike the dominating emphasis on esoteric research at many U.S. schools, often to the detriment of good teaching, Western has put more focus on the quality of instruction in class. As Dean Adrian Ryans puts it, the school "rewards good teaching through promotion and tenure and places less emphasis on research and publication." What research it does do tends to be directed toward the development of case studies. The school claims to be the second largest producer of cases after Harvard.

There are other strong business schools in Canada, including the programs at Queen's University, McGill University, the University of Toronto, and the University of British Columbia. But none of the Canadian B-schools make much of a showing in BUSINESS WEEK's surveys of corporate recruiters, with the exception of Western Business School. In recent years, applications to this school have been declining, and fell to just 800 in 1996, from a high of 1400 in 1988.

For U.S. students, time spent at Western is bound to be less of an international experience than one could gain in Europe or Asia. Americans face no language barriers in Canada, and you'd be hard pressed to find colleagues who are more like Americans than the typical Canadians in a Western classroom. Only 10 percent of the students here are not from Canada—making Western less "international" in some ways than most of the better B-schools in the United States. Indeed, Cianca doesn't really feel he is in a foreign culture. "As an American, it's not any big deal to adjust to Canada," he says. Yet the American MBA candidate believes he's getting a more global perspective on business by attending the school.

The hub of Western's efforts to think globally lies in the Center for International Business Studies, which supports research and other international programs. WBS's international elements include an active exchange program with business schools in Europe and Asia, under which students can study in Italy, Spain, Sweden, Britain, Japan, or Hong Kong for a four-month term. The exchange program, in turn, also brings foreign students on-campus, which helps to diversify the student body. WBS deliberately does not conduct any exchanges with American schools, to encourage exposure to more foreign cultures.

Each MBA class of about 225 students is divided into three sections. All of the program's first-year classes are required, and they focus on nine basic building block areas. In the second year, only one course is required: Business Policy. Then you're finally free to select from an array of electives that range from The Operating Manager to Creative Business Leadership. The former requires students to approach problems from the perspective of a young manager who must lead and operate effectively in an environment that is not under his or her control. The latter explores how business leaders can instill a stronger sense of mission in employees.

WBS is housed in a two-story, sandstone, fortress-like building that is one of the oldest on campus. Two gardens outside the building provide the settings for 500-person garden parties. Although the school offers some on-campus housing, nearly all students live off-campus in nearby apartments in and around London—a two-hour drive to Detroit or Toronto and a two-hour flight to New York.

About 206, mostly Canadian, firms recruit at WBS. But the lineup also includes such prestigious organizations as Ernst & Young (8), Deloitte & Touche (8), Toronto Dominion Bank (7); Boston Consulting Group (6); Canadian Imperial Bank (5); Nesbitt Burns (4); Bell Canada (3); Bain & Co. (2); Ontario Teachers Pension Plan Board (2); Scotia McLeod (2). The school lacks an alumni association in the United States, where about 6 percent, or 417, of its alumni make their livings.

Contact: Larysa Gamula
Admissions Director
519-661-3212
Final application deadline: April 1 for fall

INDEX

American Graduate School of International Management (Thunderbird), 10, 31, 37, 41, 43, 46–54, 197–202, 303

Babson College (F.W. Olin), 10, 34, 36, 37, 39, 41–44, 46–54, 203, 204–207
Brigham Young University, 34–42, 46–54, 208–210

Cambridge University, 299, 300
Carnegie Mellon University, 5, 7, 10, 28, 31, 32, 33–44, 46–54, 150–155
Case Western Reserve University (Weatherhead), 33, 37, 40, 46–54, 211–214
Columbia University, 10, 12, 31, 32, 38, 41, 43, 46–54, 86–91
Cornell University (Johnson), 28, 31, 32, 35, 37, 44, 46–54, 156–162

Dartmouth College (Amos Tuck), 7, 10, 12, 31, 32, 33–44, 46–54, 109–114
Duke University (Fuqua), 9, 10, 24, 28, 31, 32, 35, 37, 38, 41, 42, 44, 46–54, 115–120

Emory University (Goizueta), 32, 33, 36, 39–44, 46–54, 215–217
European Institute of Business Administration (INSEAD), 299–303, 305–307

Georgetown University, 10, 32, 33, 37, 41–44, 46–54, 218–221, 304

Georgia Institute of Technology (DuPree), 33–44, 46–54, 222–224

Harvard University, 7, 8, 10, 11–12, 25, 26, 31, 32, 33–39, 41–44, 46–54, 73–79, 304

Indiana University, 7, 9, 31, 32, 34, 37, 42, 43, 139–144
International Graduate School of Management (IESE), 305
International Institute for Management Development (IMD), 302–303, 305
International University of Japan, 300

London Business School, 301, 303–305, 308–309

Massachusetts Institute of Technology (Sloan), 1, 10, 27, 31, 32, 35–38, 40, 42–44, 46–54, 103–108, 303
Michigan State University (Eli Broad), 33–44, 46–54, 225–228

National University of Singapore, 300
New York University (Leonard N. Stern), 10, 28, 31, 32, 43, 46–54, 133–138, 300, 304
Northwestern University (J.L. Kellogg), 4, 7, 9, 10, 17, 25, 28, 31, 32, 33, 37–44, 46–54, 67–72, 303

Ohio State University (Max M. Fisher), 33–36, 38, 39, 41–44, 46–54, 203, 229–231

Pennsylvania State University (Mary Jean and Frank P. Smeal), 33–40, 43, 44, 46–54, 232–235
Purdue University (Krannert), 32, 33–37, 40, 43, 46–54, 203, 236–239

Rice University (Jesse H. Jones), 35, 39, 40, 42–44, 46–54, 240–242

SASIN Graduate Institute of Business Administration, 300
Southern Methodist University (Edwin L. Cox), 10, 31, 33–37, 40–42, 44, 46–54, 186–190
Stanford University, 1, 4, 10, 31, 32, 34, 36–42, 44, 46–54, 92–97

Texas A&M University (Lowry Mays), 33–35, 37–44, 46–54, 243–246
Tulane University (A.B. Freeman), 10, 38, 40, 43, 46–54, 247–250

University of California at Berkeley (Walter A. Haas), 10, 11, 31, 32, 33–40, 42–44, 46–54, 127–132
University of California at Los Angeles (John E. Anderson), 5, 10, 31, 32, 33–44, 46–54, 121–126
University of Chicago, 12, 25, 31, 32, 35, 38–40, 42, 46–54, 98–102
University of Florida, 25, 33–44
University of Georgia (Terry), 35–38, 40–43, 46–54, 251–253
University of Illinois at Urbana-Champaign, 33, 35–37, 40, 41, 46–54, 254–257
University of Iowa, 33–44, 46–54, 258–261
University of Maryland at College Park, 10, 32, 33, 36, 44, 46–54, 262–265

University of Michigan, 7, 10, 17, 25, 31, 32, 33–44, 46–54, 55, 61–66
University of Minnesota (Curtis L. Carlson), 33–40, 42–44, 46–54, 203, 266–269
University of North Carolina (Kenan-Flagler), 9, 31, 32, 33–41, 44, 46–54, 163–169
University of Notre Dame, 33, 34, 36–44, 46–54, 270–273
University of Pennsylvania (Wharton), 1, 7, 9, 10, 11, 23, 31, 32, 33–36, 38, 39, 41–44, 46–54, 55, 56–60, 304
University of Pittsburgh (Joseph M. Katz), 27–28, 37, 38, 46–54, 274–277
University of Rochester (William E. Simon), 7, 9, 10, 31, 32, 34–38, 40, 44, 46–54, 175–179
University of Southern California, 5, 46–54, 278–281
University of Tennessee at Knoxville, 34–36, 41–44, 46–54, 203, 282–285
University of Texas at Austin, 9, 10, 31, 32, 34, 37, 40, 44, 46–54, 170–174
University of Toronto, 299
University of Virginia (Darden), 10, 31, 32, 33–44, 46–54, 80–85
University of Washington, 33–38, 40–44, 46–54, 286–289
University of Wisconsin—Madison, 33–40, 43, 46–54, 290–293

Vanderbilt University (Owen), 10, 31, 33–40, 42, 44, 46–54, 191–196

Wake Forest University (Babcock), 10, 33, 39–42, 44, 46–54, 294–297
Washington University (John M. Olin), 10, 31, 32, 33–42, 44, 46–54, 145–149
Western Business School, University of Western Ontario, 299, 310–311

Yale University, 17, 31, 32, 38–42, 44, 46–54, 180–185

Business Week

ABOUT THE AUTHOR

John A. Byrne is a senior writer at BUSINESS WEEK. With a team of BUSINESS WEEK editors, Mr. Byrne has prepared and written *The Best Business Schools,* Fifth Edition. He has followed the business school scene for many years, and has written BUSINESS WEEK's biennial cover stories surveying the top schools since the magazine launched its rankings in 1988. Mr. Byrne is also the author of *The Headhunters; The Whiz Kids: Ten Founding Fathers of American Business—and the Legacy They Left Us;* and *Informed Consent: A story of personal tragedy and corporate betrayal . . . inside the silicone breast implant crisis,* recently published by McGraw-Hill. He holds a master's degree in journalism from the University of Missouri and a B.A. in political science and English from William Paterson College.